D1563796

BOUNDARIES

OF THE

INTERNATIONAL

BOUNDARIES

OF THE

INTERNATIONAL

Law and Empire

JENNIFER PITTS

Harvard University Press

Cambridge, Massachusetts
London, England
2018

Second printing

Cataloging-in-Publication Data available from the Library of Congress

ISBN: 978-0-674-98081-5 (alk. paper)

For Lucia and Nicholas

Contents

IF BY DESPOT we mean an absolute master, who disposes of the goods, the honor, and the life of his subjects, using and abusing an authority without limits and without control, I see no such despots anywhere in Asia. . . . I see only a certain number of places where nothing is respected, where accommodation is unknown and where force reigns without obstacle: these are the places where the weakness and the improvidence of the Asiatics allowed foreigners from distant countries to establish themselves, with the sole desire of amassing wealth in the shortest possible time, and then returning to their country to enjoy it; people without pity for men of another race, without any sentiment of sympathy for natives whose language they do not understand and with whom they share no tastes, habits, beliefs, prejudices . . . the foreigners of whom I speak are the Europeans.

A singular race is this European race. The opinions with which it is armed, the reasonings upon which it rests, would astonish an impartial judge, if such a one could be at present found on earth. Drunk with their recent progress and especially their superiority in the arts of war, they look with a superb disdain upon the other families of the human species; it seems that everyone is born to admire and to serve them. . . . They walk the globe, showing themselves to the humiliated nations as the type of beauty in their figures, the epitome of reason in their ideas, the perfection of understanding in their imaginations. What resembles them is lovely, what is useful to them is good, and what strays from their taste or their interest is senseless, ridiculous, or condemnable. That is their only measure. They judge all things by that rule. In their own quarrels they are agreed upon certain principles by which to assassinate one another with method and regularity. But the law of nations is superfluous in dealing with Malays, Americans, or Tungus.

Jean-Pierre Abel-Rémusat, 1829

Introduction:
Empire and International Law

I N 1829, Jean-Pierre Abel-Rémusat (1788–1832), who held the first chair in Sinology at the Collège de France, reflected on the ideological complex that his fellow Europeans had developed to justify their commercial and imperial depredations of societies throughout the extra-European world.[1] They read their military supremacy as evidence of their moral superiority; they looked with contempt on societies of which they lacked the most basic understanding; and with a stunning parochialism, they not only saw their own standards of beauty, right, and reason as paramount, but also expected others to embrace those supposed standards despite the Europeans' consistently abhorrent conduct. Central to this ideology was a story about law: about the supposed absence of law in the despotic empires of Asia, where tyrants dominated their enslaved subjects without any legal or moral restraints, and about the unique virtues of the European law of nations, which had tempered war with consensual rules among free and equal states and whose benefits would one day be conferred on others when they achieved "civilization." Abel-Rémusat was one participant in a minority discourse criticizing this legal ideology. As a student of the history of human culture, he particularly lamented the loss of civilizational diversity—the unique "genius" and the "spontaneous progress" of each civilization—that he feared was disappearing as there came to be "nothing left on earth but Europeans." He also eloquently condemned, and others in this vein of analysis would stress, the injustices that Europeans were perpetrating in the name of law and civilization.

This book is a study of the ideological and political work that discourses of the law of nations and international law performed during the eighteenth and nineteenth centuries with respect to relations between the imperial powers of Western Europe and states and societies outside Europe. These discourses emerged alongside the expansion and consolidation of Western Europe's global empires, although the connections between empire and international law went unacknowledged for much of the twentieth century. International law, together with structures of international governance, is in important respects a product of the history of European imperial expansion. International law also aspires to universal legitimacy. These features are in certain obvious ways in deep tension with one another. How can a set of institutions and discourses developed at least in part to sustain and justify the domination by a handful of Western European states over much of the rest of the globe hope to win the allegiance of those whose societies historically suffered under those institutions? Moreover, international law's universalism itself is more deeply bound up with its imperial features than such an observation about the tensions between universalism and domination would suggest.

The law of nations was, until the mid-nineteenth century, an almost exclusively European discourse in the sense that the texts that circulated were produced, with limited exceptions, by Europeans and addressed to other Europeans, although their theoretical questions and conceptual categories reflected the extent and significance of European states' and other agents' relations and activities outside Europe.[2] Indeed, Europeans throughout the modern period conceptualized international law through close reference to the non-European world. As a study of law of nations discourse and its imperial entanglements, this book focuses primarily on authors of the two major imperial powers of the period, Britain and France, where, until the consolidation of international law as an academic discipline in the second half of the nineteenth century, the law of nations was a language and framework for political argument used broadly in public debates and works of political thought.[3] Disputes about the scope of the law of nations and the nature of legal and diplomatic relations were not highly specialized, as they would become in the nineteenth century, but were conducted through diplomatic and travel writings, and in works of political thought, with a wide circulation. The law of nations furnished a language for thinking about the relationship between historically particular practices and universal moral principles, and was thus one of many registers in which European reflection on the place of Europe in the world took place in the eighteenth century.[4]

The implication of international law in the West's domination over other societies is an important part of a larger story of the imperial career of European universalisms. As recent studies of the mutually constitutive relationship of liberalism and empire have shown, imperial tendencies have been as internal to liberal universalism as anti-imperial, or emancipatory, or egalitarian ones, despite liberalism's ostensible commitments to the moral equality of all human beings and to the values of freedom and self-government.[5] Liberalism has often had a parochializing effect on the European imagination, thanks in large part to a linear view of progress that figured European civilization, and European commercial society, as the vanguard or the telos of world history, as at once unique and a model for the rest of the world. Even as it came to understand itself in global terms, Europe "diminished its own ethical possibilities."[6] Paradoxically, scientific and scholarly attention to global phenomena in the nineteenth century was in part driven by, and can be said to have contributed to, European parochialism, as Europe came into an understanding of itself as an entity with global reach and global significance, both because of its outsized power and because of the apparent singularity of European progress in human history. This process is particularly striking in the field of international law, which became an increasingly disciplinary, and self-consciously European, endeavor over the course of the nineteenth century, alongside the development of that parochial moral universalism.[7]

The law of nations proved a powerful political discourse in the context of European commercial and imperial expansion, in at least three respects. It supplied justifications for the actions of imperial states and their agents: from the conquest of territory, to the seizure of other powers' ships, to the imposition of unequal or discriminatory trade regimes. It also furnished resources for the criticism of abuses of power by imperial states; it had, as international law still does, both "imperial" and "counter-imperial," critical, or emancipatory, dimensions. Third, law of nations discourse could obscure the imperial nature of European states: for instance, by conceptualizing the states of the international legal community as territorially compact peoples rather than the sprawling and stratified global empires that the most powerful of them were. As accounts of the law of nations came to be structured by an idea of nations as moral communities equal in status with, and independent of, one another, they had the effect of denying theoretical space for the consideration of European imperial actions. Often they simultaneously delegitimized non-European states as atavistically imperial

in a modern world of equal nations. Such occlusions characterized dominant narratives of international law well into the twentieth century and arguably continue to shape not only mainstream international law but also
much of the discipline of international relations and to shore up the major
institutions of international governance.[9] As James Tully has argued, "the
world legal and political order is best characterized as an imperial order of
some kind," yet "our dominant languages of disclosure and research con-
ceal and overlook the imperialism of the present."[10] This book traces some
of the languages of disclosure and political argument in the eighteenth and
nineteenth centuries that contributed to the current conjuncture Tully so
powerfully articulates.

The complexity of global political interactions means that all figurations
of and narratives about those interactions necessarily abstract and simplify,
drawing attention to certain features or patterns or continuities, and rendering others obscure. Legal discourse has long been central to the project
of describing, conceptualizing, and envisioning what has come to be called
the international, and since the early modern period that legal discourse
has relied on historical narratives, whether more or less explicitly, for its
work of conceptualization. For early modern thinkers such as Grotius and
Gentili, a grasp of the principles of international law was inextricable from
a sense of its history, especially its Roman history.[11] From the time that the
first histories of the law of nations were written, in the late eighteenth and
early nineteenth centuries by figures such as D. H. L. von Ompteda (1785),
Robert Ward (1795), and Henry Wheaton (1841), historiography has been
used to stage disputes and stake claims over the normative foundations of
legal principles, to justify novel practices as conventional, and to demarcate the boundaries of the international legal community. Accordingly, this
book examines how authors deploying the language of the law of nations
and international law conceived of the international both spatially and
temporally. What did it encompass? What were its contours and limits?
How did it come into being and develop over time? What were its possible
futures? I should note that this book is a study of reflections by eighteenth-
and nineteenth-century legal and political thinkers on these questions of
scope, rather than an attempt to chart something like the scope of international law in practice over its history.[12]

Tensions between a consciousness of particularity and an aspiration to
universality have been a persistent feature of European conceptualizations
of the law of nations. The history of law of nations debates underscores the

enduring challenge of thinking about the particular and the universal together, and of accommodating perceived differences within a normative
edifice. Legal discourse itself presses toward uniform application, so that
exceptions or variations must be explained and justified. Thus, Francisco
de Vitoria (ca. 1483–1546) began his *De Indis* by canvassing the possible
reasons that the Amerindians conquered by Spain might not have had
"true dominion," for if they had, if "innocent individuals [had been] pil-
laged of their possessions and dominions, there are grounds for doubting
the justice of what has been done." Many of the key terms in international
law have had a double-edged quality: while such concepts as equality and
reciprocity are apparently inclusive, they have been used as discriminatory
standards. Legal discourse could be used to impose particular practices or
standards on others in the name of their universally obligatory nature, and
to characterize and judge societies as worthy (or not) of reciprocal treatment, or as having standing to make certain kinds of claims.[13]

The question of the relationship between particular norms and practices
and universal principles permeates the history of law of nations theorizing
most obviously and enduringly through the question of the relationship
between the law of nations and the law of nature, between positive law and
natural law. There are good reasons, as Jeremy Waldron has urged, to think
of natural law and the law of nations as inextricable, and further, to approach natural law by way of positive law. Waldron locates such an approach
in the work of Alberico Gentili (1552–1608), who wrote, quoting Cicero, that
"'The agreement of all nations about a matter must be regarded as a law of
nature.'"[14] We should not, Waldron argues, attempt to hive off our reasoning about the normative standards that guide our judgments of positive laws from the content of those laws themselves, as a common view
holds in the name of preserving moral clarity as well as clarity about what
the law is.[15] Rather, we should engage in a kind of "back-and-forth" reasoning that balances a sense of actual practices and positive laws with our
judgment of the moral quality of those practices and laws, and that allows
us to consider a principle's viability for governing social life, whether it
makes reasonable demands on people and can be stable over time. "Natural
law," as Waldron puts the point, is best understood not as something like
pure moral philosophy, but rather "as something discernable most reliably
from a careful, critical, and morally well-informed study of universal or
consensual human practices."[16] Such an approach to the law of nations represents a form of reflection that draws on actual practice to help establish

our normative standards, while at the same time always preserving an overtly critical and evaluative orientation toward practice.[17]

Waldron's reflections about how best to think about the relationship between the law of nations and the law of nature shed light on the pitfalls, the limitations, and occasionally the promise of other ways in which European legal thinkers have navigated the encounter between particular and universal, practice and norm. In what follows, I highlight a set of connected arguments that is this book's major object of normative critique. This set of arguments, which can be summarized as the view that the law of nations is Europe's distinctively successful solution to universal problems of order, entails a particular combination of particularism and universalism that, I will argue, was especially pernicious as a source of justifications for and obfuscations of European imperial domination. This was a parochial universalism that saw its own local principles as universally obligating, and put itself in a position to judge others, not just as enemies, but as "outlaws," thereby making itself both a party to conflict and the judge.

Thanks to qualities or developments unique to Europe, the argument has gone, Europeans alone managed to develop a body of legal doctrine that ought to be authoritative for the entire globe, and that they were therefore justified in imposing on others. The dominant register in which this view was expressed shifted from the religious to the civilizational, but these shared a basic narrative structure: Europe was, for the moment, uniquely in possession of universal moral and political truths. The discourses also coexisted and mingled; medieval canon law documents deploy tropes of civilizing as well as converting infidel barbarians or wild men, and international lawyers continued to insist into the late nineteenth century on the distinctively Christian character of international law.[18] Proponents of this view have suggested a variety of decisive European features, including respect for the individual as a unique legacy of Christianity; a distinctive appreciation for the rule of law as a legacy of Rome; and a varied geography that led to a plurality of states that existed in close proximity to one another and were forced by their relative equality to accommodate themselves to one another, as opposed to the steppes of Asia that encouraged vast and despotic empires.[19] Rousseau encapsulated the view in his "Abstract of Monsieur the Abbé de Saint-Pierre's Plan for Perpetual Peace," which argues that Europe shared a common culture of "maxims and opinions" based on Roman law. The position of mountains and rivers "seem to have settled the number and extent of these Nations; and one can say that the political order of this Part of the world is, in certain regards, Nature's work." Finally, the "multitude and smallness of the States" bound by commerce and intellectual culture meant that Europe produced "not merely an ideal collection of Peoples who have nothing in common but a name like Asia or Africa, but a real society which has its Religion, its morals, its customs and even its laws."[20] The blinkered Eurocentrism of such projects was noted by some Enlightenment commentators. Voltaire cheekily parochialized Rousseau's abstract with his mock commentary by the emperor of China, which criticized such peace plans not just for their futility and utopianism but relatedly for their failure to recognize non-European states as members of the international community, for their presumptuousness in placing Europe figuratively at the center of the world, and for their complicity, whether witting or unwitting, with those profiting from unjust global commercial enterprises.[21]

The universalist claim that European international law should be binding on all states and that China, or the Ottoman Empire, was a lawless exception worked in tandem with the particularist claim that international law was law of Christendom alone and that there was no community of law at all between European states and others. In both cases, the effect was to entrench asymmetries of power in legal form and to render difference from the West (that is, Western Europe and its white settler colonies) as moral and legal inferiority. As Teemu Ruskola has recounted, when Caleb Cushing, the first U.S. ambassador to China, arrived in 1844 to negotiate a commercial treaty for his country in the wake of the first Opium War between China and Britain, Cushing's ships were asked not to fire a twenty-one-gun salute, as China did not observe such a custom and it might frighten the inhabitants. Cushing was also denied an imperial audience and instead was required by Chinese officials to negotiate with the imperial envoy, commissioner Qiying, at the temple of Wanghia near Macao. Cushing was outraged about both incidents, insisting that it was his "duty, in the outset, not to omit any of the tokens of respect customary among Western nations" and predicting trouble for China if it persisted in refusing "the exchange of the ordinary courtesies of national intercourse."[22] Cushing's self-righteous response neatly encapsulated what was becoming the standard Western approach to relations with non-European states, in its appeal to supposed principle, to the ideal of mutual respect among states, and to Western customs as normative for the entire world, and its use of all these to place China in a subordinate legal position. Cushing managed to claim both universality and particularity for the European (Christian, Western) law of nations. When China declined to follow a Western practice, even one as purely ceremonial as the gun salute, it was failing to uphold a standard it ought to recognize. And yet Western states could not be expected to extend forms of legal recognition standard among themselves to China and other non-Western states.

In addition to charting iterations of that parochial universalism in eighteenth- and nineteenth-century international legal discourse, this book also examines alternative efforts to navigate the tensions between international law's universal aspirations and its particular European features. One alternative understanding has stressed that even if Europe constituted a distinct political-legal community that had emerged over time as the result of particularly dense interactions and shared history, this community had to be understood in the context of its global connections, and, moreover, Europeans ought to regard their relations with states and societies everywhere as bound and constrained by law. Although they might encounter differences in both domestic and intercommunal legal doctrines, Europeans, in their dealings with other societies, ought to look for shared legal principles. Furthermore, they ought to respect their own legal commitments in dealing with extra-European societies, and to seek mutual intelligibility, even when they could not impose their own standards on others. This approach to the tension between the particular and the universal could lead to a posture of interpretive generosity with respect to others' legal principles. Though never a dominant strain of political-legal thought, it had distinguished exponents in the eighteenth century and weaker echoes in the nineteenth, and one of the aims of this book is to recapture it.

The injustices that Europeans perpetrated in and on other societies with the help of the law of nations as a tool and justificatory discourse have sometimes been characterized as due to the exclusion of those other societies from the international legal community. But critiques that focus on exclusion are limited.[23] As Richard Tuck has argued, Asian states that had been excluded from treaty relations with Europeans by the Christian ban on treaties with infidels had good reasons to regret their later inclusion within European treaty practices—and the wars and military alliances these governed—as inclusion became more standard in the seventeenth century. Tuck sees Grotius's criticism of a ban on treaties with infidels as a feature of his imperializing bent, and he argues that it may have been

because the ban was more respected in Spanish and Portuguese discourse
that those empires lagged behind the Dutch and later the English in imperial expansion into Asia.[24] Treaties and legal recognition were instrumental
in the expansion of the British Empire in North America and the Pacific.[25]
Nineteenth-century Europeans likewise recognized the sovereignty of African rulers and concluded treaties with them precisely to facilitate their
dispossession and subjugation.[26] An apparent recognition of the validity of
non-European laws also served as the basis of one important justification
of slavery before the nineteenth century. The celebrated barrister John
Dunning, representing the slaveholder in *Somerset v. Stewart* in 1772 (the
case that established that English common law did not support slavery),
argued that the purchase of slaves in Africa rested on a recognition of the
right of African societies to make laws imposing slavery as a punishment
for offenses against society. He offered that it would be an unjustifiable
chauvinism not to recognize the legality of such enslavements:

> We are apt (and great authorities support this way of speaking) to call
> those nations universally, whose internal policy we are ignorant of,
> barbarians; (thus the Greeks, particularly, stiled many nations, whose
> customs, generally considered, were far more justifiable and commend-
> able than their own:) unfortunately, from calling them barbarians,
> we are apt to think them so, and draw conclusions accordingly. . . .
> There are of these people, men who have a sense of the right and value
> of freedom; but who imagine that offences against a society are punish-
> able justly by the severe law of servitude. . . . The law of the land of that
> country disposed of [James Somerset] as property, with all the conse-
> quences of transmission and alienation.[27]

Arnulf Becker Lorca has charted the disillusionment that semi-peripheral
international lawyers felt in the early twentieth century as they saw that the
bid for inclusion in the international community of states pursued by a
previous generation of non-European lawyers had repeatedly failed to curb
European states' use of international law to bolster and justify their dispro-
portionate power. Today, onerous sovereign debt obligations, or odious
debt, persists as another form of injustice enabled by legal "inclusion" on
unequal terms.[28] Inclusion on unequal terms arguably cannot properly be
called inclusion at all. But perhaps instead it is misleading or unhelpful to
think of exclusion as the primary problem, since the critical lens of exclusion tends to suggest that inclusion is an adequate solution. It may be more

domination, not
exclusion, is the
problem

productive to see the problem as one of domination, which more clearly enables us to see how the emancipatory and dominating sides of international law are intertwined.

The "European State System" and the Law of Nations

A conception of the international came into focus in Europe in the seventeenth and eighteenth centuries, and relations among European states had priority within this conception. It was during this period that historians and political writers came to understand Europe as a system, a "state system," worthy of analysis in its own right, rather than simply the product of actions by states and statesmen, and whose coming into being was one of the great achievements of modern European civilization. Other parts of the world were said to be unable to match this achievement, as they were characterized by, perhaps doomed to, great and oppressive empires. And yet, as Andrew Fitzmaurice has noted, "the creation of states and empires was, from one perspective, a connected, or even a single, process."[29] The relationship of this state system to the "international," to the law of nations, and to humanity as a whole was complex and ambiguous, but by the turn of the nineteenth century the European state system and its public law were coming to be seen as standing in for the international as a whole, representing a proto-international community or the germ of a global community. The law of nations was one of the most important discourses in which Europeans articulated Europe's claim to be the unique bearer of universal values.[30]

The project of creating an international order has long been commingled with that of European consolidation and informed by European exceptionalism, from Christendom's global project of conversion in medieval and early modern Church doctrine, through eighteenth-century projects for perpetual peace, to contemporary theorizations of the European Union as a democratic model for a postsovereign world. Europeans, as Martti Koskenniemi has noted, have never "thought of Europe in merely local terms, but generalized it into a representative of the universal."[31] The Abbé de Saint-Pierre reported in 1713 that he had initially conceived his project for perpetual peace as encompassing "all the Kingdoms of the World" but had concluded that "even though in following Ages most of the Sovereigns of Asia and Africa might desire to be receiv'd into the Union, yet this Prospect would seem so remote and so full of Difficulties, that it would cast an Air of Impossibility upon the whole Project."[32] He anticipated that a Christian European union "would soon become the Arbiter of the Sovereigns" of "the Indies," who would place their faith in it when they recognized that its only interest was in mutually beneficial commerce and not in conquest. The complacency of this expectation seems particularly glaring in light of the global facets of the treaty negotiations in which he was participating as a French secretary at Utrecht when the work was published, including the British acquisition of the *asiento* or permission to supply slaves to Spanish colonies, which ended the Dutch monopoly on the trade, and the recognition of various powers' sovereignty over new territories in the Americas. Immanuel Kant's federation of republics is described in universal language but is often read as a project of European federation.[33] Projects for European union have in this way long seen it as having a vocation both as a political archetype for the rest of the world and as an authoritative arbiter of the political legitimacy of extra-European states: a model for the future and a judge for the present.

To be sure, certain political developments largely internal to Europe and Christianity partly shaped the development of European understandings of the international and ideas of universal validity. As Richard Devetak has argued, Renaissance statesmen and the humanist historians who served them "helped give shape to a conception of the international as a world of states," in the course of a battle against the political theology of the Church as having supreme universal authority. Andrew Fitzmaurice has argued that the universalist gestures of the European law of nations took shape in the context of the religious warfare unleashed by the Reformation: "These rules applied between European states, but their principles necessarily had to have some claim to universality or they risked falling back into the communal ideas that had fed more than a century of war." Edward Keene has argued that the shift from naturalism to positivism, which involved an insistence that the law of nations was particular to Europe, was due as much to a counterrevolutionary context within Europe as to reflections on European states' relations with other parts of the world.[34] Yet for too long the dominant narrative of international politics was one of a system that emerged within Europe—Europe understood in isolation from the rest of the world—that then expanded in the nineteenth and twentieth to encompass the globe. The profound, and constant, role of extra-European developments in the evolution of the law of nations was long ignored.

Since the nineteenth century, such an account of the history and sources of international law has been the dominant one. That narrative said that international law had its origins within Europe, between sovereign European states that viewed each other as free and equal.[35] It saw a pivotal moment in the Westphalia treaties, which, it said, set out above all to protect states' independence from intervention by outsiders.[36] And, it concluded, this essentially European system gradually came to incorporate other states as they reached the appropriate "standard of civilization," or, as more recent language would have it, as they entered the state system or decolonized and became independent.

The Victorian historical narrative persisted well into the twentieth century. Both dismissive and defensive in the face of the challenges to international law raised by lawyers and leaders from decolonizing states, the Dutch jurist Jan Verzijl insisted in 1955 that the body of international law was exclusively the product of "the European mind"—it had been generated by a combination of European theoretical activity and European state practice, and it had integrity and coherence. With the kind of reflexive positivism that characterized Victorian international legal thought, as I discuss in Chapter 6, Verzijl offered a peremptory prediction that "it would seem very unlikely that any revolutionary ideas will appear as a result of the entrance of these new members which will have power to challenge or supersede the general principles and customary rules of law which have shown their vitality by standing the test of time and circumstance." Verzijl, that is, posited a continuity of the tradition of international law that he attributed to the essential conceptual and normative soundness of the legal totality, rather than to its imposition by and collaboration with force. He argued not simply that non-Europeans had adopted international law without materially altering it, but that they could not help but adopt without altering it, because they had no useful alternative legal traditions on which to draw. He depicted non-European resistance and critique as if these were driven by a kind of impotent *ressentiment:* something "we in the West can only regard with a certain amount of amusement because it offers curious evidence of the lasting dependence of non-Western nations in the conduct of their international affairs upon fundamental concepts of the Western world from which their political leaders nevertheless so ardently crave to liberate their States." Rather than recognizing international law as a space of contestation in the past and present, he presented it as an organic whole, "which originated in the West, but which has been adopted by the East," and he saw in this narrative of European past and global future "one of the outstanding proofs of the ultimate unity of the human race."[37]

Although it departs significantly in tone from Verzijl's smug Eurocentrism, Adam Watson's *Evolution of International Society* (1992) represents a late twentieth-century articulation of the conventional narrative that recapitulates some of the narrative's key themes and performs some of the same ideological work.[38] Watson's book was one of several prominent products of the British Committee on the Theory of International Politics led by Herbert Butterfield, Martin Wight, and Hedley Bull (the nucleus of the "English school" of international relations). Its framing narrative, that the contemporary international system is the result of the global expansion of an originally European system of equal and independent states, takes up the basic nineteenth-century narrative. This approach downplays the fact that the so-called European system of independent states was dependent on—indeed, constituted by—the global relations of politics, economy, and war in which those states were embedded, and it downplays the ongoing asymmetries of power and legal status after decolonization, because it sees the relevant story as the rise of a global society out of a European one, rather than as one of transformations of legal form within a global system characterized by domination and asymmetry.

Thus, while acknowledging the fact of European empires, Watson tells a narrative sanitized of European domination in several ways: he writes (in a Vattelian vein that I explore in Chapter 3) of the European state system of free and equal members as if this system existed independent of global imperial structures; he conceives of European relations with the Ottoman Empire and Asian states as "a compromise or hybrid"; and he summarizes decolonization as the acceptance by Europeans of all other independent states on equal terms: "When Europeans took it for granted that all other independent states should be admitted to their international society on the same terms as themselves, the European society can be said to have given way to a global one."[39] Such a gloss disregards the fact that Europeans fought during much of the twentieth century to constrict the legal rights and standing of non-European states, beginning with League of Nations members Liberia and Ethiopia in the 1920s and 1930s, by forcing constraints on sovereignty on decolonizing states, and by imposing onerous and often destructive loan conditions on Third World states through international institutions such as the International Monetary Fund and the World Bank, so that the admission on equal terms never in fact occurred.[40] If it was "taken for granted," this was arguably only in a more perverse sense than Watson intended, namely, that the very insistence that postcolonial states were incorporated as equal members itself served to obscure their ongoing legal subordination. Watson concludes that "since both the letter and the spirit of the European society of states were essentially non-imperial, and fluctuated within the independences / hegemony half of the spectrum, the nineteenth-century European dominance over the rest of the world proved to be less durable than it once seemed." The choices Watson makes to render global interactions analytically tractable—that is, his framing historical narrative and spatial conceptualization of the global order as the expansion outward of the community of equal nation-states from Europe to the world—make it hard to see some of the major phenomena of modern world history. An alternative framing would highlight the evolution of a capitalist world system in which European metropoles and extra-European states and societies, whether formally colonized or not, developed interdependently through a profoundly asymmetrical process, with international law playing an important role in justifying and stabilizing inequalities of wealth and military power.[41]

The conventional narrative, that is, disregarded the constitution of modern Europe by an imperial global order and discounted the role of domination in the history of international law by narrating that history as a product of egalitarian relations among nation-states. It largely ignored the global contexts and sources for international law—the profound preoccupation with imperial concerns by thinkers deemed foundational, such as Vitoria and Grotius; the influence of Roman legal concepts developed during the expansion of the Roman Empire; and the inter-imperial rivalries that contributed to so many of the decisive wars, treaties, and theories.[42] According to the standard account, international law emerged within Europe as a response to the problems of disorder and violence among states that understood themselves as equal in standing, even if not in size, wealth, or power. It then gradually expanded during the nineteenth and twentieth centuries to encompass ever more states as these achieved a "standard of civilization" or achieved independence under decolonization. To summarize, the conventional narrative is problematic in at least two respects. First, it depicts modern international law as developed exclusively within Europe and then exported to the rest of the world, rather than as partly forged in the course of European imperial expansion and through European interactions with extra-European states and societies. And second, it suggests that the (European) building blocks of modern international law were truly universalist, that they did not privilege Europeans or Christians but were (uniquely in the world) universal in scope. Critical histories have been challenging both pillars of the narrative.

In response to the standard narrative, Jörg Fisch has insisted that "the political aim of the European expansion, from the fifteenth to the twentieth centuries, was never to extend the international society of Europe. . . . The aim was not coordination but subordination."[43] He concludes that the "real universalization" of the system came not through the extension of European power but in its contraction with decolonization, "and this only because it contained a principle which allowed [there to be built] an international society of sovereign equals." Fisch is interested in law as a political tool rather than as an ideological structure, or rather he emphasizes the former at the expense of the latter. While his argument makes for a vitally important correction to the conventional narrative, Fisch treats Europeans as purely driven by a material impulse to dominate others for European advantage, and he treats the ideas of international law as free-floating normative principles (equality and reciprocity) that belong to everyone and were embraced by decolonizing nations because they were more attractive than the alternative of destroying the system. But the compelling principles of mutual respect, political autonomy, and humanitarian concern cannot, I would argue, be divorced from a history in which such principles were deployed to advance and justify imperial domination; to do so would be to risk failing to respond in a sufficiently critical spirit to the ideological work such ideas may continue to do to shore up or occlude global asymmetries of power, a subject I take up briefly in the Epilogue.

The Historical Narrative of the Book

This book is intended as a contribution to a growing body of literature that can be called the critical history of international law. It is a striking feature of the recent historical turn in international law that it has been deeply shaped by a postcolonial sensibility, so that the revitalization of historical interest in a field that had long lacked it has also entailed a radical challenge to international law's identity as an emancipatory project with an essentially European genealogy. The book that did more than any other to spark this process was Martti Koskenniemi's *Gentle Civilizer of Nations*

(2000), and Koskenniemi has continued to be the most influential as well as the most prolific voice in the conversation his book did so much to begin. Antony Anghie's *Imperialism, Sovereignty, and the Making of International Law* (2004), another landmark in this turn, extends back in time and systematizes the association between international law and European imperial expansion that Koskenniemi had exposed in the lives and work of the generation of international lawyers (the "men of 1873") who occupied the first university chairs of international law and founded its first associations in the name of a vision of global harmony, even as they assisted in the carving up of Africa at the 1884–1885 Berlin Conference. This work attends to the persistently hierarchical structure of the global order, what Anghie has called the "dynamic of difference embodied in the very structure, logic and identity of international institutions."[44] Koskenniemi and Anghie had important predecessors from the period of decolonization in the 1950s and 1960s, including Georges Abi-Saab, R. P. Anand, Mohammed Bedjaoui, Jorge Castañeda, and Kamal Hossain at the origins of the movement later called Third World Approaches to International Law (TWAIL).[45] The massive *Oxford Handbook of the History of International Law* is the clearest and most extensive evidence of the postcolonial turn in the history of international law; the editors view "overcoming Eurocentrism" and drawing from new developments in global history as among the book's most important tasks and contributions.[46] And while international law became the purview of specialists in the later nineteenth century, with the founding of professional societies, journals, and university chairs, the current historicizing moment has brought scholars of international law into conversation with those of other disciplines including history, anthropology, international relations, and political theory.[47] This may make possible something like a return to the predisciplinary status of the law of nations as a discourse available to a wider array of writers, thinkers, and publics.

While there has been much recent scholarship on Vitoria and Grotius, as well as on the later nineteenth century, the predisciplinary eighteenth and early nineteenth centuries have been relatively neglected.[48] And yet, even before the most recent wave of scholarship on the intersection of law and empire, a powerful revision of the standard narrative emerged in the 1950s and 1960s alongside the work of the first generation of lawyers from the so-called New States, in the historical scholarship of the Polish-British international lawyer Charles Henry Alexandrowicz. Alexandrowicz grounded his revisionist story precisely in a claim that the period around the turn of the nineteenth century was the transformative moment in the history of international law. Alexandrowicz's work had both historiographic and normative aims. He meant to set the historical record straight, from what he saw as its long Victorian detour, to show that international law both in theory and in practice had been far more inclusive than it was to become in the nineteenth century. And he sought to recover that greater inclusiveness as a means of combating "European egocentricity" in international law, with all its pernicious effects in the postcolonial period. Alexandrowicz argued that for much of the sixteenth through the eighteenth centuries, Asian states or rulers were routinely respected as fully sovereign; treaties with them were equal and binding, and these treaties were regarded by European lawyers and scholars as evidence of their participation in the law of nations. For instance, the Maratha state, a formidable military power in northwest India, was, he held, "clearly considered a legal entity in the . . . law of nations and there is no doubt as to its membership in the Family of Nations and its capacity of dealing with other members on a footing of equality and of concluding treaties in the meaning of international law." Alexandrowicz argued that this naturalist universalism was displaced by positivism beginning in the late eighteenth century. He saw authors such as Ompteda and J. J. von Moser as intermediate figures, with Ompteda seeking to defend the law of nature in a kind of rearguard action against the encroaching positivist ideology, and Moser a representative of the latter whose work nonetheless shows that the "concept of universalism was . . . capable of holding a qualified position of its own in spite of adverse doctrinal developments."[49]

As compelling and as dauntingly erudite as Alexandrowicz's argument is, it seems flawed in several respects. First, his distinction between natural law universalism and positivism is overdrawn, for theories of the law of nations have always contained elements of both: earlier so-called natural law theories relied on the practice of nations for the content of that law. Natural law remained pervasive in the nineteenth century, and even the self-declared positivists of the period who claimed to eschew natural law held on to claims of prospective universal validity for their "positive" law of nations.[50] Second, he overstated the consensus in seventeenth- and eighteenth-century Europe that Asian states were fellow members of an international legal community, for there was much greater doubt and disagreement on this question than his claims about natural law universalism suggest. In what follows I am deeply indebted to Alexandrowicz's pioneering work even as I seek to challenge aspects of his account.

Before giving an overview of the argument of the book, I will summarize a few features of the earlier history of the law of nations. In Roman law, the *ius gentium* referred to the law common to all peoples; it supplied the basis for legal decisions involving non-Romans living under Roman government, in contrast to civil law, which applied exclusively to Roman citizens. There is, then, a long history to the imbrication of empire and the "law of nations," since the Roman *ius gentium* developed within the Roman Empire precisely as a way of adjudicating relations between Romans and conquered peoples who were not Roman citizens. The *ius gentium* was considered to be based on natural reason and so to be largely in accordance with natural law, with certain key exceptions such as slavery, which was forbidden by natural law but permitted by most societies and so by the *ius gentium*. The development out of the Roman conception of *ius gentium* of an idea of a law governing relations *among peoples* is complex and contested: as Henry Maine was to note, "the confusion between *ius gentium* or law common to all nations, and *international law*, is entirely modern," because the Romans used the term *"ius fetiale"* to refer to intercommunal law governing such things as the rights of ambassadors and the proper means of declaring war.[51] The alternative phrase *"ius inter gentes"* is found in Vitoria and Suarez.[52] Jeremy Bentham sought to overcome the ambiguity of *droit des gens* or *ius gentium* with one of his few successful neologisms, the phrase "international law" (as a translation of *droit entre les gens*), which he saw as more apt because it explicitly indexed laws between states or nations.[53]

Although it was only in the nineteenth century that treatises on the law of nations began to include, regularly and systematically, treatments of the recognition of states and explicit inquiries into the scope of the international community, the question of the participation of non-European states in the law of nations was, in more oblique forms, a persistent one in law of nations discourse. First, a key argument for the claim that the law of nations tracked natural law was that it was agreed upon by all—or rather, according to the usual qualification, all "civilized"—nations.[54] The law of nations was what all civilized nations, understood as a legitimate proxy for all nations, had agreed to, either explicitly or in practice. Grotius's formulation characteristically elided the universal judgment of mankind and that of a more particular set of nations: we can "with very great Probability," he wrote, "conclude that to be by the Law of Nature, which is generally believed to be so by all, or at least, the most civilized, Nations. For, an universal Effect requires an universal Cause. And there cannot well be any other Cause assigned for this general Opinion, than what is called Common Sense." But, as Hobbes pointed out with his usual dry wit, the question of who counted among the civilized was wildly indeterminate: when writers say something is against the law of nature, he wrote, they "do allege no more than this, that it is against the consent of all nations, or the wisest and most civil nations. . . . But it is not agreed upon, who shall judge which nations are the wisest."[55] The justificatory work done by the common modifier "civilized" limited, ambiguously, the law's ostensible universality.

Furthermore, despite the universal connotations of a *ius gentium* based on natural law, medieval legal thought and practice had been structured by a notion of a unified *Christianitas* predicated on hostility to infidels, even within the more inclusive strand of thought that defended the legitimacy of infidels' property and political power (two key aspects of *dominium*), following Thomas Aquinas and the canonist Sinibaldo Fieschi (Pope Innocent IV, 1243–1254).[56] Renaissance thinkers styled Europe as a *respublica christiana*, and the figure of the infidel continued to serve as a unifying opponent for many thinkers in humanist as well as more strictly theological traditions in the sixteenth and seventeenth centuries.[57] The scholastic concept of the *impium foedus*, the prohibition on treaties with infidels, had never been absolute, for a long ecclesiastical tradition had challenged it, and over time it was increasingly regarded as an inappropriate incursion of religion into the realm of law and diplomacy. Still, into the seventeenth century, the permissibility of alliances with infidels remained the dominant idiom in which to question the nature of European states' legal relations with Ottomans and Muslims more broadly, just as the question of whether barbarians can have dominium represented the key framework for thinking about legal relations with indigenous inhabitants of the Americas. The Protestant Gentili, despite rebuffing theological authority with his famous *"Silete theologi in munere alieno"* ("Theologians, mind your own business"), held that alliances with infidels are wrong precisely because they are infidels.[58] Gentili had a complex and perhaps ultimately incoherent approach to justifying differential treatment of Muslim states. On the one hand he argued, on grounds of both universal practice and the irrelevance of religion to the *ius gentium*, that they can be legitimate states with whom it is appropriate to exchange embassies. But on the other hand he declared, though seemingly not on "theological" grounds, that it was illegitimate to make treaties of alliance with infidels, thus excluding all non-Christian powers from the most important form of interstate relations. Despite profound disagreements among medieval and early modern thinkers about Christianity's implications for law and temporal power, and about the degree to which Christendom could or should be internally united, there remained a widely shared commitment to a deep division in legal status between Christendom and its enemies.[59]

That gulf in legal status remained plausible, if increasingly contested, into the early eighteenth century. Gottfried Wilhelm Leibniz, for instance, combined a project of "universal jurisprudence" accessible to all minds with one of unifying the *respublica christiana* against "the plague of Mohammedanism."[60] Documents related to negotiations for the Treaty of Utrecht (1713) continued to refer to the *respublica christiana*, even as this language was giving way to the language of European community.[61] Yet when the East India Company sought to defend its trade monopoly in the famous 1683 case *East India Company v. Sandys* on the grounds that only an explicit royal charter could override the religious prohibition on commercial or military alliances with infidels, a lawyer for the independent English merchants fighting the monopoly rejected "this notion of Christians not to have commerce with infidels" as "a conceit absurd, monkish, fantastical and fanatical."[62] In 1758, Vattel thought that he hardly needed to address the topic at all: a treatment of treaties with infidels, he wrote, "would be superfluous in our age. The law of nature alone regulates the treaties of nations: the difference of religion is a thing absolutely foreign to them. Different people treat with each other in quality of men, and not under the character of Christians, or of Muslims."[63]

We might see the eighteenth century, then, as a period of particular fluidity in conceptions of the law of nations, when the older notion of a unified *Christianitas* or *respublica christiana* predicated on hostility to infidels was losing its hold, and the divide between civilized and barbarous was not yet as deeply entrenched as it would become in the nineteenth century. At the same time, the law of nations was coming to be identified with what legal and political thinkers began to call the *droit publique de l'Europe (ius publicum Europaeum)*. As the premise of an irreducible legal gulf between Christians and infidels was being rejected, new ways of framing the question of legal relations with non-Europeans arose. Participants in these debates were not always primarily legal thinkers but also diplomats, such as the British emissaries Paul Rycaut and James Porter, Orientalist scholars such as Abraham Anquetil-Duperron, political thinkers and legislators

such as Montesquieu and Edmund Burke, and historians such as Robert
Plumer Ward. This breadth of participation in questioning the scope of the
European legal order marks one difference with the more professionalized
late nineteenth century.

What did Europeans think were the sources of the law of nations in this
period between the waning of the Christian legal community and the rise
of a so-called positivism based exclusively on European practice? How
could one determine its content? Why, and for whom, was it authoritative,
given that there was no world state? Was it indeed universal? The major
sources for the law of nations, according to writers of late eighteenth-
century legal textbooks, were the great legal treatises (by Grotius, Wolff,
Pufendorf, Burlamaqui, Vattel) that had introduced Roman law in place of
theology and canon law as a primary source of legal principles.[64] Other key
sources were treaty collections and diplomatic memoirs and correspondence, which were thought to provide essential contextual information
about the meaning and purposes of the treaties. Treaty collecting was a
growth industry in this period, particularly after the heroic compilation
published by Jean Dumont in the 1720s. The fact that European states
signed treaties with so many non-Christian powers in the course of their
global expansion does not show, *pace* Alexandrowicz, that they saw these
treaties as foundational to the law of nations in the way that treaties within
Europe were thought to be. This is not because European states scrupu-
lously abided by their treaties with each other and violated those with
powers beyond Europe. But treaties with the Turks and other Asian and
North African powers were often treated differently from those within Europe; some collections that were seen as the basis of the law of nations did
not include treaties with non-European states, noting that they were restricting themselves to Europe. Treaties of the East India trading companies with Asian powers were usually collected separately. Some of the most
influential collections, such as Dumont's, did include treaties with non-
Christian powers, especially the Ottoman Empire and the Barbary States.
Indeed, Dumont, in justifying the usefulness of his collection, used as his
example a hypothetical English ambassador to the king of Morocco, who
would want to know the full history of Morocco's treaty relations with
France in order to "procure for his Master all the same honors, that this
African Monarch renders to the King of France." But even though Dumont's title was *The Universal Diplomatic Corpus of the Law of Nations,* his
subtitle indicated that he was including only European treaties.[65] It is this

sort of equivocation, in which "universal" and "European" operate as syn-
onyms, that suggests that we cannot assume that language of "universal"
and "mankind" in legal treatises such as Vattel's were intended to apply
globally.

As I explore in Chapter 2, the Ottoman Empire consistently represented
the most prominent fraught case, because its diplomatic and commercial
ties with Christian Europe were so dense compared with those of any other
Muslim or extra-European state. Despite the empire's considerable Euro-
pean territory and its long-standing participation in European war, com-
merce, and diplomacy, authors noted that even if it was technically part of
Europe, it was not a full participant in the European *legal* community.
G. F. von Martens, for instance, writing in the 1780s, preferred the term
"*European* law of nations" to "law of *civilized* nations," but he added that
"European" was not quite right either, because "although, *in* Europe the
Turks have, in many respects, rejected the positive law of nations of which
I here treat; and though, *out of* Europe, the United States of America have
uniformly adopted it. It is to be understood *à potiori,* and it appears preferable to that of, *law of civilized nations,* which is too vague."[66] The treaty
collections often included caveats about the differences between Ottoman
or North African treaties and standard European ones, stating that such
treaties were restricted to a few key issues, or that the procedure for
enforcing them was distinct. A British collection of maritime treaties published in 1779, for instance, noted that because the Ottomans were "unacquainted with the Treaties made by us with other Nations in Europe," the
usual assumptions and procedures could not be followed.[67]

Similarly, diplomatic memoirs regularly insisted that "the Turks" were
not fully acquainted with the European law of nations, or that they refused
to recognize it, and so were not properly part of the emerging interstate
legal system. The English emissary Paul Rycaut argued in 1666 that "though
the *Turks* make these outward demonstrations of all due reverence and religious care to preserve the persons of Ambassadours sacred and free from
violence," it was clear from their treatment of ambassadors during wars
that "they have no esteem of the Law of Nations," and it was a principle
with them to violate their treaties with unbelievers whenever doing so
would contribute to the expansion of their empire or the propagation of
their faith.[68] The English diplomat Sir James Porter likewise wrote a century
later that "the Turks have properly no idea of the law of nations."[69] Both
Rycaut and Porter were considered sympathetic observers of the Ottomans,

and Porter insisted that the regime was law-governed and not an oriental despotism. But he held nonetheless that the law of nations did not apply in Turkey. Clearly, many Europeans in the seventeenth and eighteenth centuries, despite the fact that their states and trading companies were signing treaties with Asian and Muslim powers, believed these treaties existed in a different legal space from that of the European treaties and common practices that they saw as the basis for a systematic law of nations.

At the same time, the great treatises of the law of nations in this period tended to be written in resolutely universalist language. Christian Wolff described his conception of the *civitas maxima* as encompassing "all nations," and he held that because states are equal, none has the right to impose its own interpretation of natural law on another, so that while all nations have duties of mutual assistance to one another, states cannot compel "barbarous nations" to accept their assistance. His Sinophilism, with its suggestion that "pagans and atheists could be just as moral in their daily lives as practicing Christians," led to his expulsion from his post at the University of Halle. (Characteristically, the Victorian Sir Travers Twiss would take Wolff's *civitas maxima* to refer narrowly, though "somewhat indistinctly," to "an 'Inner Circle' of the more civilized nations."[70]) Vattel, likewise, wrote of "the bonds of that universal society which nature has established among" all nations. He looked forward to the time when the principles of the law of nations would be adopted as state practice, and "the world would have the appearance of a large republic; men would live everywhere like brothers, and each individual be a citizen of the universe."[71] At the same time, given the emphatic universalism of Wolff and Vattel's language, there is remarkably little in their treatises to suggest that they seriously considered the place of treaty relations or legal practices beyond Europe as germane to the emerging doctrine of the law of nations. Like Wolff's, Vattel's language tends to be highly abstract, and his examples are drawn primarily from dealings among Europeans.[72] Beyond his claim that difference of religion has no bearing on legal obligations, Vattel wrote relatively little about how the law of nations might bind Europeans in their dealings with powers outside Europe. The ambiguity of Vattel's universalism made for diverse ramifications of his theory; he could be cited on behalf of an expansive law of nations that obligated Europeans in their interactions in Asia and the Americas just as within Europe, but he can also be seen as giving voice to invidious distinctions between law-abiding Europeans and Muslims who, though formally included within the law of nations, he often depicted as knowingly violating its provisions. Perhaps still more important for the longer-term consequences of his thought, however, was Vattel's conceptualization of the international sphere as a space inhabited by free and equal states conceived as national communities, a depiction that for Vattel represented both a normative ambition and a rough description of the world around him, although it profoundly misrepresented the character of the major European powers of his day. I explore these features of Vattel's thought in Chapter 3.

In Chapter 4, I argue that the late eighteenth century saw an unusual, perhaps unmatched, flourishing of critical approaches to the question of the scope of the European law of nations and the nature of legal relations between European and non-European states, and that these approaches emerged on the back of Vattel. The period stands out in the history of the law of nations as one of striking openness on the part of Europeans to the possibility of shared legal frameworks and mutual obligations between Christians and non-Christians, Europeans and non-Europeans. Some analysts feared that nations outside Europe would find themselves in a legal vacuum. They saw the law of nations as a discursive resource against injustice and exploitation by Europeans. They cautioned against the moral errors and political costs of a restricted understanding of the legal community. Legal and political thinkers exemplary of these critical approaches—Edmund Burke, the French Orientalist Abraham Hyacinthe Anquetil-Duperron, and the celebrated admiralty court judge William Scott, Lord Stowell—articulated a more inclusive and pluralistic understanding of the global legal order than the view that came to prevail. None was an opponent of imperial rule as such; indeed, it was precisely through imperial structures that they understood the law of nations as often operating. But they envisaged a global legal order, or network of orders, as a constraint on the exercise and abuse of European states' power. They wrote during the decades framed by the Seven Years' War and the Napoleonic Wars, a period when European states were constructing imperial constitutions of global reach, and when states as well as other actors such as trading companies and pirates competed to defend their power and interests in the terms of newly extensive legal regimes. It should again be stressed that the thinkers considered here were Europeans speaking to European audiences, often with limited knowledge of the extra-European societies, languages, and legal traditions they discussed. They drew on the ambiguous status of the law of nations as putatively universal despite its heavily European history. But they did so with the aim of chastening European power through legal limits and obligations, including constraints that Europeans should recognize as binding themselves even when they could not presume to use them to bind others.

Chapter 5 takes up later and rather different ramifications of Vattel's thought in the first half of the nineteenth century, exploring the reception of Vattel's thought in Britain, whose expanding empire, unchallenged as a global hegemon after the Napoleonic Wars, was a uniquely significant site for the production of international law, as Lauren Benton and Lisa Ford have shown.[73] Whereas the law of nations had been understood since the sixteenth century to be intimately (if complexly) connected to a universal law of nature, by the turn of the nineteenth century, self-described positivists were declaring a break from their predecessors' naturalism and universalism. The European law of nations, it was now said, was a historically particular phenomenon that had arisen in the context of dense interactions among states and their subjects; other areas of the world might have their own laws of nations, but Europeans should not consider their own legal principles binding on them in their interactions with societies in other parts of the world. In this chapter I explore these transformations in international law by tracing the question of the scope of the law of nations, and the linked question of the status of Vattel as an authority on the law of nations, from the period of the French revolutionary wars through the first Opium War. Vattel's *Droit des gens* was arguably the most globally significant work of European political thought through the 1830s, and in the changing reception of Vattel we can track the ragged transition from the intellectual world of the eighteenth-century law of nations to that of the professional international lawyers of the later nineteenth century.

From the mid-nineteenth century, as Chapter 6 argues, legal and political thinkers increasingly argued that although international law was exclusively European in origin, their law was destined, thanks to Europe's superior civilizational status, to be authoritative for all, and Europeans had the right to dictate the terms of legal interaction to backward, barbarous, or savage peoples. The tension between the European and the universal in international law, that is, came to be resolved through a view of global legality as a European order writ large. When in 1874 the Institut de droit international tasked one of its committees to examine whether so-called oriental nations were full participants in what was called "the general community of international law," it was taken for granted that international law was European in origin but prospectively authoritative for everyone, and that as non-Europeans reached the standard of civilization they would be admitted to the international community. The nineteenth-century position has tended to go by the name of "positivism," among both its proponents and later historians, and to be contrasted with an earlier natural law universalism.[74] Some claimed that unlike natural lawyers, they were not engaged in a normative project at all. They were simply interested in recording and codifying actual state practice. As Travers Twiss put it, he made "no pretension to discuss any theories of International Ethics, as furnishing rules, by which the intercourse of independent States ought to be guided. He has been content to examine into the existing usages of State-Life, and to illustrate the modifications and improvements which they have undergone from time to time, whereby they have been adjusted to the growing wants of a progressive civilisation."[75] But as the passage indicates, their theories belied their self-description in at least two ways. They were not just recording state practices but selecting the practices they considered worthy as sources of international law, and doing so on the basis of a set of poorly defended cultural and normative assumptions. Moreover, they did have universalist aspirations: they saw the European order they were codifying as the basis for a future international order that would gradually be extended to or imposed on the rest of the world, in large part through colonial conquest. I argue that nineteenth-century international lawyers placed questions of membership in international society at the heart of their theories of international law. The many late nineteenth-century efforts toward codification of international legal standards intensified the era's exclusionary tendencies by encouraging jurists to specify what might otherwise have remained vague and more implicit prejudices. The debate over the boundaries of international law ranged beyond professional lawyers and involved political thinkers such as J. S. Mill, legislators, colonial administrators, and journalists. Dissident voices in this broader public debate insisted European states had extensive legal obligations abroad. Such authors, including the moral philosopher Francis Newman, and the diplomat and Muslim convert Henry E. J. Stanley, claimed that while the increasing legal exclusions of non-Europeans neatly served an exploitative imperialist agenda, they also provoked hostility and resistance and so proved not only unjust but also foolish and impolitic.

Achieving the equality and consistency to which international law and much international political theory aspire remains tremendously difficult in the face of a global political and economic order marked by gross, and increasing, inequalities. Such tensions between global inequality and aspirations toward universality are ones we inherit from centuries of European expansion and from the political and legal thought that emerged alongside that expansion. It is my hope that an investigation of the shifting boundaries of the international, and their justifications, may help to illuminate continuing uses of ideas of international law and human rights to obscure dynamics of domination by the Global North over the Global South. There may be no untainted well from which we can draw, but recovering the perspective of ecumenical strands of the distinctive and unusual period of the late eighteenth century, as well as their occasional heirs in the nineteenth, may provide resources for the critical scrutiny of such dynamics. The history of international law has until the last two decades been a relatively minor enterprise within international law, and largely the province of international lawyers only, but it has become one of the most vibrant areas of legal scholarship and only recently has begun to be mined by political theorists and historians. This book aims to contribute both to the history of political thought and to our thinking about the lines of political, economic, and legal hierarchy and exclusion that have long marked and continue to span the globe.

TWO

Oriental Despotism and the Ottoman Empire

O VER THE COURSE of the eighteenth century, as the law of nations increasingly came to be equated with European public law, the Ottoman Empire played a role of unparalleled importance as the defining marginal case of the European international order. It was, of course, a major power on the continent and a party to frequent wars, and sometimes alliances, with European states throughout the seventeenth and eighteenth centuries. All the major European powers had permanent missions at Istanbul before the end of the eighteenth century, with some going back to the sixteenth century and the very origins of the European practice of continuous diplomacy. By contrast, none had permanent missions in Persia, China, or Japan until the nineteenth.[1]

There was no fact of the matter about whether the Ottomans belonged within what was understood to be an emerging European legal community, or more broadly how the law of nations applied to relations between Europeans and Ottomans. On the part of both Europeans and Ottomans, frequent intransigence in principle—about the possibility of reciprocal relations or genuine peace, as opposed to temporary truce, with nonbelievers or infidels—was combined with pragmatic flexibility and a well-developed and regularized repertoire of diplomatic practices.[2] This meant that there was plenty of available evidence for conflicting positions among Europeans on the question of the status of Ottomans as standing outside, or as participating in, the law of nations. What was at stake in these different accounts was not just what relations with the Ottomans would look like, but more fundamentally, how general the law of nations could claim to be, and on what grounds; what the key justifications for the limitation of its application to only some states and societies were; when and how the exercise of European states' power could be tempered by law, or, perhaps more to the point, criticized on legal grounds; and, even, what the core principles of the law of nations should be.

This chapter first reviews the history of treaty and diplomatic relations that afforded conflicting interpretations of the Ottomans' relation to the law of nations and the European legal community. It then traces evolutions in diplomatic and theoretical texts to explore the interactions between a diplomatic discourse that, although often disparaging of Ottoman practices, was also relatively flexible and pragmatic, and the starker and more uncompromising concept of oriental despotism deployed in political debates. What resulted were arguments for the legal exclusion of the Ottoman regime that seem to have exceeded the intentions of diplomats, such as the influential seventeenth-century English envoy Paul Rycaut, and those of the foremost theorist of the concept, Montesquieu. Montesquieu's theory should be read in these legal and diplomatic contexts both because he drew heavily, if selectively, on the diplomatic literature and because, whether intentionally or not, his account of oriental despotism set the subsequent terms of debate for diplomats and legal writers. His *De l'esprit des lois* (1748) influentially encapsulated a portrait of Asian states as existing outside the legal universe inhabited by European states. Sir James Porter, an English diplomat to Constantinople writing in the wake of Montesquieu's text, wrestled with and tried to roll back the legal and diplomatic implications of Montesquieu's account; his evident concern to temper the attribution of despotism to the Ottoman regime indicates the immediate impact on diplomatic discourse of Montesquieu's analysis. The most impassioned and sustained critique of the concept, by the French Orientalist Abraham Anquetil-Duperron (1731–1805), continued the debate on the diplomatic and legal terrain on which it had stood with Rycaut. In *Législation orientale* (1778), Anquetil disputed the portrait of the major Muslim regimes as lawless or arbitrary, with the purpose of calling for respect for their legal standing. As Anquetil's response to Montesquieu makes clear, although despotic regimes' foreign relations or status under the law of nations was not Montesquieu's primary concern, his remarks on the question, and more important, his overall sociological portrait of these regimes, were highly influential for European understandings of the possibility of legal and diplomatic relations with them. Much has been written about the concept of oriental despotism, Montesquieu's formulation of it, and its ramifications in European culture; the focus in this chapter is on the concept's bearing on the question of whether European states were bound by the law of nations in their relations with the Ottoman Empire. Anquetil's intervention, though it earned the admiration of contemporaries, did little to alter the growing consensus that the Asian and Muslim empires existed in a different legal universe from Europe. As we will see in later chapters, the challenge that nineteenth-century European legal writers saw themselves as facing was that of evaluating such states, now understood as outside the European-led international order, as candidates for entry into that order. While oriental despotism was a concept intended to apply much more broadly than to the Ottoman Empire only, the chapter focuses on its implications for reflections on Ottoman legal standing, given the empire's prominence, and its uniquely ambiguous status, in European war, politics, and diplomacy.

Capitulations and the Ottomans' Place in the European State System

Because legal arrangements between Europeans and the Ottoman regime often took the form of agreements that regulated foreign merchants and diplomats in the empire, called *"ahdnames"* by the Ottomans and "capitulations" in various European languages, the distinctive form these documents took played an outsized role in European understandings of the nature of their legal relations with the Ottomans.[3] The term "capitulation" referred to the chapters or articles that made up the agreements and was not, as was sometimes assumed or insinuated, an indication of Ottoman weakness. (As Henry E. J. Stanley was to note in 1865, "It is often erroneously imagined that these privileges were obtained, nay, even forced from the Ottoman Government, under treaty stipulations, on account of the name by which these privileges are known; namely, the 'capitulations.'"[4]) Only in the later nineteenth century did the Ottomans begin to call these agreements *"imtiyazat"* (privileges), reflecting their use as instruments of penetration by stronger Western powers.[5] While in a narrow sense the terms "capitulation" and *"ahdname"* referred to charters of fiscal and commercial privilege granted by Ottoman sultans and not to peace treaties, such a distinction is not always clearly drawn in the sources or the historical literature, and peace agreements also often included commercial provisions, given how thoroughly state business and private commerce were inter-mingled in early modern long-distance trade.[6] The status of European rep-resentatives in Istanbul was ambiguous, as they were often employees of trading companies rather than, or in addition to, state officials, and what would come to be seen as the exclusive prerogatives of sovereign states were long exercised by a variety of actors, especially agents of commercial companies.[7]

While the Italian maritime trading states were the first to conclude both capitulations and peace treaties with the Ottoman Empire, the latter's most enduring bond was with France. The threat posed by the Habsburgs led to a 1536 treaty of alliance between Francis I of France and the Ottoman sultan Suleiman I, against the Italian states and Charles I of Spain and the Holy Roman Empire.[8] The French also received capitulations, at first limited to Egypt, and then in 1535 (though not ratified until 1569) for the whole of the Ottoman realm, with a pact that continued to be renewed by successive sul-tans that granted privileges including French consular governance over in-ternal French lawsuits, respect on the high seas, and the right to protect other Western Christians.[9] As the sixteenth-century French historian the abbé de Brantôme wrote, "I once heard it said . . . that the kings of France had two alliances and affinities that they could never neglect and abandon [dis-traire et despartir] for anything in the world: one with the Swiss and the other with the great Turk."[10] (While Europeans routinely described the Ot-toman regime and society as "Turkish," recent scholarship has noted that the equation is mistaken, given that the identity of the empire was fundamen-tally dynastic rather than ethnic, and both the society over which it ruled and its elite officials were ethnically, linguistically, and religiously diverse.[11]) A capitulation of 1740, following the Peace of Belgrade at which the French had mediated between the Ottomans and Habsburgs, further granted the French most-favored-nation status, so that they automatically received all concessions granted other states. The French continued to be the Ottomans' steadiest European allies until Napoleon's invasion of Egypt in 1798.[12]

England's trading privileges began in 1579 when an Ottoman official vis-ited Elizabethan England with a letter from Sultan Murad III to Queen Elizabeth offering "unrestricted commerce in his country to Englishmen"; this was followed in 1583 by the visit of the first Ottoman ambassador to England and further emissaries from the sultan in 1611, 1618, and 1640. En-glish capitulations followed the form of those granted the French—ambiguously unilateral and reciprocal; as Karl-Heinz Ziegler has put it, "to the subjects of the sultan the capitulations [we]re presented as imperial commandments; to the European powers they were treaties of peace and friendship."[13]

Whereas the capitulations were originally granted from a position of strength to European merchant communities, and commercial privileges were used for a time by the Ottoman state as tools in political negotiation, it is generally agreed that as Western European states gained in economic and military power they forced the Ottomans to concede increasing trade privileges.[14] Still, political histories, beginning with Ottoman chroniclers themselves in the eighteenth century, have too readily sought the seeds of the empire's supposed centuries-long decline in episodes as far back as the empire's defeat by the Catholic powers in the 1571 naval battle of Lepanto. Recent scholarship has questioned such retrospective diagnoses of inevitable decline and instead stressed the Ottoman state's strategies of reform and reorganization, including the strategic adoption of European diplomatic practices, in response to internal and external challenges.[15] The Ottoman rivalry with the Habsburg Empire, in which the Ottomans had seen gains in the sixteenth and early seventeenth century, issued in the failed second siege of Vienna of 1683, and ultimately defeat in their long war with the Holy League of the Habsburgs, Poland, Venice, and Russia (1683–1699), ending with the 1699 Treaty of Karlowitz, in which the Ottomans ceded Hungary and other Central European territory to the Habsburgs and Dalmatia to Venice. The negotiation process leading to the treaty marked the Ottomans' first participation in a multilateral peace conference.[16] That Ottoman negotiators at Karlowitz recognized the European legal principle of *uti possidetis* (which enabled a belligerent party to claim territory acquired in war) is one indication of their participation in European diplomatic practices.[17] The resulting treaty "established a number of precedents in Ottoman diplomacy that accelerated the incorporation into the European system, including diplomatic equality of the sultan and his Christian counterparts, the monarchs of Europe."[18]

A mixed record of gains and losses continued over the following century. In the Treaty of Passarowitz (1718), the Ottomans lost further Balkan land to the Habsburgs, including Belgrade (regained in 1739), but also reclaimed the Peloponnese from Venice. In 1720 they ratified a peace treaty with the Russian tsar Peter I in which the two powers pledged "permanent and perpetual peace," the first such pledge the Ottomans made with a European power, and the model for future treaties. No such lasting peace took hold, however, for the Russian Empire soon replaced the Habsburgs as the Ottomans' main rival. The period saw the Ottomans begin to establish formal alliances with Christian powers, which Ottoman officials defended as being in the interest of the empire even if technically in violation of the prohibition in Islamic law against alliances with non-Muslim states.[19] Russian victory in the war between the two powers from 1768 to 1774 led to the notorious Treaty of Küçük Kaynarca (1774), which recognized the independence of the Khanate of Crimea (a prelude to its annexation by Russia in the following decade, the first time the empire had ceded a mainly Muslim territory to a European power) and which the Russians interpreted as establishing a Russian "right of protection" over the Ottoman Empire's Christian subjects, a claim that would itself generate extensive conflict in the nineteenth century.[20]

With further losses in European conflicts at the turn of the eighteenth century, the Ottomans began to undertake more assertive diplomacy. While the regime did not install permanent embassies in European capitals until the 1790s, eighteenth-century Ottoman ambassadors on temporary missions were men of higher administrative standing and greater diplomatic responsibilities than had been the case for previous envoys: the task of gathering information was increasingly assigned not to non-Muslim translators but to highly placed Muslim officials.[21] Among the most significant was the almost yearlong embassy to France in 1720 to 1721 by the official who had been Ottoman plenipotentiary at Passarowitz, Yirmisekiz Çelebi Mehmed Efendi. The purposes of his mission were both to study French society, economy, and military practices and to investigate the possibility of an alliance with France against the Habsburgs. His ambassadorial report reflected on the importance in European affairs of diplomatic representation:

> The Christian states have always been in communication, sending each other ambassadors. In this manner, they are kept well-informed on each other's intended course of actions and true state of affairs. In particular, all Christian nations have sent ambassadors to the Exalted [Ottoman] state to draw and communicate information. As the advantage [to these states] of sending ambassadors was certain and incontestable as stated above, and as the Ottoman state could not neglect this advantage, the noble Grand Vezir reflected upon this (advantage) and decided to send an ambassador to the lands of the French.[22]

Such ambassadorial reports were an increasingly important source of information for the Ottoman regime about European interstate relations and diplomatic protocol, among other subjects, as embassies became more frequent and ambassadors became increasingly higher-ranking officials. Further embassies included those of Ahmed Resmi to Vienna in 1758 (and comparable embassies to Russia and Poland) to announce the accession of a new sultan, and to Berlin in 1763 in the hopes of establishing a defensive alliance with Prussia.[23]

The years of French revolutionary warfare further integrated the Ottoman Empire into the European state system. Under Sultan Selim III, officials began to adopt some European diplomatic terminology (such as "status quo," first used in an official Ottoman document in 1789).[24] The empire's first permanent resident ambassador to a European state, Yusuf Agha Efendi, was sent to London in 1793 and served for three years.[25] Permanent envoys to Vienna, Berlin, and Paris soon followed.[26] Selim III's efforts to formalize diplomatic relations in these years were complicated by the instability of a Western Europe in the throes of war. Even as Britain sought to strengthen its connection with the Porte, Selim III continued the Ottoman regime's posture of friendliness to revolutionary France, declaring neutrality in the conflict between France and the "First Coalition" of Britain, Austria, and Prussia. When James Gillray, in a satirical print of 1793, depicted Yusuf Agha Efendi's presentation of his credentials to George III, he imagined the Ottoman emissary, surrounded by Jacobins and their British sympathizers, presenting to a horrified king and queen a document reading "Powers for a new Connexion between the Port [sic], England & France."[27] Napoleon's invasion of Egypt in 1798, however, led to the Ottoman state's first breach with France and precipitated its alliance with Britain, Austria, and even Russia, with whom it had concluded its most recent war in 1792. Selim III's 12 September 1798 manifesto announcing the rupture with France after the invasion of Egypt noted his government's hitherto constant posture of neutrality in France's conflict with the major powers of Europe, out of respect for a friendship since "time immemorial," even as the revolutionary government had increasingly come to "inspire horror."[28]

Several documents associated with the Ottoman declaration of war on France in September 1798 invoke the law of nations, indicating that officials considered their state a participant in the law of nations and saw the French as having violated its principles by the Egyptian invasion.[29] "Demon-

strating to all nations that they no longer recognized public faith or treaties, that they made no distinction between friendship and enmity,"
France had "like pirates, with contempt for the law of nations and contrary to the laws respected by all peoples, suddenly invaded and seized by
armed force Egypt, the most precious province of the Ottoman Empire,
from which France had only ever received evidence of friendship."[30] Even
a legal directive that Selim III first circulated to his officials in the European provinces, a document thus directed at an Ottoman audience and not
a European one, called the French invasion a violation of the law of nations
(bi-gayr-i kaide-i düvel) and warned that it had caused grievous damage to
the Muslim world.[31] The so-called War of the Second Coalition against
France (1798–1802), and the 1799 defensive alliance into which the Ottomans entered with Britain and Russia, have been called a "diplomatic revolution" for the Porte, both because it had broken with its most constant
European ally and because it committed to greater mutual obligations
than ever before with European powers.[32] Some have seen the 1802 peace
treaty of Paris between Napoleon and Selim III as another important moment because of its official instantiation of reciprocity, though the peace it
established was short-lived, and the Ottomans again joined a defensive
treaty against France in 1805 as part of the Third Coalition.[33] During these
conflicts, the Ottomans arguably shared with other Europeans an understanding of the laws governing prisoners of war.[34]

Very different constructions could be put on this dense history of Christian Europe's legal, diplomatic, and treaty relations with the Ottoman
Empire.[35] On one hand, long-standing practices of treaty making could
be drawn on to show that the Ottomans had long been a part not only of
the European political world but also of its emerging legal order.[36] On the
other hand, it was common to portray the Ottomans as irreducibly alien
in religious belief, constitutional principles, and norms of interstate relations, and therefore not full members of the European legal community.
Capitulations were read by European interpreters in two conflicting ways:
either as generating a reliable legal and diplomatic environment like those
supported by other sorts of treaties, or as instruments whose peculiar features revealed an anomalous and inferior form of interstate law.

Ottoman capitulations were indeed, as Europeans often stressed, formally unilateral grants by sultans to foreign sovereigns whose envoys sought
trading privileges within the empire, rather than bilateral treaties. As
Porter wrote, "They are called capitulations, and not treaties, because they

are mere concessions for privileges of trade, granted by the Porte, and no reciprocal concession, but merely a stipulation of friendship on the part of Great Britain."[37] They were thus in principle revocable at any time by the sultan. Later European writers took the unilateral form of the capitulations as a key piece of evidence that as they were not reciprocal agreements, they could not be sources of the law of nations in the way that other treaties were. But despite their unilateral form, the capitulations were framed explicitly as vehicles of reciprocal obligations.[38] They were granted on condition that the representatives of the nation comport themselves peacefully. As the English capitulations of 1662 stated,

> And as long as the said Queene of England according to the present agreement of sincere friendeship, & good correspondence shall shew herself, & remaine with us, in peace, friendship, league, firme, constant, & sincere, *wee doe promise also on our parts reciprocally,* that this peace, frindship Articles Capitulations, & correspondence in the fore written forme shall be for ever of us maintained, observed, & respected & of no man any part thereof shall bee contradicted, or infringed all which above mentioned Articles of peace, & friendship were concluded, signed, & an Imperiall Capitulation granted & confirmed by our Ancestors of happy memorie.[39]

Reciprocity was also specifically invoked in relation to encounters between the respective states' ships, with the pledge that when Ottoman ships met ships from the relevant European state, "they will reciprocally give all sorts of testimony of friendship," as the 1740 French capitulation put it.[40] Capitulations shared other qualities that could have made them readable as generating a regular legal community with Europeans. They were regularly renewed, often with extensions of the privileges granted in earlier versions; the English capitulations first concluded between Queen Elizabeth and Sultan Murad III were reissued several times by his successors. Further, a unified capitulatory system emerged over the course of the eighteenth century as the practice of granting something like a most-favored-nation clause came to be standard in these agreements.[41] Thanks to their form, then, capitulations could appear to be transient and idiosyncratic, unilateral grants of privilege offered personally by a particular sultan to the subjects of a given foreign sovereign. Taken as a practice, however, the capitulations system generated a fairly stable form of interstate law: a regularized and generalized system with rules for the allocation of jurisdiction between

European officials and local Ottoman judicial officers and a standard set of privileges for European diplomats.

How, then, did capitulations, and more broadly, Ottoman-European relations, come to be seen as part of an altogether separate legal universe from the treaties that governed European relations and that were coming to be seen as one major source for the law of nations? As I noted in Chapter 1, by the late seventeenth century a consensus began to emerge that the conceptual rubric that had structured debates about relations between European states and the Ottoman Empire—the question of whether it was permissible to make treaties with infidels—was no longer a meaningful one, because confessional difference was now held to be irrelevant to interstate legal relations. The terrain of the debate shifted and came to be constructed on the conceptual ground of the category of oriental despotism. Oriental despotism thus emerged as the organizing category for the question of what sort of diplomatic and legal relations were possible between European states and the Ottoman Empire as well as the Persian, Mughal, and Chinese Empires.

The exclusion of these regimes from full participation in an interstate legal structure as conceived by Europeans may seem overdetermined, so that the specific language in which such exclusion was debated and justified may appear to be mere superstructure or pretext. There are clearly continuities between the Christian posture of suspicion toward treaties with infidels and the view that properly legal and reciprocal interactions with despotisms were impossible, as well as with the nineteenth-century claim that nations had to reach a certain standard of civilization before they could be admitted to the family of nations. These discourses share a proselytizing universalism as well as the claim that conversion to Christian or European standards is in the interest of the subjects who suffer under the infidel or despotic regime. With the replacement of the *respublica christiana* by the law of nations, the presumptively universal authority of a historically European configuration remains, based not on divine revelation but ostensibly on rational principles accessible to all.

At the same time, conversely, the connections between the legal inclusion or exclusion of non-European regimes and European states' imperial aspirations seem underdetermined. Projects of imperial acquisition could be supported by arguments for legal inclusion as well as by arguments that Europeans could have no properly legal obligations to non-European states, and even the most avid defenders of the legal respectability of Asian states could accept or even promote their states' imperial aspirations. As we will see later in this chapter, Anquetil-Duperron, an insightful critic of the discourse of oriental despotism and a prominent defender of the legal recognition of the Ottoman, Persian, and Mughal states, was adept at using such claims to criticize British imperial expansion; but he also, at times, supported French imperial aims.

Paul Rycaut and Ottoman Legal Standing

The concept of oriental despotism itself was the product of traffic between diplomatic writings and legal and political theory; while it was applied to various societies including China, Persia, and Mughal India, it had particularly important ramifications for the question of Ottoman participation in the law of nations, given the unique diplomatic history just described. An Aristotelian conceptual framework that continued to be used fairly abstractly by medieval Christian thinkers was given greater specificity, and greater practical bite, by late sixteenth-century Venetian diplomats who took up the category to criticize the Ottoman regime whose power they had, until recently, admired. English observers at that time, as Gerald MacLean has noted, expressed a combination of "imperial envy," a sense of the Ottomans as "potential allies in the great game of international intrigue," and interest in the regime as patriarchal despotism, through much of the seventeenth century.[42]

The most important source for eighteenth-century treatments of the Ottoman Empire, including Montesquieu's, was Paul Rycaut (1629–1700), whose two major books, *The Present State of the Ottoman Empire* (1667) and *The History of the Turkish Empire (1623–77)* (1680), ran to many editions and were translated into most major European vernaculars.[43] The first edition of *Present State* was printed in August 1666 (postdated 1667), and though most copies were destroyed in the Great Fire of London, the book made an immediate impression. Rycaut, the London-born son of Dutch Protestants (of Huguenot origins), served as secretary to the English ambassador in Constantinople from 1660 to 1666. Rycaut's career illustrates the intersection of state and commercial agency in early modern long-distance trade. The ambassador, Heneage Finch, third earl of Winchilsea, was also the consul in Constantinople for the Levant Company; although he was appointed by the newly restored Charles II, his salary and those of his staff were paid by the Company. Rycaut handled the secretarial duties for both royal and Company affairs, and he attested to seeing his work for the Company as service to the nation.[44] Rycaut took advantage of his unparalleled access to official correspondence and his contacts within the Ottoman state in writing *Present State,* published during his temporary return to London in 1666. As he wrote, "I had opportunity by the constant access and practice with the chief Ministers of State, and variety of Negotiations which passed through my hands in the Turkish Court, to penetrate farther into the Mysteries of this Polity, which appear so strange and barbarous to us, than hasty Travellers could do, who are forced to content themselves with a superficial knowledge."[45] His account in *Present State,* though persistently hostile in its political commentary, was empirically rich with historical and ethnographic detail that gave substance to his promise to provide an unprecedentedly authoritative portrait of Ottoman government and society.[46] Rycaut's extreme portrait of Ottoman tyranny may have been, as Linda Darling has compellingly argued, intended as an intervention in the politics of Restoration England, just as Montesquieu's was in French disputes over royal power. As a royalist and a Protestant, Rycaut may have intended his picture of insecure Ottoman property rights and of the Ottoman ruling class as slaves to the sultan, but also restive and rebellious, to warn Charles II against absolutism and abuse of his power.[47]

Although he did not use the terms "despotic" or "despotism," Rycaut supplied the empirical detail for subsequent debates about Ottoman despotism. (Pierre Bayle, who is generally credited with coining the term "despotism" in his essay by that title published in 1704, used Rycaut as his major source of information about the nature of the Ottoman regime, citing him as evidence against those who imagined that in the Ottoman regime the monarch was entirely above the law, and arguing instead that despotism is a matter of degree.[48]) Rycaut introduced all the major questions that would come to be at issue in debates over the legal standing of the Ottoman and other Asian and Muslim states: the extent to which such a state could be said to be governed by law internally; the ruler's views of relations with other states; and the regime's observance of standard European practices of foreign relations, especially its treatment of ambassadors. Rycaut also broached two more specific questions that came to dominate discussions of the status of capitulations as binding treaties: whether the Ottoman ruler could be said to be bound by laws or by his own agreements, and what the implications were for the capitulations' standing as international legal agreements that they were officially unilateral grants of privilege by the sultan rather than reciprocal arrangements between equal partners.

Rycaut had already begun to address these questions in his publication of the *Capitulations and Articles of Peace* between Britain and the Ottoman Empire in Constantinople in 1663. In his dedicatory letter to the governor of the Levant Company, Rycaut laid out some of the central claims he would develop in *Present State* and that would become leitmotivs in European discussions of legal relations with the Ottomans. He placed the capitulations in the framework of the "law of nations."[49] But he also described the key respects in which he considered these agreements anomalous in relation to standard European treaties. These agreements were, he wrote, not like any "practiced in the Courts of Christen-dome," and were of such "different forme, in matter & proceeding, as will render an experienced Minister in the treaties of other countries a Novice in this, until time & conversation hath instructed him in a new science & unacquainted Maximes of State, & policie." He noted their distinctive unilateral structure: "The Capitulations of the Grand Signor to us, & other Christians that traffick with him are (in my opinion) of an other nature & forme, then articles of peace are usuall to bee betweene two nations, for hee requires no counterpart from his Majestie, whereby to oblige him to performe the same conditions with himself." Rycaut also stressed the need for diplomatic experience particular to the country because of the alleged wiliness of the "Turks," whose "malitious invention" was "ingenious in nothing but in matters of their interest"; he thus called attention to the virtues of his employer the ambassador and identified the need for precisely the book he would publish in London three years later, one capable of explaining the "peculiar Maxims" of the Ottoman polity and their implications for diplomacy.[50]

In *Present State,* Rycaut set out to replace what he saw as frivolous and misleading accounts of the Ottoman Empire generated by European ignorance and contempt for its supposed "Barbarity" with a solidly grounded account of the regime's power. In doing so, he furnished empirical details that would be mobilized by participants on both sides of the debate about relations with, and the legal otherness of, the Ottoman regime. It was in Rycaut's interest to show both that diplomatic relations with the Ottomans could be successful and had been so under the prudent supervision of his employer, and that recondite knowledge of the sort provided in his book was indispensable to successful relations. Ordinary diplomatic knowledge acquired in European courts was insufficient, he argued, and thus relations with the Ottomans could not be entirely subsumed within the diplomatic and legal canons of European intercourse. The rhetorical positioning of his book, in other words, disposed him to take precisely the ambiguous stance he did on the Ottoman Empire's legal standing.

On the one hand, he supplied much material for the position that the Ottoman Empire was a tyrannical antithesis to European freedom and moderation. He described the Ottoman state as "absolute and unlimited," where the sultan was owner of all property in the state and no one else had more than "usufructory" property.[51] He contrasted the "Oppression, and Cruelty of that State, wherein Reason stands in no competition with the Pride and Lust of an unreasonable Minister" and the "Liberty and Happiness" enjoyed by the European, and more specifically the British, reader. He suggested that the vices of the regime infected and shaped its subjects, who exhibited a greediness "above all people in the World," though "what they labour for is but as Slaves for their great Patron and Master"; the "whole Turkish Government" was "such a Fabrick of Slavery that it is a wonder if any amongst them should be born of a free ingenuous spirit."[52] On the other hand, Rycaut also portrayed the empire and its inhabitants as less barbarous and alien than they were generally understood to be by Europeans, and argued that historical circumstance rather than natural or deep-seated cultural differences had produced the distinctive vices of the regime. The key causes of Ottoman absolutism were the state's origins in war, the adaptation of customs to that circumstance, and the large territorial extent of the empire, which necessitated "the quickness and severity of their justice." As "Men of the same composition with us," Rycaut argued, Ottoman subjects "cannot be so savage and rude as they are generally described." Although he declared them to fall short of Christian civilization, learning, and moral virtue, they, too, like "all mankind," followed the law of nature that prescribes mutual good offices to all human beings. Even the Ottomans' history of conquest and war could be said to have helped to instill principles of mutuality in them, by "having procured them in conversation with other Nations, and their Wars and Treaties with Christians, having refined their Minds."[53]

On the first question noted above, whether the regime was law-governed, Rycaut provided characteristically ambiguous evidence. He reported that Ottoman legal experts commonly recognized the sultan as above the law, both in the sense of having the "power of an infallible interpretation" of the law, and in the sense, as "some maintain," "that the very Oaths and Promises of the Grand Signior are always revocable."[54] Because legal experts gave the sultan leave to dispense with the civil laws and his own agreements when these were an "obstacle to his Government" or "any great design of the Empire," the sultan "can no more be said to be bound or limited, than a man who hath the World to rove in can be termed a Prisoner." But he resisted the conclusion that such ideas of the ruler's power were either utterly distinct from European practices or uncontested within the empire. He looked to the Roman law compendium, the *Institutes* of Justinian, for a similar picture of royal prerogative, in which the king, though not bound by law, adheres to it from a recognition that only rule by law is secure. He described the ceremonies by means of which each new sultan similarly "obliges himself to govern within the compass of Laws," and to be answerable to God for the "execution of the *Mahometan Law*."[55] There was, then, a recognized system of law, even if, as a matter of principle, the sultan was considered not to be bound by that law. Rycaut contrasted the strength lent by this absolute but not arbitrary power to the weakness of the Holy Roman Emperor, forced to solicit the cooperation of independent princes and the Imperial Diet.[56]

Rycaut managed to argue both that Islamic principles jeopardized legal relations between Europeans and Ottomans, and that Europeans could trust in agreements with the Ottoman state to address the distinct challenge of legal relations with Muslims. He began his discussion of the "regard the Turks have to their Leagues with Foreign Princes" with a stark contrast between a Christian commitment to kind and fair dealing with human beings as such ("all that are within the Pale of Humane Nature") with a Muslim principle "not only to abhor the Doctrines, but also the Persons of such whom they term not Believers." He thus attributed to the Ottomans a "Maxim, that they ought not to regard the Leagues they have with any Prince, or the reasons and ground of a quarrel, whilst the breach tends to the enlargement of their Empire, which consequently infers the propagation of their Faith." While acknowledging that Christian states had violated treaties and waged war "on frivolous and slight pretences," and also that a long-standing Christian theological debate questioned whether it was appropriate to keep faith with infidels, he held that faithlessness as a principle was unique to Muslim law, as practiced and commanded by Muhammad.[57] He depicted justice for individual Christians as threatened by Muslims' willingness to give false witness in cases against Christians, "so that I believe in no part of the World can Justice run more out of the current and stream than in *Turkey*."[58] And yet he showed precisely that such practices did not make legal arrangements between Ottomans and Christians impossible. He reported that an English ambassador was led by this Ottoman practice to "insert an Article of Caution against the testimony of Turks" into the capitulations, and that this wise provision "hath proved of admirable consequence and security to the Trafique and Merchants Estates." Rycaut portrayed the capitulations, then, as a reasonably well-functioning and reliable set of legal arrangements that had effectively governed commerce between English merchants and Ottoman subjects, to their mutual benefit, and despite significant obstacles in Islamic jurisprudence.

On a second key question about the capitulations, whether their being asymmetrical grants of privilege by the sovereign vitiated their status as treaties—and more broadly, whether they could be taken as evidence that Europeans' legal relations with the Ottoman Empire were not reciprocal in the way that interstate relations should be—Rycaut again supplied evidence for both lines of argument. As we have seen, he noted the asymmetrical feature of the agreements in his introductory text to the 1663 *Capitulations*. In *Present State*, Rycaut contrasted the capitulations with the sultans' meticulous recognition of reciprocal relations with the Holy Roman Emperor. Because their territories were contiguous and their relations primarily military, Rycaut argued, the sultan regarded himself as obliged to the performance of symmetrical responsibilities with the emperor: "as bound" to defray the imperial ambassador's costs in traveling to his court and "to recompence the Embassie with another from himself, and to adorn it with Presents of equal value." The fact that the actions that accompanied capitulation agreements were not similarly reciprocal (for instance, that the sultan regarded foreign consuls' gifts as his due) stemmed from the fact that these were primarily commercial agreements with distant countries—not, as later authors would assert, because the Ottoman state could not in principle recognize other states, or Christian states, as equals and as appropriate partners in mutually binding agreements.[59]

The treatment of ambassadors proved to be a persistent theme in treatments of the Ottoman state's international legal standing, and here, as elsewhere, Rycaut's evidence cut both ways. He opened his discussion of the question by ruling out, in principle, the possibility that the Ottomans might utterly ignore the particular respect due ambassadors, since "there was not Nation in the World ever so barbarous, that did not acknowledge the Office of an Ambassadour sacred and necessary"; and he quoted Islamic and

Ottoman laws that explicitly endorsed such a principle.[60] But he went on to highlight differences between Ottoman and European customs regarding ambassadors that, he asserted, amounted to evidence of the regime's disdain for the law of nations. They regarded ambassadors not just as representatives of their sovereigns but also as potential hostages in cases of misconduct. He narrated instances, "injurious to the Law of Nations," of Venetian and French ambassadors imprisoned upon the threat of war for assisting the escape of the Ottomans' enemies, or, as with one French ambassador, for debts that he had accrued in order to buy presents for the sultan and other "couvetous and craving Turks," as well as to bribe the seraglio's eunuchs to gain access to the sultan's mistresses. In the last case, Rycaut wrote, the ambassador having "wholly discredited and lost the Honour and Authority of his Embassie," the French king tried to recall him, "but the Turks gave a stop to his return, pretending that their Law which was indulgent to the persons of Ambassadours, did not acquit them from payment of their Debts . . . contrary to that rule of Grotius, who not only exempts the Persons, but the Servants and Moveables of Ambassadours from Attachements."[61] Rycaut recognized a certain logic in the Ottoman position (though his "pretending" called into question their sincerity) and acknowledged that Europeans abused the law of nations regarding the protection of diplomats to shield misconduct, but he suggested that European law of nations principles were non-negotiable.

Despite the obstacles that he claimed "Turkish" principles and character posed to diplomatic relations with the Ottoman state, Rycaut insisted on the particular success of the British mission. Thanks to their skill as diplomats in this challenging environment, which required "courage and circumspection, wisdom to dissemble with honour, and discreet patience" and a willingness to take no notice of the affronts that this "uncivilized people" could not avoid, they had not had the trouble other Europeans had. The society's lack of refinement and its habituation to hierarchy meant that "Turks of all Nations in the World, are most apt to crush and trample on those that lie under their feet; as on the contrary, those who have a reputation with them, may make the best and most advantageous Treaties of any part of the World." Flexibility, ordinarily a diplomatic virtue, "is of little use to a publick Minister in his Treaty with *Turks*," who, lacking the virtue of self-control, would take any concession as an invitation to demand more and were likely to be impressed by "obstinacy."[62]

Finally, Rycaut's work illustrates the work that a notion of oriental despotism could do to justify European imperial or global power through ostensibly anti-imperial rhetoric. In an ideological move that Montesquieu and many nineteenth-century authors would echo, Rycaut associated empire and conquest with oriental tyranny, and European states with freedom and commerce.[63] He held that the glory of a great empire was incompatible with that of political freedom, while suggesting that it was precisely their freedom and respect for law that entitled European states to power on a global scale. Echoing the admiration that was conventional among earlier Venetian ambassadors to Constantinople, who described the impressive discipline and unity of the Ottoman regime as enabling the empire's greatness, he asserted throughout *Present State* that the extent of the Ottoman Empire demonstrated that absolute power had been beneficial; it was hard to imagine, he writes, that a state would ever "be termed the Mistress of a great Empire, or a Prince be said to have a long arm, or embrace a large compass of the Globe, who is pinioned with the bands of his own Laws." British subjects contemplating the impossibility of attaining an empire to rival the Ottoman, he suggested, should console themselves with the "greater glory" of being free from indiscriminate punishment and oppression.[64]

Yet, as he elaborated in a later work, it was precisely the English sovereign's respect for law that justified his state's increasing global power. Between his diplomatic post in Constantinople and a final posting to the Hanseatic states, Rycaut undertook a translation of Garcilaso de la Vega's *Royal Commentaries of Peru,* published in London in 1688, a work that exercised its own influence on eighteenth-century English thought. He dedicated the work to James II, whose "Dominions being adjacent and almost contiguous to the Countries which are the subject of his History, make Your Majesty a Party concerned in the Affairs of the new World, and so supreme an Arbitrator in the Government thereof, that to suppress the Robberies and Insolence of certain Pirates who infest those Coasts, your Majesty's Royal Arms are called for."[65] Rycaut stressed the repeated violation of diplomatic norms by the Spanish, and the Incas' persistent attempts to abide by their agreements with the Spanish as a matter of principle. Here the Spanish replaced the Ottomans as the lawless and violent foil against which the English could be depicted as the custodians of a globalizing legal order, guardians of law on behalf of vulnerable people inclined to follow norms of peaceful negotiation but incapable of defending themselves.

Rycaut's work was the most influential firsthand account of the Ottoman regime and its relations with European states, not only within England but across Europe, including in France, despite his expressed enmity for the French. Its rich detail combined with its ambiguous position on key questions ensured that it was cited by all participants in debates on the Ottoman Empire's legal status. The abbé de Mably used Rycaut as his main source on the nature of the Ottoman regime in his chapter on European treaty relations with the Sublime Porte in his handbook of European public law, *Le droit publique de l'Europe fondé sur les traités* (1746).[66] Mably cited Rycaut regarding the Ottomans' supposed religious opposition to keeping faith with non-Muslims whenever its empire could benefit, though he also quoted Rycaut's acknowledgement of Christian states' routine violation of their treaties and concerns about treaties with infidels, and his view "that it would be more glorious and more advantageous for Christians never to have practiced the first nor doubted the second."[67] Mably drew on Rycaut to portray the Ottoman regime as one whose "despotic" features were the source of its weakness and decline vis-à-vis a Europe that was increasingly united by shared principles of statecraft and diplomacy. The Porte would continue with its old maxims of caprice and "no end but a vague aggrandizement," with the ruler at the mercy of the soldiers on whom he depended to oppress his people, and the country devoid of the "arts, commerce, and all the industry that makes a state flourish": "the most intolerable despotism has produced in the Ottoman Monarchy all evils of which it is the germ."[68] In the book's expanded 1776 edition, Mably contrasted his picture of Ottoman decline with one of an increasingly "enlightened" Europe that, as feudalism waned, "began to conduct itself by less unreasonable principles." While asserting that the Porte, mired in "superstition" and "despotism," was unlikely to change its policy, he took the liberty of suggesting that it more deliberately and actively participate in the European state system. As he cheekily pleaded with his European readers,

> May I not be charged with a crime for revealing to an infidel court its true interests relative to Christian powers; political writings will in no way change the face of the world; for they will not change its passions. My work will hardly be taken to Constantinople, and if it, instead of a Persian tale, were in the hands of the Grand-Seigneur or the Vizir the politics of the Seraglio would remain the same. So I continue. . . . [69]

If alliances with the Porte became more regular, Mably proposed, re-maining European prejudices against agreements with unbelievers would be moderated: "Let us count on alliances with the Porte, and soon we will seek its friendship. After four or five repeated examples, we would no longer find it extraordinary that a Christian Prince would seek from Constanti-nople aid that they cannot ask today without causing a sort of scandal."[70] Mably's book, whose first edition appeared before Montesquieu's *Spirit of Laws* radicalized the portrait of oriental despotism, shares Rycaut's ambiv-alent judgment about the Ottoman state's relation to Christian Europe: alien, hostile, weakening, but capable with careful management of stable participation in European public law.

As claims about the despotic features of the Ottoman state moved out of a specifically diplomatic literature concerned with facilitating relations with that regime, and into the more abstract realm of political and legal philosophy, the diplomat's flexibility was lost, and the category became starker, more categorical, and more exclusive. Montesquieu, in creating his tripartite typology of republic-monarchy-despotism, entrenched a categor-ical distinction between the moderate regimes of Europe and the despo-tisms of Asia. Rycaut's account of Ottoman caprice and tyranny, as taken up and systematized by Montesquieu, could be used to support the posi-tion that the Ottomans should have no legal standing because law and binding obligations had no place in their political system.

Montesquieu and Oriental Despotism

Although the phrase *"despotisme oriental"* may not have come into usage until after the publication of the *Spirit of Laws,* an "oriental" association was implicit in the concept of despotism already at its ancient Greek ori-gins.[71] While the Greek term *"despotes"* originally referred to the private power of a father over his family, or a master of his household, Aristotle initiated the enduring association of despotic power with a distinctly Asian "barbarian" political regime. Voltaire strategically overlooked this long history when he wrote in his *ABC* (1768) that

It has pleased our authors (I do not know why) to call the sovereigns of Asia and Africa *despots*. In days gone by, it was understood that by despot was meant a minor European prince, a vassal of the Turk, a

disposable vassal, a kind of crowned slave governing other slaves. Originally this word *despot* signified among the Greeks master of a household,
father of a family. Today we make free with this title for the Emperor of
Morocco, the Grand Turk, the Pope, the Emperor of China.[72]

By the end of the eighteenth century the concept of oriental despotism did
considerable work to mark the Ottoman regime as standing outside the European legal and diplomatic community. Eighteenth-century political argument also saw the development of the idea that despotism is a violation
of universal standards of right, or of the natural rights of humanity, further entrenching the idea that such regimes existed beyond the pale of an
emerging global legality. Fénélon declared in 1747 that "le Despotisme
tirannique des Souverains est un attentat sur les Droits de la Fraternité
Humaine. C'est renverser la grande & sage Loi de la Nature, dont ils ne
doivent être que les Conservateurs."[73] The physiocrat, colonial adminis-
trator, and defender of enlightened absolutism Pierre-Paul Le Mercier de la
Rivière wrote that the word "despotism" "peint toujours une chose odieuse,
contraire à l'ordre, aux droit naturels de l'humanité." Mercier linked despotism as a violation of natural right with the insecurity of property, since
the right of property, an essential natural right, was the "first principle of
all rights and all the reciprocal duties that men have toward one another,"
but he did not single out Asian or "oriental" regimes as distinctively violators of those natural rights.[74]

Montesquieu's account of despotism, in contrast, placed the "oriental"
associations of the concept at its heart. The *Esprit des lois* was an influential, though persistently ambiguous, intervention into debates about abuse
of power by the French monarchy, and much of the debate sparked by
Montesquieu, in keeping with his own main intentions, concerned the
implications of the category of despotism for understanding the internal
workings of European states. And yet his account proved decisive for European understandings of "Eastern" societies throughout the later eighteenth century. Because his treatment of despotism was saturated with an
oriental reference point, in his hands the question of the threat of despotism within Europe was also a question about how to characterize Muslim
and Asian regimes, and his work intensified debates about what Europeans
could know about those regimes and societies, and how they should interpret evidence about them. Were there degrees of despotism, such that Asian
regimes were recognizable as existing on a spectrum of regimes also oc-

cupied by European states, or were they different in kind, in their very nature? Although Voltaire's response to Montesquieu might be said to be driven primarily by his interest in defending enlightened absolutism in Europe, it is striking that his first published commentary on Montesquieu's work in his *ABC* was devoted to a critique of Montesquieu's misuse of exotic sources, his profound ignorance of Asian states, and his misleading interpretation of evidence to the detriment of the Ottoman and Chinese regimes. Voltaire's *Commentaire sur l'Esprit des lois* (1777) further criticized Montesquieu's rendering of the Ottoman Empire, his use of Rycaut, and the implications of his account for European self-understandings in relation to non-European states.[75]

Montesquieu's own interest was in the internal workings of his three regime types—republic, monarchy, and despotism—in their natures, or basic structures, and their principles, or motive passions. The category in which he was most interested, monarchy, was also the most unstable: monarchies tended toward either republic or despotism, and the *Spirit of Laws* pursues the worry that Montesquieu had broached nearly thirty years earlier in the *Persian Letters* (1721): that the French monarchy was becoming despotic.[76] As he wrote in the *Persian Letters,* "Asia and Africa have always been afflicted by despotism [*accablés sous le despotisme*]" but even in Europe monarchy can devolve into despotism, since monarchy is "a violent state that always degenerates into a despotism or republic."[77] In the *Spirit of Laws* Montesquieu likewise noted that "neither mores nor climate" would protect Europeans against despotism in the wake of a "long abuse of power or by a great conquest."[78] For this reason, although he identified despotism with Asian regimes, in an important sense he drew the dichotomy between Orient and Occident only to challenge it.[79] Melvin Richter has described Montesquieu's denigration of Asian peoples and societies as an unintended consequence of his more direct purpose of elaborating oriental despotism as a rhetorical weapon in political contests internal to Europe, in criticism of the aggrandizement of the French monarchy under Louis XIV and what Montesquieu saw as the dangerously reduced power and independence of the aristocracy. In distilling a "painting" of despotism, which he acknowledged was not an exact account of any actual regime, Montesquieu sought to capture a logic of unchecked power.[80] But in supplying apparent evidence from actual Asian regimes, and in engaging the diplomatic literature, he also altered understandings of what kinds of relations were advisable with such regimes.

In introducing his three regime types, Montesquieu noted that his definitions were utterly conventional, that the "least educated men" have an adequate idea of the nature of each, suggesting that a conception of despotism was by this time widely available. In this typology, despotism is lawless by definition, since its lawlessness is what distinguishes it from monarchy: "in despotic government, one alone, without law and without rule, draws everything along by his will and his caprices."[81] It is sustained, among the subjects, by fear and by a slavish adherence to religion and custom, rather than a reasoned acquiescence to a normative order. The people have no private property, and the monarch is the heir to all his subjects (though he will generally temper his claims to their property according to custom). Subjects are considered, and come to have the spirit of, slaves. At the same time, in Montesquieu's portrait, despotic power is in key respects illusory, for the despot is weak and fearful, and, because he holds power only by means of violence, is himself dependent on his soldiers.

An Orientalized concept of despotism was used by members of the aristocratic Fronde to criticize abuse of power by Louis XIV, and it developed in the context of debates over the question of what constituted appropriate limits to monarchic power: Did there have to be a separation of legislative and executive power? Was an independent nobility necessary? In such debates the category had a double-edged quality: on the one hand, its power within the European polemical context came from its usefulness as a device of critique or warning against the abuse of power. At the same time, it marked out Asian archetypes of despotism, whose despotic features were exaggerated for polemical effect, as categorically, and systematically, different from monarchy. This double-edged aspect of the device accounts for the continuing controversy over the implications of the concept in the hands of a thinker such as Montesquieu.[82] Moreover, criticisms of the inaccuracy or tendentiousness of the category as a description of actual Asian states were among the earliest reactions to the book.[83] Although the status of such regimes under the law of nations was not often explicitly addressed in such debates, these conceptual disputes about how stark or categorical the difference was between monarchies and despotisms, and between Asian and European political orders, would profoundly affect the diplomatic and legal literature.

A key feature of Montesquieu's account of despotism was the claim that it was systematic: not the result of occasional abuses of power by corrupt governors, but a feature of the regime itself, and therefore ineradicable and in a sense legitimate, though radically inferior to free or law-governed regimes. Rycaut was an important source for this account, in that he showed absolute power to be the state's "chief principle" and supplied many of the details Montesquieu would use to construct his portrait.[84] And while Montesquieu's selective use of his sources in the travel literature was immediately criticized, he drew faithfully on Rycaut for some of his central claims about the arbitrariness, lawlessness, and tyranny of the Ottoman regime. There are profound continuities of theme between Rycaut and Montesquieu: the claim that the sultan's caprice, and not law, governs; that there is no private property; and that the subjects are effectively an undifferentiated body of slaves, without any intermediary powers or independent sources of authority that might check the power of the ruler. Yet Rycaut's evidence could be used to support contradictory positions. Montesquieu and Bayle cited to opposite effect Rycaut's discussion of the idea that the sultan is formally above the law, although, as in Justinian, he often governs by law. Bayle cited this passage to refute what he saw as the extreme portrait of despotism as an utterly lawless condition different in kind from other regimes, and to claim that there are degrees of despotism. Montesquieu quoted the same passage to demonstrate despotism's radical difference from moderate regimes: fear being the fundamental principle of despotism, the despot must always have at his disposal the power to "instantly destroy those in the highest places." Montesquieu himself acknowledged the presence of law in such regimes, as when he noted that in despotisms "the people must be judged by the laws, and the important men by the prince's fancy."[85] But his more ideal-typical treatments of despotism as guided by fear and caprice in contrast to law had the effect of making despotism, and the actual Asian regimes that he saw as embodying it, appear deeply anomalous in relation not merely to other societies but even to nature itself.[86]

Montesquieu identified a variety of structures or patterns in despotic governments with implications for interstate relations. They are unaccustomed to negotiation; they wage wars more fiercely and with few of the legal restrictions on the conduct of war that emerge in the context of more moderate regimes; and because they lack continuity from one ruler to the next, they are incapable of making stable commitments to other states. Despotic states are antipolitical in their simplicity: among their component parts, they lack relations of mutual accommodation, constraint, resistance, and negotiation. Power is always delegated in a despotic state (to the infamous vizir) as the ruler gives himself over to the pull of pleasure and passion.[87] The more extensive the empire, the less attention does the prince pay to government. This delegation of despotic power differs radically from the independent "channels" through which monarchic power flows in a moderate regime. Despotism is by nature antipluralist, incapable of making space for alternative claims or normative principles, such as "natural feelings," family affections, or laws of honor. In despotic states, Montesquieu argues, "the prince's will, once known, should produce its effect as infallibly as does one ball thrown against another. No tempering, modification, accommodation, terms, alternatives, negotiations, remonstrances, nothing as good or better can be proposed."[88]

A consequence of this antipolitical quality of despotism was that such regimes were equally incapable of engaging other states on terms of mutuality. Oriental despotism, in Montesquieu's depiction, was thus the antitype to international law and diplomacy. The despotic monarch, accustomed to "to meeting no resistance in his palace," has no sense of magnanimity or "true glory," so that "wars have to be waged there in all their natural fury, and the law of nations has to be less extensive than elsewhere." The court life of monarchies cultivates dispositions toward flexibility and mutual respect in a community of those deemed worthy to belong. Monarchy's signal virtue, honor, is "eccentric," Montesquieu argued, in the sense that it stubbornly challenges the normative scheme of the ruler. These qualities had prepared Europe's moderate regimes to coexist in a community of relatively equal states that, because of their close proximity, had to tolerate one another, negotiate, and come to terms, even if they also engaged in war and commercial exploitation.[89]

Despotic states, in contrast, operated through conquest and engaged in a fundamentally different mode of interstate interaction than republics and monarchies; they were ill suited to coexistence with other equal and independent states. Unlike compact European states whose proximity had developed in them the capacity for diplomacy and negotiation with their adversaries, despotisms conquered vast hinterlands and relied on those extensive frontiers and dependent vassal states to separate them from rivals. Despotic states provided for their security not by uniting, as republics did, but by holding themselves apart, sacrificing a part of their territory, and placing distant provinces under feudatory princes. A despotism "will be in the best situation when it is able to consider itself as alone in the world, when it is surrounded by deserts and separated from the peoples it

calls barbarians" (the suggestion that Asian despotisms are incapable of regarding foreigners as anything other than barbarians would become a
standard trope of nineteenth-century British accounts of China, as we will
see in Chapter 5). This is in part because the ruler cannot rely on the loyalty and obedience of the militia; the hinterlands exist to be sacrificed for
the survival of the regime in the absence of a reliable military.[90] Despotism
also entailed a radically different conception of the very identity of the
state from that of moderate regimes, in the sense that the state had no
existence independent of the ruler. Because the ruler was at once "the
laws, the state, and the prince," treaties made with a deposed ruler had
no force; this made despots' interstate relations as unstable as their domestic
condition.[91]

With this argument Montesquieu developed an ideological picture of
European states as inherently anti-imperial, as the preserve of freedom, as
forming a unique community of states capable of tempering their hostility
through the law of nations and diplomatic flexibility.[92] If Europe were to
succumb to despotism, "in this lovely part of the world, human nature
would suffer, at least for a time, the insults that it has suffered in the three
others."[93] Still, notwithstanding Montesquieu's critique of conquest as
characteristic of despotisms, rather than as a thoroughgoing critic of empire, he should be read, in keeping with a line that we have seen proposed
by Rycaut, as developing an imperial model that was commercial and maritime as an alternative to the empires of conquest and extensive territory
that he associated with Asian despotisms.[94]

Moderate and Radical Critiques of Montesquieu: Porter and Anquetil

The transformation of the diplomatic discourse on the Ottoman Empire
that Montesquieu's work effected is apparent in the late eighteenth century's
major successor to Rycaut's work of reportage and diplomatic advice, the
Observations on the religion, law, government, and manners of the Turks
(1768) by Sir James Porter, England's ambassador to Constantinople from
1746 to 1762.[95] Porter's views about the Ottoman state were in many respects
similar to Rycaut's, as was his professional stance as a diplomat concerned
to convey both that it was possible to engage the Ottomans diplomatically,
and to profit from commercial dealings with them, and that his own

specialized knowledge was indispensable in dealing with a society so unfamiliar—"an uncommunicative people," as he put it with a classically Orientalizing metaphor, "concealed and wrapped up in the veil of their own obscurity."[96] Like Rycaut, he combined a degree of disdain for supposed "Turkish" vices (from the "absurdities of the Koran," to a relentless "pursuit of their own interest," to tempers at once "passive," "vindictive," and "ungovernable") with a purpose of disabusing European readers of their worst prejudices against the Ottoman state and society.[97] But, writing in the wake of Montesquieu, he chose to frame his account of the Ottomans as a refutation of the category of oriental despotism as applied to that state.

The importance to Porter of repudiating Montesquieu's account is particularly evident in the new introduction that he wrote for the second edition, in which he attacked the historian William Robertson's brief and categorical dismissal of the Ottoman regime as a despotism on the grounds provided by Montesquieu: the sovereign is not bound by any law; there are no intermediary powers to check the capricious and arbitrary rule of the sovereign; and the sovereign governs through fear, thanks to the "absolute command of a vast military force."[98] Robertson somewhat glibly set aside the evidence of those, like Porter, with more intimate knowledge of the Ottoman Empire than he himself had, to insist that the regime was a despotism, "the genius of [whose] policy continued to be purely Asiatic," and like Montesquieu, he quoted Rycaut to support a far more relentless portrait of despotism than Rycaut himself had intended. Central to Porter's response to Robertson and to the "ingenious president Montesquieu, led by precarious authorities," was the claim that Ottoman regime was law-governed. Not only was it "more perfect and regular, as well as less despotic" than most writers had claimed, but it was also "much less despotic, than the government of some Christian states," and a regime that one could be confident from its long duration had "some parts of its constitution wisely regulated" by religion and law.[99]

A key point at issue between defenders and critics of the category of despotism was the significance of religious limitations on the exercise of sovereign power. Montesquieu's very acknowledgment of the limiting role of religion had had an exoticizing effect. On Montesquieu's account, despotisms differed from other regimes in being limited only by religion and custom: these were alternatives to the rule of law rather than sources of law.[100] Although Porter, too, placed religion at the center of structures of Ottoman obligation, he insisted that these structures made the regime not an "absolute despotism" but a "limited monarchy" comparable to European states, and like them, founded on a social contract that produced obligations between ruler and people. This meant that ruler and subjects alike followed legal forms and precedents, and the judgment of independent legal authorities, in all important matters of state, including foreign affairs.[101] The sultan was "limited and circumscribed by the Koran," which was a "code of laws between prince and people, a compact binding both, and sealed in heaven."[102] Porter countered Montesquieu's claim that the regime lacked anything like a monarchy's intermediary powers with references to the ulema, "a body of men equal, if not superior to any nobility, jealous of their rights and privileges, and who stand as an intermediate order between the prince and people," and to the mullahs, "the perpetual and hereditary guardians of the religion and laws of the empire" as independent authorities capable of relying on law to limit the power of the sovereign. While Montesquieu and Porter disagreed to some extent in their empirical claims, more important is the construction they put on these facts. Both regarded religion as the key source of political obligation in the country, but where for Montesquieu Islam supplied a radically inferior alternative to systems of civil and political law, for Porter it was instead a reliable basis for such systems: "Whatever defects may be in the political system of the Turks, their empire is so solidly founded on the basis of religion, combined with law."[103] Thus, in Porter's account, the Ottomans had laws to secure property and regulate commerce: the source of the country's problems was not its laws but the corrupt administration of them. *Contra* Montesquieu, such abuses were neither systematic nor necessarily worse than abuses in European states, but rather as incidental as they are anywhere else.

In his account of treaty relations between the Ottoman regime and European states, Porter depicted the former as both attentive to treaty obligations and savvy and determined in extracting the maximum benefit from its agreements with other states. Porter quoted the Ottoman ministers to the negotiations around the 1739 Treaty of Belgrade, negotiations with the Russians and Habsburgs mediated by the French, describing their regime as "more *republican*" than was commonly believed in Europe. They noted, he wrote, that whereas in Petersburg or Vienna foreign affairs depended on one or two men with no accountability to anyone else, "the Grand Seignor could not offer preliminaries of peace without the concurrence of the Moulahs . . . however despotic he might be supposed."[104]

(While it is possible that Ottoman ministers of 1739 were aware of European disagreements about the character of their regime, the imputed quotation seems more likely Porter's projection onto the earlier moment of the debates provoked by Montesquieu.) He noted structural disadvantages under which the Europeans labored, and their lack of leverage with the Ottoman regime, in that they relied on commercial ties as the Ottomans did not: "As the trading powers remote from the Turks have no reciprocal advantages to grant them, their ambassadors in Turkey must submit to such terms as the government pleases to allow; and it is more surprising their capitulations or concessions have been so well observed, than if they had been totally neglected." The capitulations, as he later added, were "mere concessions; there is not, as we have already observed, nay, there cannot be the least reciprocation: the only way to support them is by prudence, and a circumspect behavior."[105] Porter's conclusion from the observation that the agreements were not reciprocal was primarily the pragmatic one that Europeans had little leverage to enforce such agreements; like Rycaut, he did not conclude as later legal writers would that their nonreciprocal quality placed such agreements in a separate legal universe from the reciprocal treaties that formed the basis of the European legal order.

Despite his insistence on the legal structure of the Ottoman regime and on the reliability of treaty relations with the Ottomans, Porter did endorse several claims that would underlie later arguments that Ottomans stood outside the European legal community. He asserted the Ottomans' ignorance of the law of nations and indeed suggested their contempt for the very possibility of such a law: "The Turks have properly no idea of the law of nations: they consider themselves the only nation on earth, and regulate their whole conduct with others on positive compact, spontaneous concessions, or usage and custom. Foreign ambassadors, therefore, have no other security but written concessions, of which they have copies, or such privileges unwritten, as their predecessors made use of."[106] He noted "the hatred and contempt they bear to all people in the universe who are not of their own persuasion." And he maintained that Ottoman policy toward ambassadors was to receive them "only conditionally at the Porte, as guests to the Grand Seignor," and when contemplating war against another power, to "insult [the ambassador's] person" as a means of conveying their hostility to the opposing sovereign.[107] Although Porter presented such observations as advice for those who sought successful relations with Ottomans and not as arguments for their exclusion from European law, it was precisely this set of claims—that the Ottomans disregarded the law of nations, maintained a formal hostility to nonbelievers, and rejected the European principle of ambassadorial immunity—that would furnish arguments for their inferior legal status in the nineteenth century.

The most radical and thoroughgoing critique of Montesquieu's account of oriental despotism, *Législation orientale,* published in Amsterdam in 1778 by the French Orientalist Abraham Hyacinthe Anquetil-Duperron (1731–1805), drew on Porter for evidence of the law-governed nature of the Ottoman Empire but used that evidence to insist that the Ottomans did respect the law of nations. Anquetil left France for India in 1755 at the age of twenty-three and made a three-year overland voyage from Pondicherry to Surat, where he remained studying Zoroastrian manuscripts until 1761.[108] He stayed with his elder brother, Etienne Anquetil de Briancourt, a merchant in the service of the Compagnie des Indes and later the French consul at Surat, until a violent conflict with a French merchant led Abraham to seek protection in the British factory at Surat.[109] Anquetil-Duperron returned to France with a collection of nearly 200 Indian manuscripts and fragments.[110] His best-known work, a translation of the Zoroastrian text known as the *Zend-Avesta,* was published in Paris in 1771, prefaced with a verbose and self-promoting account of his voyage and his dedication to scholarship that remains one of the major sources of biographical information about him, and which was partly responsible for the egregiously hostile reaction the work provoked in the republic of letters.[111]

Législation orientale was a refutation of Montesquieu's theory of oriental despotism by way of a detailed account of the legal frameworks of the Ottoman, Persian, and Mughal Empires. Anquetil presented abundant evidence to show, against Montesquieu, that the rulers of these states recognized legal obligations, both toward their own subjects and toward foreigners and Europeans. As he summarized the Montesquieuan position, "Government is despotic in the Orient; Princes are reproached with a conduct opposed to that dictated by the law of nations [*droit des gens*], the laws [*loix*] of humanity: thus this conduct is particular to and inherent in Despotism. That is the objection."[112] The title page captures Anquetil's call for impartiality and justice in the evaluation of Asian regimes with an image of a hand reaching down from the clouds, holding a balanced scale; the work is dedicated to the "peoples of Hindustan." Anquetil's epigraph from the *Aeneid* invokes Jupiter's call for impartiality between the natives of Italy and the Trojans, one of Europe's oldest tropes of Eastern alienness, who in the *Aeneid* are of course also Rome's ancestors: "I will draw no distinction between them, Trojan or Rutulian." In what follows, I highlight two features of Anquetil's critique that structure and inflect his substantive claims about the legal structure of these Muslim empires and the nature of their legal relations with Europeans. These are his critique of the ideology of oriental despotism and his approach to the interpretation of the necessarily flawed evidence available to Europeans about non-European societies. In 1776 Anquetil sent the French foreign minister, the comte de Vergennes, the manuscript that served as the basis for *Législation orientale*. The manuscript was titled *Despotism considered in the three states where it is thought to be the most absolute: Turkey, Persia, and Hindustan.* In contrast to the manuscript title, which challenges the purported despotism of these societies, the title of the published work more affirmatively stresses their lawful structure.[113]

Anquetil's central objection to the theory of oriental despotism was that it depicted as systematic, as a system of government, what was in fact nothing more than abuses of power such as might, and do, happen under any government. As he suggested, profound implications followed from the depiction of despotism as systematic. First, if Asian princes could be shown as consistently violating the law of nations and the "laws of humanity," they would have no claim to inclusion in the system of mutual respect and obligation governed by the law of nations, and no claim to law-governed treatment by other states. Further, because these systems were depicted as settled, naturalized, and in a sense even legitimate, doubt was cast on the capacities of the subjects of these regimes to live under moderate and lawful government; it came to seem as though despotic regimes were suited to their populations and that these populations were little better than beasts.[114] Both the regimes and their subjects, then, were depicted as categorically different from the normative European regime, and not, as in his view they should be, as variations on a universal type sharing the basic structures of law and order that exist in all societies, and that in all societies are sometimes defied, abused, and neglected by the powerful. Injustice and violence occur in all states at all times, he argued; every state has officials who act in bad faith and laws that "violate natural law more or less," including, significantly, European laws regarding serfdom and the *Code noir*.[115] On the subject of slavery, Anquetil noted sardonically, in response to Montesquieu's claim that only small-scale trade was possible under despotisms: "I admit that the Indians neglect certain means of enriching themselves that Euro-

peans could direct them to. For example, they have not yet tried to erect into
a regulated commerce those *Sales of human flesh* that in Europe are called
the *Traite des Nègres*. In this they are less advanced than we are."[116]

In his polemical introduction to the work, Anquetil offered an angry
summary of what he regarded as the standard European portrait of oriental
despotism epitomized in the *Esprit des lois*.[117] He criticized Montesquieu's
presentation of the supposed facts of Asian regimes, the conclusions he had
drawn about despotism as a type, and the selective use of sources by Montesquieu and other theorists of oriental despotism, such as Boulanger.[118]
Anquetil objected to Montesquieu's caricaturing of Asian regimes as simple
despotisms reducible to a handful of basic principles ("deux ou trois idées")
and characterized above all by the absence of law. He identified three fundamental sets of questions, on all of which he opposed Montesquieu's
conclusions. Most generally, does despotism reduce a society to a state of
barbarism by annihilating law, knowledge, industry, and commerce, and by
"dissolving ties of reciprocity" between sovereigns and subjects, and between states? More specifically, are there written codes in existence, and in
force, in the Orient? And do subjects hold private property in land and
goods? Anquetil accepted the terms of the debate in the sense that he agreed
it was relevant to show that these regimes were societies organized according to law, and so legally intelligible to European societies, that they
practiced reciprocity and respected the law of nations, and that they respected private property. This, then, is an argument for legal recognition
and inclusion in the law of nations community that is limited to agricultural and commercial states with written legal codes, rather than a more
thoroughgoing critique of the premises of such a conception of intersociety
law. When Anquetil wrote what we might see as a parallel defense of Native American societies against standard European misconceptions and
prejudices, *Considérations philosophiques, historiques et géographiques sur
les deux mondes,* he did not make a case for their recognition as participants in an expansive law of nations.[119]

Arguably, Anquetil's greatest contribution in *Législation orientale* was
his diagnosis of the causes of what we might call the legal ideology of oriental despotism, or legal orientalism: the combination of ignorance, self-
indulgence, and interest that, as he argued, produced a tendentious account
of Asian regimes as so lawless that Europeans had no obligations toward
them.[120] Anquetil argued that the portrait of oriental despotism arose from
the interaction between travelers' reports that concentrated on abuses

of power and Montesquieu's systematizing, which led him to read the travelers' reports selectively and for polemical purposes.[121] The reasons for Europeans' misapprehensions about, and bias against, Asian regimes and peoples included the desire for inappropriate wealth acquisition and territorial conquest, a natural human tendency to regard the alien as inferior, and distinctly European forms of cultural and racial self-conceit. Travelers were given to describing cruelties and massacres, not laws; when they noticed reasonable or useful institutions they treated them as "*hors d'œuvres,*" anomalies, details outside the general character of the regime and people.[122]

While Anquetil relied to some extent on the same reports (though in the case of India he also relied on his own observations and on primary documents), he stressed the significance of one's interpretive posture toward such evidence. The thought that we must continually combat our own natural tendency to denigrate our fellows—"rabaisser son semblable"—is one that lies behind a number of Anquetil's works. As he put it in his *Considérations philosophiques,*

> The same mental disposition that causes [man] to see monsters in whatever is foreign to his mores and habits, degrades in his eyes the thinking being that does not share those tastes or faculties of body or soul that belong to his own circle. . . . most often, regarding himself with complaisance, he will reduce an entire people, a considerable portion of the human species, to the state of brutes, because he makes incidental things the foundation of the human species.[123]

In *Législation orientale,* Anquetil targets that denigration in a particular legal idiom. The book is a call for interpreting ambiguous evidence generously, in a way that assumes continuities rather than discontinuities with familiar European cases, that seeks analogies and commonalities rather than tendentiously combining evidence of governmental formalities and abusive practices to produce the most pejorative picture possible of these states.[124]

In a satirical portrait of the European traveler looking to get rich and determined to blame everything that stops him on tyranny and bad government, Anquetil exposed Europeans' tendency to attribute to Asian despotism state policies that they accepted as part of the rule of law when they encountered them in Europe. It is worth quoting at length for its encapsulation of so many of Anquetil's themes:

An individual, a merchant, a statesman, soldier, even a man of letters, full of the ideas that he has formed for himself of the excellence of European governments, goes to India, always to make his fortune, that is to say to amass in four years what his homeland would not give him in a hundred. The difficulties that he faces upon arrival embitter him. The soldier is stopped in his conquests by what he calls *a troop of blacks*. What a scandal! The least of these soldiers considers himself greater than their Leader. The businessman, the politician finds in the country other Europeans in contestation with the natives, always for money: the latter have the bad grace not to let themselves be despoiled without protest. . . .

Our traveler has possessions [*des effets*]. As a European everything ought to be permitted him. Yet his possessions are stopped by Customs, duties imposed, contraband seized. What an affront! and on his return, he encounters many others in his country, of which he does not complain.

What is bad in Asia is always an effect of Government. Locusts have devastated one province; war has depopulated another; the lack of rain causes a dearth that obliges the father to sell his child to live (I saw this in 1755 in Bengal): again the Government. The traveler composes his work in Paris, in London, in Amsterdam, where one may say anything against the Orient. The same obstacles [*inconveniens*], in his homeland, he attributes to the land, to heaven, to human malice; because it is reason that has dictated the laws.[125]

The vignette captures a profound critique of the ideology of legal orientalism and its cultural and material contexts. These contexts included a European sense of superiority and privilege both cultural and racialized, and unrealistic financial expectations generated by the practice of commerce underwritten by increasingly preponderant military power. The fact that European publics had little access to counterevidence or refutations from members of the societies in question, Anquetil showed, meant that the discourse of oriental despotism had taken flight from reality: "one may say anything."

Much of the evidence Anquetil presented in the book was designed to show that the Ottoman, Persian, and Mughal monarchs, far from exercising arbitrary or despotic power, were constrained by, and themselves recognized, detailed and rigorous codes of law interpreted by independent legal authorities.[126] As we saw with Porter, to some extent Anquetil's dispute with Montesquieu and the account of oriental despotism turned on what various authors made of the status of Muslim law, since all agreed that Muslim law partly regulated these governments but disagreed on the implications and significance of this fact. For Montesquieu, the supposed absence of "civil law" meant that such regimes could rely only on religion and custom for any sort of regulation; he made clear that these were inferior forms of regulation. For Anquetil, as for Porter (and Burke, as we will see in Chapter 4), the fact that the Qur'an and its commentaries served as the basis for civil decisions ("covering all cases that might concern persons and goods") did not make the Ottoman state different in kind from other legal systems.[127]

For much of his argument about the essentially reliable structure of the Ottoman legal system, and for the claim that instances of fraud indicate abuses of the law, "not the vice of the Law itself," Anquetil relied on evidence from Porter and took Porter to be an ally. His critical difference from Porter arose with respect to the question of whether the Ottomans could be said to respect the law of nations. Against Porter's claim (quoted above) that the Ottomans did not respect the law of nations, he wrote, "I ask whether the law of nations, distinguished from natural law, has other foundations than treaties and the accords made among nations. The Turks observe these Treaties, they govern themselves by [se règlent sur] these agreements, thus they have an idea of the law of nations."[128]

He enumerated instances in which Turkish leaders insisted on upholding treaties when interest might have dictated breaking them. It was clear, he wrote, that "the law of nations, the law of war, public faith, the security of property, that of commerce, in sum that the laws of humanity and of reason are respected by the Ottoman Monarchs as well as by their representatives." He cited as an example Sultan Ahmed I, who had signed a treaty in 1604 with Henri IV of France reaffirming earlier agreements between the two countries. Anquetil observed that "to show such a singular respect for Treaties made by his predecessor was as much as to say to [European] nations [les nations] 'I have the same principles of equity as you do; the Ottomans share the same public law.'" This was one of a number of instances in which the dispute between those who would include or exclude the Ottomans from the law of nations turned on interpretation of an agreed set of facts. Anquetil agreed, that is, with the conventional account that Ottoman policy dictated that all treaties expire with the death or removal of the sultan who had signed them. But rather than reading such a policy as evidence of a radically different conception of foreign relations that placed the Ottoman regime outside the law of nations community, he looked to the standard practice of treaty renewal to suggest instead a shared understanding of the force of treaty obligations: a substantive agreement behind different legal forms.[129] His evidence, that is, was precisely the actual practice of states that later positivist jurists would insist restricted international law to Europe. He also took up the question of the Qur'an's supposed ban on permanent peace with non-Muslims, rejecting Rycaut's claim that Muslim rulers believed themselves "authorized . . . by the Law of their Prophet" to break treaties or alliances when doing so would increase their empire or the reach of Islam, which later authors would cite as evidence that Muslim states themselves ruled out anything like legal community with Europeans. Anquetil instead quoted from the ninth sura of the Qur'an to show that "the Alkoran formally orders the observation of Treaties made with Infidels who abide by their agreements."[130]

Anquetil took ironic pleasure in using instances of Asian cruelty as evidence that these societies recognized the laws of nations and would punish European violations of those laws. He noted that in 1775 the Marathas had given the Europeans "some rather cruel lessons in the law of nations." The English had committed atrocities in the course of seizing the island of Salsette near Bombay in the previous year, after agreeing to come to the aid of the Marathas in a local power struggle. These atrocities "revolted all the people of the country, even the Marathas who had called the English to their aid. . . . Indignant to see Europeans violating at this point the laws of war and of humanity, they avenged themselves by cutting off the ears and the noses of the English who fell into their hands."[131] Similarly, he showed up the contradictions in accounts that accused Asians of both stupidity and wiliness, and he pointed to details in travelers' reports that belied their own claims, such as that of Turkish servility. He noted that the secretary to the French embassy in 1670, Edouard de La Croix, insisted on the "blind obedience of the Turks" even while undermining his own picture with evidence of the penetrating and independent-minded advice one of the sultan's advisors gave him about managing his conquests. Anquetil commented: "Is this the language of a slave, of the prime minister of a Despot whose government knows no laws, destroys sentiments, leaves men hardly an animal, even a vegetative, life?"[132]

In *Législation orientale*, law was the primary discourse through which Anquetil insisted on human unity; the legal argument was in service of a project of universal sympathy that he expressed in the opening in the following terms: "I am a man, I love my fellows [*mes semblables*]; I would like to further tighten the bonds by which nature unifies the human species, and that the distance of times and places, and the variety of languages, customs, and opinions have but too greatly weakened, if they have not altogether broken them."[133] Anquetil suggested that law had a privileged position in the European imagination: he recognized that the possession of and respect for law, both internal and interstate, was becoming important in marking Europe out in relation to the rest of the world as, paradoxically, both unique and in keeping with nature's purposes for all of humanity. As he recognized, the discourse of oriental despotism allied European civilization with the law of nations and the rights of humanity; his detailed exposition of the legal principles that governed the major Asian empires internally and externally was intended to challenge the suggestion that particular European practices were privileged representatives of universal principles. Anquetil reiterated this point in notes that he took on Bossuet's *Politique tirée des propres paroles de l'écriture sainte,* a work that had defended the legitimacy of Louis XIV's absolutism by distinguishing it from the "arbitrary government" practiced in some unnamed but culturally distant societies "quite far from our customs": "It suffices for us to say that it is barbarous and odious," Bossuet had written.[134] Anquetil commented that if one read the book carefully, one could find "correctives" to the "explanations about all the places that might seem unfavorable to the liberty that is natural and inherent in the human species." He added, on the theme of despotism in Bossuet's fifth *Avertissement aux protestants,* that while its principles were generally good, "they are not always well applied to the people of God and other governments of the Orient."[135]

In a still later work, *L'Inde en rapport avec l'Europe,* written in 1798 in the wake of the revolution, Anquetil offered a more jaundiced account of the law of nations as "nothing but the resource of the weak," who, when they lack the necessary force to stand up to a greater power, "confide their rights to the publicists and jurisconsults" but are ultimately invaded anyway.[136] "Among Europeans, or rather among all peoples," he wrote, "particular interest has always prevailed over considerations of decency." Commercial nations were particularly guilty of bad faith in treaty making, he suggested; like merchants, they ruined their neighbors with "*sang-froid*" and saw all others as competitors to be bested; they "subordinated" truth and obligation "to gain." These evils of commerce could be counteracted in the case of individual merchants by laws and courts, but such tools "have no force against such a nation." The practice of European merchants in Asia and the states that underwrote their activities gave the lie to the narrative in which European modernity and civility were indexed by respect for property rights, respect for contracts, and peaceable commerce.

Législation orientale had little impact in its day, and Anquetil's profound critique of European provincialism and racism and their connection to abuses of power were largely forgotten, although his philological scholarship was vindicated in the early nineteenth century, and admirers such as Jules Michelet celebrated him as an archetype of the intrepid scholar single-mindedly dedicated to the pursuit of knowledge. Michelet described him as the young man who set out to "verify" where others only "discussed": threatened by tigers, beset by the "maladies of the climate," he closed his eyes to the seductions of "luxurious Asia." "His bayadère, his sultana, was the old and indecipherable book."[137] Siep Stuurman has argued that Anquetil's "global egalitarianism," an egalitarianism recognized in passing by Edward Said as merely "eccentric," was not as anomalous as Said suggests, but was rooted in the same combination of historicism and natural-rights universalism that can be found in Diderot and Raynal. While Said criticized Anquetil's biographer Raymond Schwab for choosing, in the celebrated *Oriental Renaissance* (1934), "to see the East-West relationship as basically an equal one—whereas in fact, of course, it was no such thing," he did not note that criticism of the exploitation of Asia by Europe was one of Anquetil's own primary intentions.[138] Stuurman attributes the relative obscurity in the nineteenth century of Raynal's *Histoire des deux Indes,* one of the great bestsellers of the Enlightenment, to same cause as Anquetil's, namely, the European triumphalism of the historiography and anthropology of the later period. As he writes, "transcultural equality became almost unthinkable to the nineteenth-century mind."[139] I will argue in Chapter 4 that such a dynamic also accounts for nineteenth-century misinterpretations of the legally inclusive posture of British authors such as Edmund Burke and William Scott, Lord Stowell, though it must be acknowledged that such an explanation does not account for the relatively marginal status of *Législation orientale* even in its own day.

Conclusion

As *oriental despotism* came to replace *infidel* as a key analytic lens through which Europeans regarded legal and diplomatic relations with some of their major trading partners in the eighteenth century, the concept did important work to justify the idea that the law of nations was both uniquely European in fact and presumptively authoritative for the world as a whole. Alongside the growing importance of the category of despotism was a shifting understanding of the nature of diplomatic relations with states such as the Ottoman Empire and of the legal instruments known as capitulations; these came to be seen as anomalous and inferior in relation to reciprocal treaties among European states, and as evidence of the inferior capacity for sovereignty of the states that issued them. As the German scholar August Wilhelm Heffter was to put it, "The oriental state must be distinguished from the European state. The oriental state is that of resignation and bondage, in which despotism or oligarchy is allied with hierarchy. . . . States' international sovereignty rests essentially on the organization of an independent and regularly constituted power."[140] Even as the term itself fell into disuse, the conceptual framework of oriental despotism underlay the insistence by Western European legal writers throughout the nineteenth century that the Ottoman Empire and China were internally lawless regimes unable to provide adequate legal protection for their European residents, and arrangements for consular jurisdiction once granted as a privilege to merchant communities by a powerful state, without implying any derogation of its sovereign powers, evolved into expansive extraterritorial jurisdiction imposed through unequal treaties.[141] As the states with whom Europeans had long had a variety of treaty and diplomatic relations came to be conceived as internally lawless, and as unwilling or unable to bind themselves by law to other states through bilateral treaties, and therefore as different in kind from European states, European discussions of the law of nations changed. Questions of admission into the community governed by the law of nations became paramount for nineteenth-century international lawyers in a way that would have been surprising to law of nations theorists of the previous century, although the way for this new preoccupation was paved by the discourse of oriental despotism.

European accounts of oriental despotism tended to be at once anxious and triumphalist: the worry that oriental despotisms represented a condition to which European monarchies might always succumb fed a desire to mark them as utterly alien and radically inferior to European regimes, whatever their flaws. The challenge posed by writers such as Anquetil-Duperron to this way of thinking took the form of both legal argument and cultural critique. In contrast to the parochial universalist mode of seeing law and the law of nations as the exclusive prerogative of Europeans and a source of justification for their exercise of power over others, for Anquetil, Europeans were as likely to violate the law of nations as those they declared incapable of living up to its precepts. Moreover, they were uniquely guilty of using the moral authority of the law of nations to vindicate self-interested actions, their own complacent self-conception, and their contempt for racialized others, whether Indians, Muslims, or simply "blacks." While Anquetil concluded that the law of nations was a weak tool with which to confront state violence or the misdeeds of merchants and envoys, he sought at least to call attention to its misuse in the service of such violence or misdeeds and perhaps to repurpose it for more critical ends. Reading the actions of non-European states—even, or especially, those that others labeled barbarous—*as if* they embodied principles of the law of nations was one way he did so. As we will see in Chapter 4, Burke would adopt the same strategy for similar ends in the impeachment trial of Warren Hastings.

"Oriental despotism" created a false narrative that was used to justify the West's abuse of Eastern sovereigns.

Napoleon & 7 yrs' War. major infl on Vattel
but more German than Fr.

THREE

Nations and Empires in Vattel's World

THE CATACLYSM OF the Seven Years' War was remarkably generative for international thought—for reflection on the idea of the European state system, the rights and obligations of states under the law of nations, the connections between commerce and war and the belligerent nature of modern commercial societies, and Europe's role in the world.[1] The English translator of Rousseau's *Projet de paix perpetuelle* lamented in 1761 that it would be nearly impossible to divert sovereigns from the "imperious pleasures of disturbing the tranquility of human kind, of wasting the blood and treasure of their subjects to satisfy sanguinary resentments, and of acquiring glory and dominions by filling the world with terror and desolation."[2] Subsequent works, from Smith's *Wealth of Nations* to Raynal's *Histoire des deux Indes* (both 1776), bore the traces of the conflict. For the first time, Europeans witnessed the spread of European conflict and power on a global scale.[3] Understandings of Europe itself were altered by the perception that Europe and its modern history could only be understood in light of its global commerce, wars, and imperial conquests. The war began with battles in 1754 between the French and British over control of the Ohio Valley before spreading to Europe, where Minorca was captured by the French in the spring of 1756, as well as to the Caribbean, West Africa, and the Philippine archipelago. In India, French-British hostilities reignited conflict among powers on the southeastern Carnatic coast, as British East India Company forces and their allies captured the French settlements of Chandernagore and Pondicherry and ultimately ended French aspirations to an Indian empire.[4]

Emer de Vattel's *Droit des gens*, though published early in the course of the long war, can be read as one of the most influential intellectual products of the conflict, and yet it is an anomalous one in relation to the war's global scope. Vattel (1714–1767) was personally implicated in the war and unusually attuned to its profound implications.[5] His native Neuchâtel, a hereditary principality, was chafing at domination under Prussia, with whom it shared a king although it was arguably an independent sovereign state, as Vattel himself insisted. After a brief and disappointing stint in Berlin, the Prussian capital, Vattel worked as a *conseiller d'ambassade* to the elector-prince of Saxony, whom he tried to persuade to negotiate with the Prussian king Frederick II for the sovereignty of Neuchâtel.[6] The war began on the continent in August 1756 with Frederick II's invasion of Saxony, Austria's ally, in anticipation of a campaign by Austria and Hungary to recover the province of Silesia, which had been lost to Frederick.[7] Although France and Britain had already declared war on each other (in May 1756) after two years of fighting in North America, it was the battles of the European continental theater of the Seven Years' War that were of most urgent interest to Vattel.[8] The imperial concerns of France and Britain that were such a dominant part of those states' experience of the Seven Years' War and subsequent decades through the fall of Napoleon were muted for Vattel in a way that shaped his influential framing of the "universal" law of nations, as much in his occlusions and omissions as in his overt arguments.[9]

Vattel's text was both a culmination and a beginning. While he understood himself as the product of the German academic tradition of *ius naturae et gentium* that had produced Pufendorf and Christian Wolff, Vattel departed from that tradition in regarding his work as a contribution to a broad public discourse—that of "les gens du monde"—rather than a narrowly doctrinal one.[10] Although his political context was arguably "German" rather than French, as a Protestant citizen of a francophone Swiss principality, Vattel was a participant in a French public sphere who read and commented on Voltaire and Rousseau and wrote literary essays and dialogues in addition to his legal writings.[11] His book exercised tremendous, immediate influence, especially in the anglophone world, with ten translations published in England between 1759 and 1834 and a further eighteen translations or reprints published in America from 1796 to 1872.[12] As early as 1765, Vattel could boast that "Mon *Droit des gens* a fait grande fortune en Angleterre."[13] It was cited as a major source on international law during the American Revolution, British debates on the French Revolution, the Napoleonic Wars, and the Congress of Vienna, and it remained canonical through the nineteenth century.[14] It was especially warmly embraced, as has been well documented, among the founders of the new United States of America.[15]

Vattel's work marked a beginning, too, in its use of modern history rather than classical examples and Roman law as its main source material for reflecting upon the principles of the law of nations. What might be called his incipient historicism links him to the decisive turn to historicism in the law of nations discussed in subsequent chapters of this book, though unlike later thinkers, he did not present a historical narrative of the development of the modern law of nations. Natural law was a source of moral standards for the law of nations, according to Vattel, though he famously displaced its authority in practice by asserting that while natural law was binding "internally," on nations' consciences, nations were externally bound only by positive laws, laws to which they could be said or presumed to have consented; they could be held to account by others only on the basis of positive laws. As equal and independent sovereign bodies whose chief duty is to their own development and perfection, nations were in most cases the sole judges of their own conduct: "Each possess the right of judging, according to the dictates of her conscience, what conduct she is to pursue in order to fulfill her duties."[16] This meant, for Vattel, that no foreign power had the right to "set himself up for a judge" of the government of another state or its internal conduct. The principle that nations had no right to judge one another applied globally, and specifically barred Europeans from appointing themselves judges of extra-European states as violators of natural law: "Those ambitious Europeans who attacked the American nations, and subjected them to their greedy dominion, in order as they pretended, to civilize them, and cause them to be instructed in the true religion,—those usurpers, I say, grounded themselves on a pretext equally unjust and ridiculous."[17] Thus Vattel argued that the "Spaniards violated all rules, when they set themselves up as judges of the Inca Atahualpa," since the Incas had not "violated the law of nations with respect to them."[18]

Vattel's distinctive version of dualism—the view that the law of nations depends on both natural and positive law—has been the central subject of interpretive efforts and disputes in the reception of and scholarship on his thought beginning in the late eighteenth century, and has produced widely diverging interpretations. He is often seen as a transitional figure between traditional natural law theory and nineteenth-century positivism, as paving the way for positivism while (unlike most later positivists) holding

Natural law, in the form of the conscience, was for you & your own nation; positive (voluntary) law was only expected of all others.

onto the normative aspiration of natural law thinking by seeing natural law as imposing duties on the consciences of states or nations. He described the "natural or necessary" law of nations as "originally no other than the *law of nature applied* to nations." While the natural must be "distinguished from" the positive or voluntary law of nations that "proceed[s] from the will of nations," they should not be "treated separately." The former is "always obligatory in point of conscience" and should guide a nation in its deliberations about how to act, but when determining what "she may demand of other states," a nation must consult the voluntary law.[19] Many commentators have praised Vattel for combining normative principle with hardheaded acknowledgement of the realities of interstate relations: for preserving something of Christian Wolff's cosmopolitanism, with its robust duties to all of humanity that do not disappear altogether with the creation of independent states, while wisely (it is often said) giving up what Vattel called Wolff's implausible "fiction" that the *civitas maxima* or world community was anything other than a moral ideal.[20] Others have criticized Vattel's dualism as ultimately incoherent, either because its normative commitments ultimately give the theory too little purchase on state behavior, or, conversely, because Vattel grants too much latitude to state interest.[21] Philip Allott follows a line of thought in twentieth-century international law that saw Vattel's theory as so uncompromisingly state-centric that, in Allott's words, it licensed murder, oppression, misery, and indignity "of kinds, and on a scale, that [human beings] could not tolerate within their internal societies. . . . Such was, and is, the Vattel tradition and the Vattel reality flowing from it."[22] Ian Hunter has neatly summarized the interpretive divergence among Vattel's critics as being between those who "treat Vattel's project of applying natural law to the relations between states as idealistic and impracticable, and those that treat its idealism as fatally undermined by political expediency."[23]

In this chapter I address a different though related interpretive conundrum, on the question of Vattel's universalism. A striking feature of Vattel's treatise is its apparent ambiguity about the scope of the international community—whether the law of nations applies within Europe or across the globe—and also its relative silence on European imperial and commercial expansion. Vattel has been read as both a characteristic exponent of an eighteenth-century natural-law universalism committed to the view that, in the words of Alexandrowicz, "non-European State entities . . . enjoyed a full legal status," and, in contrast, as a thinker narrowly concerned with theorizing relations among European states and justifying one political form, that of the Protestant agricultural-military republic.[24] Vattel's language is resolutely universal: he routinely writes of the law of nations as applying to the world, to mankind, to the "universal society of nations,"[25] and he opens his book by justifying a new work on the subject with the complaint that most writers "confine the name of the Law of Nations to certain maxims and customs which have been adopted by different nations," which is to confine "within very narrow bounds a law so extensive in its own nature, and in which the whole human race are so intimately concerned."[26] At the same time, his illustrative examples are generally, though not exclusively, drawn from modern European interstate relations, and his text has often been read, in the decades after it was published as well as in later scholarship, as an account of the modern European state system. As the admiralty court judge Sir William Scott wrote in 1799, "For this proof I need only refer to Vattel, one of the most correct and certainly not the least indulgent of modern professors of public international law. . . . Vattel is here to be considered not as a lawyer merely delivering an opinion, but as a witness asserting the fact,—the fact that such is the existing practice of modern Europe."[27]

In light of the great divergence among readers regarding the scope of Vattel's theory, I make two main interventions in this chapter. First, I argue that the universalism of Vattel's language must taken more seriously than has been the case in recent literature: we should not conclude that his subject was simply the European state system, even as we must qualify Alexandrowicz's view that Vattel exemplified an eighteenth-century natural-law universalism that took for granted the equal legal standing of European and non-European states. While Vattel rejected Christianity as the ground of legal principle or a criterion of legal recognition, and while he assumed non-European polities to be members of the society of states bound by the law of nations (and turned to them for evidence of agreement on basic principles), his legal system was unselfconsciously European in origin. Through Vattel I explore questions about canons of generalization and universalization in European law of nations thinking in the eighteenth century. Second, I suggest that Vattel's influential account of the state or nation as a moral person, and of the international arena as an egalitarian society of such persons, produced a distinctive, we might say deceptive, picture of the international realm that was to serve an important ideological function in the context of European imperial expansion. It rendered theoreti-

pretended European countries to be on 'equal footing' w others?

Vattel's attention was focused on Europe, particularly the sovereignty of Neuchâtel [handwritten annotation]

cally opaque the fact that some of Europe's most important powers were global empires rather than simply territorially bounded communities of citizens engaged in a shared, and implicitly republican, political project, and it largely disregarded the violence of European commercial and imperial expansion. It thus effaced the features of hierarchy and imperial extension that characterized the world system in Vattel's day, and from his day through to the present.[28]

Vattel's *Droit des gens* is a work that emerged from and was then taken up in multiple and very diverse contexts, complicating efforts to interpret the text.[29] It is worth stressing that the book that was to exercise such profound influence in the intellectual and political circles of Europe's major imperial and commercial powers, Britain and France, at the height of their global rivalry, was written by a diplomat most concerned with continental politics in the German states. As a Swiss subject of the Prussian king, preoccupied by the fate of his vulnerable homeland ("a country of which liberty is the soul, the treasure, and the fundamental law"), Vattel's attention was arguably less drawn to the global features of European states and their wars than was true of his French and British contemporaries, or had been true of Vitoria and Grotius as subjects of major imperial powers.[30] Whereas on crucial questions Vitoria and Grotius started with European empires and developed abstract claims about the law of nations from the dilemmas thrown up by imperial expansion, Vattel, with the exception of his reflections on settling "vacant" land, largely ignored the very significant imperial facet of the states he described as territorially based moral persons. Scholarship on Vattel's thought about empire and the non-European world has, consequently, focused on his views about the legitimacy of settlement and his contributions to agriculturalist justifications for the expropriation of native peoples in the Americas and Australia.[31] It is the contention of this chapter, however, that we should also attend to the implications of Vattel's argument for other questions of relations between European states and the rest of the world, both within the text and in its reception.

Although little has been written directly on the geographic scope of Vattel's theory, existing understandings diverge widely. For Alexandrowicz, Vattel exemplified, and concluded, a tradition running from the Spanish Scholastics and Grotius through the late eighteenth century, which saw natural law as the basis of the law of nations, with two crucial and related implications. The first is that the law of nations and the family of nations

[handwritten margin note: recognition unnecessary for sovereignty]

are universal.[32] The second is a declaratory rather than constitutive view of the recognition of sovereignty, such that a state's sovereignty exists prior to and independent of its recognition by others (others' recognition declares an existing status rather than constituting a new one): "for the family of nations could not be universal if its members were allowed to recognize or not to recognize newcomers to the family of nations employing recognition as a discretionary instrument of making or unmaking sovereign entities."[33] For Alexandrowicz these features mark the fundamental difference between natural law universalism and the Eurocentric positivism that replaced it at the turn of the nineteenth century, when the family of nations was restricted to Europe in legal discourse, and the constitutive view of state recognition prevailed, placing European states in the position of arbiters of membership in the international community.

Recent scholarship has mounted a significant challenge to Alexandrowicz's reading by asserting the highly particular nature of Vattel's apparently universal claims. For Ian Hunter, who has developed this line of argument most comprehensively and forcefully, Vattel's substantive account of the nation and the law of nations was not only distinctively European. It was also, more particularly, "a concrete historical order—that of a Protestant agricultural-military republic sourced from his Swiss homeland," which it raised "to the abstract level of a model of the virtuous national republic."[34] Hunter and others stress the importance of Vattel's diplomatic career and Swiss context for his theoretical arguments in the *Droit des gens*. Tetsuda Toyoda argues that "Vattel's seemingly 'theoretical' arguments in *Le Droit des Gens*" are far more "politically loaded" than they have been recognized to be. He points in particular to Vattel's defense of mercenaries (an important Swiss industry), his great "flexibility" on the question of preventive attack, about which he was far more permissive than Wolff, and his account of citizens' right of resistance against tyranny.[35] According to this reading, Vattel's was an abstracted rendering of the practices of the European state system and diplomatic community, and more specifically an abstraction of Swiss republican commitments, rather than a theory with more universal scope or implications.[36] However, the strongest version of such a claim, that Vattel's thought was "intra-European in its sources and concerns" because it was "wholly internal" to a "specifically European political history," neglects the fact that the European political history in which Vattel's thought was situated was not sealed off from but rather deeply tied to global commercial and political developments, as so many of Vattel's contemporaries made clear.[37]

The *Droit des Gens* in French Writing before Vattel

Much of the recent literature takes for granted that the classical law of nations, *droit des gens,* or *ius gentium,* was continuous with European public law, or the *ius publicum Europaeum.*[38] Throughout the eighteenth century, however, indeed, from the late sixteenth, political writers routinely referred to the law of nations as a body of globally applicable principles that bound states in their relations with one another and that excluded pirates and bandits but could include non-European states. Martti Koskenniemi has argued that France lacked a robust law of nations tradition of the kind that we find in German universities of the time, because the dominant strand of official French thought about interstate relations was the *raison d'état* tradition, in which the prince was bound by the imperatives of the preservation of the state, by the logic of statecraft, rather than by the rules of common law or natural jurisprudence. He argues further that the German tradition of *ius naturae et gentium* itself did not tend to designate a special sphere of interstate relations but instead referred to a more general project of public law as a technique for securing the happiness of the state.[39] Still, in broader French public discourse, the law of nations or *droit des gens* was frequently referred to as a body of principles governing interstate interaction, and its presence in works for general audiences suggests the degree to which the *droit des gens* was a language of moral and political thought rather than a narrowly legal and academic doctrine.[40]

Furthermore, it is striking how frequently the language of the law of nations was invoked precisely to address questions of European relations with states outside Europe, as Vitoria had earlier used it. So Michel de Montaigne, in his essay "Of Coaches," one of several essays he devoted to questions generated by the encounter with the New World, employed the phrase *"droit des gens"* in relation to Spanish conduct in Mexico. In the course of his argument that Europe had discovered a great new world whose people, to their own tremendous disadvantage, surpassed Europe in their "devoutness, observance of laws, goodness, liberality, loyalty, frankness," Montaigne wrote that the Spanish, having besieged and then captured the king of Mexico, "against their word and against all *droit des gens,* condemned the king himself and one of the principal lords of his court to the torture in one another's presence."[41] In a more ambiguous instance suggesting that the law of nations in principle applies among Muslim states, though they, like others, are sometimes warranted in deliberately breaking the law, Jean Bodin approvingly noted a violation of the law of nations in the war declared by "Tamerlane, Prince of the Tartars," on "Pajazet, King of the Turks," to chastise his tyranny. It is magnificent, he argued, for a prince to take up arms to avenge a whole people unjustly oppressed by the cruelty of a tyrant; there is more honor in attacking him like a "murderer, a parricide, a thief, rather than following the law of nations" ("plustost que d'user envers lui du droit des gens").[42] Nicolas Lenglet Du Fresnoy argued in *L'histoire justifiée contre les romans* (1735) that it is only through history that we can learn the "maxims of the law of nations, so necessary, so essential in themselves ... graven in the hearts of all peoples." These laws, he wrote, are not normally established by public acts, but rather certified by notorious facts, so that it is only history that can instruct us in them; relevant historical sources included the Bible and narratives of rulers from Alexander the Great to the Romans to, once again, Bajazet, emperor of the Turks. The Marquis d'Argens's epistolary novel *Lettres juives* of 1736 has a character assert that the "Moscovites, once less polished and less affable than the Turks, were ignorant of even the simplest proprieties, and knew only moderately [*médiocrement*] the *droit des gens*."[43] In sum, in this literature—political, historical, and literary writings that invoke the law of nations—questions of which states at Europe's borders and beyond recognized the *droit des gens* arise regularly. This suggests that we should read the *droit des gens* not as a discourse that originally was understood to apply only to Western Europe and was later extended, or as one simply assumed to apply universally, but rather as a discourse that was sometimes used to frame questions about the possibility for legally governed relations with states and peoples perceived as potentially very different in laws and mores.

Such questions were set aside by some of Vattel's contemporaries in their explicit narrowing of attention to European public law or the "European law of nations." The abbé de Mably tracked the process by which "the people of Europe were united, in some degree, together by a constant correspondence." In his disillusioned portrait of interstate relations, Mably proposed that "it was ambition, avarice, and fear, that obliged all nations to court each other. ... The same passions still direct their commerce, and engage them to receive ambassadors"; his story would have none of the moral ambitions of Saint-Pierre. Mably portrayed the discovery of the New World and the Portuguese rounding of the Cape of Good Hope that initiated maritime commerce with Asia as revolutionary events that radically and profoundly affected the European system by making commerce a new source of power, so that "money became the sinew of war and policy," and England, the country that made the best use of the new opportunities for wealth, developed unprecedented power. While Mably understood modern Europe to have been built on global commercial and imperial enterprises ("ships . . . factories . . . and colonies"), the political and diplomatic "system" that interested him was restricted to Europe, in which the Ottoman Empire participated as an important but only incompletely assimilated member. Although Vattel, too, described Europe as so closely united that it formed "a kind of republic," he analyzed it as a political system based on the balance of power rather than as a distinct legal universe or the sole domain of the law of nations.[44]

Vattel's Universalism in Question

In light of such developments, why did Vattel make such extensive use of universal language in his treatment of the *droit des gens*? How consciously did he do so—that is, to what extent was he aware of the genre of a more specifically European law of nations? What is the significance of this universalism for his argument? Why would it be important to Vattel to couch his normative principles in universal terms, and why would it be important to him to couch his law of nations principles likewise in universal terms? Finally, what are the substantive positions said by Vattel to have universal purchase, and what are the implications of these for thinking about relations with non-European states?

Universalisms, of course, always take a particular form, with respect to the metaphysical framework in which universal claims are made as well as the anthropological qualities asserted to be universally human. Several different, though interacting, forms of universalization play important roles in Vattel's argument. The most important framework of universalization within which Vattel operated was that of the *ius naturae et gentium* tradition, which presupposes a law of nature rationally derivable from human nature, and, in Vattel's words, "obligatory on every man possessed of reason, independently of every other consideration than that of his nature."[45] Modern Europeans had inherited this discourse from Roman law and Stoic cosmopolitanism, whose universalism was intimately connected with Rome's imperial ambitions.[46] This universalist language remained an attractive vehicle for those concerned with justifying European imperial

terra nullius

object = mutual assistance

expansion on moral grounds, as Vattel did in defending the settlement of "vacant" lands. Further, the universalist form of the law of nature enabled claims about the principles governing states' interactions to appeal across the religious divide within Christianity in the wake of the Protestant Reformation, bitter religious warfare, and the breakdown of a singular church as the authoritative framework for European morality.[47] For Vattel, the morally necessary law of nature guides human beings, as individuals and collectives, in their task of self-perfection: "The object of the natural society established between all mankind is that they should lend each other mutual assistance in order to attain perfection themselves and to render their condition as perfect as possible." The law of nature provides a normative standard by which we may judge the justice, injustice, or moral indifference of the voluntary law of nations, the law deriving from human will through custom or treaty. A conception of what nature requires of us, Vattel argued, should be able to guide us in determining when positive laws or customs are obligatory, if useful or even indifferent, or when they are prohibited, if unjust.[48]

Ian Hunter argues that Vattel universalized particular European practices—"the concrete history of European public-law treaty practices and conventions"—by claiming to ground them in natural law principles and by using them as the basis for arguments about the nature of political community.[49] Hunter likewise argues that Vattel's supposed universal law of nature is really the statement, in abstract terms, of a particular kind of political community, exemplified by Vattel's native Neuchâtel and other Swiss republics: territorial communities that valued intensive agriculture and citizens armed in self-defense. Readers of Vattel are commonly misled, Hunter argues, into reading natural law as "the unifying philosophical foundation" for Vattel's account of obligation, and so take for granted the idea of the state as a "self-perfecting nation-person." Hunter urges us to see Vattel's use of natural law not as a philosophical foundation for the law of nations, one whose tension with the principle of national self-interest is either philosophically incoherent or "a prelude to philosophical synthesis." Rather, we should understand the "irreconcilable normative tension" between the natural law principle of the reciprocal self-perfection of nations as moral persons, and the "maxims of individual national self-interest drawn from diplomatic history," as the setting for a practice of diplomatic casuistry, in which natural law principles are continually adjusted in relation to maxims of national self-interest. Vattel's "practice of abstraction works by elevating into 'political thought' a diverse array of technical languages and cultural traditions . . . through their annexation to the arbitrarily privileged metaphysics of self-perfecting personhood."[50]

To say that self-perfecting nationhood is an arbitrarily privileged metaphysics is to argue that Vattel does not, perhaps cannot, give reasoned arguments for his account as a political ideal; it is to suggest, as Hunter does elsewhere in relation to Kant, that mere subjective preference is the ultimate basis for all normative political arguments.[51] (Hunter does note elsewhere that for Vattel, the replacement of universal justice with diplomatic casuistry had a normative dimension in that it was seen as the only way to mitigate the violence of Europe's wars of religion.[52]) Hunter is right to point out that Vattel's account of the state as a moral person is based on a particular vision of human flourishing, one closely associated with Swiss republicanism. But it is one that Vattel offers not simply arbitrarily, as Hunter suggests, but rather as a moral ideal that does important argumentative work. He presents an ideal of naturally free individuals whose reason tells them to form political communities dedicated to furthering their happiness and the development of their rational and moral faculties. The idea of the state as moral person establishes the principle that nations' primary duties are duties to themselves, and it shapes and constrains their rights, a "right being nothing more than the power of doing what is . . . proper and consistent with duty." Nations' rights are rights to pursue their members' happiness and self-perfection autonomously, without the interference of outsiders. Vattel derives from the natural principle of human equality the idea that "nations composed of men, and considered as so many free and persons living together in the state of nature" are likewise equal, that (in his often cited analogy) "a dwarf is as much a man as a giant; a small republic is no less a sovereign state than the most powerful kingdom."[53] Hunter's analysis entails a kind of hermeneutics of suspicion: though he is sensitive to the discursive particularities of the text, rather than using these to understand the move in an argument that the thinker is making, he instead uses these to unmask the thinker.

Hunter's skeptical account should be supplemented with one that takes Vattel's universalism more seriously on its own terms. His description of Vattel's project as one of "diplomatic casuistry" is insightful, but his use of the concept largely as a shorthand for the idea that Vattel supplies diplomats with resources to argue whatever side of a question they see as being in their state's interest fails to do justice to the philosophical and normative work that casuistry does for Vattel. We can read the work as casuistical in a more specific and less pejorative sense, for the *Droit des gens* is shot through with the language of the case and with casuistical argumentation, in the sense that it is structured in terms of general rules supplemented by consideration of various circumstances that make deviations from the rules appropriate and is particularly interested in extreme cases and extenuating circumstances.[54]

Adam Smith's exactly contemporary (1759) treatment of casuistry helps us to see why Vattel might have been attracted to casuistry as a mode of reasoning for the law of nations as he understood it, among states that he conceptualized as having two key attributes: that they are mutually independent and thus charged with making their own judgments about their conduct, and that they are "moral persons" with a conscience. The concluding chapter of Smith's *Theory of Moral Sentiments* gives a brief history of casuistry and compares it to jurisprudence, which also seeks to "lay down exact and precise rules for the direction of every circumstance of our behavior." According to Smith, the key difference lies in the nature, and the enforceability, of their judgments. Jurisprudence concerns principles of right, or "what the person to whom the obligation is due, ought to think himself entitled to exact by force." Casuists instead ask what "the person who owes the obligation ought to think himself bound to perform from the most sacred and scrupulous regard to the general rules of justice, and from the most conscientious dread, either of wronging his neighbour, or of violating the integrity of his own character."[55] Smith, arguing for a non-rule-based practice of moral judgment by means of sentiment, rejected casuistry as misguided and corrupting with respect to individual morality. He concluded that casuistry "ought to be rejected altogether," leaving "Ethics and Jurisprudence" as the only "useful parts of moral philosophy."

But Smith's account shows precisely why casuistry would be useful for a theory of obligations between Vattelian states. For Vattel, one might argue, the task for an account of interstate justice is precisely to restrict the scope of what Smith calls jurisprudence—judgments properly backed by force.[56] States' conviction that they are justified in using force to carry out their judgments of others' violations of natural law or the law of nations is, according to Vattel, a major source of violence and bloodshed. The Vattelian international arena, composed of nations as "free and independent" moral individuals, is well suited to casuistry precisely because there is no global magistrate to enforce law, as Smith says systems of positive law do in trying to replicate natural jurisprudence, where instead of allowing each man to vindicate his rights by violence, they place violence in the hands of the magistrate. Even as casuistry was coming to be seen as outmoded and inadequate for questions of personal morality, then, we can see why Vattel would have found it appropriate as a framework for questions of international justice: its purpose is to inform thinking about how general rules are to be applied in particular situations, when there is no question of rights to be vindicated by violence.[57] Casuistry guides states' judgment about their duties, without giving them a license to prosecute their judgments by force. Further, casuistry has been described as entailing a mutual definition of the normative and the declined case; not only is the case evaluated in relation to the norm, but the norm itself is judged, evaluated, and refined. This dual movement parallels the mutual constitution of the natural law and the law of nations in practice.[58]

Perhaps the language of casuistry is not necessary to make some of the claims I make here about the nature of Vattel's arguments about what law of nations obligations entail. Emmanuelle Jouannet in her recent reconsideration of Vattel has made similar arguments without reference to casuistry, arguing that "for a jurist like Vattel, legal treatises are above all ethical codes of good conduct," rather than lists of "juridical prohibitions in the strict sense" or "unconditional imperatives," and that such a conception has been misread by later jurists because its "graduated conception of the juridical" affronts their desire to mark a stark boundary "between the juridical and the non-juridical."[59] But it may be worth recovering casuistry as a key register in which Vattel moved between the particular instance and the universal rule, using the universal rule to guide evaluation of the case while leaving room not only for exceptions to the rule but also for its adjustment in light of state practice. We next should ask how geographically extensive were the state practices that Vattel believed could legitimately inform the universal norms.

Universalizing Moments in Vattel

It is not surprising that the majority of Vattel's examples illustrating law of nations principles refer to intra-European relations, given that their "frequent intercourse" had given rise to a thick set of rules and customs for interstate relations and that they made up the bulk of the practice with which he and his sources were familiar. To the extent that Vattel took distinctly European practices and universalized them by claiming that they expressed principles of natural law, there may be several ways to understand what he was doing. He could have been arguing that key features of European practice can be shown to be compatible with natural law, without claiming that European practice, in all its specificity, is normative for others. This is a line of argument that his younger contemporaries Edmund Burke and William Scott developed, sometimes drawing on Vattel, as I will argue in Chapter 4. He could have been attempting to create an aspirationally universal law based on European principles, implicitly imposing duties on others who might have no reason to recognize such duties, as I argue in Chapters 5 and 6 was the dominant mode of universalization employed by nineteenth-century international lawyers. He could have been interested only in supplying rules or guides to judgment for European diplomats, as Hunter suggests, in which case the universal language may do discursive work in a Europe riven by confessional disputes but would not intend to refer to the world beyond Europe. A question to keep in mind as we evaluate these various possibilities is that of how non-European practices serve as source material of the law of nations for Vattel. Should we read them as corroborating claims that are derived mainly from European sources? Are they significant in their own right as sources of knowledge about the content of the law of nations? Does he ever use them to criticize or correct European practice?

In an effort to address these questions, I begin by canvassing four respects in which Vattel's account of the law of nations and the family of nations appears not to be restricted to Europe but to have broader or even universal application; I will also highlight the ambiguity of this universality. Most obvious is the universalist language already noted: Vattel's frequent references to the "universal society of mankind," "*l'amour universel du genre-humain*," and his claims that that if the "benevolent precepts of nature" were followed, the "world would take on the appearance of a great Republic, all men would live together as brothers, and each would be a citizen of the universe." Second is the related claim that nations' mutual obligations owe nothing to religion but are due to others simply as fellow human beings, as when Vattel writes that the obligation of performing the offices of humanity is founded solely on the "nature of man. Wherefore no nation can refuse them to another, under pretence of its professing a different religion: to be entitled to them, it is sufficient that the claimant is our fellow-creature."[60] Third is Vattel's source material from non-European state practice and precepts. And fourth are instances concerning relations between Europeans and non-Europeans, including those in which Vattel draws attention to European failures to respect principles of justice or the law of nations in their relations with non-European societies.

After setting out the general principle that we are bound by the law of nature to respect and work for the benefit of all other members of human society (quoting Cicero, *"pro omnibus gentibus"*) Vattel explicitly includes the "American nations" among those nations who are "absolutely free and independent" and protected by the law of nations from the unwarranted intrusions of others. His cursory treatment of China and Japan likewise indicates that he assumes them to be participants in the law of nations, whose actions with respect to foreigners have been perfectly in accordance with that law.[61]

The ambiguity of Vattel's universalism arises especially in relation to Muslim states, for although he includes them among the family of nations and suggests that Europeans are bound by the law of nations in dealing with them, his examples cumulatively suggest that Muslim states are distinctly untrustworthy and pose a particular threat to international society. With regard to two of the most important obligations of the natural law of nations, the fulfillment of treaties and the inviolability of ambassadors, Vattel makes a point of noting that that Christian-Muslim differences are irrelevant to the law of nations and of referring to Muslim recognition of the principle. Addressing the question of whether "treaties made with the enemies of the faith are valid," Vattel argues with some impatience that such a question should "be superfluous in the present age" because "difference of religion is a thing absolutely foreign" to treaty obligations, which are regulated only by the law of nature. He substantiates the claim that the fundamental principle that nations should observe their promises and treaty obligations is "generally acknowledged by all nations" with reference to Mohammed's injunction to his followers to observe treaties. Similarly, his argument that ambassadorial inviolability is a principle of the "natural and necessary law of nations" draws on evidence from Mexico, China, India, Arab societies, and the Qur'an, and "even among the savage tribes of North America."[62]

And yet Muslims and "Turks" appear repeatedly as aggressors against whom European nations rightly allied for mutual protection, and as violators of these universal principles.[63] Vattel's choice of illustration for his critique of Grotius's principle of punitive war, on the grounds that it "opens a door to all the ravages of enthusiasm and fanaticism," is the desolation wreaked across Asia by "Mahomet and his successors." He illustrates his argument for the irrelevance of religious affiliation to duties of humanity with an account of Christian cooperation against Muslims: Pope Benedict XIV was admirable in his willingness to protect Protestant Dutch ships as well as those of his fellow Catholics from Algerian corsairs. Likewise, when the Ottomans were reaching the height of their power, he argues, "all Christian nations ought, independent of all bigotry [*toute bigotterie*], to have considered them as enemies," given that they "made it their profession to subdue by force of arms all who would not acknowledge the authority of their prophet."[64] Vattel thus largely preserves the Christian-European alliance against Muslims, while displacing religion as a legitimate ground for that alliance. The cumulative effect of such examples seems to cut against the overtly universal language to present instead a European society routinely at odds with Muslim assailants.

After establishing that Christian-Muslim differences should have no bearing on treaty obligations, he includes the caveat that "if the maxims of a religion tend to establish it by violence, and to oppress all those who will not embrace it," the law of nature forbids alliances with its followers. The "common safety of mankind invites them rather to enter into an alliance against such a people,—to repress such outrageous fanatics." Here Vattel does not specify Muslims as such a people, though the trope of Islam as a fanatical religion spread by violence was not only a well-established one but also, as we have seen, one that Vattel himself had already invoked earlier in book 2. Thus, in the casuistical form his argument so often takes, he makes available principled grounds for taking either position, for including Muslim states in the network of treaty relations or for excluding them, leaving it to the statesman or diplomat making use of the text to establish the relevance of the abstract category for the case at hand. Although Vattel thus rejects an invidious religious distinction, replacing it with a universalistic principle based on the obligations of all nations to contribute to the peace of the society of nations, the force of his examples goes some way toward reinscribing the traditional exclusion of Muslims from the European/universal society of nations.

Similarly, when Vattel gives examples of those who "elude the true sense" of an agreement by adhering underhandedly to its strict letter, they are Muslims bent on violence: the Turkish sultan Muhammad II, who "having promised a man to spare his head, caused him to be cut in two through the middle of the body," and Tamerlane, who having extracted a capitulation by promising to shed no blood, had all the soldiers buried alive. Vattel's European examples also include descriptions of breach of principle.[65] But his most provocative examples tend to come from outside modern Europe. The rest of the examples of perfidy in the chapter just mentioned are ancient ones, aside from an anecdote about an Englishman who married three wives to avoid the penalty of the law that forbids marrying two, which Vattel dismisses as "doubtless a popular tale, invented with a view to ridicule the extreme circumspection of the English."[66] We do not find the same questioning of the veracity of reports about Muslim practices. The relative absence of provocative accusations against contemporary Europeans projects a harmonious vision of the European system that is notable, and was perhaps doing ideological work, in the context of the Seven Years' War.

As with the fulfillment of treaty obligations, Vattel's account of the universal obligation to respect the inviolability of ambassadors is supplemented with a series of examples that seem to throw into question the respect of Arabs, Muslims, and other non-Europeans for such universal legal principles, even as they assert a shared commitment to them.[67] The passage is worth quoting at length to convey the cumulative effect of the examples in the wake of the stated "universally acknowledged" principle of respect for ambassadors, for in each example Vattel has chosen, he confirms the general agreement on the principle by way of an example of its breach by various Asians and Arabs, or their abuse of its protections, and contrasts these with examples of scrupulous, even ostentatious, respect for the principle by Christians.

> Turn to the other extreme of the globe and you will find that ambassadors are highly respected in China. They are also respected in the Indies, though less religiously so, it is true. The King of Ceylon has sometimes imprisoned ambassadors of the Dutch East-India Company. He knows that because cinnamon grows in his dominions the Dutch will overlook many things in favor of a rich commerce, and like a true barbarian he takes advantage of the fact [il se prévaut en Barbare]. The Koran commands Muslims to respect public ministers; and if the Turks have not always obeyed the precept the failure to do so is rather due to the ferocity of certain princes than to the principles of the Nation. The rights of ambassadors were well known among the Arabs.[68]

The point about the Qur'an and its violation is double-edged: on the one hand Vattel is appealing to the Qur'an to assert a shared principle, and arguing that violations of that principle by "the Turks" should not be taken as evidence that basic Muslim values regarding interstate relations are radically different from European values. On the other hand, he presents those violations as a litany of abuses by Asians and Muslims. He adds two examples of Arab-Christian interactions in which Arab ambassadors exploit diplomatic privilege to speak "insolently" to their Christian counterparts, who respond by calling attention to their own restraint and respect for the principle of ambassadorial immunity.

Vattel's use of the term "civilized" is likewise ambiguous: while certain passages suggest that he did not in principle limit it to European countries, others seem to have an implicitly European referent. His argument is not for the most part a strongly progressive one, but he occasionally introduces a progressive narrative in which the principles of natural law, long hidden from view, come to be revealed among "civilized" nations.[69] The principle of mutual benevolence, for instance, was not recognized among the ancients, who "had no notion of any duty" to nations with whom they had no treaty ties, but "at length the voice of nature came to be heard among civilized nations; they perceived that all men are brethren. When will the happy time come that they shall behave as such?"[70] Here he asserts Europe's failure to live up to principles he seems to gloss as distinctively European. Likewise, in noting that the expedient of making hostages of women and children is rarely practiced in Europe, he invokes the protection of women and children as evidence of a distinctively civilized and European moral practice, one that he presents as superior, though not universally obligatory.[71]

Vattel's treatment of global commerce suggests that he did not consider in detail questions of law of nations obligations outside Europe that this commerce might well have raised for him, as it did for some of his contemporaries. He notes in passing that although monopolies in general constitute violations of the rights of citizens to engage freely in the nation's commerce, certain commercial enterprises can be undertaken only with considerable capital, and it was for this reason that many countries chartered monopoly companies for the East Indies trade. Here, like Mably, Vattel registers (briefly) the remarkable impact that global trade and conquest have had on the European political system, without pursuing questions of whether European conduct in Asia has conformed, or should conform, to principles of the law of nations. He notes the power, wealth, and glory amassed by the English and Dutch in the East Indies—it is thanks to its global commerce that England holds "in her hand the balance of Europe," while "a company of [Dutch] merchants possesses whole kingdoms in the east, and the governor of Batavia exercises command over the monarchs of India"—but neither here nor elsewhere does he address whether those Eastern possessions, or the relationship of command over Indian monarchs, are in conformity with the law of nations.[72]

Even at those relatively infrequent moments that Vattel addresses legal questions arising from European commerce in Asia, the text generally remains ambiguous as to whether it is giving an account of a law of nations operating among European states on a global stage or also between European and non-European states. In his chapter on rights regarding the open sea, Vattel mentions three examples around European commerce in Asia that raise legal questions: the attempt by the Portuguese to "arrogate . . . to themselves the empire of the seas of Guinea and the East-Indies"; the Austrian treaty renouncing commerce in Asia in favor of England and the Netherlands; and the question whether "the pearl fisheries of Bahrem and Ceylon may lawfully become property [*puissent légitimement tomber en propriété*]." The second is a question of intra-European treaty obligations, although the theater is Asian. The first and third are not as clearly specified but appear to have to do with relations among Europeans rather than with Asian sovereigns. He writes that the "other maritime powers" (not specifying whether he took Asian states to be among those powers) "gave themselves little trouble" about the Portuguese pretension to possess the open seas. This seems far too glib, given the strenuous efforts by the Dutch, especially, to undermine Portuguese claims to monopoly, including the seizure by a Dutch East India Company (VOC) ship of the Portuguese ship the *Sta. Catarina*, and the justifications of this seizure by Grotius in the text he called *De rebus Indicis (On the Affairs of the Indies)* that has come to be known as *De Jure Praedae (On the Law of Prize and Booty)*, one chapter of which was published in 1609 as *Mare liberum* and provoked responses by English, Portuguese, and Spanish jurists. Vattel's phrasing in discussion of the pearl fisheries, suggesting that they may in future be possessed rather than that they are currently, for instance, might suggest a claim by a new European power rather than an existing local power, but the passage is ambiguous as to which states would count as legitimate possessors under the law of nations.[73]

Despite Vattel's universal language and his repeated insistence on the irrelevance of religious differences for legal relations, then, the text nonetheless marks out those whose habitual violence places them outside the protections of the law of nations, a legal otherness that he often aligns with distinctions framed in terms of civilization or religion—Tamerlane and Genghis Khan, "savage Tartars," and barbarous Indian rulers. His influential description of nations that should be considered "monsters, unworthy the name of men" and "enemies to the human race" because they make war gratuitously includes "Turks and other Tartars," though it also seems to gesture at unnamed Europeans ("those supposed heroes" "among the most civilized nations"), and would be drawn on by British advocates of war against revolutionary France.[74] He likewise argued for a collective right to punish any nation that "by its manners and by the maxims of its government" encourages mistreatment of foreigners, such as "the nation of the Usbecks," or fosters piracy, such as the Barbary States.[75] As commentators have noted, the violence Vattel permits against such nations is extreme: "All nations have a right to join in a confederacy for the purpose of punishing and even exterminating those savage nations."[76] In contrast, Vattel's account largely obscures the violence of European imperial expansion, which would receive increasing attention from critics in France and Britain in the coming decades, among them the Abbé Raynal and Diderot in the best-selling *Histoire des deux Indes* (1770), Smith in the *Wealth of Nations* (1776), and Edmund Burke in parliamentary speeches beginning in the 1780s. In these senses—his proscription of the sort of "savage" violence associated especially with Islam, and his effacing of the violence of European expansion—Vattel serves as a blueprint figure for later treatments that shift from religion to violence as the ground of otherness. At the same time, for those who were concerned about the European infliction of violence on others, Vattel could be a useful resource precisely because of the universal terms in which he couches his argument, as we will see in the next chapter with Edmund Burke's use of Vattel during the Hastings impeachment trial.

Vattel's account of the state as a juridically independent moral person can be seen as a drawing together of two strands in early modern legal thought: state sovereignty and the moral personhood of the political community. That his conception of sovereign equality and independence was an aspiration rather than a plausible description of his world, even within Europe, is clear from the complex legal status of his native Neuchâtel, which epitomized the dependence of many states on outside powers and the heterogeneity of states in post-Westphalian Europe, though Vattel himself argued that Neuchâtel was a perfectly free and independent sovereign state.[77] As Daragh Grant has argued, the emergence in Europe in the latter half of the sixteenth century of an understanding of the sovereign state as the subject of the law of nations profoundly affected European perceptions of the legal nature and legal status of non-European polities. Whereas Spanish and English adventurers in their early encounters with indigenous American peoples often described them as "civil" and orderly, the rise and entrenchment of a conception of sovereignty narrowed the range of acceptable political forms to independent states with exclusive jurisdiction over their territories.[78]

Nonetheless, although contemporary commentators often write as though the "society" of states governed by the law of nations was, for Vattel, coterminous with Europe, it seems closer to his view to describe Europe as a political system that was a subset of the larger society of states.[79] What distinguished Europe from other parts of the world was not the law of nations, nor even, primarily, a separate and more detailed body of legal conventions, though he noted that various regions of intense interstate interaction would have their own particular legal norms, but rather a set of political and diplomatic practices: above all, the "scheme" of the balance of power.

> Europe forms a political system, an integral body, closely connected by the relations and different interests of the nations inhabiting this part of the world. It is not, as formerly, a confused heap of detached pieces, each of which thought herself very little concerned in the fate of the others, and seldom regarded things which did not immediately concern her. The continual attention of sovereigns to every occurrence, the constant residence of ministers, and the perpetual negotiations, make of modern Europe a kind of republic, of which the members—each independent, but all linked together by the ties of common interest—unite for the maintenance of order and liberty. Hence arose that famous scheme of the political balance, or the equilibrium of power; by which is understood such a disposition of things, as that no one potentate be able absolutely to predominate, and prescribe laws to the others.[80]

Vattel's conception of state sovereignty is not confined to Europe; indeed, his first illustration of the right of sovereign rulers not to be judged or interfered with by outsiders is the example, noted earlier, of the Inca ruler Atahualpa, whose rights under the law of nations were violated by the Spanish when they killed him in 1533. In a discussion of the formalities required by the law of nations for starting a war, he added that the "unfortunate Montezuma" would have been justified in using violence to free his people from the Spanish after "Ferdinand Cortes attacked the empire of Mexico without any shadow of reason, without even a plausible pretext."[81] Vattel's picture of states as free, equal, and independent moral persons would, however, go on to serve additional ideological functions in later international thought, especially in supporting the idea that states must meet certain normative standards to qualify as legitimate members of the family of nations. Although Vattel would seem to rule out such a course with his insistence that states are not in a position to judge one another's internal constitutions or governance, his idea of the self-perfecting community would, as I argue in Chapter 5, become a criterion by which later legal writers purported to judge states or societies, so that insofar as peoples were held not to fit the description of a nation, they were deemed illegitimate and unworthy of the respect or the rights due to legitimate states.

Conclusion

Vattel assumed a legal universality that was nonetheless largely situated in the specificities of European norms and practice. His account of universal principles seems to generate invidious distinctions, and while he specified grounds of supposed tendencies toward violence rather than religion or civilization, his examples tend to track European discourse about Muslim states as particularly violent. Vattel shows little of the preoccupation with the scope of the law of nations that was to become so pressing a question for the authors of nineteenth-century treatises of international law, and his casuistical method makes his argument about the scope of the law of nations, as on other topics, remarkably flexible. As we will see in Chapter 4, contemporaries of Vattel did indeed raise very explicitly the question of the implications of the universality of the law of nations for Europe's relations with Asian and especially Muslim states. As such questions migrated from texts by diplomats in states such as the Ottoman Empire reporting back to European publics, into broader political and philosophical debates, and then to more narrowly legal debates, Vattel's extraordinarily influential book proved a powerful resource for both those arguing for an international community restricted to Europe and those who sought to appeal to a universal law of nations to chastise and rein in European agents they believed were abusing their growing military advantage in the course of their commercial and imperial expansion in both hemispheres.

FOUR

Critical Legal Universalism
in the Eighteenth Century

A s WE SAW IN Chapter 1, the mid-twentieth-century historian of
international law Charles Henry Alexandrowicz argued that
eighteenth-century understandings of the law of nations, as they appear in
both treaty practice and theoretical accounts, assumed the law of nations
to be universal, and in particular to bind European states in their interactions with Asian commercial ones. Chapters 2 and 3 have attempted to
show that eighteenth-century conceptions of the law of nations were not
as inclusive of Asian powers as Alexandrowicz claimed. The evolution of
the category of oriental despotism over the course of the eighteenth century
in diplomatic and political writing made for persistent questioning about
the capacity of Asian commercial states to participate fully in the international legal community. The formal universalism of Vattel's account,
while significant in its inclusion of non-European states in both hemispheres as presumptive participants in the law of nations, was undercut by
several features of his account: a heavy reliance on European practice as the
source of a detailed account of legal norms, a tendency to reinscribe the
exclusion of Muslim states on the grounds of their supposedly habitual
violence, and an account of the state as a moral community that effaced the
imperial quality of the major European powers.

But the contrast Alexandrowicz drew between an earlier legal universalism and later "European egocentrism" gets at something both historically and normatively important.[1] The notion that the law of nations was
not exclusively European but was based on reciprocal, binding legal arrangements among a host of diverse polities had a presence in eighteenth-
century political debate and could serve as a powerful basis for criticism of

European imperial conduct and the cultural presumptions that underlay it. This critical posture arguably was not the dominant view, but its exponents could, and did, draw on both diplomatic practice and the most influential legal thought of the day to make their case; and their arguments had a resonance in broader public debates that they would not have in the following century. We encountered in Chapter 2 an instance of such a line of thought in Anquetil-Duperron, who presented his account of the legal structures of the Ottoman, Persian, and Mughal Empires in part to show that Europeans ought to respect such states as counterparts under the law of nations.

In this chapter I explore two other figures who maintained that the law of nations obligated Europeans in their dealings with states that stood outside the emerging European legal community: Edmund Burke, particularly in his 1794 closing arguments in the impeachment trial of Warren Hastings; and the influential admiralty court judge William Scott, later Lord Stowell (1745–1836), who developed the position in a series of opinions from the 1790s through the 1810s around maritime controversies involving Europeans and subjects of the Ottoman Empire and the Barbary States. Elsewhere I have written at greater length on Burke's arguments over the course of the Hastings impeachment.[2] Here I propose that the impeachment trial of Warren Hastings marked a fertile moment of what might be called the politics of legal pluralism.[3] I focus particularly on Burke's use of the idiom of the law of nations and his claim that the British were bound by the law of nations in their dealings with powers in India, above all in his 1794 closing speech, which developed these themes to a greater extent than Burke had done in any earlier trial material. The closing speech is the culmination of Burke's efforts in the trial to elaborate an account of the interlocking legal orders, including the law of nations, that should be considered to bind British agents in the fraught interactions unleashed by global commerce and global imperial expansion. Both Burke and Scott drew attention to a history of European treaty relations with various extra-European powers, treaties that they thought should be understood to be among the sources of the law of nations. Although not without its own dangers and limitations, discussed below, this strand of legal inclusion could be a powerful tool with which to criticize the conduct of European empires.

Where Burke's pronouncements on the law of nations were political as much as juridical, intended to influence government and East India Company policy and the public perception of British conduct in India as much as to inform the Lords' decision in the impeachment trial, Scott's were more particularly juridical, intended to justify his decisions, particularly regarding prize cases, during the intense maritime conflicts of the Napoleonic Wars. Their respective influences in the nineteenth century reflected this difference, with Scott having an influence on later international jurists that Burke did not. Conversely, there is a polemical edge to Burke's, like Anquetil's, appeals to the law of nations that makes more explicit than Scott did the role that law of nations discourse could play in a broader cultural critique.

Burke and Anquetil argued that imperial depredations had been made possible by the European powers' contempt for the legal standing of Asian states, and they used similar strategies for making the case that the law of nations was as strictly binding on Europeans beyond as within Europe. Unlike the later civilizing international lawyers discussed in Chapters 5 and 6, they tended to direct their critiques inward rather than outward: they were interested mainly in criticizing European abuses rather than the inadequacies of non-Europeans or non-Christians. They turned to the language of the law of nations primarily to chasten European power rather than to legitimate it. They shared an attention to the limits of European knowledge and European authority, a sense of humility and respect in the face of complex civilizations of which Europeans had only the most superficial knowledge, and, especially in Anquetil's case, a belief that Europeans had much to learn from these societies, which, he held, they were in the habit of seeing merely as potential markets or as curiosities rather than as true interlocutors about politics and morals. This posture of autocritique in the face of increasing European power and the triumphalism that accompanied it was a characteristic element of the political discourse of this era, as in the writings of Denis Diderot, Johann Gottfried Herder, and Samuel Johnson, among many others, though it more rarely took the form of legal argument, as we find in the figures under discussion here.[4] Anquetil argued that one of the major causes of the arrest of human knowledge—along with brute ignorance and religious dogmatism—was Europe's "presumptuous science": scholars were sure that their acquaintance with Greek and Latin meant they knew everything worth knowing, even though, having been "raised in the knowledge of four to five hundred leagues of country, the rest of the Globe is foreign to us." Merchants at least had the curiosity that is driven by desire for profit, but they were indifferent to the human beings and the moral worlds they encountered, rather than seeking to learn from their laws, customs, and opinions.[5]

These authors focused on European relations with Asian and Muslim agricultural and commercial states, and it might be said that in insisting on a shared legal community with Asian commercial societies, Burke and others were simply moving the boundary of exclusion further along a spectrum of development, so that societies deemed "savage" were still outside it.[6] When Burke wrote about Native Americans, between the 1750s and 1770s, his characterizations of them as "fierce tribes of Savages and Cannibals" are often crude and disparaging.[7] Anquetil wrote a long manuscript defending indigenous Americans against their European denigrators, but this was a work of sympathetic ethnography rather than an argument for legal inclusion.[8] Moreover, their arguments were not necessarily anti-imperial: Anquetil wavered on the question of whether European empires were justified, and at some stages of his career he was certainly criticizing the British with the aim of defending French claims in India.[9] Burke, too, is read by some as seeking (successfully) to reform the British Empire so as to entrench its power more deeply, though he also intimated that British rule in India might be irredeemably unjust.[10]

Although he knew of Anquetil, Burke does not seem to have cited him in his writings and speeches on India, and Anquetil's writings had neither the prominence in their day, nor the longer-term influence or theoretical originality, of Burke's.[11] But the marked affinities in their legal and moral arguments make it clear that Burke was not unique in basing his account of a law of nations with broad scope on an argument that European and various other legal systems were mutually intelligible and shared basic principles of legal and political order. Both Burke and Anquetil insisted on the fundamental similarities between European legal regimes and other systems widely regarded as the antithesis of legal order. Both argued, against Montesquieu's account of oriental despotism, that these rulers recognized themselves as bound by law both internally, with respect to their own subjects, and in their external relations. Indeed, both argued, no society of any durability could be habitually, constitutionally lawless, as oriental despotisms were said to be. Both used such arguments to insist that these states were parties to the law of nations, and that Europeans dealing with them were bound by its key provisions, such as respect for the sovereignty and the internal constitution of other states, and an obligation to abide by treaties and contracts entered into with them.

Treaties and accords between European and Asian "nations" had, of course, long been mediated by chartered companies with shifting and ambivalent relations to their sponsoring states: the Portuguese Estado da India, the English Levant Company, the Dutch Vereenigde Oost-Indische Compagnie (United East India Company, or VOC), and the English East India Company (EIC).[12] The last, chartered by Elizabeth I in 1600, was, as Philip Stern has argued, a "body politic" and "political community" in some ways typical in early modern England's complexly "interlocking matrix" of commonwealths, corporations, and associations, when the prerogatives of sovereignty had not yet been deemed the exclusive province of the state.[13] Its officials quickly concerned themselves not simply with commercial imperatives but with the responsibilities and prerogatives of sovereignty: governance of territories and populations, war, and diplomacy. But tensions among its commercial interests, its responsibilities as an Indian sovereign, and its status as a representative of the English and then British state and nation, perceived by the Company's critics and its own agents from the start, came to seem intolerable to many observers, especially after the Company's acquisition of vastly greater powers and territory by the end of the Seven Years' War.[14]

Burke's Global Web of Law

Goaded by an army of pamphleteers, including disgruntled former Company employees and independent merchants, Parliament attempted to exert greater control over the Company's activities, from its "first major inquiry into the [Company's] affairs" in 1667, through Lord North's Regulating Act of 1773 establishing the position of governor-general, Charles James Fox's failed East India Bill of 1783, and a series of select committees convened to investigate allegations of corruption, despotism, and abuse of power by the Company.[15] These efforts culminated in 1786 with a vote in the House of Commons to impeach Warren Hastings, the former governor-general of Bengal, before a committee of the House of Lords, for "unwarrantable criminal practices" that threatened the well-being of the natives of India, the fortunes of the East India Company, and the honor of the British nation and the Crown.[16] Burke, the chief manager of the prosecution on behalf of the House of Commons, was hailed as a humanitarian during the early stages of one of the greatest political dramas of eighteenth-century Britain, as the public grew increasingly anxious over the Company's practices of widespread bribery and corruption, aggressive war making, and mistreatment of Indian rulers. By the time Hastings was finally acquitted in 1795, he was regarded as the victim of Burke's vindictive and monomaniacal crusade. Burke's spectacular oratory, by turns powerful, theatrical, and overwrought, was the object of both admiration and ridicule from the large public who followed it in person and in the daily press. Much has been written since about the many rhetorical registers and lines of attack that Burke took up over the course of the trial: his Whig assault on the power and patronage of the Crown; his sometimes sentimental defense of traditional hierarchies in India and England against the novel wealth and power of Company agents; his anxiety over the seemingly incomprehensible alienness of Indian society to the British public; his chivalric defense of vulnerable Indian women against the "errant masculinity" of the Company; and his lurid detailing of Company misdeeds.[17] Scholars have long read the trial for evidence of Burke's motives and psychology; more recent work has recovered a compelling moral and political theory from his India speeches.[18]

However ultimately self-defeating his presentation of the case against Hastings and the Company, Burke's aim in the trial, it has been rightly emphasized, was as much moral suasion as legal conviction.[19] And yet a central element of Burke's project of persuasion was his effort to prompt a reconception of law itself, specifically the role of law in global commercial and political encounters.[20] Burke himself understood the trial as a peculiar and potent form of global legal encounter: it mobilized British law, through the rarely used mechanism of impeachment, to check the abuse of British power abroad, and it might help to transform an overly insular British law by way of encounter with other legal orders. This required soliciting from his British audience both a new respect for unfamiliar legal and normative systems and an unaccustomed sense of doubt about the adequacy of their own. As was typical of Burke, this was a project of both transformation and conservation, in the sense that he argued both that British legal traditions were parochial and inadequate to a global politics, and that they contained the seeds of their own reform.

By the end of the trial, during his nine-day closing speech in 1794, Burke had come to characterize his dispute with Hastings as at bottom a controversy about law.[21] Given at a time of despair for Burke, when it was clear that the legal case against Hastings was all but lost, this speech (400 pages in the modern edition) is one of his least successful performances: rambling, repetitive, exaggerated, convoluted, and often vindictive. At the same time, it was in this speech that he most fully and powerfully elaborated his vision of legality in the imperial and inter-imperial space that India had become. Although part of Burke's purpose may have been to reform imperial structures, as Nicholas Dirks and Robert Travers have argued, his conceptualization of British-Indian relations cannot be reduced to that aim.[22] Rather, in offering an account of the ways in which British actions in the world beyond Europe were constrained by a complex web of laws—including positive law of both British and Indian origins as well as natural law and the law of nations—Burke was articulating a distinctive vision of the international legal order.

Burke was one of the first to rely on Vattel's *Droit des gens* as an authority in parliamentary debates.[23] But he attended more closely than Vattel did to its potential implications for engagements beyond Europe. Burke had invoked the law of nations, as based in the law of nature, on several occasions during the American war. He argued in 1777 that the Americans should be understood, and that British policy had recognized them, as parties to "the unhappiness of civil dissension" rather than traitors, and therefore they were "in possession of the law of nations." In his 1781 speeches on the British seizure of the neutral Dutch Caribbean island of St. Eustatius, he appealed to the law of nations to condemn Britain's expropriation of merchants, especially Jewish merchants whose statelessness made them particularly vulnerable to abuse.[24] At both moments he invoked the law of nations in a call for restraint on the part of British imperial power in relation to weaker counterparts of uncertain legal standing. His reflections on the scope of application of the law of nations point us toward a notion of global legal orders different from the view that was emerging among thinkers as different as Vattel and Bentham, which would triumph in the nineteenth century—the view that international law applied to states understood as equal and independent sovereign entities.[25] As we have seen, Vattel's work was the most influential articulation in Burke's time of the idea that states are equal, free, and independent, and the exclusive subjects of the law of nations, though as I note below, Burke found useful in the Indian context Vattel's principle that a weaker state in an unequal alliance still retains its status under the law of nations.[26] In more generally stressing the uniformity of the international legal space and of the states that filled it, however, Vattel's theory may have facilitated the emergence of the view that only certain sorts of states can qualify for that status: states that fit a particular institutional and cultural description that for most nineteenth-century thinkers turned out to exist only in Europe. Such claims are not necessarily implied by Vattel's theory—indeed, they may contradict its universalistic spirit—but his insistence on legal uniformity may have made difficult the more flexible and political legal pluralism that Burke developed during the Hastings trial.[27] Bentham's late notes toward a code of international law likewise began with the principles of equal and independent states, as I discuss in Chapter 5.

Burke, in contrast, emphasized the multiplicity of legal orders within and among states; the term "interpolity law," which can encompass a more diverse set of actors in relations beyond formal independence and equality, may better capture the complexity of the legal landscape Burke observed.[28] With respect to Europe, he complicated Vattel's international landscape of independent sovereigns in his late *Letters on a Regicide Peace* of 1796– 1797 in response to what he saw as the unprecedented challenge of revolutionary France, an expansionary "sect" rather than a conventional state. Those who viewed the war with France through the lens of simple interstate law were, he urged, mistaken. After finding Vattel's more restricted theory of intervention unsuited to his purposes, Burke defended a radically new standard for intervention in France based on Roman private law remedies, arguing that the principles that governed interactions among European states were more particular than the law of nations, grounded as they were in a common religion, common origins in the Roman Empire, and a shared feudal past. He styled a European commonwealth or community as "virtually one great state having the same basis of general law." This "grand vicinage of Europe" was governed, he argued, by a sort of "Law of Neighbourhood" or "law of civil vicinity."[29] He similarly accepted the coexistence and interpenetration of multiple legal systems in India, without insisting, as Hastings and others did, that what was needed was an authoritative hierarchy or code of jurisdictions, with Europeans as the ultimate arbiters.

In what follows I highlight Burke's two key arguments in his closing speech about the legal structures that bound Hastings and the Company in India. First, like Anquetil, Burke insisted in opposition to the theory of oriental despotism that Indian society was structured by dense webs of laws that the Europeans were obliged to recognize and respect. The British duty to obey the law of nations in relation to Indian powers was partly due to this fact, namely, that these were societies in which sovereigns were assumed to have duties to respect the law internally (with respect to subjects' rights and property) as well as externally, and so could be expected to abide by treaty obligations and other customary rules of engagement among foreign powers. Second, Burke went to particular lengths to insist on the standing under the law of nations of Indian "foreign" powers, a point he argued most thoroughly with respect to Chait Singh, the raja of Benares, whom Hastings had treated as a subject of the British and had punished as a rebel against British power. In his opening speech of 1786 Burke had asserted that "in Asia as well as in Europe the same Law of Nations prevails, the same principles are continually resorted to"; he now provided a more elaborated account of how and why the law of nations was binding on the British in India.[30]

Hastings's Hierarchical Legal Pluralism

Warren Hastings's defense was inconsistent with respect to questions of the legal structure and legal standing of the Indian polities. Far from rejecting outright the notion that the law of nations applied in India, Hastings's lawyers invoked the law of nations in his defense, especially regarding principles of treaty making, drawing comparisons with intra-European conflicts that suggested that the cases were equivalent.[31] At the same time, the defense counsel also argued that Indian society was internally lawless, on the Montesquieuian model of oriental despotism, and that Indian states routinely violated basic principles of treaty making, such as that a treaty was binding on successor regimes. As Hastings testified, "I know not how we can deny the Existence of many *despotic principles* in the Mogul system of government; but wherever *those* exist the *powers* of the Prince will be every thing, and the *rights* of the Subject nothing."[32] Hastings later disowned the most notorious passages about Asian despotism in his testimony before the Commons as having been written not by himself but by his supporter Nathaniel Brassey Halhed, translator of the 1776 *Code of Gentoo Laws*. (Burke noted that it was alarming that the man responsible for the *Code,* which he admired, had penned these "horrible doctrines" about lawlessness in India.) But Hastings delivered the words, and as Burke pointed out, his defense lawyers continued to repeat similar arguments. This aspect of Burke's case, then, although it responded to Hastings's testimony, was arguably something of a caricature of Hastings's own views. Burke's insistence on arguments that Hastings himself had not actually drafted, and that stood in marked contrast to Hastings's own statements while governor-general about the sophistication of Indian laws, may have cast their disagreements in something of a false light.[33]

In combating the defense's claim that Indians had "no laws [and] no rights," Burke appealed to a variety of legal and normative orders in Indian society, from property and inheritance regimes to "hereditary dignities" and systems of "honour and distinction." Whereas Hastings and his lawyers held that disorder was endemic in India, for Burke, order was apparent in these overlapping normative systems, and it was the British who represented the irruption of disorder. Burke stressed the antiquity of Indian jurisprudence, as in his claim in the closing of the Hastings impeachment trial that "We have shown you that *those* people [in India] lived under the Law, which was formed even whilst we, I may say, were in the Forest, before we knew what Jurisprudence was," and that the British were "bound to know and to act by these Laws." He suggested that India had a long history of functioning legal pluralism, disrupted by the British and their contempt for and ignorance of local structures of obligation.[34]

There were undoubtedly greater affinities between Burke and Hastings than Burke's rhetoric of excoriation—or, it should be added, Hastings's own defense—allowed. The adversarial context of the trial heightened the opposition between Burke and Hastings and effaced the points of similarity, as the defense was driven to exaggerate Indians' unreliability and Burke to overstate the stability of the pre-British order in North India. As an admirer of Indian civilization, and a great patron of scholarship about it, Hastings wrote sensitively and powerfully about the virtues of Indian literature and about the obstacles to its proper appreciation in Europe.[35] The notorious passages about oriental despotism in his opening speech belied his more complex recognition as governor of the desirability of accommodating Indian law. In a 1774 letter to Lord Chief Justice, Lord Mansfield, Hastings, sounding very much like Burke during the impeachment, had criticized the view that Indians were "governed by no other principle of justice than arbitrary wills, or uninstructed judgements," and had called Muslim law "as comprehensive, and as well defined, as that of most states in Europe."[36] Hastings saw himself as having undertaken to govern Indians as far as possible by their own laws, whether Muslim or Hindu.[37] Like the Orientalist Sir William Jones, he fought factions in Parliament that he believed intended to supplant Indian law with English law. The legal reforms that Hastings instituted in 1772, in which he established civil and criminal courts in Bengal staffed in large part by Indians and reliant upon Hindu and Muslim precedent as Hastings understood it, were intended precisely to entrench Indian legal systems in the territory under British authority.[38] And in 1781 he established a madrassa in Calcutta to cultivate among Indian Muslims "erudition in the Persian and Arabic Languages, and in the complicated system of laws founded on the tenets of their religion."[39] Burke himself, in the course of criticizing Hastings for opportunistically appealing to Muslim law when it suited his purposes, noted that "the thing Mr. Hastings values himself upon" was "to keep the Law of England and the Law of Mahomet upon a just par."[40]

Notwithstanding Burke's more extreme portraits of him, then, Hastings attempted to further a form of legal pluralism in India, one that recognized the complexity of Indian legal systems and regarded them as valid sources of legal principle. Still, Hastings's approach to British-Indian legal relations, though more nuanced than it appeared in Burke's rendition and even Hastings's own defense, represented a vision at odds with the view that Burke came to hold by time of his 1794 closing speech in the impeachment trial. Unlike Hastings, who invoked multiple legal systems as means of authorizing and channeling British power, Burke appealed to those systems as constraints on that power. He criticized the Company's use of legal structures and arguments to deny Indians recourse against abuses of power, and Company officials' efforts to arrange and appeal to plural legal orders in order to enhance their own power.[41] He warned of the danger of Hastings's opportunistic version of legal pluralism when he urged that the judges not judge Hastings "by Laws and institutions which you do not know, against those Laws and institutions which you do know, and under whose power and authority Mr Hastings went out to India."[42] Whereas Hastings sought to use law, including Indian legal systems, in the service of the Company's projects of administration and revenue extraction, Burke emphasized the function of laws as constraints on the powerful, and as resources available to the vulnerable. And for all his vilification of Hastings as an individual, Burke was equally troubled by structural aspects of British involvement in India: above all, the inaccessibility to Indians of the main political processes by which the Company's power was checked.[43] Parliament's virtual representation of Indians, and its use of both legislation and impeachment, were one channel for the redress of abuses, though Burke had little faith in its adequacy, given his belief that the British people and their legislators had little knowledge of or interest in Indians.

Three differences between Hastings's formulation of a plural legal order in India and Burke's approach in his closing speech are worth highlighting:

differences in the characterizations they offered of multiple normative orders, in the reasons they gave for recognizing those different systems, and in the structure they thought a plural legal order should take. First, Hastings presented Indian legal systems as evidence of a cultural chasm between India and Britain.[44] For all his admiration of Indian civilization, and his fostering of research into Indian law, Hastings often pointed to Indian laws and legal practices as evidence of the country's backwardness and stagnation, and as betraying the unreliability of Indian legal experts. His 1772 Judicial Plan for Bengal justified its reforms in part on the basis of the "Litigiousness and Perseverance of the Natives of this Country," the "Chicane and Intrigue, which Passions amongst these People often work to the Undoing of their Neighbours."[45] His letter to Lord Mansfield insisted, in a common trope of the time, that Hindu laws had "continued unchanged from the remotest antiquity," an implicit contrast with Britain's more supplely evolving law.[46]

Second, the reasons Hastings gave for taking Indian laws into account were pragmatic rather than principled: doing so would make it simpler— indeed was indispensable for making it even *possible*—for the British to administer a large territory and complex societies. The small number of British agents in India meant that the Company was reliant on local elites, who would only be willing to act according to familiar laws. A related argument was that Indians, who were peculiarly hampered by custom and religious strictures, were incapable of recognizing the force of alien laws. Hastings, again like Jones, believed that unfortunate but deep-seated cultural limitations on the part of Indians made the preservation of local law imperative.[47] Moreover, he believed that in order to make local law viable and usable in the empire, it had to be fixed, codified, and translated in authoritative editions, so that British officials could have direct access to authoritative law, rather than having to rely on native legal experts, whom he suspected as corrupt and liable to mislead the court whenever it was in their interest to do so.

Third, Hastings proposed a hierarchical form of recognition, in which British law and government was authoritative but could elect to make use of local laws when it was feasible or convenient.[48] He argued in his opening speech that British sovereignty over Indian provinces would become a burden instead of a benefit, unless "the whole of our Territory in that Quarter shall be rounded and made a uniform compact Body by one grand and systematic Arrangement."[49] He lamented "the Informality, Invalidity, and Instability of all Engagements in so divided and unsettled a State of Society; and . . . the unavoidable Anarchy and Confusion of different Laws,

Religions, and Prejudices, moral, civil, and political, all jumbled together in one unnatural and discordant Mass."[50] Hastings is often characterized as a late exemplar of the colonial order of corrupt Company officials superseded by an improving colonial state that is said to owe much to Burke's vision of a benevolent empire. These officials were replaced, it is often said, by a more orderly, and self-consciously improving, type of colonial official that conformed better to Burke's own vision of empire. But it was Hastings's hierarchical version of legal pluralism, centered on the colonial state, which ultimately triumphed.[51]

Burke's Political Legal Pluralism

Over the course of the trial, Burke came to insist that the British should respect Indian laws not because Indians themselves were incapable of moving beyond them, as Hastings argued, but because those laws independently obligated the British. Most directly this was so for contractual reasons, as an implicit element of the agreements that, Burke claimed, underlay the Company's power in India, the 1765 granting of the diwani of Bengal to the Company by the Mughal Empire being the most consequential such agreement. But while he sometimes made it clear that he meant that these local laws imposed obligations on the British *as governors,* he also regarded them as constraints on Hastings's more general "relations with the people of that Country," which is to say, those outside British territory as well as those the British considered their subjects. The British were not operating in a legal vacuum beyond their own territory in India. One reason, in Burke's view, that these legal systems all had normative standing is that they had been worked upon and reformed over a long period of time: they should be presumed to be distinctive but valid approximations of what he called the eternal law.[52]

Like Anquetil, Burke argued that Indian society was as thoroughly structured by laws as any European society: that they "have laws; that they have rights; that they have immunities; that they have property moveable and immoveable. . . . In short, that every word that Montesquieu has taken from idle and inconsiderate Travellers is absolutely false."[53] This was the first of his key legal claims.

> We do assert that Mr. Hastings went into India under a Law and under a discretion. We contend that when he acted according to discretion that

he was bound to act according to the solid established rules of political morality, humanity and equity; that when he acted under a Law, as I contend that he did act under a Law, that with regard to all foreign powers he was obliged to act under the law of Nature and under the Law of Nations; that when he acted under the Law with regard to his relation to this Country, he was obliged to act according to the Laws, statutes, and Acts of Parliament of Great Britain. . . . next that with regard to his relation to the people of that Country, that he was obliged to act according to the laws, rights, usages, institutions and good customs, according to the largest and most liberal construction of them.[54]

While the articles of impeachment and Burke's earlier speeches had stressed the Company's "fraud and duplicity" and its repeated "violation of faith" in relation to Indian allies and dependents, the closing speech presents a more abstract argument for the basic communicability between Eastern and Western law, as well as a more precise case for the standing of "foreign powers" in India under the law of nations.

Burke's second key legal theme was that Hastings had violated or denied the sovereignty of various Indian powers in the multilayered political structure of the subcontinent. In the articles of impeachment and in his opening speech, Burke had addressed the violation of treaties as a facet of Hastings's general "Breach of Faith" with various Indian agents. He contrasted Hastings's reduction of native states to British subjects to the practice of the early Muslim conquerors of India, who, though he characterized them as cruel religious fanatics, "left the ancient people in possession of their states; and left the ancient Sovereigns of the Country possessed of an inferior Sovereignty; and where the nature of the Country would permit it, they suffered them to continue in a separate state of Sovereignty from them."[55] In the closing speech Burke used the occasion of such charges to maintain that the law of nations bound the British "with regard to all foreign powers," in India as well as in Europe.[56] And he argued that the British were obligated to extend the benefit of the doubt to powers that "appear to be sovereign" or that had recently been sovereign. He now framed the treaty violations not simply as a problem of bad faith or opportunism, but as the product of a dangerous legal theory. He rebuked Hastings for having questioned, in testimony before the Commons, "the validity of any Treaty that can be made at present with India."[57] In evidence before the Lords on 25 February 1788, Hastings had argued that "all the governing Powers of Hindostan are extremely averse to any Treaties or Agreements which are declared to be binding on Posterity; and I have had frequent Difficulties in many Negociations with the native Princes on this Head; they have always pleaded 'that it was against the Custom of their Country.'"[58] Anquetil, as we saw in Chapter 2, had rejected a similar charge against the Ottoman Empire, which was commonly cited as a reason to disavow European treaty obligations to the Porte.

Hastings, Burke argued in response, "is bound in all transactions with foreign Powers to act according to the known, recognized rules of the Law of Nations, with regard to all powers that are Sovereign, or appear to be Sovereign, whether dependent or independent."[59] Burke developed the implications of this claim most interestingly with respect to Chait Singh, the raja of Benares, the subject of the first article of impeachment, whom Hastings had ordered arrested after he refused to pay an additional tribute or rent to support troops that the Company imposed on his territory, ostensibly for the defense of the Company and its allies. At issue in the impeachment was the question of Chait Singh's political status: was he a "mere zamindar," as Hastings insisted or, as Burke maintained, "a person cloathed with every one of the attributes of Sovereignty, with a direct stipulation that the Company should not interfere in his internal Government"?[60] Where Hastings insisted on the "Company's sovereignty over Benares" and cast Chait Singh as a rebel whose conduct warranted punishment from the Company, Burke described him as a ruler who maintained his sovereign status under the law of nations despite being the weaker party in an unequal treaty relationship.[61]

Whereas the Hastings defense accepted in principle the relevance of the law of nations to British dealings in India, they worked to undercut its applicability, whether by denying legal standing to the Indian agents in question or by accusing them of habitually violating treaty protocol. Burke charged that the British were obliged not merely to follow the law of nations in their dealings with Indian rulers, but also to attempt to construe those rulers' actions as if they might be in accordance with shared legal principles, and to look for evidence of shared principles in their practice and their legal documents.[62] For this purpose, he drew on Vattel as a means of interpreting and justifying the actions of Indian actors such as Chait Singh. It was sensible to do so, on Burke's account, because the law of nations was natural (and therefore universally valid) law that had been "recognized and digested into order by the labour of learned Men"; natural law invariably took concrete form by way of a particular intellectual tradition.[63]

But even if they were not familiar with the precise legal texts that had articulated these universal principles in Europe, Indian rulers could be expected to follow a similar logic; and Burke maintained that their own jurisprudential authorities had similarly articulated particular versions of natural law. He therefore invoked Vattel to defend Chait Singh against Hastings's imputation that the raja was "guilty of a great crime" in fomenting a resurrection against the Company. Burke read the raja's actions as reasonable in light of Vattel's theory of agreements between greater and subordinate powers. According to such authorities, Burke argued, Chait Singh in fact had done "that which his safety and his duty bound him to do," and Hastings had acted illegally in deeming Chait Singh's actions a rebellion and crushing them. Burke argued that Chait Singh had not been rebelling but had been freed from his treaty obligations as a result of failures by the British to live up to their own. He argued that the British were obliged to recognize "the rights of natural equity, of the Law of Nations which is the birthright of us all." Burke's strategy was to presume and to seek agreement at the level of principle, to assume that the British were bound by the law of nations, and to interpret Indian actions as if they might also be acting in accordance with its principles.

Burke envisioned English law itself as being transformed by these global encounters. We find this in his repeated calls for an expansive approach to evidence and judicial procedure in the impeachment trial.[64] It was, of course, in Burke's interest in the trial to argue for the widest possible latitude in collecting evidence. But in this instance as in many others, he capitalized on a line of argument that suited his immediate purposes to make a point of broader theoretical interest. He had argued in his opening impeachment speech that rules "formed upon municipal maxims" were inappropriate when what was at issue was justice for "various descriptions of men, differing in language, in manners and in rites, men separated by every means from you."[65] He developed this line of argument most fully in his *Report on the Lords Journal* of 1794, where he argued that law would stagnate if it were to hew narrowly to existing doctrine. Law evolved and progressed with developing social organization—by "keep[ing] Pace with the Demands of Justice, and the actual Concerns of the World," "our Jurisprudence [must conform] to the Growth of our Commerce and of our Empire."[66] Adherence to the strict letter of the law was appropriate to simpler societies, but the complexity introduced by empire and global commerce, he argued, made a more flexible sense of equity imperative.[67]

Admiralty Court Judge William Scott, Lord Stowell

A related strain of cosmopolitan legal thinking emerges in the opinions of
the admiralty court judge William Scott (1745–1836; after 1821, first Baron
Stowell).[68] Educated at Oxford and the Middle Temple, Scott chose the path
of civil rather than common law at a time when prize cases generated by the
American war were bringing renewed prominence to the civil law–based
admiralty courts after a long decline. Scott was an acquaintance of Burke's,
briefly a counsel for the Hastings prosecution, and a fellow member of
Samuel Johnson's circle and of the Club, the London dining club that
Johnson founded with Joshua Reynolds, whose members included many of
the era's leading political and literary figures. Along with his brother John
(later Lord Eldon), Prime Minister William Pitt's solicitor general, and
Robert Chambers, one of the first justices of the Supreme Court of Calcutta, Scott also founded the "distinctly Tory" University College Dining
Club.[69] In 1788 he was appointed king's advocate general, the state's chief
authority on maritime and international law. He served in Parliament from
1790 until his elevation to the Lords in 1821, and as judge of the High Court
of Admiralty from 1798 until 1828. Scott's highly respected admiralty opinions on the frequent maritime controversies of the Napoleonic Wars, the
first such judgments to be regularly collected and published, quickly became an authoritative source for maritime and international law in both
Britain and America. As a civil lawyer, he was widely and deeply read in
Roman law, canon law, and the continental law of nations tradition.[70] The
English civilian tradition was committed, as the common law was not, to
comparative law, foreign sources of law, and the development of law with
transnational and perhaps universal validity, in a tradition going back to
judges such as John Cowell and Richard Zouche.[71] It looked to the past as a
source not of legal authority, as did common law, but of conceptions and
practices against which to judge contemporary principles. Scott was a
member of the last great generation of English civilians in ecclesiastical and
admiralty law; although his judgments were much admired by nineteenth-
century international lawyers, it appears that they misunderstood his views
on the scope of the law of nations, as I argue below.

Scott's civil law orientation and his early training at Oxford in a natural-
law perspective on the law of nations continued to influence his thought,
and there are important affinities between his and Burke's views of the law
of nations, which both men saw as resting on universal principles acces-

sible to reason. Both called for the recognition of the sovereignty and legal standing of various extra-European states in Asia and North Africa, notwithstanding certain differences between European standard practice and the practices of other states. And both believed that frequent contact in war and diplomacy among European states had led to a more particular set of legal principles that only European states could be held to, and indeed that they could be held to even in interactions with extra-European states that could not be so held, a position I discuss below as "deferential asymmetry." Finally, Scott, like Burke, often invoked the law of nations as a constraint on abuses by British agents in the course of global conflict.

An early example of his sense of the duties imposed on Britain by the law of nations can be seen in correspondence between Scott, then advocate general, and Henry Dundas, then home secretary, on the subject of punitive levies imposed on the residents of St. Lucia after it was captured from France in 1794. This was a situation much like the 1781 British seizure of St. Eustatius, in response to which Burke had invoked the law of nations to denounce British abuses. Dundas, on behalf of the ministry, had requested Scott's opinion as to the appropriateness of the levies under the law of nations (though he had already written to General Sir Charles Grey to say that the levies seemed to him "perfectly proper" as a temporary measure). Scott responded that according to the "Modern Law of Nations," the British policy of confiscating the property of civilian residents of St. Lucia "appears to be utterly unjustifiable, and ought to be revoked"; he professed to be so shocked by the policy (in contrast to Dundas's complacency about it) that "I can hardly bring myself to believe, that such a step can have been taken."[72] It was with this sense of the authority of the law of nations to check the conduct of British officials that Scott took up the admiralty court judgeship.

Scott described his court as a tribunal of the law of nations and his role as an impartial adjudicator of that supranational and universal law. As he wrote in a 1799 opinion:

> What is it that the duty of my station calls for from me;—namely, to consider myself stationed here, not to deliver occasional and shifting opinions to serve present purposes of particular national interest but to administer with indifference that justice which the law of nations holds out, without distinction to independent states, some happening to be neutral and some to be belligerent. The seat of judicial authority is, indeed, locally *here,* in the belligerent country, according to the known

law and practice of nations: but the law itself has no locality.... If, therefore, I mistake the law in this matter, I mistake that which I consider, and which I mean should be considered, as the universal law upon the question.[73]

As at once an admiralty judge purporting to adjudicate impartially according to universal law, and also a British subject (and member of Parliament) hearing cases that arose in the course of his country's punishing, even existential, war against revolutionary and Napoleonic France, Scott was placed in a demanding position. His biographer maintains that he generally succeeded in issuing unbiased judgments, notwithstanding a significant departure from his stated policy of impartiality in a series of opinions in which he backed the British government's blockade policy despite its violation of what he had earlier declared to be the law of nations.[74]

More important for present purposes than whether Scott always succeeded in rising above British national interests in adjudicating cases was his conception of the supranational law as "universal," without locality, and based on principles of natural reason, though elaborated by way of state practice and therefore necessarily also particular, historically conditioned, and evolving. In a parliamentary speech Scott noted that the admiralty courts

> are not restricted within the narrow limits of municipal institution: the law of nature, and of nations, is the foundation on which they build; all the subjects of foreign states, on the general principles of justice and humanity, have a right to redress for injuries received upon the high seas, and look for protection to these establishments.... The character and honour of every country, in a great measure, depends on the regard which is paid to the just demands of individuals, placed in the most remote regions of the world.

In a typically counterrevolutionary trope equating French revolutionary and Barbary lawlessness (one we will encounter again), Scott called the capacity of the British admiralty court to protect the rights of foreign subjects under universal laws precisely what made British justice superior to the "the laws of Algerine piracy, or the institutions of revolutionized France," a rhetorical flourish that belied his more general refusal to treat the North African states as beyond the pale of law.[75]

It was in opposition to seeming innovations by the French revolutionary regime that Scott articulated his defense of "the ancient and universal practice of mankind" as filling in the content of the law of nations, beyond its fairly abstract underlying principles: he argued that the French could not justify an unprecedented practice with reference to principle alone (in this case, the condemnation of a prize ship by a French consul "pretending to be authorized" in a neutral port rather than by an official tribunal in the belligerent country).[76] "A greater part of the law of nations stands on no other foundation [than the 'usage and practice of nations']: it is introduced, indeed, by general principles; but it travels with those general principles only to a certain extent," and a state is required to "confine itself to those modes which the common practice of mankind has employed, and to relinquish those which the same practice has not brought within the ordinary exercise of war, however sanctioned by its principles and purposes."[77] Yet, despite the anti-French or counterrevolutionary tenor of some of his statements on the sources of the law of nations, Scott also argued more impartially against certain principles of British common law that the court was obliged to determine cases "upon equitable principles, and according to the rules of natural justice."[78]

While the cases discussed so far concerned disputes among Europeans, Scott heard many involving North Africans (generally, concerning the seizure of European property by North African ships, and vice versa).[79] In these cases he maintained that Europeans were obliged to recognize the sovereignty of the Barbary States, and he held that certain very fundamental legal principles could be considered to bind them as well as Europeans. He cited the jurist Cornelius van Bynkershoek's judgment, against Gentili, that Europeans owed the Barbary States legal recognition, rather than treating them as pirates, since they met all the criteria of legal sovereignty.

> Certain it is, that the *African* States were [considered pirates] many years ago, but they have long acquired the character of established governments, with whom with whom we have regular treaties, acknowledging and confirming to them the relations of legal states. . . . Although their notions of justice, to be observed between nations, differ from those which we entertain, we do not, on that account, venture to call in question their public acts. As to the mode of confiscation, which may have taken place on this vessel, whether by formal sentence or not, we must presume it was done regularly in their way, and according to the established custom of that part of the world.[80]

That is, neither the concern that those states departed in various respects from European legal norms nor their violation of treaties in pursuit of their own interest should, as some held, place them beyond the bounds of the legal protection, nor should their sovereignty be considered compromised. He noted that within Europe as well, states could not always find unanimous agreement on the principles of the law of nations.[81]

Scott, then, rejected the conclusion that because the Barbary States failed to follow European law of nations in its particulars they were lawless, or that Europeans had the right to force European standards on them. Rather, Europeans should regard the Barbary States' actions as regulated by their own law of nations and as therefore to be respected even if they deviated from European law. In some instances where European claimants might assume the conduct of both the Algerian ruler and his subjects to be irregular, Scott noted the analogies between their actions and those of European and American agents.[82] Yet the fact that North African law of nations practice did differ in some important particulars from the European generated distinctive considerations; in such cases his court might be able to offer only "*rusticum judicium,* or a coarse sort of equitable arbitration," rather than definitive adjudication according to a thick record of shared practice. Europeans should, in such cases, exercise "a more than ordinary caution, and regularity of proceeding." Barbary States, for instance, followed a practice considered inappropriate under European law of nations in demanding immediate compensation from any countrymen of those who had seized their property. If Europeans wanted to do business with such countries, he noted, they would have to accept the vulnerabilities that came with that business, and should themselves be particularly scrupulous in their observance of legal forms in order not to render their compatriots vulnerable to the summary justice particular to the "law of nations" observed by the Barbary States.[83]

At the same time, he argued for some deference toward others' laws and practices when it came to the finer points of the European law of nations. He called this law "a pretty artificial system, which is not familiar either to their knowledge or their observance."[84] Ruling for the Algerian claimants in a case involving the seizure of Algerian property by Britons, he wrote, "I do not . . . mean to apply to such claimants the exact rigour of the law of nations as understood and practiced among the civilized states of Europe; it would be to try them by a law not familiar to any law or practice of theirs," and "we must pay some attention to the rules of morality and law that prevail amongst such people." He excepted from this rule what he considered certain widely known and long-standing principles, such as the principle of respecting blockades: "I must hold that they are bound to the observance of this most ancient principle, on which nations have acted in every state of civilized society, since the first records of mankind."[85]

Scott, then, saw the law of nations as a complex practice that combined broad principles that he believed were universally binding, with historically European rules that could not be said to obligate non-Europeans. But he also held those European laws to be binding on Europeans in their dealings with at least some extra-European states, even when those same laws did not bind the other party. We thus find in Scott, as in Burke, what we might see as a kind of deferential asymmetry in the application of the laws. Scott's version of this argument is as follows:

> In the first place it is to be recollected, that this is a Court of the Law of Nations, though sitting here under the authority of the King of Great Britain. It belongs to other nations as well as to our own; and what foreigners have a right to demand from it, is the administration of the law of nations, simply, and exclusively of the introduction of principles borrowed from our own municipal jurisprudence, to which, it is well known, they have at all times expressed no inconsiderable repugnance. In the case of a British subject it is different. To him it is a British tribunal, as well as a Court of the Law of Nations; and if he has been trampling on the known laws of his country, it is no injustice to say, that a person coming into any of the Courts of his own country, to which he is naturally amenable, on such a transaction, can receive no protection from them.[86]

Similarly, even as Scott acknowledged that encounters with those outside the historical bounds of the European law of nations might be freighted with additional risk for Europeans—they would be bound by their own legal rules even when dealing with those they could not legitimately oblige by the same rules—he resisted the temptation, which would come to dominate later nineteenth-century accounts, to insist that European law should become authoritative for all.

Finally, Scott's judgments in the wake of the Haitian Revolution and Haiti's declaration of independence in 1804 show him pushing as far as he thought British law would allow toward recognition of Haiti as an independent government. In 1808 he took up the question of the "national character" of the parts of the island of St. Domingue wrested from French control.[87] Citing a pair of cases decided in 1805 (the *Dart* and the *Happy Couple*), in which "it was held that notwithstanding the unsettled state of St. Domingo, it was still in point of law under the dominion of France, and must be considered as an enemy's colony," he argued that the situation had since changed.[88] Despite the fact that the judges in the 1805 cases had decided that they could not recognize an independent Haiti because the British government had not officially declared its recognition, and although the subsequent government's Orders in Council on which Scott based his judgment also declined to recognize Haiti as a sovereign nation, Scott concluded that there were grounds for seeing recent developments as tending to establish Haiti's independence. The question of Haiti's "national character" had been raised, he argued, by the

> peculiar circumstances of that island, which are well known . . . several parts of it had been in the actual possession of insurgent negroes, who had detached them, as far as actual occupancy could do, from the mother country of France and its authority, and maintained within those parts at least, an independent government of their own. And although this new power had not been directly and formally recognized by any express treaty, the British Government had shewn a favourable disposition towards it on the ground of its common opposition to France, and seemed to tolerate an intercourse that carried with it a pacific and even friendly complexion.

Julia Gaffield has shown that the actions of merchants, local colonial governors, metropolitan governments, and courts in the key European imperial states produced more extensive, though still ambiguous and unreliable, European support for Haitian independence than the states' refusal to grant formal diplomatic recognition would suggest.[89] Scott's decision in the *Manilla,* by reading the noncommittal Orders in Council as a showing a "favourable disposition" and "friendly complexion," took an expansive reading of the legal implications of the Orders for Haiti's international standing. He added that however anomalous the new government, the regularity of the new power's official acts and declarations indicated that its possession of its territory was more than simply military.[90] Gaffield shows the influence of Scott's decisions on later civil and admiralty court cases, which cited him in support of the view that the Haitian ports were neutral ports, not part of belligerent France. The legal space he had created for recognition was not decisive, however, given the advantages to Britain—in commercial profit and political control—of maintaining an ambiguous policy of economic engagement and diplomatic nonrecognition; Britain would withhold formal recognition until 1839.

Conclusion

An inclusive understanding of the law of nations as "universal," or at least as applying to many societies beyond Christian Europe, was double-edged for those included, since it also morally freed Europeans for a newly aggressive imperial interventionism through treaties of alliance and military aid that once would have been forbidden as treaties with infidels. A further danger of the broad legal inclusion through equivalence, of the kind exhibited by Burke, is that it may too readily assimilate the unfamiliar into one's own framework, and so not recognize or give due respect to genuine differences or alternatives. Burke might be said to have done this when he claimed that he could try Hastings by any law, from the Institutes of Tamerlane to the Qur'an, and get the same result as under English law.[91] But whatever the limitations of their approach, Burke and Anquetil were persistently self-critical, aware of the ever-present dangers of parochialism, complacency, and what Anquetil called Europe's "presumptuous science." They were alert to the ways in which the powerful may use the law as yet another tool at their disposal, and they saw the effort to secure common legal frameworks as a means of restraining abuses. Their expansive conception of the law of nations provided the framework for a powerful line of critique of imperial injustices during this formative period for both European empires and international law. According to this critique, religious and cultural difference was no justification for differential standards of legal and political obligation. Europeans had a duty to treat their engagements outside Europe—with powers and societies that might not share European legal principles and customs in all their particulars—as just as binding, just as much a part of a global legal framework, as those within Europe.

Despite the considerable stature and influence of Burke and Scott during the nineteenth century (the same cannot be said for Anquetil), the views adumbrated here left remarkably little trace in later European legal thought.[92] An increasingly hegemonic understanding of the international realm as made up of free, equal, and independent states eclipsed the earlier, more complex legal landscape of corporate polities and dependent and divided sovereignty, superannuating Burke's complexly political legal pluralism.[93] Europe's increasing self-confidence in light of the Industrial Revolution and its "great divergence"—its apparently decisive technological superiority over Asian societies whose cultural achievements had earlier commanded European respect—also surely contributed to the tendency to regard the world as divided into hierarchized legal spheres, with Europe representing the archetype and future for the rest.[94] And if Burke's and Anquetil's legal arguments were largely ignored, Scott's view was seemingly misunderstood, or misrepresented, by later thinkers. The anonymous entry on Scott in the famous eleventh edition of the *Encyclopaedia Britannica* identified as one of his "chief doctrines of International law" that "the elementary rules of International Law bind even semi-barbarous States," citing Scott's opinion in the *Hurtige Hane*, quoted above.[95] The Victorian jurist Sir Travers Twiss cited the same ruling to argue that the law of nations was binding only within Europe, and that because Christian powers could not expect Muslims to follow the European law of nations, there could be no legal relationship between them at all, but only, as Twiss wrote, citing Friedrich Carl von Savigny, a "purely moral" one.[96] Where legal relationships may be said to generate "perfect" obligations, producing standing for each side to demand that the other fulfill its duties, the idea that a relationship was "purely moral" implied that the Europeans were entitled to judge for themselves the content of their duties to extra-European societies. In different ways, both of these readings missed the subtlety of Scott's opinion and assumed that his ruling implied legal inferiority for non-Europeans and a European right to dictate the normative terms of interstate encounters.

The substance of Scott's view, I have argued, is closer to Burke's and Anquetil's: that whatever the particular differences among legal systems, they were united by certain very basic common principles and were mutually intelligible as law, and moreover that Europeans were bound by their own laws when encountering others. Still, Scott's emphasis on the peculiarities of European law may have laid the ground for the later arguments. Indeed, the arguments of his contemporary and acquaintance Robert Plumer Ward, discussed in Chapter 5, illustrate the ambiguous implications of the decision to deny the universality of the law of nations. That move made possible a pluralist version of the critique of European presumptuousness.

For Ward, there were many legitimate law of nations communities, and the political and legal task facing his contemporaries, as interactions among these different communities around the globe became denser and more frequent, was to work to find legal common ground to stabilize those interactions and make them more just, not to impose on others a particular set of norms through specious universalism. But too often, those who claimed to have overcome the false universalism of their predecessors merely smuggled in their own unacknowledged, as we will explore in Chapters 5 and 6.

FIVE

The Rise of Positivism?

T HE TURN OF THE nineteenth century is widely seen in histories of international law as a watershed moment, when naturalism gave way to positivism: when theories of the law of nations as based on the law of nature were rejected in favor of the view that the only relevant source for international law was state practice. Many nineteenth-century writers on the law of nations took such a view of the moment, as have subsequent historians from divergent perspectives, from Alexandrowicz in the 1950s and 1960s to Stephen Neff in 2014.[1] The decades around the turn of the nineteenth century clearly represent a key turning point in a number of respects, including the gradual adoption of the very term "international," coined by Bentham in the 1780s.[2] Martti Koskenniemi has gone so far as to argue that there is no continuity between eighteenth-century law of nations discourse and the discipline of international law that emerged in the nineteenth century.[3] Despite the general sense that the period represents a key transitional moment, the first half of the century has been relatively neglected in recent historiography, which has focused on the professionalization of international law in the latter part of the century.[4] Moreover, too great an emphasis on the transformation of international law from naturalism to positivism obscures other developments that are closely linked with but conceptually distinct from that shift and from one another, namely, the rise of historicism and the entrenchment of Eurocentrism in accounts of the law of nations.[5]

In this chapter I explore these transformations in international law by tracing the question of the scope of the law of nations, and the linked question of the status of Vattel as an authority on the law of nations, from the period of the French revolutionary wars through the first Opium War of 1839–1842. Vattel's *Droit des gens* was arguably the most globally significant work of European political thought through the 1830s, and in the changing reception of Vattel we can track the ragged transition from the intellectual world of the eighteenth-century law of nations to that of the professional international lawyers of the later nineteenth century. I begin with a brief consideration of the influential treaty collector and professor of the law of nature and nations G. F. von Martens, whose efforts to demarcate a distinctly European positive law of nations were shadowed by the recognition that a substantial body of positive law in the form of treaties linked European states with counterparts in Asia and North Africa, and could be differentiated from the "European" law he claimed to elucidate only through vague claims about a shared European culture. Distinctly European practices were likewise at issue in the historicist turn in English-language writings on the law of nations signaled by Robert Ward's 1795 *Enquiry into the Foundation and History of the Law of Nations* and James Mackintosh's 1799 *Discourse on the Law of Nations*. What we might see as the incipient historicism of Vattel's approach—which relied heavily on historical examples but drew on them as disarticulated precedents or instances of given principles rather than seeing the development of the law of nations as a historical phenomenon—gave way, with these works, to a new evolutionary account of the law of nations. Vattel's text continued to serve as the primary authority for legal principles, particularly in Britain, where it was made newly relevant for the dilemmas thrown up by imperial expansion thanks to a new edition published by Joseph Chitty in 1834 that supplemented Vattel's original text with principles and precedents from British admiralty law and imperial experience. Yet, as I will argue, a universalist reading of Vattel as applying to states outside Europe proved so problematic for the dominant prowar position in the British debates leading to the first Opium War that this moment marked the end of his position as the primary authority. The text that most immediately superseded it, *Elements of International Law* by the American Henry Wheaton, first published in 1836, was insistent, and increasingly so in later editions, that the law of nations applied exclusively to European states until others were explicitly admitted to the international community.[6] When public figures from states outside Europe, such as the Algerian Hamdan Khodja and the Chinese official Lin Zexu, drew on translations of relevant passages from Vattel to justify their positions in conflicts with European imperial states in the 1830s, they were appealing to a text whose authority in Europe was being supplanted at that very moment, arguably in part precisely because its universal scope made it so apt for their critical purposes.[7]

Vattel's *Droit des gens* quickly became the authoritative source of legal principles for interstate relations throughout Europe, in the newly independent United States, and in Spanish America and the many new republics that declared independence there in the 1820s and 1830s; he was the "current oracle of writers and politicians," as Anquetil-Duperron put it in 1798.[8] At the same time, his name was becoming a byword for useless and even dangerous pieties about law. Kant's famous description in *Toward Perpetual Peace* of Grotius, Pufendorf, and Vattel as "sorry comforters," writers whose precepts are trotted out in justification of offensive wars but have never been known to restrain state violence, was preceded by similar dismissals by Voltaire and others.[9] Bentham similarly derided Vattel as "old-womanish and tautological": "[His propositions] come to this: Law is nature—nature is law. He builds upon a cloud." At the same time, he saw Vattel as the authority to be displaced, writing, "Vattels [sic] the most accredited work on this subject—it's [sic] inadequacy to this purpose."[10]

A satirical verse similarly mocking the futility of the naturalist tradition, first published in the ultra-Tory weekly *The Anti-Jacobin* in 1798, proved irresistible to later British commentators, and can be found echoing across the nineteenth century, quoted by figures from Palmerston to Thomas De Quincey and many others.[11] While contributions to the newspaper, founded by the young M. P. George Canning and edited by the satirist William Gifford, were anonymous and often multiauthored, many of its most celebrated verses were by Canning, whose own copy attributed this poem to himself, Gifford, and John Hookham Frere. The original verse ridiculed the French revolutionary government's consul to Algiers, who, it said, was threatened with execution by the dey after he tried to foment revolution among the "Moors" by translating Paine's *Rights of Man* into "language *Mauritanic*." The verse initially placed the action in Tunis, then self-mockingly called attention to such ignorance about, and indifference to, extra-European societies. It also sardonically equated the French revolutionary regime and North Africans as "Pagans" ("Every friend of Humanity will join with us, in expressing a candid and benevolent hope, that this business may not tend to kindle the flames of War between these two Unchristian Powers") and expressed the "wish that the head of [the consul] should be reserved for his own *Guillotine*." In response to the dey's threat of decapitation,

The Consul quoted Wicquefort,
And Puffendorf and Grotius;
And proved from Vattel,
Exceedingly well,
Such a deed would be quite atrocious.[12]

Some uses of this verse, which became a ubiquitous shorthand, a kind of Victorian meme, indicate later nineteenth-century legal writers' understanding of themselves as positivists who restricted themselves to reporting state practice, in contrast to an earlier, overly ambitious prescriptive natural law tradition.[13] As *Chambers's Encyclopaedia* summarized what had become the conventional wisdom by 1870, "Like all his predecessors in the same field, V[attel] based his whole system on an imaginary law of nature, and it would be easy to enumerate a large number of false conclusions to which he came in the absence of light thrown on the law of nations by practice, and by the principle of utility in our time, so generally adopted as the test of international morality." Those relatively few later nineteenth-century international lawyers who considered themselves defenders of naturalism could look to Vattel as a precursor, the passing of whose authority marked a great intellectual loss. One such jurist, James Lorimer, wrote, "As Vattel (1714–67) was the last of the philosophical, Moser (1701–86) appears to have been the first of the empirical jurists." He lamented that Vattel failed to save "the science from the rising tide of empiricism," concluding, "It is only when the necessary law is lost sight of in its concrete manifestations, that empiricism, utilitarianism, and the like, degenerate into mere objectless groping amongst lifeless facts and life-destroying fictions." And yet, as we will see in Chapter 6, self-understood naturalists of the later nineteenth century shared with their positivist colleagues a conviction that the law of nations was an exclusively European possession.[14]

The rise of positivism, historicism, and Eurocentrism beginning around the turn of the nineteenth century were linked phenomena, and an increasingly stark positivism tracked a progressively obdurate Eurocentrism. The early historicist and positivist G. F. von Martens, who, like Vattel, acknowledged a natural basis for the law of nations even as he quickly dispensed with it for practical purposes, was also more equivocal about the distinctiveness of Europe and recognized the awkwardness of the line he was trying to draw. The later outright rejection of naturalism, in contrast, was accompanied by an uncompromising Eurocentrism, as Chapter 6 will discuss. But these three tendencies could also pull in contrary directions. Ward, a thoroughgoing historicist interested in the evolution of distinct law of nations communities, had none of the scientific aspirations of the positivist turn, and his insistence that Europeans had no right to impose their own parochial moral schema on others contrasts with the views of most of the historicist and positivist thinkers who followed. Bentham was profoundly idiosyncratic, but his thought also exercised an influence on the positivist turn, particularly by way of his disciple John Austin. Bentham's obsession with reformist codification contrasts with the direction taken by mainstream international law positivists after the mid-century, as they gave up on utopian schemes of legal reform and stressed their own deference to state practice. Although Bentham was an unsparing critic of natural law thinking, his expansive notion of the international community, his overtures to non-European collaborators, and his critique of European imperial conduct contrasted sharply with the later positivists' European triumphalism. This chapter, then, stresses the ways in which positivist, historicist, and Eurocentric strands of international legal thought could diverge even as a consensus came to be built by mid-century that international law was a body of positive law historically European and presumptively authoritative for the world, given the superiority of European civilization.

Martens's Positive Law of Nations

The Göttingen law professor G. F. von Martens took it to be his task to "prov[e] the existence of the positive law of nations" and to establish its content, in his *Précis du droit des gens de l'Europe* and by way of his influential collections of treaties.[15] For Martens, the law of nature was inadequate as a source of rules for the "frequent commerce" that characterized European interactions: it was too rigorous and abstract, and its insistence on the equality of rights was unrealistic. He celebrated Vattel as one of a handful of modern authors who had paid attention to the positive law of nations, as opposed to the universal.[16] Martens opened his account of states' rights and duties with a perfectly conventional reference to natural law as the universal and necessary law that governs all nations, "even against their will," and he argued, again in a familiar vein, that because the law of nature was too indeterminate to provide sufficient guidance for states in frequent interaction, they were obliged to generate more specific rules, through conventions and custom. As Koskenniemi has argued with Martens in mind, "Far from [their] being opposed to each other," the relationship between naturalism and positivism "is better seen as that between framework and routine. If natural law provides an overall image of the world, positivism labours with its details."[17] Martens's positivism thus did not entail a rejection of natural law, although his treatment of the natural foundations of the law of nations was perfunctory, and he saw the "science" of the positive law of nations as having been properly launched only when it was "separat[ed] entirely from the universal law of nations," something Vattel had not done.[18]

What is more striking about Martens's account than its departure from naturalism, and what distinguishes it more markedly from Vattel's, is his insistence on restricting the scope of the law of nations to Europe. The authors Martens cited as contributing to the positive "science," above all, Johan Jacob Moser, addressed a specifically European law of nations.[19] He recognized the awkwardness of the category, noting that "I thought it necessary to confine my title to the *nations of Europe:* although, *in* Europe, the Turks have, in many respects, rejected the positive law of nations of which I here treat; and though, *out of* Europe, the United States of America have uniformly adopted it. It is to be understood *à potiori,* and it appears preferable to that of, *law of civilized nations,* which is too vague." He also noted that the "connection between the Ottoman Empire and the Christian states of Europe is much less general, and more feeble in many respects, than that which subsists between the greatest part of the Christian states." And yet Martens routinely included the Ottoman state among the European powers when enumerating them, and discussed its practices as he did those of other (European) states.[20] And although in the *Précis* he restricted the positive law of nations to the "society of European nations," his treaty collections included treaties with powers beyond Europe.[21] Given such ambiguities about the scope of the law of nations, Martens did not simply *assume* that it applied only to Europe but rather felt it necessary to argue for the existence of a European society of states with its own law of nations. He acknowledged that "all the nations of Europe" had never agreed by treaty upon a common positive law of nations and possibly never would. The European society was like a people before they form themselves into a republic, but while he predicted that they would "never" take that final step, still, the connections among Christian European states were close and robust in a way that their connections with others were not. Given the absence of any

record of uniquely European positive law, and an extensive body of treaties reaching outside Europe, Martens leaned on a notion of European
culture to substantiate his account of a "positive" European law of nations.
He cited tacit consent, shared history and custom, and patterns of treaty
making to assert that the European powers could be seen to have accepted
a shared set of rights and obligations that constituted the positive law of
nations.[22] Thus, from the start, positivism was, as it were, not strictly positivist—it did not restrict itself to the existing record of written agreements
and state practice—but introduced principles of selection according to
which some treaties and some diplomatic practices, namely, those between
European and extra-European states, were not relevant sources of the law
of nations.

The Advent of Historicism: Ward, Mackintosh, Wheaton

Roughly simultaneously with the beginning of explicit calls for a science
of the positive law of nations such as we find in Martens was the flourishing
of a new genre, the history of the law of nations. Robert Ward's *Enquiry into
the Foundation and History of the Law of Nations in Europe from the
time of the Greeks and Romans to the Age of Grotius* (1795) is significant
as the first history of the subject written in English, with only a few recent
predecessors in German, most notably D. H. L. von Ompteda's *Litteratur des
gesammten sowohl natürlichen als positiven Völkerrechts* (1785).[23] Ward
himself was conscious of the novelty of his project, writing that while the
historical facts he adduced were familiar—for the "same collection of facts"
had been used to tell a variety of histories, "of man . . . of the progress of
society . . . the effects of climate . . . laws in general"—they had "never yet"
been used to narrate "a History of the Law of Nations."[24] Ward's pluralism
and his consciousness of the provincialism of European law sharply distinguish his historical narrative from the developmental historicism based
on an account of progressive civilization that, as we will see, characterized
James Mackintosh's work, and that would come to dominate nineteenth-
century international law. Ward insisted on the validity of a plurality of
legal systems around the globe, though his pluralism was compromised by
his belief in the unique truth of Christianity, which he saw as the basis of
the European law of nations. (Ward's pluralism may, however, bear comparison to J. G. Herder's, which also was grounded in Christian belief and

a faith in providence: such thinkers can accept a diversity of moral beliefs among cultures as an aspect of a benevolent divine plan.)

Although a young and untested lawyer when he wrote the *Enquiry*, Ward had a cosmopolitan upbringing. He was born in 1765 in London to an English merchant based in Gibraltar and his wife, a native of Spain from a Genoese Jewish family, and he lived in Spain for his first eight years. After studying at Oxford and then enrolling at Lincoln's Inn, he left for France for his health around 1788 and remained there until the beginning of the Revolution. His nineteenth-century biographer, quoting Ward, recounts his arrest at the hands of the revolutionary regime when he was apparently mistaken for another Ward and "ordered without trial to Paris, to be guillotined," only to be released when the "real traitor" was found. But he was "banished from the republic merely for my name's sake," returning to London by the last packet boat allowed to sail for England in 1790. In 1794, passing by a London watchmaker's shop with a revolutionary placard in the window, Ward entered the shop and engaged the watchmaker in argument against the "horrors" of revolution; the man, ultimately convinced, revealed to Ward a revolutionary plot and persuaded Ward to accompany him to the authorities, who took them directly to Prime Minister William Pitt. Pitt took an interest in the young lawyer and ultimately recommended him for a pocket borough seat in the House of Commons, which he took up in 1802. Pitt's circle included the attorney general Lord Eldon and his brother William Scott, whom we encountered in Chapter 4, who apparently suggested that Ward write a history of the law of nations. Perhaps not surprisingly, the history that Ward told would have certain clear affinities with Scott's judicial opinions, above all in the position that Europeans had no right to assume that the finer points of their international jurisprudence obligated states that had not consented to such principles or participated in their formulation.[25]

The only extensive critical study of Ward's thought gives prominence to his counterrevolutionary views, describing him as a spokesman for an "Ultra-Tory orientation" and as a representative of modern conservative ideology at its inception.[26] Some critiques of the French Revolution, as we have seen already in the *Anti-Jacobin* verse and in Martens, took the form of skepticism about the Revolution's universalist aspirations or pretensions, whether these were seen as impotent or alternatively as a screen for old-fashioned power politics. When Pitt asked why he had entered the watchmaker's shop, Ward is said to have responded, "I, sir . . . am not long returned

from France, and have there seen in practice what sounds so fine in theory."
His biographer later surmised that his "late residence in France, in which
he was so near being the victim of a harsh, if not a wrong, construction of
international law," may have sharpened his interest in that law.[27] But while
Ward was indeed a critic of the French Revolution when he wrote the *Enquiry,* and while he criticized what he saw as the misguided universalism
of natural-law accounts of the law of nations, the arguments he developed
in the *Enquiry* cannot, I would argue, be reduced to or particularly well
explained by either the idea of an incipient conservative ideology or his opposition to the French Revolution. His few asides critical of the Revolution
are moderate, and Ward did not portray revolutionary France as a mortal
threat to civilization or the European order; he blamed French aggression
as much on geopolitical as ideological motivations—namely, the desire to
extend French territory to the Rhine.[28] He was committed to the legitimacy
of plural moral judgments. Such a commitment to moral pluralism is certainly compatible with strands of conservatism and defenses of traditional
social orders, and Ward's thought did develop in a conservative direction
in later years. Still, his pluralism as expressed in the *Enquiry* is neither
distinctly conservative nor particularly counterrevolutionary. And given
Ward's departure from Burke's universalist account of the law of nations,
he cannot, I would argue, be marshaled into a "Burkean" counterrevolutionary tradition.

Ward's central argument in the *Enquiry* was that the law of nations had
to be understood historically, because normative diversity was so profound
both within and among communities, and normative commitments so
thoroughly shaped by custom and education, that no principles could be
said to oblige human beings universally. For "those who take their ideas of
universal morality, solely from their own," he wrote acerbically, such a historical investigation might seem unnecessary.[29] Those of a more self-critical
and less presumptuous frame of mind had to acknowledge that humanity's
grasp of the universal principles of natural law could only come about
through education and habit, and therefore that diverse understandings
of those principles were intrinsic to the human condition.[30]

The implication of this pluralism for legal obligations among states was
that "we expected too much when we contended for the *universality* of the
duties laid down in the Codes of the Law of Nations." He proposed instead
that laws that oblige nations in their interactions must arise among "different divisions or *sets* of nations" connected by "particular religions, moral

systems, and local institutions." This was a theory that had to be "proved from history, if proved at all." He wrote that he had decided to test his theory from the history of Europe, "as that in which we are most interested"; not, at least here, because it was normatively superior to others. Ward would go on to argue for the truth of Christian principles as well as for the superiority of many principles of European law of nations over those of various predictable others such as "Turks" and "Tartars," though he criticized both Europe's principle of balance of power and its obsession with commerce as being of mixed value. The distinctively European institution of the balance of power led European states to "join cheerfully in the most dreadful conflicts to which the lot of Humanity is liable," though precisely this tendency to war had also necessitated Europe's relative "polish and mildness."[31]

Ward wrote of being struck by the conflict between the universal language of the law of nature and the historical fact that what was called "the system of the Law of Nations was neither more nor less than a particular, detailed, and ramified system of morals"; in other words, that "what is commonly called the Law of Nations, falls very far short of *universality*." He argued that general terms such as "'the *Law of Nations*,' or '*the whole World*,'" should not be taken "in the extensive sense which is implied by those terms," but rather should be understood to mean "nothing more, than the law of the European Nations, or the European World." Importantly, the particularism of the European law of nations meant, for Ward, that even as Europeans should understand themselves to be morally bound by its precepts, they had no "right to act toward all other people as if they had broken a law, to which they had never submitted, which they had never understood, or of which they had probably never heard." If others followed precepts that threatened European "happiness and just rights," they might be treated as enemies, but never as if they were "punishable for *breaches* of those laws." Europeans were not justified in appealing to their own legal principles as if they were universally obligatory.[32]

Ward affiliated himself with Vattel, and he can be seen as a dualist in the tradition of Vattel in the sense that he accepted reason and natural law as the distant bases for the law of nations, but found them inadequate for the purposes of establishing external legal duties.[33] At the same time, his pluralism constitutes a substantial departure from the presumed universality of Vattel's law of nations. Ward's far greater stress on cultural and normative diversity evidently owes a great deal to the example of Montesquieu, who had likewise argued that different peoples have different laws of nations. He quoted Montesquieu as holding that the law of nations depends on the principle that different nations ought to do as much good in peace and as little harm in war as possible. While such a principle might be fine as a starting point, Ward wrote, when we require a more "detailed scheme of duties, it is obvious that much more is necessary to render it definite," and the fundamental question then becomes "*who is to judge?*" It is here, in his insistence on the question of judgment, and on the inappropriateness of any peoples' presumption to judge on behalf of others, that the distinctiveness of his argument in relation to both Vattel and later civilizational theories lies. Vattel, for his part, seems to have been indifferent to the question of diversity of judgment. The universality of his law of nations is taken for granted; he begins mostly with European principles and practices, looks for confirmation in the practices of others, and maintains that all are obligated by the same principles in their interactions. This universality could provide a useful basis for criticism of European violence and abuse of power outside Europe, as we have seen with Burke. But it could also serve as a means by which to foist parochial normative judgments on others; it is this latter facet of Vattel's thought and the tradition for which Ward thought he stood that Ward's stress on normative diversity and judgment enabled him to criticize. He criticized the use of "civilization" as a criterion used by Europeans to coerce others to conform to parochial European precepts: "It is fair to suppose that uncivilized, as well as civilized nations believe the religious notions which inspire them, to be the dictates of their nature; although *civilized* reason should demonstrate, ever so much to its own satisfaction, that uncivilized minds are wrong in their ideas, yet unless the latter agree that they are wrong, nothing satisfactory can be determined." Not only did those who understood themselves as civilized have no legal grounds for requiring the "uncivilized" to abide by their rules, but there was great diversity of moral and legal principles among so-called civilized nations and even among different sects of the same religion.[34]

Ward recognized a history of interaction among disparate societies alongside their normative differences, and he saw treaties as a means of drawing together societies that otherwise fell into different communities or "classes" of the law of nations. The "horrid enmity" between Christian and Muslim nations was generated on both sides by prejudice due to unfamiliarity, as well as by more active ideological manipulation within Europe, where the popes had sought to gain power over certain monarchs by

castigating their alliances with the Ottoman Empire. He saw the "deso-
lating wars of the Crusades" as an illegitimate Christian assault on territory "fairly possessed according to the maxims of the world," as indicated
by long-standing Christian acceptance of "Infidel" possession.[35] He critically canvassed the history of the European prohibition on alliances with
"infidels," showing it to be ill founded from the outset and always contravened by a more flexible practice of treaty and alliance across religious divisions, as well as obviously obsolete by Ward's own time.[36] "Treaties once
begun," the two sides developed regular principles of interaction and came
to consider each other *"legitimate States,"* an example of "the manner in
which Convention came to change and to amend the errors of the Law of
Nations." He claimed that just as the Russians and Poles used to stand
"upon the verge" of the European legal community, so now did the
Ottoman Empire, whose first permanent ambassador to Britain, as we
saw in Chapter 2, was fascinating London society at just the moment of
Ward's writing.[37]

Finally, Ward singled out for criticism the presumption of Vattel's claim
that nations have a duty to cultivate commerce: he objected that if commerce's utility is the source of the obligation, "its universality must entirely depend upon this, that all mankind consider commerce in the same
light with Vattel, which is known not to be the case." Ward's pluralism led
him, that is, to reject the imposition by philosophical fiat of a particular
European law of nations and the values in which it was embedded onto
peoples that had not consented to them. At the same time, he was interested in the historical processes by which nations of different international
legal communities could come to share principles and respect one another's
legal standing. Although Ward's book was well received, and he had a
modest political career and some popularity in later years as a novelist, the
Enquiry, with its distinctively pluralist historicism, was not influential.[38] Its
significance lies instead, I would suggest, in its suggestive articulation of a
path not taken: a pluralism critically oriented against European pretensions to impose their own principles on others and to constitute themselves arbiters of acceptable international conduct for the whole world.

A nearly contemporary work, James Mackintosh's brief *Discourse on
the Study of the Law of Nature and Nations,* published in 1799 in the course
of his own counterrevolutionary turn, was more representative of the developments that were to take place in early nineteenth-century thought
about the law of nations. Mackintosh is best remembered for his eloquent

expression of his early support for the French Revolution in his *Vindiciae Gallicae: A Defense of the French Revolution and Its English Admirers* of 1791 (a moderate, liberal response to Burke's *Reflections* admired by those uncomfortable with the democratic radicalism of Paine's *Rights of Man*), and his subsequent repudiation of that support and newfound admiration for Burke by 1796. His published *Discourse* was essentially the text of the first of a series of lectures he delivered at Lincoln's Inn in early 1799 that were intended as a public declaration of his change of view: while the published work treats what he calls "that part of morality, which regulates the intercourse of states," the course of lectures, the rest of which remained unpublished, ranged more broadly across jurisprudence.[39] He served as judge in the British court at Bombay, and also as a judge on the new vice-admiralty court there, adjudicating prize cases such as those that William Scott decided at the admiralty court in London; taught law at the East India Company's college at Haileybury (what appears to have been a light task he took on for the salary, while he continued to write); and served in the House of Commons from 1813 until his death in 1832, as a major Whig and defender of reform causes including the abolition of slavery, the abolition of capital punishment, Catholic emancipation, and parliamentary reform.[40] He also supported Latin American independence.[41] Mackintosh's significance for our story lies in his turn to historicism in the service of an argument for the European law of nations as having uniquely universal significance. While Mackintosh's *Discourse* bears some resemblance to Ward's argument in its turn to history and its interest in the "positive" facet of the law of nations, alongside a basic commitment to the law of nature as the ultimate foundation of the law of nations, its preoccupations differ in crucial ways.

Mackintosh's historicism was progressive, and his preference for Christianity was based not simply on religious principle but on an elision of "Christendom" with civilization. He utterly lacked Ward's skepticism toward self-serving appeals to the idea of civilization. For Ward, the history of any collection of polities would provide evidence for its positive law of nations; he presented his choice of Europe as due to local partiality rather than to its universal significance. Mackintosh, in contrast, found the positivist refinement of the law of nations a distinctively European achievement: what "we now call the law of nations has, in many of its parts, acquired among our European nations much of the precision and certainty of positive law." Mackintosh presented the law of nations in a "gradation"

running from the most basic, "necessary, to any tolerable intercourse between nations," "some traces" of which can be "discovered even among the
most barbarous tribes"; to a second class of principles more advantageous
and more advanced, which might be found among "the Asiatic empires"
and "the ancient republics"; to the most advanced "law of nations, as it is
now acknowledged in Christendom." Mackintosh's essay, although it was
reprinted as a preface in a number of later French and Spanish editions of
Vattel's *Droit des gens,* was remarkably dismissive of him as a legal authority,
and his criticisms of Vattel's legal thought seem to be tied, in a way that is
not true for Ward, to a rejection of Vattel's republican politics.[42] To his original description of Vattel as "ingenious, clear, elegant, and useful," Mackintosh added a footnote the following year, noting, "I was unwilling to have
expressed more strongly or confidently my disapprobation of some parts
of Vattel. . . . His politics are fundamentally erroneous; his declamations
are often insipid and impertinent; and he has fallen into great mistakes
in important practical discussions of public law" and "adopted some
doubtful and dangerous principles."[43]

Mackintosh's judgment of Vattel was cited approvingly by the American
legal writer and diplomat Henry Wheaton, who first undertook a history
of international law—using the new Benthamite term—in a speech in 1820,
"History of the Science of Public or International Law."[44] Wheaton drew
on this account in his *Elements of International Law,* the book that by the
1840s would replace Vattel as the standard reference work. His later invocation of another judgment by Mackintosh—"Vattel, a diffuse, unscientific,
but clear and liberal writer, whose work still maintains its place as the most
convenient abridgment of a part of knowledge which calls for the skill of a
new builder"—seems to herald the advent of his own treatise.[45] Wheaton's
Elements, first published in 1836 and then in numerous subsequent editions
in English, French, and Spanish, shared Mackintosh's progressive account
of the law of nations as an element of the moral and cultural progress represented by post-Reformation Europe.

> So entirely distinguished is the international law of Christendom, from
> that which prevails among the other classes of nations which people the
> globe, or between those other nations and Christendom itself, that it may
> with truth be asserted, that there is no law of nations universally binding
> upon the whole human race; or, to speak more properly, no other than
> that of reciprocity—of amicable or vindictive retaliation, as the particular

case may require the application of either. There is no universal and immutable law of nations, which all mankind, in all ages and countries, ancient and modern, savage and civilized, Christian and Pagan, recognise in theory or in practice, profess to obey, or in fact obey.

Wheaton held that the "science of international jurisprudence" was, like the sciences of morality and government, "entirely of modern structure," the product of a now racialized European civilization that shared "Teutonick origin and ancestry" and Christianity along with the legacies of Roman law, feudalism, and chivalry. He distinguished "civilized nations" of Western Europe from the "Eastern Empire, [where] the Mohammedan conquerors remained separate from the vanquished race," relying solely on the "Koran [as] their all-sufficient institute of ethical and political science."[46] Wheaton took for granted the utter separation of European developments from those of the rest of the globe in a way that Martens had not done, for all his sense of the distinctiveness of the European law of nations. Later, in a section of his *History of the Law of Nations* (1845) titled "Relations of the Ottoman Empire with the other European States," Wheaton suggested not simply that the European law of nations was the product of a discrete European history, but indeed that it was precisely in distinction from the Muslim world that this law of nations was formed and identified.[47]

Wheaton also remained preoccupied by the idea of the Ottomans' racial and religious aloofness. In describing the heterogeneity of the Ottoman Empire in the *History*, Wheaton quoted a passage from Burke's "Speech on Conciliation with America" that stressed differences in the structures of government in various parts of the Ottoman Empire. But where Burke was making a point about the role of sheer distance in weakening government over extended territories, and likening the Ottoman, Spanish, and British Empires as all subject to this universal experience ("In large bodies, the circulation of power must be less vigorous at the extremities. Nature has said it"), Wheaton misleadingly cut Burke's reference to distance and used the passage to suggest that the Ottoman Empire was, by implicit contrast with European states, not "completely blended into one nation" but rather riven by "indelible distinctions of race and religion," and for that reason, among others, alien to the European community of nation-states.[48]

In his 1820 history, Wheaton similarly cited a passage from William Scott but interpreted it in a way that departed from Scott's own meaning and supported a more triumphalist reading of European civilization. Scott had written, as we saw in Chapter 4, that a "great part of the law of nations stands upon the usage and practice of nations. It is introduced, indeed, by general principles; but it travels with those general principles only to a certain extent." Recall that Scott was arguing that Europeans were obliged to suspend some of the details of their interstate legal principles when dealing with North African states that had not consented to them. On Wheaton's gloss, Scott's passage supported the view that "the customs which regulate the intercourse between barbarous communities, are much wider deviations from that law *which is written on the hearts of men,* (as we civilized nations read its precepts,) than the voluntary or conventional law of civilized nations has shown even in the most unfortunate periods of European history." Wheaton had asserted, in something of the spirit of Scott and Ward, that European precepts were not binding on those to whom they were entirely foreign:

> The public law of Europe is no more obligatory upon the Asiatic and African nations, than the municipal code of any one state of the world is applicable to another; and it would be as absurd to apply it to them, as it was to punish a Hindu bramin for violating a law enacted on this side of the Cape of Good Hope, by a foreign legislature, and in an unknown language.[49]

He did not inquire, however, as Burke and Scott had done, into Europeans' own obligations to abide by the law of nations in their conduct beyond Europe, and the suggestion of his generally enthusiastic account of European commerce and colonization was that little criticism on this score was necessary. As with Mackintosh, the implication of Wheaton's progressive history, with Europe playing a privileged role as the sole source of the science of international jurisprudence, was that the law of nations was historically unique to Europe but had a claim in the future to general authority on the grounds of its basis in superior civilization.

European Imperial Expansion and Vattel's Global Reception

Meanwhile, Vattel was briefly given renewed life as an important authority for an increasingly hegemonic Britain in Joseph Chitty's English edition of 1834, which Chitty greatly expanded with commentary referring to British colonial law and citations from admiralty, prize, and other courts, adapting Vattel for an imperial state.[50] Vattel was routinely cited in support of Britain's right to settle New Zealand in mid-nineteenth-century debates, as when Lord John Russell argued in the House, "You must say that New Zealand shall be treated as inhabited by a civilized people . . . [or] you must apply the principle of Vattel, who alleged that savages could only hold the land they occupied, and beyond that they should have no favour whatever."[51] Chitty's heavily amended text is typical of nineteenth-century editions of Vattel published in Europe and Latin America, such as Andrés Bello's *Principios de Derecho de Jentes [Gentes]* (Santiago de Chile, 1832), and the Portuguese philosopher and diplomat Silvestre Pinheiro Ferreira's *Droit des gens, revue et corrigée avec quelques remarques de l'editeur* (Paris, 1838), whose title, like that of the 1863 French edition by Paul Pradier-Fodéré (in which Vattel's text was *"augmented"* with a new translation of Mackintosh's *Discourse* and *"complétée par l'exposition des doctrines des publicists contemporains mise au courant des progrès du droit public moderne"*), announces the editor's extensive interventions.[52] Like Chitty, Pinheiro Ferreira and Pradier-Fodéré larded their editions with extensive commentary, drawing heavily on Martens, Johann Ludwig Klüber, and Wheaton to bring Vattel "up to date." Pradier-Fodéré's revision included a lengthy discussion of the membership of the international community (in comments on book 1, chapter 1 that dwarf the original text), a rebuttal of Vattel's defense of China's right to restrict commerce, and a celebration of the expansion of the French Empire: "In less than fifty years, France has recovered the rank that the carelessness of governments or the misfortune of the times had taken from her."[53] In these editions, Vattel's text sometimes seems to serve as little more than scaffolding for nineteenth-century commentary that departs considerably from his arguments.

Chitty's edition was well timed to contribute to British debates leading up to the first Opium War, in which Vattel's text was a ubiquitous point of reference, "constantly quoted by advocates of war," as one of their critics noted, and invoked likewise on the antiwar side. The key questions around which Vattel was invoked were whether China was justified in prohibiting the opium trade; whether China had violated the law of nations in confiscating and destroying millions of pounds of opium in 1839, and in detaining the British merchants of Canton in order to force British traders to hand over the opium on their ships off the Canton coast; and whether Britain was justified in demanding compensation for the destroyed opium and, ultimately, in going to war to exact repayment and to force China to permit the opium trade. For those who supported the use of military force to compel China to allow the opium trade, Vattel's arguments about commerce were inconvenient because Vattel so categorically supported every state's right to regulate commerce in whatever way it deemed to be in the best interests of its people.[54] Some prowar authors quoted Vattel, straining his meaning to claim that nations are obliged to engage in commerce and to suggest that China's conduct had implied a tacit agreement to "carry on trade with us on equitable principles."[55] But others, recognizing that Vattel contravened their position, bit the bullet and argued for excluding China from the community protected by the law of nations:

> It is laid down by all writers on public law, that it depends wholly on the will of a nation to carry on commerce with another, or not to carry it on, and to regulate the manner in which it shall be carried on (Vattel, book i.§ [i.e., chapter] 8). But we incline to think that this rule must be interpreted as applying only to such commercial states as recognize the general principles of public or international law. If a state possessed of a rich and extensive territory, and abounding with products suited for the use and accommodation of the people of other countries, insulates itself by its institutions, and adopts a system of policy that is plainly inconsistent with the interests of every other nation, it appears to us that such nation may be justly compelled to adopt a course of policy more consistent with the general well-being of mankind.[56]

Indeed, the pressure brought to bear on the prowar position by a universalist application of Vattel's principles might be seen as a contributing factor in the movement toward the exclusion of China from the "family of nations," as well as in the displacement of a universalist Vattel as an authority.

Such a development can be seen in not only the British but also the American response to the war. Former president John Quincy Adams, in the course of his forceful defense of the war (which was unusual at that moment in relation to American public sentiment generally in favor of the Chinese position),[57] felt the need to reckon with Vattel's unqualified defense of a nation's right to order its commercial policy as it sees fit.[58] Adams, by then a congressman, argued first that an unrestricted such right contradicted Vattel's own principle that nations have a general moral duty to engage in commerce, and second that in any case, the Chinese followed a "churlish and unsocial system" that contravened the principle of equality among nations that was the cornerstone of the European law of nations. Giving a thumbnail sketch of the history of the law of nations, Adams proposed that there is

> a Law of Nations between *Christian* communities, which prevails between the Europeans and their descendants throughout the globe. This is the Law recognized by the Constitution and Laws of the United States, as obligatory upon them in their intercourse with the European States and Colonies. But we have a separate and different Law of Nations for the regulation of our intercourse with the Indian tribes of our own Continent; another Law of Nations between us, and the woolly headed natives of Africa; another with the Barbary Powers and the Sultan of the Ottoman Empire; a Law of Nations with the Inhabitants of the Isles of the Sea wherever human industry and enterprize have explored the Geography of the Globe; and lastly a Law of Nations with the flowery Land, the celestial Empire, the Mantchoo Tartar Dynasty of Despotism, where the Patriarchal system of Sir Robert Filmer, flourishes in all its glory.[59]

Adams rejected as a "fallacy" what is arguably the structuring principle of Vattel's dualist system, that while nations have a duty in conscience to contribute to the happiness and perfection of others, a nation's first duty is to itself, and it is the exclusive judge of that interest. The *Chinese Repository*, an American missionary publication in Canton, reprinted the lecture because it showed "in a lucid manner one of the strongest reasons why the Chinese government has not the right to shut themselves out from the rest of mankind, founded on deductions drawn from the rights of men as members of one great social system."[60] This claim, issued alongside Adams's extravagant proliferation of "separate and different" laws of nations governing relations among Europeans and their descendants, versus between Europeans and other societies, illustrates the typical dual movement by which Westerners simultaneously declared that they adhered to universal laws—so the Chinese were violating general principles in supposedly contravening them—and also that the European law of nations was historically particular and so did not pertain to relations with extra-European states.[61]

For their part, antiwar texts appealed to Vattel in their rejection of attempts to exclude China from the law of nations. One such pamphlet asked, "Now what says Vattel[,] a high law authority, constantly quoted

by the advocates of war?," responding with Vattel's principle that foreigners are obligated to obey local laws.

> And yet in direct contravention of this equitable rule, which regulates
> our own government in regard to foreigners, and is submitted to by the
> subjects of England in every other part of the world; and to support the
> monstrous proposition,—that the Chinese are without the common
> rights of other nations,—is a criminal withheld from justice, momentous
> interests involved in inextricable embarrassment, and hundreds of lives
> have already been sacrificed.[62]

The Chinese authorities likewise had recourse to Vattel to defend their
actions. When Commissioner Lin Zexu arrived in Canton in March 1839
to enact the emperor's anti-opium policy, he employed a number of agents
and translators to gather and translate information about the foreign
traders there; one of his early requests was for the translation of several passages from Vattel in relation to commercial prohibitions, the right of a state
to confiscate contraband, and the right to wage war.[63] Lin obtained translations from the American medical missionary Peter Parker, who recorded
the request in his medical report, as well as from his senior interpreter,
who had been educated in English and who may have been the one to alert
Lin to Vattel's text. As Parker wrote, "His first applications, during the
month of July, were not for medical relief, but for translation of some quo-
tations from Vattel's Law of Nations . . . sent through the senior hong-
merchant; they related to war, and its accompanying hostile measures, as
blockades, embargoes, &c."[64] The opium contraband that Lin proclaimed
later that year was entirely in keeping with Vattel's principle that states have
perfect liberty to set and change at will their commercial policy. Lydia Liu
argues that "Lin's use of international law in these transactions was strategic," on the grounds that he had selectively translated passages "strictly
confined to the issues of how nations go to war and impose embargoes,
blockades, and other hostile measures," rather than taking the text as a
whole.[65] But this is to mark too stark a boundary between opportunism and
a willingness to engage sources the British themselves considered authoritative, on a subject on which Lin considered himself in the right and on
which Vattel unambiguously supported his position.

Lin gave the two sets of translated passages to a fellow official, Wei Yuan,
in Beijing, who included them in a compilation of texts about the conditions and views of foreigners, the *Hǎiguó Túzhì*, or *The Illustrated History*

of the Maritime Countries. The compilation, including the Vattel passages, was printed and circulated to officials across China in 1844 and expanded to two further editions over the next decade (1847 and 1852), and it played an important role in development of Chinese foreign relations over the subsequent decades, as Qing officials responded to the increasingly aggressive European and American commercial and quasi-imperial expansion across maritime Asia.[66] But, in a development indicating Vattel's waning authority in the West in subsequent decades, when the American missionary W. A. P. Martin set out to translate a text of international law into Chinese in the early 1860s, he decided against Vattel and in favor of Wheaton's *Elements of International Law.*[67] The Opium War thus arguably marks an important turning point, when the implications of Vattelian universalism sat so uncomfortably with a dominant political position in a European imperial state that Vattel had to be argued away or dismissed.

Like Lin Zexu, the Algerian businessman and scholar Hamdan ben Othman Khodja (ca. 1773–1842) found it useful in the early 1830s to obtain translations of some key passages in Vattel in order to challenge abuses of power by a European imperial power. After the French conquest of the city of Algiers in 1830, Hamdan Khodja had a complex series of encounters with French officials in Algeria before choosing to depart for Paris in the spring of 1833. He sent his son, Hadj Hassan, to negotiate with General Bourmont the capitulation of Algiers, a treaty whose immediate violation by the French was to become one of Hamdan Khodja's most insistent grievances.[68] He also served, under some duress, as an intermediary between the French and one of their most formidable opponents, Ahmed Bey, the Ottoman governor of the eastern province of Constantine.[69] Giving up any hope of influencing the intransigent colonial officials, he arrived in Paris in the spring of 1833, at the height of French parliamentary and public debates over the "Algerian question," and in a series of letters and memoranda, and a book titled *Le Miroir,* appealed directly to the metropolitan authorities and French public opinion. He seems to have produced *Miroir* in collaboration with a fellow Maghrebi liberal, Hassuna D'Ghies of Tripoli, through whom Hamdan Khodja had met Bentham in the early 1820s, and possibly also with the assistance of French critics of the conquest.[70] In *Miroir* he argued for an independent Algeria that would take its place in a nineteenth-century Europe of emerging nationalities and engage with European states as a diplomatic equal. He recalled the struggle of the 1820s for an independent Greece, the French participation in the liberation of Catholic Belgium from domination by Holland, and the widespread interest in the "Poles and the reestablishment of their nationality." He repeated such analogies in a letter of October 1833 to the French commission of inquiry into the conquest (la Commission d'Afrique):

> I congratulate myself on my honorable step when I recall that the Greeks owe their independence to the French, that the Belgians owe them their liberty, and that proud and unfortunate peoples have always found in the French the warmest sympathy. No, the Algerians do not deserve to be thrown out of society; they are part of the human family. Blood flows in their veins, Gentlemen, with the same heat as in your own.[71]

The *"question d'Alger"* had generally been taken in French debates, even by the *"anti-colonistes,"* to be the question of what colonial policy would best serve France's interests; Hamdan Khodja reframed it as one that "has to do with the vitality of an entire nation, composed of ten million individuals." While granting that the country had been placed, in the deferential language of his appeal to the king, under "Your Majesty's guardianship [*tutelle*]," he proposed that the king "emancipate the Algerians [and] restore harmony between the two peoples," for "Algerians, too, have rights that should permit them to enjoy liberty and all the advantages that European nations enjoy."[72] Where French ethnographies tended to insist that the regency's inhabitants were not a single people but an assortment of disparate and hostile populations, *Miroir* describes Algerians as *"un peuple," "une nation," "mes concitoyens," "mes compatriotes."*[73]

Hamdan Khodja submitted a memorandum to the French commission of inquiry into the conquest of Algiers in 1833, arguing that continuing the war of conquest would be a strategic disaster for France, as well as unjust, dishonorable, and a violation of France's liberal principles. He concluded with a protest against the French violation of fundamental principles of the "laws of war and peace" in the course of the conquest. Rather than treating the Algerians as the fellow members of human society and the commercial partners they were, the French had "fixat[ed] [*s'attacher*]" on differences of religion and custom and considered themselves free to violate the "customs of all civilized countries" in Algeria. He cited two passages from Vattel, the first arguing that "justice" is "indispensably binding on nations" even more stringently than on individuals, and the second that not only are agreements made during the course of war inviolably binding, but it is particularly "unjust and scandalous" as well as imprudent for conquerors to violate capitulation agreements with those that surrender to them.

> Finding myself one day with a general [Clauzel], this illustrious personage declared to me that the French were not at all obliged to the observe the rules of the capitulation, which was nothing but a ruse of war. This is the source of all our troubles, since the French soldiers, those who hold power, think themselves free to do anything and have acted thus as long as they have been in my country.
>
> Even so I am astonished that the heads of the French army are oblivious to [*ignorent*] the existence of the laws of war and peace that govern the civilized world. . . . As for me, I do not read French, but I certainly know the faithful translation into Arabic that the Sherif Hassuna Deghiz has made of the treatise on the law of nations by Vattel, and I think I may cite here the provisions contained in Book 2 chapter 5, para 63 and book 3 chapter 16 para 263, which I will not report here.
>
> Can these principles be denied? Are Africans excluded from human society [*la société humaine*]? Would liberty properly understood approve the morals of this illustrious general? No. In any other common [*vulgaire*] man, one could excuse this manner of reasoning, but in a leader representing the French nation, such language is unpardonable.[74]

Hamdan Khodja saw three possible measures in the interests of France: either to clear the countryside by repelling the population into the desert, "if the law of nations approves such a measure, and if it is compatible with the liberal principles that characterize the French nation," or—in true accordance with the law of nations—to select a Muslim prince known to France in whom to confide the fate of the people, "to govern them with the aid of liberal principles, compatible with the laws and mores of these peoples." Even better, as he concluded *Miroir*,

> Evacuate the country and renounce all idea of conquest in establishing a free and independent indigenous government, as was done in Egypt, which has the same religion and follows the same customs, and conclude with this government treaties favorable to both peoples. France would undoubtedly find far greater advantage this way than if Algiers remained her colony. . . . This liberal emancipation, all the more because the Algerians do not profess the same religion as the Europeans, would further add to the celebrity of our century.[75]

Such a course would entail a "conquest of men's hearts," the only form of conquest appropriate to an age of "enlightenment, civilization, and justice," and the only prudent as well as lawful measure. The French conquest, far from securing Algeria's wealth for France, as the French had assumed, was destroying the orderly countryside and long-standing commercial ties that had made Algeria the "granary of Europe," and inciting the population to "fanaticism." General Clauzel, or his allies, found it necessary to publish an extensive "refutation" of *Miroir* that sought to discredit Hamdan Khodja personally in classically Orientalist terms as wily, duplicitous, and motivated by a religious "fanaticism," and also to undermine his case for an Algerian nation-state. As a *"maure,"* or member of the Turkish-allied elite, the refutation argued, Hamdan Khodja was illegitimate as a spokesman for the whole population, and his very idea of an "Algerian" people was incoherent.[76]

In elaborating his idealized portrait of French and European liberal civilization and legal principles, Hamdan Khodja did not simply present the French with their own ostensible standards as a critique of their colonial depredations. He also performed the sort of act of interpretive generosity that he asked of his French readers vis-à-vis Islam. He suggested that both Islam and European civilization had been betrayed by their agents. Ottoman and other Muslim rulers had abused their power, and it was this, rather than anything inherent in Islamic legal principles, that had given some substance to the European stereotype of the Oriental despot.[77] But European "civilization" had been equally ill served by its self-professed representatives. Having demonstrated the extent to which officials in Algeria had violated French ideals, Hamdan Khodja nevertheless declared himself an ally of those ideals. He implicitly asked his French readers to respond with similar imagination and sympathy to what he acknowledged was an idealized portrait of Islam.[78]

Bentham's Failed Alternative

Hamdan Khodja's proposal that the French work with a native ruler to install constitutional government in Algeria recalls his friend Hassuna D'Ghies's collaboration with Bentham on a project of constitutional reform for his native Tripoli. D'Ghies, whom Bentham referred to as "my disciple and an adopted son of mine," had lived in France and England beginning in 1815 and introduced Hamdan Khodja to Bentham in 1822. Bentham hoped to work with Hamdan Khodja to promote political reform in Algeria, and he encouraged him to send reports from Algiers that Bentham would try to place in the British press. Only one report seems to have resulted, which Bentham summarized as follows: "The Algerines are tyrannized over by about 10,000 Turks. The object is, by flattering the Dey, to engage him to listen to European advice, and seek European assistance for delivering his country from that tyranny, and concur in establishing a better form of Government."[79] The summary may well represent Bentham's (or D'Ghies's) aspirations rather than Hamdan Khodja's, though the latter did lament in *Miroir* that the French had all but dashed his hopes that their expedition might represent a liberation from Ottoman misrule.[80] Together with D'Ghies, Bentham devoted substantial time and energy to the project of drafting legal codes for a constitutional regime that he hoped might replace the pashalik that ruled the regency of Tripoli, a former dependency of the Ottoman Empire.[81] The respect with which Bentham approached the prospect of the indigenous crafting of a constitutional, representative government in a non-European and Muslim society is unusual, and his writings and letters surrounding this episode are striking for their detailed consideration of the questions Bentham believed might be involved in attempting such a project in a Muslim country. Bentham's writings on North Africa from the 1820s show that positivism did not necessarily entail an understanding of the international community as restricted to Christian Europe, as he suggested that the countries of North Africa should be integrated into the European system. In a draft letter to Mohammed Ali, Bentham urged the Egyptian ruler to declare independence from the Ottoman Empire: "Declare yourself *independent*," he wrote, "there are no foreign powers with whom you could not right away make whatever treaties you liked. . . . You would then take your place among the Sovereigns of Europe. And why not? Look at them in population and in revenue—if you find some that are your superiors—you find more that are your inferiors."[82] Bentham's awareness of the widespread hostility to reform among the ruling classes of Europe contributed to what seems to be his almost gleeful sense of the political possibility latent in the peripheries.[83]

This sense of possibility reflects the ambitious and idiosyncratic vision that Bentham had offered in his radical critique of international law's entanglements with European imperial domination in the 1780s, when he coined the term "international" and began to write, at first in French, the texts that would later be stitched together by his nineteenth-century editors into the essay known as "A Plan for an Universal and Perpetual Peace." Writing in the wake of the Seven Years' War and the American Revolutionary War, Bentham argued that the most fundamental precondition for global peace was that all states must emancipate their colonies. These writings from the 1780s show the extent to which (in contrast to Vattel) Bentham conceived of the international realm as a space of empires—and saw imperial ambitions and imperial violence as the greatest threats to international peace. Bentham had been no great friend of the cause of the American revolutionaries, whose natural rights arguments he rejected as empty posturing, just as he would later criticize the imprescriptible natural rights of the French Revolution as "nonsense upon stilts," and "bawling on paper." So although in that conflict he had supported Britain's imperial claims, largely because he thought natural rights arguments were so flimsy, Bentham was already coming to see the conflicts driven by imperial ambitions as the greatest threat to international peace.[84]

Bentham's writings of the 1780s depict the international politics of his era as dominated by the effects of colonial expansion. Colonization was, in Bentham's words, the "race of vulgar ambition" and a "war against mankind."[85] Above all, he saw colonies as the chief cause of war in the modern world. He cited as recent examples the war against Spain in the 1740s (the War of Jenkins' Ear), and the Seven Years' War, whose violence, he said, stretched from "North America to the East Indies," and which, in the needless destruction it caused Britain, demonstrated "the extreme folly, the madness of war." Bentham saw a global system dominated by empires as structurally doomed to incessant violence. Colonies provoked wars not only by multiplying the possible sources of conflict but also because in their newness, and distance from Europe, they were fraught with uncertainty, which Bentham saw as a key source of instability and aggression. His project for the codification of international law was driven by the aim of quelling conflict by reducing uncertainty. A code would do so, he thought, in part by minimizing the many offenses against international peace that were committed by sovereigns unsure of, or in good-faith disagreement about, what constituted their obligations toward one another. But the greater danger to peaceful commerce and cooperation was empire. Bentham's attention to the imperial nature of the world's major powers allowed him to see, and to make explicit, what remains possibly implicit, but certainly obscure in Vattel: that a legal system premised on the reciprocity and equality of independent states must require first of all that they give up their empires and become, in fact, the territorially compact political communities that Vattel had hypothesized.[86]

Nearly fifty years later, when, at the age of eighty, Bentham returned to the subject to sketch a plan of "International Law," he took the radically different position that the first rule of international peace was that states should stay out of each other's colonies. In the notes on international law that he sent to the barrister and former colonial judge Jabez Henry in 1827, in the hope that Henry would develop them into a treatise or code, Bentham accepted a number of the essential features of Vattel's picture of the international realm: states must recognize each other as equals; each pledges to respect the regime, religion, and customs of all the others; and each is oriented not only toward keeping peace with the others, but also toward "mutual good will" and "mutual good offices." This is all quite faithful to Vattel's account, perhaps more than Bentham would have acknowledged. But now Bentham limited the community of states under international law to "all civilized nations[,] which at present is as much as to say, all nations professing the Christian Religion."[87] This was a radical departure from both Vattel's and his own earlier presumptive universalism as well as his overtures of the early 1820s to Muslim North Africa.

Bentham was now also far more modest in his aspirations for the international legal code than he had been in the material that became the essays on perpetual peace. Above all, he gave up the hope of taming imperial ambitions. In describing the "Utility of a body of International law," he first noted the "Good which it is not capable of effecting—preventing a Sovereign who has purposes for conquest from endeavouring to carry them into effect." Rather, the code's main function would be to reduce uncertainty about states' respective rights and duties, so that inflated ideas of "rights violated" might be kept from "stir[ring] up angry passions and anti-social affections." Along with this greater modesty went a complete abdication of Bentham's original prescription for international peace, the emancipation of all colonies. Instead, the principle of universal equality now required (just as Chitty did) that states not interfere in one another's colonies, or as Bentham put it, "Fundamental principles to be agreed upon by all the States: (1) universal equality. No State to pretend to any authority over any other State (a) on sea, (b) on land in the territory of a barbarous nation not being a member of the Congress. (2) All States to be upon a par in Congress, whatsoever the form of government."[88]

Bentham, then, made an about-face on international law and empire. He gave up on the key prescription for global peace that he had made as a young man, he accepted the restriction of the international legal community to Christian Europe, and he accepted that the system's major powers would be vast global empires with utter legal impunity—at least with respect to international law—in their conduct in their colonies. For help in turning this sketch into a code of international law, he turned to a man whose reputation was built on his work as a colonial official. Bentham's motivations can be obscure, and it is hard to account for what may have happened within his own mind from the 1780s to the 1820s to bring about this change. It may have had partly to do with the shift of the center of gravity of imperial domains from the settler colonies of the Americas—which had mostly established their independence by the late 1820s—to India and other nonwhite populations. But it is worth stressing that in the earlier period, Bentham had insisted on the emancipation of all colonies, India specifically included, and not just colonies whose loudest voices were white settlers.

Whatever his own reasons, there is no question that the change in Bentham's thinking tracks a more general development in European thinking in this period, one that we also see in the shift from Vattel's original text to the Chitty edition of the 1830s. We begin with a universal vision of an international community that is not limited to Europe, one made up of states understood as moral communities protected by political autonomy to work out their collective life. We end with a vision of an international community of equal states limited for the time being to Europe; states understood in a dual way as legal equals vis-à-vis each other but also as global empires controlling vast territories and populations as they see fit. Both Lin Zexu and Hamdan Khodja drew on Vattel to argue that European states had the same stringent legal duties to their states that they had within Europe, at the very moment that the principle of the universal application of the law of nations was coming to be seen as obsolete in Europe, and Vattel as an outdated authority in relation to newer sources that recognized the uniquely European character of the law of nations. International law speaks, in the later model, only to the interactions between European states; it is not well equipped to analyze those states as empires, to hold them to legal account, or to recognize the global order as one that is structured hierarchically. Henry Wheaton's *Elements of International Law* quickly replaced Vattel as the standard reference work. As we have seen, Wheaton was a thinker in whom the strands of historicism, positivism, and Euro-centrism worked in tandem. In an 1845 author's preface to *Elements,* Wheaton wrote, "If the international intercourse of Europe, and the nations of European descent, has been since marked by superior humanity, justice, and liberality, in comparison with the usage of the other branches of the human family, this glorious superiority must be mainly attributed to these private teachers of justice" beginning with Grotius, who articulated its principles.[89] Among the key features of Wheaton's text that made it more in tune with its times than the outdated Vattel—especially for Martin's purposes of bringing Western international law to China—was Wheaton's insistence that the law of nations was not universal. This was an argument that he made ever more insistently in the editions of his text published after the first Opium War, in which he argued that international law "has always been, and still is, limited to the civilized and Christian people of Europe or to those of European origin." His revisions to later editions also newly stressed, however, that the European order would and should expand to encompass the extra-European world.

> The more recent intercourse between the Christian nations of Europe and America and the Mohammedan and Pagan nations of Asia and Africa indicates a disposition, on the part of the latter, to renounce their peculiar international usages and adopt those of Christendom. The rights of legation have been recognized by, and reciprocally extended to, Turkey, Persia, Egypt, and the States of Barbary. . . . The same remark may be applied to the recent diplomatic transactions between the Chinese Empire and the Christian nations of Europe and America, in which the former has been compelled to abandon its inveterate anti-commercial and anti-social principles, and to acknowledge the independence and equality of other nations in the mutual intercourse of war and peace.[90]

As international law came in the latter half of the nineteenth century to be increasingly a self-conscious discipline, its major practitioners came to argue that international law had to be understood as a historically particular system that had arisen under the distinctive circumstances of early modern Europe and was constantly adjusting to the "growing wants of a progressive civilization."[91] They were, consequently, preoccupied in a way that earlier theorists of the law of nations such as Wicquefort, Wolff, and Vattel had not been with delineating the scope of the international community, expounding the criteria for admission into that community, managing its gradual expansion to encompass some excluded states, and specifying the legal status of various societies they deemed inadmissable. Anxious to establish the scientific credentials of their discipline, most shared with figures in other emerging social or human sciences of the period a conviction that the intellectual advances made over their eighteenth-century predecessors lay precisely in their historical approach to their subject. International law could be scientific and progressive only by being historical.[92] The resulting constellation of beliefs—in the historical particularity of the European law of nations, the normative validity of the European legal system for the future of the world as a whole, and the possibility of rendering international law scientific—distinguished nineteenth-century international legal thought from its eighteenth-century sources and left a marked legacy for international law in the twentieth century.

SIX

Historicism in Victorian
International Law

It was an apt remark on the part of his Excellency Kuo-Taj-in, the first
Envoy-Extraordinary and Minister-Plenipotentiary accredited from China
to the Court of St. James, that he found the European Law of Nations to
be "a very young Law"; but he had also observed that since the age of Grotius wars had been less frequent in Europe, and less sanguinary.

S IR TRAVERS TWISS (1809–1897) thus began a narrative that encapsulated the received wisdom of his European contemporaries about the
history of international law, in the introduction to the revised 1884 edition
of his major treatise, *The Law of Nations Considered as Independent Political Communities*.[1] In the space of a paragraph, Twiss managed to announce all the major themes that structured European international law's
self-understanding at the time. In Twiss's summary, the European state
system was founded on the principle of the independence and legal equality
of all states, notwithstanding their obvious inequalities of wealth and
power. The practical realization of such a system in the Treaty of Westphalia was possible only because of Grotius's prior conceptualization of
territorial sovereignty and its attendant rights. The establishment of these
principles through a foundational juridical text and in diplomatic practice
had successfully tamed state violence. Grotius's genius had been to accept
the moral truth that universal principles of natural law apply to states as
well as to individuals, while also recognizing that natural law principles in
their abstract generality had to be filled out by a systematic account of the
actual practices of states; accordingly, since Grotius, European legal writers
had increasingly emphasized positive over natural law.

By introducing his account with an ostensible observation from the Chinese ambassador, Twiss purported to supply unbiased confirmation of the superiority of Europe's system. He matched the ambassador's oblique compliment to Europe with his own backhanded tribute to China, as an old and venerable civilization with the good judgment to recognize that progressive Europe had developed an international system of universal significance. Twiss's introduction went on to trace the theoretical developments that had brought international law from Grotius's day to his own: most importantly, the further articulation of the idea of a body of positive as distinguished from natural law (which he attributed to Richard Zouche); treaty collections that furnished the material for the study of the positive law (Leibnitz, Dumont, Schmauss); the notion of the law of nations as a science; and the idea, which he misleadingly attributed to Christian Wolff, that the international community was divided into an outer circle of "less cultivated" nations and an inner circle of European nations among whom alone special obligations of reciprocity applied.[2] Arguing that Wolff and Vattel had "exhausted" the subject of the natural law of nations, Twiss maintained that what was left to their successors was to systematize a specifically European public law, and then went on to describe the relevant states as Christian. But he downplayed the significance of the religious classification—it was merely "used for the sake of convenience"—in a way that belied the anxieties he expressed elsewhere about the obstacles that differences of religion posed to legal community.[3] According to Twiss, the result of this history of increasingly precise attention to European law within a tradition of thought that had once seen the law of nations as an elaboration of the law of nature was that European lawyers now faced the question of the scope of the law of nations:

> In what sense are we to interpret the phrase "Law of Nations"? Are we to extend its meaning as widely as Professor Bluntschli, who has laid it down that "International Law is not restricted to European nations. Its domain extends over the whole surface of the globe"? or shall we adopt Professor Frederic de Martens' view, that reciprocity is a cardinal principle of contemporary international Law, and that the application of the Law of Nations, as a system distinguished from the Law of Nature, is confined to such civilised States as recognise in their international relations the obligations of reciprocity.[4]

As his opening invocation of the Chinese ambassador suggests, Twiss himself resolved this apparent dilemma of the universality versus the

European particularity of the law of nations by means of a progress narrative whereby a particularly European history came to have universal authority.[5] In this account, because the European law of nations, "which reason has moulded in conformity with the progress of civilisation," "has been found to conduce to the general welfare of the community of civilized States," its "observance . . . is obligatory upon every Nation that claims to participate in the common advantages of that civilisation."[6] In the thought of Twiss and others, that is, the progress narrative enabled a tautology whereby recognition of the validity of the European law of nations was indispensable evidence of a state's worthiness as legal subject. Toward states that remained outside the community, Europeans bore moral but no legal obligations, or only the barest duties such as abiding by one's promises.[7]

Twiss used his preface to insert a brief for the cause of his then employer, King Leopold of Belgium, by arguing that international recognition of the Congo under the control of a private "philanthropic" organization should not be controversial. He had the temerity to suggest that the recognition of Liberia was a clear precedent for the recognition of the sovereignty of the Belgian Association Africaine Internationale over Congo, on the grounds that Liberia, too, was first founded by a private association and supported by its funds, despite the evident differences between Liberia's mission as a colony of freed slaves and King Leopold's project of conquest, which was soon to become notorious for its brutal atrocities.[8]

Twiss's 1884 introduction was, finally, typical in its apparently modest claims to undertake only to describe state practice rather than to prescribe normative standards. Twiss smuggled normativity into his account unacknowledged, both in his principle of selection, in that only "civilized" Europe counted toward relevant "state practice," and in the related notion that the facts themselves were progressive, that a developmental dynamic was embedded in the law of nations as state practice, so that ethics need not be imposed from without, by legislating lawyers. Legal writers had only to "illustrate" the progress that was actually taking place. While Twiss was willing, as some of his positivist contemporaries were not, to acknowledge a distant basis in natural law, an unacknowledged prescriptive moral universalism in the form of progress narratives survived even in thinkers more explicitly critical of natural law.[9]

In 1878 Guo Songtao (Kuo Taj-In) attended, as did Twiss, the meeting of the Association for the Reform and Codification of the Law of Nations in Frankfurt, where he made the remarks that Twiss freely paraphrased in his introduction. His statement read:

The Law of Nations has existed since very remote times. It did not form a distinct science until the seventeenth century, when most of the European nations began to adopt it. European countries have within these two hundred years made daily progress in their national prosperity and civilization.

Although the Association for the Reform and Codification of the Law of Nations is quite a young institution, yet its object, which is to improve the law for the benefit of all governments and peoples, is a very grand one.

The administrative system of China differs in some points from that of any of the European countries. China is not in a position to adopt the Law of Nations at once. With respect to its diplomatic and commercial relations with other countries, China has never gone beyond the International Law. I am very desirous of attaining a knowledge of this science, in the hope that it will be beneficial to my country.[10]

As Arnulf Becker Lorca has noted, the hopes that Guo and the Japanese delegate, Kagenori Ueno, held for the abolition of the unequal treaties their countries suffered "were rapidly shattered" by the hostility of the European delegates to the legal equality of their states. As the American David Dudley Field put it, "so long as there was not something like a parity of civilization in the East and West," legal disabilities such as consular courts must remain in place.[11]

This chapter examines the intellectual developments in the latter half of the nineteenth century that led the new professional class of European international lawyers to a preoccupation with the question of international law's scope, and that produced the theoretically fraught but ideologically powerful response to that question that Twiss's narrative encapsulates, in which Europe had uniquely forged a solution to the universal problem of reciprocity among peoples. This was a response that drew together positivism (and often a critique of natural-law universalism) and a stress on Europe's exceptionality, with scientific aspiration and a conviction in the universal validity of European values. The irony that these thinkers demanded "reciprocity" from others while themselves violating the spirit required for reciprocity, such as a generosity of engagement or a willingness to subject oneself to those others' judgments and standards of judgment, was not lost on the critics that I discuss at the end of the chapter, who lamented the way in which ideas of civilization and European uniqueness had been used to pervert international law from more inclusive and just implications of the discourse's premises. According to these critics, often nonlawyers who used the language of international law in public forums, it was Europeans who had failed in the duty of reciprocity.

As we have seen, Robert Ward had maintained in his *History of the Law of Nations* (1795) that international law could be understood only as a historical phenomenon, and William Scott, in his admiralty court jurisprudence, had shared Ward's historicist sense of a "law of nations" as a social construct that developed out of a long history of dense commercial ties among a group of nations, such that Europe's law of nations was one of many such systems. And yet neither Ward nor Scott held the view that was to become standard among the Victorian jurists: that the European law of nations was a global legal system in embryo, that other nations were lawless insofar as they failed to participate in the European system, and that a key task of European jurists was to construct a process by which those others might be granted admission to the European-global legal community. The subsequent generations of international lawyers that forged the discipline in the second half of the century shared a set of presuppositions that would profoundly mark modern international law. These included, above all, the belief that international law, though historically particular to Europe, was prospectively authoritative for the globe: that only Europe could claim to have produced and experienced the progressive civilization that was ostensibly humanity's vocation and destiny. Despite imagining a developmental process by which other societies would gradually be admitted to legal standing in the system of civilized states, these thinkers often naturalized the differences they asserted between Europeans and others. Finally, despite regarding Europe's system of international law as both an index and an engine of progress, they professed a certain impotence in the face of European imperial expansion, even when they recognized European actions as unjust, and they expressed fear that Europe's material civilization in the form of increasingly destructive technologies of war might overwhelm the normative achievements of European civilization.

Chapter 5 analyzed how the idea that the international community is composed of free and legally equal states became entrenched, and was deployed on behalf of European commercial, imperial, and quasi-imperial expansion. We encountered some of the chief elements with which later nineteenth-century disciplinary international law was constructed. These included: (1) the downplaying of international law's natural-law basis, but generally not its outright rejection;[12] (2) the claim that the task of lawyers and treatises was to document the positive law of nations, which could only be discerned through *patterns* of European treaty making (rather than as the sum of all agreements), so that assumptions about the content and meaning of shared European cultural norms lay behind the inclusion or exclusion of any given treaty as relevant; (3) the notion that because international law is not promulgated by an authoritative body, academic treatises have a juridical role in articulating, even codifying, the law; and (4) above all, the assertion that the truth of the equality and independence of states was something that only European states had understood and practiced, in contrast to the imperial structures of the rest of the "civilized" world—that while there were many law of nations communities, the European one alone had global normative authority.

In this chapter I focus on the writings of British international lawyers of the latter half of the nineteenth century, given the dominance of Britain as the major imperial power and as the leader of quasi-imperial commercial expansion in Asia. Particularly in light of the 1857–1858 Sepoy Rebellion in India, Britain saw intense public debate about the consequences of imperial expansion in which claims about the scope of international law played a role. British theorists of international law also faced distinct intellectual challenges due to the predominance of the common law tradition and the relative lack of a robust Roman and civil law tradition, although certain prominent figures including Twiss, Sir Henry Maine, Sir Robert Phillimore, and the Scot James Lorimer were trained as civilians.[13] I trace Maine's historicist critique of Austinian positivism and revisit the debate between analytic and historical jurisprudence to argue that behind that apparently deep divide was a shared historical narrative that united aspirationally scientific and universal claims about humanity as such, encapsulated in the paradoxical assertion that Europeans uniquely exemplified certain universal human tendencies or qualities, including social progress, a recognition of the rights of the individual, and a commitment to relationships of reciprocity among independent states.

As it was for other social sciences such as anthropology and political science, this was a period of disciplinary consolidation for international law, which saw the establishment of some of the first university chairs in the subject, the publication of unprecedented numbers of treatises, and the formation of professional societies and the first academic journals.[14] The nascent profession of international law in Victorian Britain was intimately linked to counterparts on the European continent, particularly through professional associations: the first periodical of international law, *Revue de droit international et de législation comparée*, was established in 1869 by the Belgian Gustave Rolin-Jaequemyns, the Dutch legal scholar Tobias Asser, and the British John Westlake, who were all instrumental in the founding a few years later of the Institut de droit international. Westlake, who had been briefly a Liberal MP as well as a cofounder of the Working Men's College and a champion of progressive causes such as women's emancipation, later succeeded Maine in the Whewell chair in international law at Cambridge, where he taught from 1888 to 1908, and from which he dominated the field.[15] The profession in Britain was also distinctively British and sometimes English in its concerns, thanks to factors including the country's insularity, its global dominance as the foremost imperial power, its relative lack of a civil law tradition, and the outsized influence of the new tradition of analytical jurisprudence associated with the utilitarian tradition and especially with Bentham and John Austin.

Even as the field became more highly technical and doctrinally complex, writers on international law saw it not as the exclusive province of professionals but as the instrument of an educated citizenry, largely enforceable only by public opinion. As Westlake wrote, "International law being the science of what a state and its subjects ought to do or may do with reference to other states and their subjects, everyone should reflect on its principles who, in however limited a sphere of influence, helps to determine the action of his country by swelling the volume of its opinion"; the "chief justification" for teaching it was "to prepare men for the duties of citizenship."[16] John Stuart Mill made the same case in his 1867 address to the University of St. Andrews on the purposes and appropriate subjects of a "complete scientific" university education. There he called for the teaching of international law as part of "direct instruction in that which it is the chief of all the ends of intellectual education to qualify us for—the exercise of thought on the great interests of mankind as moral and social being."[17] International law, that is, continued to play the role noted in earlier chapters of a key discourse for the articulation of normative claims about politics, as well as for claims about the trajectory of human history and for reflections on the relationship between social and cultural particularities and a common humanity.

The rapid succession of conflicts that beset the political landscape during this period shaped the key preoccupations of Victorian international lawyers.[18] The Crimean War (1853–1856), seen as the result of Russian belligerence and Ottoman weakness, entrenched in British observers a belief that the community of civilized Western European nations bore responsibility for maintaining peace in the face of threats from an uncivilized European periphery. The 1856 Treaty of Paris that concluded the conflict was described as having formally inducted the Ottoman state into international society, though many jurists continued to question its capacity to participate as a full member of the European "family of nations." Western European military intervention in the Ottoman Empire, both private and state-sponsored, spanned the century.[19] The Sepoy Rebellion in India shone attention on the status under international law of the Indian states not formally subject to Britain, and more generally on the question of whether Europeans had any obligations under international law in their relations with Asian states. The American Civil War generated controversies around the question of recognition of belligerents and the rights and duties of neutral states and heightened the British public's interest in international law, through celebrated cases such as the *Trent* and the *Alabama*.[20] The unforeseen violence of the Franco-Prussian War of 1870–1871 provoked in the community of international lawyers a sense of their profession's vocation to tame and civilize modern states with alarmingly destructive military arsenals, and prompted the founding in 1873 of the Institut de droit international.[21] And at the watershed imperial negotiations at the Berlin Conference in 1884–1885, international lawyers served as energetic agents of the participating European states and associations.[22] Their understanding of all these events was framed by accounts of the evolution of societies toward civilization and of the historical trajectory and extension of the system of international law.

A New Discipline, Historical and Scientific

At the height of the Crimean War, in April 1855, Henry Maine (1822–1888) delivered a paper titled "The Conception of Sovereignty, and Its Importance in International Law" before the new Juridical Society, which was founded, according to its first president, to redress the traditional indifference of law professors to the advancement of their field, in contrast to "the anxiety shown by those who are engaged in other departments of science," and despite the fact that lawyers' "pursuits and studies are so intimately connected with the progress and well-being of mankind."[23] Maine's paper, the first delivered before the new society, was an opening salvo in what would prove to be a highly influential campaign by Maine to historicize the British understanding of law, including international law. Maine had taught civil law at Cambridge before taking up a position in Roman law and jurisprudence at the Inns of Court in London, where he was lecturing on the material that would become his most influential book, *Ancient Law*. He lamented that "the great majority of contemporary writers on International Law tacitly assume that the doctrines of their system, founded on principles of equity and common sense, were capable of being readily reasoned over in every stage of modern civilization," when in fact "the true explanation of those ambiguous dicta . . . is entirely historical."[24]

Maine's lecture was an ambitious attempt to assert "the great speculative and practical importance" of a properly historical understanding of key legal concepts such as sovereignty in the face of perilous contemporary conflicts from the 1848 revolution in Germany to the looming battle between the American states to the Crimean War's combat between the Russian emperor and the Ottoman sultan, which had drawn in much of the rest of Europe. By the end of his career, Maine would come to characterize the Ottoman Empire and its inevitable breakup as "the most hopeless of all the problems which the civilised world has to solve."[25] This portentous sense of responsibility was characteristic of international lawyers who by the late Victorian period would come to see themselves and their discipline as indispensable to the maintenance of order and the progress of civilization within the European "family of nations," and to the management of European imperial and commercial expansion around the globe.

Maine published little on international law between his early paper on sovereignty and his posthumously published inaugural lectures, delivered in 1887, as Whewell Professor of International Law at Cambridge.[26] But his historicist program for the study of law, developed in *Ancient Law* (1861) and *Village-Communities in the East and West* (1871), not only profoundly influenced British jurisprudence generally but also significantly shaped the emerging discipline of international law. Maine's call to study law as a historical phenomenon, as a social construct responsive to and dependent upon other social institutions, faced the particular hurdle in British legal studies of the influence of the relatively ahistorical analytical tradition.[27] Despite early efforts such as Ward's, during the first half of the nineteenth century historicism had less of a presence in Britain than it did elsewhere in Europe, thanks to the influence of the analytical jurisprudence associated with Bentham and his disciple John Austin.[28]

Austin's famously restrictive definition of laws as the commands of a sovereign raised the question whether international law could justly be considered law at all, since it was clearly not promulgated in that way. Nearly all British theorists of international law felt obliged to respond: both historicists who rejected Austin's account of law as narrow and wrong-headed, and analytical jurists who admired his rigor and yet wished to salvage international law as law. And this was the case even though Austin himself granted that international law could be understood as "analogous to jurisprudence" and "treated . . . in a scientific or systematic manner."[29] A sense of the force of the Austinian view was a distinguishing feature of British international law thinking in this period, in contrast to the Continental colleagues with whom British theorists worked closely in bodies such as the Institut de droit international, for whom Austin was largely irrelevant. Austinians such as T. E. Holland argued that international law was law by analogy: "the vanishing point of Jurisprudence; since it lacks any arbiter of disputed questions, save public opinion, beyond and above the disputant parties themselves."[30] Westlake, though he quickly dispensed with Austin's command theory of law, shared his goals of parsimony and scientific rigor, and wrote somewhat dismissively about historical approaches to law that collected ingenious discoveries about "remote state[s] of society" without first analytically establishing the meaning of law.[31]

Maine's agenda no doubt partly owed its great success, despite that hurdle, to its congruence with the general philosophical historicism that characterized social and political thought both in Britain and on the Continent, in the work of thinkers as diverse as Auguste Comte, the Saint-Simonians, J. S. Mill, and Karl Marx.[32] For all their differences, these thinkers shared an aspiration to establish the study of society and politics on a scientific basis, and they did so by means of narratives of human progress that, though universal in scope, also posited the historical uniqueness of European civilization. Maine's work also followed the more specifically legal historicism pioneered in Germany by Friedrich Carl von Savigny's critique of Enlightenment abstraction and the artificiality and inflexibility of codification. By mid-century, then, Maine's historicist agenda was timely—in keeping with major intellectual trends in Europe—but also required a distinctive sort of work in Britain.[33]

From Maine's perspective, Austin's account of law was misguided precisely because it was analytical at the expense of any proper historical understanding. Austin's theory, in form, proposed a sweeping, a priori definition of law (as the command of sovereign) that seemed to have little to say about historical change or the situatedness of law in a historical context. Maine held that Bentham and Austin's command theories of law "tally exactly with the facts of mature jurisprudence" but are unhelpful as a picture of law in early stages of society, as well as of international law.[34] Maine's early paper on sovereignty began with a polite nod to the analytical power of Austin's approach. There he adopted most of Austin's definition of sovereignty, though he offered his own distinctively historical account of the emergence of that conception of sovereignty under feudalism from the rival forms that had existed earlier (nonterritorial "tribal sovereignty," and the idea of universal dominion). In *Ancient Law* Maine more directly took on Austin along with other figures and lines of argument he regarded as misguidedly a priori, especially Rousseau's state of nature and natural rights claims that relied on such a device. Such "plausible and comprehensive" theories of the origins of law in natural law or social contract had "obscure[d] the truth" about the origins of law; indeed, it was their very plausibility and thus their power over the modern imagination that had enabled them to so mislead modern thinkers about the true origins of law, which, he argued, could be understood only through "sober research" into primitive history.[35]

Maine further argued, against Austinian ahistoricism, that only a properly historical study could salvage the powerful but precarious system of international law:

> If international law be not studied historically—if we fail to comprehend, first, the influence of the theories of the Roman jurisconsults on the mind of Hugo Grotius, and next, the influence of the great book of Grotius on International Jurisprudence,—we lose at once all chance of comprehending that body of rules which alone protects the European commonwealth from permanent anarchy, we blind ourselves to the principles by conforming to which it coheres, we can understand neither its strength nor its weakness, nor can we separate those arrangements which can safely be modified from those which cannot be touched without shaking the whole fabric to pieces.[36]

He used his historicist account of international law as a demystifying device, meant to strengthen the force of an ill-understood social construct by dispelling illusions, such as that international law is a reflection of an abstract and universal law of nature or a reflection of fundamental principles

of human nature. Rather, and more humbly and idiosyncratically, international law's "rapid advance to acceptance by civilised nations was a stage,
though a very late stage, in the diffusion of Roman Law over Europe," a
fact that only historical research could reveal.[37]

Some of the misapprehensions at the heart of the older ahistorical tradition of the law of nations had fortuitously proven salutary, Maine argued. Seventeenth-century jurists' view that natural law corresponded to a
fundamentally pacific and sociable human nature gave a false picture of a
period that had in fact been "excessively inhuman" in war, as demonstrated
by new research into "the actual childhood of the human race." But, though
it was based on an "imaginary reconstruction" of the remote past, the early
modern law of nations system "more and more calmed the fury of angry
belligerency, and supplied a framework to which more advanced principles
of humanity and convenience easily adjusted themselves." On the basis of
poor historiography, then, Grotius and his successors had erected a powerful
system for the maintenance of peace by "creat[ing] a law-abiding sentiment" among European sovereigns.[38] The task of scientific histories of
law in Maine's day was to perpetuate that system by placing it on firmer
ground. He argued the English were in particular need of a properly historical understanding of international law, because in taking seriously the
Austinian question of how international law comes to have authority in
particular countries (through legislative fiat, for instance), they placed
themselves outside the consensus of "civilized nations" that international
law is simply binding on nations as a condition of their membership in that
privileged circle.

Maineans who insisted on the historicity of law against what they saw
as the static universalism of Austin nonetheless felt obliged to respond to
its implication that international law was not properly law at all.[39] Indeed,
in the hands of Maine and his followers, historicism was the method by
which to vindicate international law against the Austinian challenge to its
status as law. T. J. Lawrence, who taught international law at Cambridge,
the University of Chicago, and the Royal Naval College, began his *Essays
on Some Disputed Questions in International Law* (1885) by responding to
Austin with an essay titled "Is There a True International Law?" As Lawrence put it, "Our notion of law is a development. This is a fact which once
fairly grasped would save us from many historical and philosophical errors. The Austinian analysis of law into command, obligation and sanction
applies with fair accuracy to the condition of some societies under strong

and civilized governments; but it fails altogether if we attempt to bring under it the legal phenomena of earlier stages of human progress."[40] Likewise, international laws "do actually regulate human conduct . . . even when no definite punishment is annexed to the breach of them." Indeed, the efficacy of international law despite the absence of reliable sanctions was precisely an indication of Europe's advanced civilization: "As man progresses, the notion of force as the most necessary element in the conception of law, tends to fall into the background." Like maturing children (the classic developmental trope), "so states in their development towards moral and intellectual manhood, need less and less the discipline of compulsion."[41] In this way a developmental narrative could subsume and transcend Austin, accepting his theory as a usefully scrupulous account of law within civilized societies while defusing its potentially destructive implications for the authority of international law.

While Austin and Maine did offer radically different accounts of the place of historical reasoning in legal theory, even Austin's ostensibly ahistorical approach invoked an implicit developmental narrative. In defining an independent political society as one whose members were "in a *habit* of obedience to a *certain* and *common* superior," for instance, Austin noted that it might not be possible to establish a determinate test. But he envisioned a spectrum, with "England, and . . . every independent society somewhat advanced in civilization" at one extreme of obviously political societies, and at the other extreme of obviously natural or nonpolitical societies, "the independent and savage societies which subsist by hunting or fishing in the woods or on the coasts of New Holland."[42] More important, international legal theorists of both Austinian and Mainean bents generally sought some way to synthesize what they took to be the opposing analytical and historical approaches. Whether they identified more with Austin or with Maine, Victorian theorists of international law shared the broad set of assumptions about the uniqueness and exemplarity of European progress and civilization that undergirded the period's distinctive brand of historicism.

The Victorian Narrative: European Past and Global Future

Victorian international law, then, rested on a historical narrative beset by a distinctive tension. The human being, it was held, is an inherently historical animal, so that we cannot understand human nature without understanding how human society and human individuals in their wants and needs change over time. At the same time, Europe was seen to have a uniquely historical, and a uniquely progressive, nature. Maine's account, if unusually thoroughly theorized, was characteristic. He saw the progress from "primitive" to "modern" society as of great general theoretical interest and as normative, while at the same time he insisted that both progress and progressiveness were extremely rare, achieved only by ancient Greece and Rome and their modern European heirs. As Maine famously put it, "Except the blind forces of Nature, nothing moves in this world which is not Greek in its origin." J. S. Mill likewise noted the rarity of societies that have in them a "spring of unborrowed progress."[43] James Lorimer made the argument overtly biological in aspiring to distinguish between progressive and nonprogressive races and arguing that there were "ethnical differences which for jural purposes we must regard as indelible."[44] For all of them, Europe's unique progressiveness, whether or not it indicated any inherent qualities (it did not for Maine or Mill), legitimated differential legal status and imperial rule. As Maine went on:

> A ferment spreading from that source has vitalised all the great progressive races of mankind, penetrating from one to another, and producing results accordant with its hidden and latent genius, and results of course often far greater than any exhibited in Greece itself. It is this principle of progress which we Englishmen are communicating to India. We did not create it. We deserve no special credit for it. It came to us filtered through many different media. But we have received it, so we pass it on. There is no reason why, if it has time to work, it should not develop in India effects as wonderful as in any other of the societies of mankind.[45]

Ancient Law, where Maine presented his argument that "the movement of the progressive societies has hitherto been a movement *from Status to Contract*," traces the legal mechanisms of progress through which the rights-bearing individual rather than the family comes to be the fundamental legal subject.[46] Maine regarded his historical method as scientific and believed that the progress followed by European civilization could be given a scientific account, in terms of general laws. But he also noted that "it is only with the progressive societies that we are concerned, and nothing is more remarkable than their extreme fewness."[47] Like others, Maine acknowledged the obvious sophistication of Chinese and Indian civilizations while insisting that theories of progress did not apply to these societies. He exploited the distinction between material and normative facets of civilization to deny that material was a necessary index of moral or legal progress: "There has been material civilisation, but instead of civilisation expanding the law, the law has limited the civilisation." Maine speculated that the reasons for failure of progress in "the East" included the tendency of Eastern legal codes to bear religious rather than civil authority, the large populations and territories of Eastern societies, and the codification of their laws at a later and more "perverted" stage than was the case for Roman law: "Even now, Hindoo jurisprudence has a substratum of forethought and sound judgment, but irrational imitation has engrafted in it an immense apparatus of cruel absurdities."[48] But in the end, he simply restricted his "scientific" theory to progressive societies, settling for the observation that the "difference between the stationary and progressive societies is . . . one of the great secrets which inquiry has yet to penetrate. . . . The stationary condition of the human race is the rule, the progressive the exception."[49] European civilization was thus the only properly historical civilization as well as the only one amenable to scientific study. As Karuna Mantena has argued, the logic of Maine's argument was more binary than evolutionary; he produced a picture not so much of a "ladder of civilization" but of a "spatial frontier where bounded societies live side by side, yet, significantly, in different temporalities": traditional (Eastern) societies governed by culture alongside modern (Western) societies. As Mantena shows, Maine's framework enabled colonial administrators to rationalize their disillusionment with projects of imperial liberal reform by turning to culturalist explanations that located the failures of liberal projects, and political rebellion and resistance to them, in the nature of "native" societies, "as stemming from deep anthropological, racial, and cultural imperatives."[50]

The tension we find in Maine's narrative between European civilization's unique past and its universal future, and likewise the tension between an evolutionary narrative and the dichotomization of human societies as progressive or traditional, structured the dominant Victorian accounts of international law. John Westlake, for instance, could write of international law that "as English law is the law of England and French law that of France, so international law is that of a certain part of the world," and also that the subject comprised "all that can be said with some degree of generality about human action not internal to a political body."[51] William Edward Hall began by positing European international law as simply one particular system in a world with multiple civilizations; but because he recognized only Europe's system as "law-governed," he granted Europeans gatekeeping authority over what turns out to be, in his account, the world's only such system:

> As international law is a product of the special civilisation of modern Europe, and forms a highly artificial system of which the principles cannot be supposed to be understood or recognized by countries differently civilised, such states can only be presumed to be subject to it as are inheritors of that civilisation. They have lived, and are living, under law, and a positive act of withdrawal would be required to free them from its restraints. But states outside European civilisation must formally enter into the circle of law-governed countries. They must do something with the acquiescence of the latter, or of some of them, which amounts to an acceptance of the law in its entirety beyond all possible misconstruction. It is not enough consequently that they shall enter into arrangements by treaty identical with arrangements made by law-governed powers, nor that they shall do acts, like sending and receiving permanent embassies, which are compatible with ignorance or rejection of law.[52]

Hall's account exemplifies the way in which the conception of civilization that governed these narratives operated in at least three registers at once: as an analytic or descriptive category, as a universal normative aspiration or telos, and—in the guise of the "standard of civilization"—as a mechanism of exclusion.[53]

As a descriptive category, civilization comprised individualism, contract relations, cognitive complexity, and intricate social interdependence; it was capitalist and liberal. As a normative category it entailed the refinement of distinctively human faculties of moral judgment, artistic achievement, and scientific reasoning. As J. S. Mill noted in his influential 1836 essay "Civilization," the term, "like many other terms of the philosophy of human nature, has a double meaning"; it could mean, in a normatively charged sense, "farther advanced in the road to perfection: happier, nobler, wiser," but it also applied particularly to complex modern society, and in that sense it was a descriptive and normatively neutral term, such that one could speak of the "vices or the miseries of civilization."[54] Travers Twiss used both of these meanings of civilization, writing in the more purely descriptive sense that "one feature of the present civilisation is that the application of steam-power to ships has not only rendered an armed ship a more formidable engine of War than heretofore" but also enabled unarmed ships to threaten enemy territory—technological developments that posed major new threats to international peace.[55] In the evaluative vein, he wrote of the "common advantages of that civilisation" of the "States of the Western Hemisphere" that had over several centuries of progress learned to follow rules that conduce to the general welfare.[56]

For Westlake, international law was based on the "common civilisation" of Europe and America, by which he meant—mingling the descriptive and normative facets of the term—that

> the same arts and sciences are taught and pursued, the same avocations and interests and protected by similar laws, civil and criminal, the administration of which is directed by a similar sense of justice. The same dangers are seen to threaten the fabric of society, similar measures are taken or discussed with the object of eluding them, and the same hopes are entertained that improvement will continue to be realised.[57]

Although Turkey, Persia, China, Japan, and Siam "must be recognised as being civilised, though with other civilisations than ours," international law was founded upon a "common and in that sense an equal civilisation" among European states. Turkey, geographically but not civilizationally a part of Europe, occupied an anomalous position. "She may benefit by European international law so far as it can be extended to her without ignoring plain facts, but her admission to that benefit cannot react on the statement of the law, which is what it is because it is the law of the European peoples." "This civilisation," Westlake wrote, had "grown up by degrees, and populations have become included in it among whom it did not originate."[58] European civilization was at once fixed and developing; the civilization had a stable identity over time, even as its membership was changing progressively to include new members. Admission to the community under international law, that is, did not put non-European states in a position to question or alter the content of that law.

Overlapping Criteria of Exclusion and Subordination

In his 1859 essay on non-intervention, John Stuart Mill argued for a strict distinction between the legal and political standards applied within Europe and those reserved for the treatment of so-called barbarian societies, though, as I discuss further below, the basis for his distinction between the groups was flimsy and undertheorized.

> To characterize any conduct whatever towards a barbarous people as a violation of the law of nations, only shows that he who so speaks has never considered the subject. A violation of great principles of morality it may easily be; but barbarians have no rights as a *nation,* except a right to such treatment as may, at the earliest possible period, fit them for becoming one. The only moral laws for the relation between a civilized and a barbarous government, are the universal rules of morality between man and man.[59]

Mill's relatively casual approach to the determination of the boundary between the "communion of civilised nations" and the rest of the world can perhaps be attributed partly to his belief, following Austin, that international law could not properly be thought of as law at all.[60] The law of nations, he held, is "simply the custom of nations . . . a set of international usages, which have grown up like other usages, partly from a sense of justice, partly from common interest or convenience, partly from mere opinion and prejudice."[61] Since this "falsely-called law" was not promulgated by any sovereign and so could not be repealed, the only way for members of the international community to improve it was to attempt to establish new principles by violating the existing customary rules. Given that Mill conceived of international law as nothing other than a vague set of customs established out of convenience and prejudice as much as from principle, it is not surprising that he believed its boundaries were of little theoretical interest. While he invoked the language and recommended the study of international law, Mill was attempting to determine what political or administrative arrangements were most conducive to human progress as he understood it—"the permanent interests of man as a progressive being," as he put it in *On Liberty*—not to develop a coherent doctrine or code of international law.

If Mill was more satisfied than many jurists with an underspecified legal community, there was little dissent among the jurists about the fundamental justifiability of the legal distinctions, however vague or poorly theorized, between civilized and barbarous, or improving and stationary, societies. The grounds jurists offered for the legal exclusion or compromised legal standing of other societies overlapped and reinforced one another, making the distinctions appear overdetermined and so all the less in need of carefully elaborated justification. In addition to the so-called standard of civilization, these included the notion of a religious (and therefore ethical) community that bound Europeans to one another and guided their interactions even absent explicit agreements, and purported racial or biological incapacities of certain human groups that were said to pose obstacles to their achievement of sufficient self-development to participate fully in a regime of reciprocal rights and duties. Even thinkers who were not avowedly racist appealed to persistent differences among groups, or noted that science had not progressed far enough to determine the role of race in politics.[62]

The centrality of the question of international law's scope is apparent in the agendas of the new international law societies that were forming in the 1870s. At the suggestion of the American legal reformer David Dudley Field, the Institut de droit international formed a commission in 1874 to consider the question "To what extent, and under what conditions, is the unwritten international law of Europe applicable to Eastern nations?"[63] Field himself hoped to see the issue addressed in the broadest terms. He held that neither Christianity nor "civilization" supplied a convincing justification for the exclusions of international law as they stood in his day. Field began with the tendentious assertion that the European law of nations had always aimed at "the intercourse and community of nations," whereas "the object of all people outside Christendom has been conquest or isolation and non-intercourse," but he soon worked his way around to a more historicized and less judgmental account of the peculiarity of European law. He noted the unreasonableness of radical differences in legal standing between Russia and China, despite the apparent similarities in degree of civilization throughout much of their territories. Of China, he asked, "Can it be justly claimed that a nation which has maintained a regularly administered government, over hundreds of millions of human beings, for thousands of years . . . is uncivilized? It must be admitted, I think, that the point of civilization is not the one on which the question of international law, in its application to China, should turn."[64] While Field was unusually articulate in his skepticism about the use of "civilization" as a criterion, other jurists occasionally voiced similar doubts. A vote was later held to remove the language of "civilized" and "uncivilized" states from the commission's report; after some discussion the words were replaced by "Christian" and "non-Christian," although it is clear that many doubted the justifiability of this distinction as well.[65]

The institute's commission on Oriental nations concluded that Field's question was unmanageably broad, and chose to restrict its agenda to the narrower question of how to organize the European consular tribunals abroad. Twiss, as the commission's rapporteur, held that it was not yet possible to abolish consular jurisdiction in Asia, but that the consular and mixed courts must be reformed, for they allowed Europeans at times to "escape justice altogether," causing scandal and ill will in the host countries.[66] The commission had sent a questionnaire to European and American diplomats in Asia as well as some Asian diplomats in Europe, asking these experts whether there was "such a radical difference" between Asian and European views of duties toward foreign peoples and individuals, and obligations to abide by treaties, "that it would seem impossible to imagine permitting these nationals to enter the general community of international law."[67] Although respondents to the questionnaire maintained that views in Asia's commercial states about treaty obligations were similar enough to those in Europe to pose no obstacle to these states' inclusion in international law, the commission declined to pursue that broad agenda further.[68]

The commission's failure to address the broader and more philosophical question of legal relations between Europe and Asia (not to mention Africa) did not go unchallenged. The Swiss jurist Joseph Hornung protested that the commission's decision to limit itself to legal arrangements tailored to the needs of Europeans abroad was symptomatic of a more general European egoism: "In our relations with non-Christian humanity, Europe never sees anything but its own interest. . . . It is time for Europe to raise itself to better and more disinterested perspectives. Before speaking to Oriental nations about their duties toward us, it would do to think about those we bear toward them."[69] Hornung's approach to non-European societies was by no means egalitarian, and he regarded Europe's duties toward Asia as those of superiors to inferiors.[70] Yet he was a more astute critic than most of his colleagues of the interested motivations that prompted ostensibly scientific inquiry among the European jurists. As he saw it, the broader question of mutual obligations under international law tended to collapse into the less challenging question of what Europeans could demand of those to whom they extended membership in the international system.

Another group formed in the 1870s was the Association for the Reform and Codification of the Law of Nations, which, though it was organized by Americans (including Field), met in Europe and had a large European membership.[71] This group, too, formed a committee to study the application of international law to non-European states, but whereas the Institut de droit international, as we have seen, settled on the self-interested question of European legal rights abroad, the Codification Association framed the problem as one of European attitudes of lawlessness. As the committee reported at the association's meeting in 1876,

> The root of the evil lies in the fact that even such imperfectly defined principles of international law as exist are not regarded as binding by Christian, in their intercourse with non-Christian, states. China and Japan have now been happily received into the comity of nations; and it is to be desired that other countries similarly situated should also be invited to enter into diplomatic relations with Europe and America. It is doubtless the duty of civilized governments to employ moral influence to induce a non-Christian people to reform its laws, when these are characterized by injustice or barbarity; but to interfere with the administration of its affairs by force is not only to do violence to the rights of an independent power, but to run the risk of undermining an authority which is probably the only barrier between order and anarchy.[72]

The member who had proposed taking up the question—an American, like Field—was the Congregationalist minister and Egyptologist Joseph Parrish Thompson (1819–1879), who lived in Berlin in the 1870s and involved himself in various European reformist schemes. Pointing to the contrast between the universal European horror at Ottoman atrocities against Bulgarian subjects, and the widespread acceptance of British troops' burning of villages in Ashanti and Dahomey in West Africa as "punishment and warning," Thompson noted "how far Christendom yet is from unanimity as to what constitutes brutality in war, or what measure of brutality would justify protest and intervention in the name of humanity." Thompson's project was in one sense broader in scope than the Institut's, "at once more comprehensive and more radical," as he put it, in that he sought to codify principles of interaction between Europeans (or, in his terms, Christians) and *all* non-Christian "peoples," whether they were states or "roving hordes . . . not recognized as states."[73] Thompson noted (drawing on his travels among bedouins in the Arabian Peninsula) that even if nomadic tribes did not mark boundaries as sedentary societies do, nonetheless, they have "some notion of territorial limits and public law," which should be drawn upon in codifying European relations with them.[74]

A recurrent "criterion" for inclusion within the scope of international law was said to be the ability to engage in reciprocal relations, rendered variously as an ethical notion particular to certain religions, or as a capacity of cognition or will, whether determined by race, or, as in Mill's thought, by civilizational stage. Relations between civilized nations and "barbarians" could not be governed by the law of nations, Mill argued, because "barbarians will not reciprocate. They cannot be depended on for observing any rules. Their minds are not capable of so great an effort."[75] Twiss similarly stressed the capacity of societies' members for reciprocity (rather than, say, the structure of their governments) when he argued in his Institut report that the question of the scope of international law could not be addressed until one had addressed "a prior question that is very serious, and that concerns the oriental peoples themselves, that of knowing whether they are capable, to the same degree as Western peoples, of admitting a moral basis of reciprocity with other peoples who do not accept the same religious sanctions." For Twiss the question was one not of mental ability but rather religious precept; he maintained that the moral code of the Qur'an is at the same time a code of international law, "which prohibits relations of equality and reciprocity between the house of Islam and infidel countries."[76] Twiss conceded that the Ottoman Empire had, under Sultan Abdülmecid I (Abdul Mejid), "submitted to the influence of the general civilization of the nineteenth century," and had reinterpreted its duties under the Qur'an, with results such as the proclamation of 1839 that all subjects of the empire enjoyed equal rights, irrespective of religion. Still, while Twiss proposed that China and Japan posed no cultural obstacles to reciprocity, and that major reforms in the Ottoman state counteracted Islam's suspected refusal to engage in reciprocal relations, he himself concluded that these states could not yet be considered full members of the international community, which he continued to equate with the "system of public law, which has grown up amongst the Nations of Christendom" and the "European concert of public law." In a chapter added for his treatise's second edition, Twiss justified the capitulation regime as indispensable to "qualify" the Ottoman state to participate in the European law of nations. While he noted that there had been "from the earliest times" two schools of Muslim thought, and that the "larger and more liberal views have obtained the ascendant" in the Ottoman Porte over the belief in permanent hostility with non-Muslims, he continued to stress the "religious abyss, which separates Islam from Christendom."[77]

In a series of articles written in the 1870s, Twiss did make a more emphatic case that, as he put it in a pamphlet on conventions governing lighthouses, "Asiatic and African states . . . have recently been admitted into the

European concert of public law."[78] These articles illustrate how international law could be mobilized as an aid to the expansion of European commercial and imperial power not only by excluding non-European states from the international legal community, and thus justifying European violation of otherwise applicable norms of respect for sovereign independence, but also precisely by including them on compromised terms. Twiss's argumentative move was akin to that of John Kasson, the American delegate to the Berlin Conference, in which sovereignty was attributed to African rulers in treaties ceding territorial rights to the Europeans.[79] Andrew Fitzmaurice argues that in the lighthouse pamphlet, "Twiss was making the quite remarkable claim for equality between European states and the Muslim states of Africa in international law,"[80] and that both Twiss and Field "argued for the equality of non-European nations precisely in order to extend European and American empires," through arguments stressing not the rights but the duties of sovereignty. "One might ask whether, in all such instances, arguments for equality could also become premises of dependence," he concludes. As Fitzmaurice acutely observes, for such thinkers, legal incorporation served as a technique of domination and imperial expansion.

But we might also ask whether these were indeed arguments for equality. Twiss assumed the one-sided duty of non-European states to accept the rules already developed by European states, and presupposed their subordinated position in various respects, including, most notably, extraterritorial privileges for resident Europeans, which he and others saw as indispensable for the time being, as well as other forms of supervision such as an East Asian maritime customs regime that, Twiss himself noted, was "entirely under the direction of European officers." The "two great civilised nations of the far East," Twiss wrote, had "acceded effectively to the established practice of the nations of the Western world." This acquiescence, as Fitzmaurice has noted, "sanctioned their submission to an international regime, where necessary, in order to meet those obligations."[81] Twiss described it as the duty of the Statesmen of Europe "to mould the future international relations of the Mussulman and the Christian races," and suggested that "steadfast adherence to the principles of Public Law" was "the best guarantee" for the improvement of those relations.[82] Twiss, then, envisioned Europeans inhabiting the controlling role in the international legal system, and as unilaterally representing the "interests of humanity" in their interactions with extra-European states that could gain recognition only by accepting European law and leadership.[83]

Article 7 of the 1856 Treaty of Paris formally "declare[d] the Sublime Porte admitted to participate in the advantages of the Public Law and System (*Concert*) of Europe," with the signatories pledging "to respect the independence and the territorial integrity of the Ottoman Empire." Yet discussions of the abolition of extraterritoriality during the Paris conference led nowhere, and the treaty promised that the powers would revisit the question in a future conference that never took place. Even if it had, as Turan Kayaoğlu has argued based on British and American official documents, the powers would have rejected the abolition of extraterritorial privileges, even while those privileges undermined the Ottoman state's capacity to carry out the very reforms the Western powers were demanding.[84] And so the Ottoman Empire's admission to the Concert of Europe was "a pyrrhic victory," even a sham.[85] While some lawyers, such as Phillimore, insisted that Turkey had been formally and unambiguously inducted into international society and the European "family of nations," members of the Institute of International Law were still disputing the question two decades later. Even those who were prepared to recognize that the Ottoman Empire had been "received as a Peer into the European Parliament of States" before 1856 did not regard it as a legal equal, as the extraterritorial privileges still held by Europeans in the Ottoman Empire indicated.[86]

In contrast to colleagues who purported to recognize the Ottoman Empire as a peer while subverting its legal equality through support for continued extraterritorial privileges, James Lorimer insisted that the recognition of what he called a "phantom state" had always been a farce that was best abandoned for frank acceptance of Europe's duty to civilize the place by conquest.[87] Lorimer, who held the Regius Chair of Public Law and of the Law of Nature and of Nations at the University of Edinburgh, devoted several of his annual introductory lectures in public law during the 1870s to the impossibility of any reciprocal relations between European and Muslim states. "To talk of the recognition of Mahometan States as a question of time," Lorimer wrote with characteristic dispatch, "is to talk nonsense," for Islam, whatever its truth or falsehood, "is always false when seen from an international point of view. . . . We are thus driven to assume towards it the same uncompromising attitude which it presents to us."[88] He maintained that capitulation treaties demonstrated the absurdity of any claims of Ottoman sovereignty.[89] The "Turks," on largely religious and racial grounds, were "bankrupt . . . of every quality of a nation." Lorimer had idiosyncratic preoccupations and unusually explicit prejudices compared with his more conventionally positivist colleagues. His international thought was overtly racist.[90] He rejected the notions, fundamental to the emerging positivist dogma, of the legal equality and independence of European states; the "insincere recognition of [the] jural equality" of great powers and minor European states had "doomed" the latter to exclusion from international politics, whereas honest recognition of their separate but inferior status would earn them genuine, if modest, influence ("Half a loaf is better than no bread," he remarked).[91] Despite these differences of language and political program, however, Lorimer's arguments are revealing in that he articulated openly what often remained more implicit in others' work. He placed the doctrine of recognition at the heart of international law, and regarded the capacity to reciprocate as the key criterion for recognition, thus making the foundational moment of international law the judgment by insiders of the fitness of outsiders for inclusion in their community of mutual obligation.[92] While Lorimer's insistence that the law of nature underlies international law made it especially clear that his universalist legal aspirations were compromised by his European particularism, such a tension was present throughout this literature.[93] Ostensibly general and abstract theoretical provisions, such as Lorimer's criterion that a state have the capacity for "reciprocating will," proved to be the exclusive province of European states for an indefinite, though in principle, limited period.[94]

Lorimer himself claimed, with some justice, to be simply attempting to theorize explicitly the political reality of states' unequal status that others recognized but attempted to veil with legal fictions. Like the critics of legal exclusions of Asian states whom I discuss below, though from a very different political perspective, Lorimer recognized the hypocrisy of Europe's legal posture toward Turkey and other Asian powers. Rather than calling as the critics did for political practice that might live up to international law's universal pretensions, he sought the revision of the legal framework to reflect what were, in his view, justifiably unequal practices.[95] Lorimer, though unusual in his embrace of (an idiosyncratic) naturalism, made particularly plain an impulse he shared with many positivist legal thinkers of the period—the insistence that they were basing their legal theories on bare "fact." Legal sovereignty, for instance, was merely a declaratory recognition of an independent reality: "International law can no more create a State, add to it, or diminish it, than it can create a man, or increase or diminish his stature."[96] This insistence on "fact" as the basis of law led Lorimer and others to naturalize the conventional and so to deny the idea that practices of sovereignty were not simply conventions but—as Ward, for one, had recognized—peculiarly European conventions whose exclusions and hierarchies remained unacknowledged and unjustified.[97]

Lorimer called on Europeans to give up the sham by which they pretended to regard the Ottoman Empire as a legal equal, and instead conquer Constantinople and use the city as the home for a new international legislature, executive, and judiciary body, which, given Lorimer's restricted notions of international membership, was really more a European community. Thus, he argued, with a remarkable combination of cynicism and utopianism, "in the only possible answer which I can see to this Eastern Question, I am not without hope that we shall find the only possible answer to the central question of International Jurisprudence.". Only such a world government would make possible the "conversion of International Law from a positive system in the scientific sense, into a positive system in the practical sense."[98] Lorimer's project to "denationalize" Constantinople was more audacious and bizarre than most. But he was characteristic in his confidence that European experiments in the "semi-barbarous" societies at Europe's periphery could furnish solutions to the greatest challenges of international society.[99]

Lorimer's overt preoccupation, even obsession, with biological race distinguished him from most of his international law colleagues, but on this and other subjects his eccentricity masks a deeper affinity with more conventional colleagues, as well as what Gerry Simpson describes as his chilling and uncanny "prescience."[100] He tied his scientific aspirations for international law to his hopes for a science of race: "No modern contribution to science seems destined to influence international politics and jurisprudence to so great an extent as that which is known as ethnology, or the science of races."[101] He issued diagnoses of societal infancy and senility even more casual than Mill's: "I would give up the farce of pretending that he [the 'Turk'] was *sui juris* when, if not in his dotage, he was plainly in his minority."[102] His racial essentialism meant that he was less interested in specifying his developmental claims than were perfectionists such as Mill or Maine, though he shared Maine's worry that civilizing projects disrupted traditional societies without improving them.[103] But his sense that racial differences as yet uncomprehended by science might perhaps underlie political differences, and influence political and legal relations, was more widespread, and his naturalizing arguments were more widely shared by liberals.[104]

The Naturalization and Racialization
of International Hierarchy

One notable device of naturalization was the tendency in Victorian accounts of progress, in both legal writing and social and political theory more broadly, to individualize the developmental narrative. Societal development was commonly conceptualized as, at root, the result of the improved faculties of individual members of a society: their capacity for abstract thought, their willpower, their ability to delay gratification, their ability to subjugate individual desires to the needs of the collective. Not only were nations analogized to individuals as having infancy, maturity, and senility or dotage, but also individual members of societies seen as being at an early stage of development were understood as having deficiencies of mind and character. This view of progress as a matter of individual cognitive development, as opposed to an irreducibly social phenomenon (as it was, for instance, in the work of Adam Smith), had direct implications for understandings of these societies' legal standing.

Sometimes this tendency—for instance, to speak of "the savage" or "the barbarian" in the singular—seems a mere quirk of language. In the course of his argument that Western European progress is the exception to the rule of human stagnation, Maine wrote that "much the greatest part of mankind has never shown a particle of desire that its civil institutions should be improved since the moment when external completeness was first given to them by their embodiment in some permanent record," as though societal progress could be accounted for at the level of individual will or desire.[105] Mill, similarly, proposed that "the savage cannot bear to sacrifice, for any purpose, the satisfaction of his individual will. His social cannot even temporarily prevail over his selfish feelings, nor his impulses bend to his calculations." After characterizing the failings of savages and slaves in their extreme forms, Mill extended the argument to peoples who "approach to the conditions of savages or of slaves" to explain, for instance, why civilized belligerents usually defeat their less civilized foes. He argued that the reason for such patterns is that cooperation, like other attributes of civilization, "can be learnt only by practice," and he described this learning process as one undergone by individuals.[106] Like Maine, Mill held that such deficiencies in powers of mind and will justified a suspension of legal norms in European relations with non-European societies. His essay on non-intervention is striking in its use of this casual and speculative philosophical anthropology to justify the exercise of vast coercive political and military power.

Mill withheld application of law to relations with "barbarians" and justified civilizing despotism not simply on the grounds that such rule was necessary to undermine the power of entrenched and oppressive political structures and social hierarchies. Rather, his claim was that the rational capacities of individuals in such societies were so immature that they were incapable of being "guided to their improvement by conviction or persuasion," as he put it in *On Liberty*.[107] Even if Mill largely resisted biological racism, the naturalization of difference between Europeans and members of other societies suggested in his individualization of their differences undermined the universal trajectory implied in the liberal narrative of progress and incorporation.[108] Further, while the "civilized" continued to bear moral obligations to such people—"the universal rules of morality between man and man"—the implication of the contrast between legal rights and such rules of morality is that only the civilized are in a position to judge the content of their own moral duty; such duties generate no claims on the part of others, and their violation does not constitute an injury that might generate a right of resistance.

Others who invoked the distinction between legal and moral obligations rhetorically minimized the implications of legal exclusion by glossing law as a kind of trifling formalism, as when T. J. Lawrence maintained that

> the area within which the law of nations operates is supposed to coincide with the area of civilization. To be received within it is to obtain a kind of international testimonial of good conduct and respectability; and when a state hitherto accounted barbarous desires admission, the leading powers settle the case upon its merits. In addition to the attainment of a certain, or rather an uncertain, amount of civilization, a state must have possession of a fixed territory before it can obtain the privilege of admission into the family of nations. . . . For there are many communities outside the sphere of International Law, though they are independent states. They neither grant to others, nor claim for themselves the strict observance of its rules. Justice and humanity should be scrupulously adhered to in all dealings with them, but they are not fit subjects for the application of legal technicalities. It would, for instance, be absurd to expect the king of Dahomey to establish a Prize Court, or to require the dwarfs of the central African forest to receive a permanent diplomatic mission.[109]

Several features of this passage are worthy of note: the author's admission of the flimsiness of the standard of civilization (and his acceptance of it, nonetheless); his suggestion that the exclusion of African and other unspecified societies from the sphere of international law is self-imposed; and his racialized gesture at the self-evidence of the exclusion.

John Westlake was characteristic in presenting a racialized account without advancing a theory of biological racial difference, as when he glossed international law as "the rules which are internationally recognised between white men." He went on:

> But wherever the native inhabitants can furnish no government capable of fulfilling the purposes fulfilled by the Asiatic empires, which is the case of most of the populations with whom Europeans have come into contact in America and Africa, the first necessity is that a government should be furnished. The inflow of the white race cannot be stopped where there is land to cultivate, ore to be mined, commerce to be developed, sport to enjoy, curiosity to be satisfied. If any fanatical admirer of savage life argued that the whites ought to be kept out, he would only be driven to the same conclusion by another route, for a government on the spot would be necessary to keep them out. Accordingly international law has to treat such natives as uncivilised. It regulates, for the mutual benefit of civilised states, the claims which they make to sovereignty over the region, and leaves the treatment of the natives to the conscience of the state to which the sovereignty is awarded, rather than sanction their interest being made an excuse the more for war between civilised claimants, devastating the region and the cause of suffering to the natives themselves.[110]

Such naturalizing language reinforces the impression of the impotence of law in the face of "fact" and of possibly innate differences among peoples: "Natives in the rudimentary condition supposed take no rights under international law," because, Westlake asserted by means of a telling metaphor, "a stream cannot rise higher than its source." In such accounts, the exclusion of Africans from the purview of international law appears overdetermined; Westlake implies, without interrogating, mutually reinforcing disparate grounds for limiting international law to the "mutual benefit of civilised states." His tacit developmental narrative suggests that a state apparatus to regulate commerce and land use is a telos of societal evolution, as well as a necessary condition for international recognition, but because Africans cannot supply such government independently, their subjection to the sovereignty of a European power is inevitable. International law cannot prohibit economic exploitation and colonization by Europeans; to try not only would be futile but also would involve a bizarre fetishization of "savage" life. International law within Europe was both enforced and developed by means of public opinion; a "justly offended state" may be left "to fight its own battle, but it receives a moral support from the general recognition that its resort to arms was the exercise of a right," and the "offender is made to feel the loss of sympathy which his conduct has occasioned."[111] In insisting on the limited scope of application of international law, Westlake rendered it impervious to emendation or expansion to encompass either African claims or African interests. For all their aspirations that international law might serve as the "juridical conscience of the civilized world" and as an ever more potent mechanism for taming the power and violence of the modern state, jurists abdicated responsibility by declaring the impotence of law in the face of European colonial aspirations.

Critical Uses of International Law

In addition to the resistance mounted by lawyers from the "semi-periphery" that Arnulf Becker Lorca has explored, a small number of European writers dissented against the exclusion of extra-European states, particularly Asian commercial states, from the scope of international law.[112] In faint echoes of a recurrent trope of earlier centuries (among thinkers such as Montaigne and Diderot), a few writers lambasted the instability and presumption of the very language of civilization.[113] Henry E. J. Stanley (1827–1903), a gifted linguist, sometime diplomat, and Muslim convert, presented a series of powerful arguments against such legal exclusions in an edited volume titled *The East and the West: Our Dealings with Our Neighbours* (London, 1865).[114] Stanley's collection of unsigned essays denounced the hypocrisy of the discourse of civilization and its pernicious consequences for international law, asserting that Europeans had long cultivated "anti-humanitarian" habits of lawlessness in Asia.[115] Stanley regarded the "perversion of ideas" through the use of terms such as "civilization" and "expediency" as one element of the European arrogance that engendered contempt for international law, bullying and violent abuse of Asian states from Turkey to Japan to Siam, and the widespread acceptance in Britain of a "rapidly increasing number of little wars."[116] What is perhaps most striking about these essays is their historical self-consciousness: their criticism of the peculiar form that European hypocrisy and aggression had taken in the nineteenth century, and their nostalgia for an earlier understanding of the law of nations as based on universal moral commitments. In this sense Stanley was an Alexandrowicz avant la lettre; using Vattel as a touchstone, and alluding, with reference to the Stoic Seneca, to a natural law grounding for international law, he regarded nineteenth-century European understandings of international law as derogations from an earlier universalist international law more truly grounded on principles of state equality and reciprocity.

The East and the West began with a critique of consular jurisdiction and extraterritoriality as arrangements that typified nineteenth-century Europeans' exploitation of older legal forms and their misinterpretation of history to justify their abuses. Consular jurisdiction was not, as Europeans now insisted, "an abstract right which can be claimed," but a concession that had been made by host governments for the mutual convenience of themselves and foreign residents, always revocable if it did not serve the host's interests. Similarly, the British notion that a Roman precedent (encapsulated by *"civis romanus sum"*) legitimated the exercise of British power around the world to "protect" British subjects rested on a poor reading of Roman history.[117] Compounding such convenient historical errors, the volume suggests, was the deeper problem of a tendentious developmental narrative that undermined the international rights of non-European states. Thus, "One of the first principles of international law is, that all nations are equal, without regard to their size or importance, or to the form of their government"; nineteenth-century Europeans were guilty of "setting aside [the] principle of equality amongst nations, by fanciful divisions of civilised and uncivilised."[118]

The volume's essay titled "The Effects of Contempt for International Law" deconstructed the rhetorical moves by which contemporaries had dismantled the earlier, more properly reciprocal, international law (the repetition of themes from the preface suggests Stanley as the likely author of this essay). Authors blurred the descriptive and normative meanings of "civilization" in order to claim Europe's moral superiority with reference to its technological achievements: "Perhaps the improvement of the nineteenth century is only material, and there is a falling off in the respect felt for legality and the rights of others." Stanley contended that the nineteenth century had replaced an older religious rhetoric of exclusion with the "watchword" "civilization," which served simply to proscribe those who differ from the persons who utter it, and to deprive them of those rights which all men possess in common, and to get rid of those obligations which all members of the family of mankind owe to one another. The modern term is more vague, more elastic, more unjust; and it serves to deprive the Chinese of the rights of international law and its mutual obligations, equally with the Feejee Islanders, or other cannibals.

There had in fact, Stanley argued, been a moral decline in the substitution of "civilization" for Christianity as the pretext for aggression, since the underlying motive of commercial dominance was undisguisedly selfish, whereas religion, for all the evils perpetrated in its name, had at least mobilized a few "to plead for the vanquished." The essay pointed to the variability and irrelevance of European "standards" of civilization: De-Maistre limited it to "nations which study Latin," Richard Cobden looked to "miles of electric telegraph" and numbers of daily newspapers. The Chinese, with as much justice, the essay argued, could point to "respect for the law, and the most ancient annals," the Japanese to the absence of pauperism. More important than the elasticity of the standard of civilization, however, was its irrelevance to legal status: "Since civilisation confers no rights over the uncivilised, it is not strictly necessary to inquire what is civilisation, or by what it is tested."[119] Despite that claim, the line dispensing with Fijians and "other cannibals" suggests that Stanley, for all his criticism of the emptiness of the language of civilization, and like others who defended the inclusion of Asian commercial societies within the scope of international law, was willing to move the boundary of the community of legal reciprocity further along a spectrum of development to exclude ostensibly savage societies (as Burke had also arguably done, as we saw in Chapter 4). Still, his insistence on the indefensibility of the "standard" of civilization and the power that the term's elasticity gave states such as Britain to justify aggression toward its trading partners throughout Asia, and his demand for a more truly reciprocal international legal order (figured as a return to an older model), represents a provocative moment in the Victorian debate over the scope of international law.

Stanley's volume was unusual in its hostility to the system of consular jurisdiction and insistence upon the full legal personality of Asian states, but we find its arguments echoed in the London *Times*, in several unsigned articles by the correspondent and leader writer Antonio Gallenga published in the summer of 1868. These pieces called in acerbic tones for a reform of

[handwritten marginal note: ridiculous markers of civilisation?]

the system of consular jurisdiction in the Ottoman Empire and Egypt; they castigated Europeans' cultural arrogance, "bigotry," and "hypocrisy," and charged that Europe's patent violations of international law and standards of reciprocity stemmed from European contempt for Muslim societies and legal institutions.[120] The legal argument of these articles was unambiguous: whereas all international law could be established only on the basis of "spontaneousness and reciprocity," Europeans "enjoyed and claimed rights, privileges, and immunities for which their respective Governments offered no reciprocity." Extraterritoriality was grounded in nothing but the chauvinistic "opinion of the Europeans [that] no fair award of justice could be expected from a Mussulman Tribunal, while the Consular Courts were so vastly above all reproach and suspicion that Mahomedans, as well as Christians, might rely on their infallibility and incorruptibility."[121] It was within the rights of the Ottoman government under international law to demand that Europeans either submit to local jurisdiction or leave the country; any other legal arrangements, such as the mixed tribunals recommended by the author, had to gain the approval of the Ottoman authorities. These articles were strikingly more inclusive in their understanding of international law and the duties it imposed on Europeans than were the prominent international lawyers of the time. They suggest that there was a place in the broader public debate about international law for the position that Europeans were obligated under international law to treat at least certain non-European states with the respect and reciprocity due to sovereign states, and for the inclination to question European cultural confidence and the categories of barbarous and civilized.[122]

While the Ottoman Empire's status, especially after 1856, was the case most persistently debated, the political and legal status of the hundreds of Indian principalities that remained outside direct British rule was similarly in dispute during this period.[123] Were they, as the British parliament sometimes put it, "princes and states in alliance with Her Majesty," whose sovereignty had to be respected under international law, or were they, as other statutes had it, under British "suzerainty" and therefore without any international standing whatsoever? Was the language of sovereignty and international law that the British state sometimes used evidence of these states' true status, or meaningless rhetoric? In the wake of the Sepoy Rebellion of 1857 to 1858, some of those who held the former view charged that Britain's aggressive policy of annexing Indian principalities, which had intensified under the governor-generalship of Lord Dalhousie (1848–1856), not only was a violation of international law but also was in large measure responsible for provoking the rebellion and might ultimately lead to the violent overthrow of British rule in India.

The polymath scholar and writer Francis W. Newman (brother of John Henry, Cardinal Newman) argued in a series of articles between 1858 and 1863 that the Indian principalities were independent states whose relations with Britain were "international," and toward which Britain had (and perpetually violated) strict obligations to fulfill its treaties. In a *Westminster Review* article of 1858, Newman argued that Dalhousie's aggressive annexation policy had been a principal cause of the Sepoy Rebellion. While Newman lacked the international lawyers' professional concern to establish the scope of international law, he pointedly described Lord Dalhousie's annexation measures as an aspect of "foreign policy" and spoke of the "national rights" of the peoples annexed or slated for annexation.[124]

Newman noted the hypocrisy with which the British had appealed to law in their dealings with Indian states: they had extorted agreements by force and then piously insisted on the treaties' terms; or they turned to accounts of Indian immaturity or degeneracy when the letter of a treaty was inconvenient. Typical of this approach, he suggested, was Dalhousie's avowed strategy of using the policy of lapse to take (in the governor-general's own words) "any *just* opportunity for consolidating the territories that already belong to us." Newman commented: "The word *just*, thus used by English statesmen towards Asiatics, means *in accordance with treaty*, quite regardless of the questions whether that treaty was obtained by unjustifiable violence, (as were *all* our treaties with Oude,) and whether the party who made the treaty had any legal or moral right to make it." Newman noted that British writers dwelt on sensational but irrelevant descriptions of Indian princes' personal vices in order to obscure "the fact, that we have entered into solemn public treaties with these dynasties."[125]

Although Newman shared the nearly universal British view that Indians as a whole were still "unfit . . . for democratic representation," he regarded as a "gratuitous and illogical insult" the suggestion that there were no Indians fit for the civil service and for high judicial and bureaucratic office.[126] He believed that immediate extension of citizenship and political rights to Indian elites would make broader democratic participation and self-government imminently possible, and he looked forward to Indian independence in the not-too-distant future with equanimity.[127] While he hoped such self-government might be accomplished without bloodshed, he warned that British injustices would almost inevitably provoke violent rebellion; respect for Indian states as participants in international law was both just and prudent.[128] Newman's arguments for the jural independence and international subjecthood of those states represented a minority view in Britain, even though the British parliament remained content to refer to the Indian princes as allied states, at least into the 1870s. Legal texts rarely discussed the status of the states, and those that did regarded the states as dependent entities with nonexistent, or, occasionally, nominal international status.[129]

Conclusion

Victorian international lawyers converged around a distinctive historical narrative despite apparently deep divergences among thinkers on key theoretical questions, particularly concerning the relative merits of natural law versus positivist, and historical versus analytical, approaches. Conceptions of civilization and barbarism, rendered in the scientific idioms of sociology and legal positivism, offered thinkers a means by which to assert the universal validity of European moral and political norms while forestalling inquiry into that assertion. Although they sometimes recognized Europe as a major source of violence in the world, in both wars within the continent and colonial and commercial expansion, they saw Europe as the vanguard of human progress and therefore granted it the benefit of the doubt as to its alleged pacific "tendency" and also its right to continue to deploy violence through its "police authority over barbarous races." T. J. Lawrence noted, with some acerbity but also a typical dismissal of the effects of European violence on its victims, a different propensity of European commerce: "to cause little wars by forcing at the sword's point upon barbarous tribes the blessing of cheap calico and adulterated rum."[130] Legal writers, like contemporary social and political theorists such as Mill who shared their progressive historical theory, thus routinely combined a series of narrative and argumentative moves. They registered anxiety about the state of European civilization while nonetheless affirming its progressive "tendency," which then underwrote Europe's right to adjudicate international legal norms and to deploy violence in an administrative (rather than either political or legal) mode over those societies Europeans deemed not yet candidates for legal inclusion.

These thinkers saw international law itself as both an index and a source of progress. Laws were becoming ever more precise and authoritative with the progress of civilization in a teleological process, so that the existing framework of international law was the partial realization of a historical trajectory and the harbinger of the complete system that would someday emerge.[131] In this sense, the state of international law was a reflection of the state of human progress. International law could also drive that progress by securing the peace that would enable further material, cultural, and intellectual development and also by codifying, entrenching, and therefore speeding, the "progress of opinion."[132] International lawyers' accounts of the development of nations and of international practice were thus, as Koskenniemi has shown, also narratives in which they, as international lawyers, figured prominently as those who could "articulate and . . . represent" Europe's evolving *conscience*—in the sense of both its moral conscience and its consciousness, its knowledge of objective truth.[133]

Although Europe was understood to be the source of progressive civilization, peace and order within the continent were seen as precarious. International law needed to be codified and extended precisely because the increasing sophistication of destructive weaponry and the increasing power at the disposal of states produced a constant threat of escalating violence. Peace and civilization thus stood in a relationship of tension. International law figured as a key means by which the morally progressive features of civilization, including a perceptible tendency toward peace (thanks, in a typical formulation, to commerce, democracy, and Christianity), might be brought to triumph over its vices.[134] Maine's posthumously published *International Law* (1888) exemplified concerns that tendencies to peace implicit in the development of an increasingly integrated European system of states were simultaneously threatened by technological developments that increased the destructiveness of war. The buoyant view following the long peace that had held from 1815 up to the outbreak of the Crimean War— that "Captain Pen had vanquished Captain Sword"—had, Maine worried, been tested by the succession of subsequent conflicts that testified to the "prodigious forces which seem now to make for war. . . . We know of no limit to the power of destroying human life."[135] Indeed, Maine argued that Europeans had lately abandoned a long-standing inclination to ban the most horrific new weaponry, in part because technological innovation was so quick that it was rarely possible to ban particular weapons before others more or differently destructive were invented. Maine held out hope that the "thrill of horror through the civilised world" that would follow an action such as the torpedoing of a neutral or friendly ship (though not horror at human suffering or death as such) meant that it was still possible to use public opinion and the international law that embodied it to tame state violence.[136] But he shared the late Victorian anxiety that civilization as a matter of material development posed a potentially lethal threat to civilization as a moral achievement.

What the Victorian lawyers rarely interrogated were the ways in which their normative idea of civilization itself enabled violence and domination. The narrative of a progressive European order that had succeeded in taming violence among "civilized" states belittled the brutality of late Victorian imperial rule and expansion by regarding imperial conflicts as "little wars" incidental to the international system. It also obscured the systemic connections between the violence that Europeans inflicted outside the boundaries of their continent and aggression within and between European states themselves. As W. E. B. Du Bois would write in 1917, when many Europeans were perceiving the First World War as an unprecedented and almost inexplicable eruption of irrational violence,

> As we see the dead dimly through rifts of battle smoke and hear faintly the cursing and accusations of blood brothers, we darker men say: This is not Europe gone mad; this is not aberration nor insanity; this *is* Europe; this seeming terrible is the real soul of white culture. . . . Is then this war the end of war? Can it be the end so long as its prime cause, the despising and robbery of darker peoples sits enthroned even in the souls of those who cry peace? So if Europe hugs this delusion then this is not the end of world war—it is the beginning.[137]

Epilogue

T HE IMAGE ON this book's cover is a detail from a study by William Rothenstein (1872–1945) for his mural *Sir Thomas Roe at the Court of Ajmir, 1614,* in St. Stephen's Hall in the Palace of Westminster. It depicts the durbar at which the Mughal Emperor Jahangir received England's first ambassador to India, who was named by the English East India Company and approved by King James I and was thus typical of the marriage of corporate and state power that characterized modern Europe's expansion into the extra-European world.[1] However unintentionally, the study conveys, in a way that the ornate and rather static final painting in the Houses of Parliament does not, something of the tentative, unfinished, and unstable nature of the international legal order that was emerging out of such encounters between early modern empires. Roe's mission had ambiguous resonances in Britain in 1925, when the painting was commissioned. Part of a sequence conceived by the poet, historian, and government advisor Sir Henry Newbolt to commemorate great events in "The Building of Britain," the scene could be read as prefiguring the British Empire's rise to global hegemony: a representation, as Newbolt wrote in the painting's inscription, of Roe's success "by his courtesy and firmness at the court of Ajmir, in laying the foundations of British influence in India."[2]

But Rothenstein may have regarded the event differently. An ardent promoter of Indian art and artists in the face of what he saw as British contempt for Indian artistic achievement past and present, he had founded the India Society in 1910 to educate the British public about the fine arts in India. Throughout his life he urged greater recognition of and official commissions for contemporary Indian painters.[3] During a visit to India in

1910–1911 to study fifth-century Buddhist frescoes in the Ajanta caves and learn about Indian aesthetics, Rothenstein met Rabindranath Tagore, who became a lifelong friend and correspondent; his nephew, the painter Abanindranath Tagore; and other members of what came to be called the Bengal School, all fellow participants in an emerging global modernism. The Bengal School emphasized the importance of engaging both Asian and European aesthetics and of placing them on equal footing, rather than turning to premodern Indian art in an indigenist resistance to modernism. Rothenstein was attracted to their modernist vision, at once cosmopolitan and contextual, and he drew inspiration from their work and from historical Indian painting and sculpture in the sketches he made in India. It has been argued that he remained disappointed, however, at his own inability to "incorporate any sense of Indian aesthetics as he had understood them" into his more formal painting. That failure may partly account for the difference between Rothenstein's sketch for the *Roe* mural, whose fluid lines and washes of vivid color evoke the work of Abanindranath Tagore that he so admired, and Rothenstein's more rigid final mural.[4]

Though never an overt advocate of Indian independence, Rothenstein was receptive enough to Indian nationalism to dismiss warnings before his journey by a friend at the India Office that "my sympathy for Indians and for things Indian would encourage the Nationalists, now beginning to be heard through Gokhale and Tilak," and he met with Gopal Krishna Gokhale, a leader in the Indian independence movement, toward the end of his stay.[5] Rothenstein's distance from formal politics, and also his efforts to participate in egalitarian forms of community with Indians in spite of an imperial domination he deplored, are suggested by a letter from the Bengali philosopher and poet Brajendranath Seal, who met with Rothenstein in London after participating in the 1911 Universal Races Congress, at which W. E. B. Du Bois and Gokhale both spoke. Seal wrote to the painter after his return to Calcutta,

> These are the first lines I write on reaching home, and my heart turns instinctively to what impressed me most profoundly in my recent visit to the West,—more even than the meeting of representatives of fifty nationalities at the Universal Races Congress;—for in my relations with you and yours, I had a genuine experience of life in one of its finest phases—the capacity of human love and sympathy to transcend all external barriers that divide man from man—indeed to convert the marks

of division themselves into fresh sources and occasions of a joyous self-expression.[6]

Rothenstein's own efforts to find mutuality within the empire are conveyed in a letter he wrote in September 1914 to the author and scholar of Bengali literature Dinesh Chandra Sen, whose work he was trying to get published in Britain:

> We are all, as you may imagine, dominated by our absorbing interest in the grave events across the channel. That India should have shown us how fraternal her feelings are towards us has been a very moving thing to me, who have always loved your country with a deep affection. That your grievances should be so generously forgotten at the first token of our need has touched the whole of England.[7]

Not long after his return to Britain, Rothenstein had initiated the translation of a selection of Rabindranath Tagore's poems by the India Society, published as *Gitanjali* in 1912, which Tagore dedicated to him and which precipitated the poet's global reception and his receipt of the Nobel Prize in 1913. When, in protest against the Amritsar massacre in 1919, Tagore resigned his knighthood in an open letter to the British viceroy "giving voice to the protest of the millions of my countrymen, surprised into a dumb anguish of terror," Rothenstein wrote him to express admiration for Tagore's letter as well as something of his own political perplexity.

> You have not put off, but have put on dignity . . . I too have had no easy task & know something of the difficulty of yours. We are expected to be pros or antis; as a matter of fact we can never be consistently either. . . . One hopes the years, be they few or many, still left to one will allow one to make up for past weaknesses. How to serve it is not always easy to see.[8]

Such perplexity may explain Rothenstein's largely apolitical efforts to "serve" by way of several decades' engagement in the work of the India Society to promote Indian arts and letters. He also seized upon the 1926 Parliamentary commission as an opportunity to revisit his Indian material. Perhaps the constraints of the official task conspired with his own felt inability to bring Indian aesthetics into his painting, for the final and better-known mural, in its stolidity and conventional Orientalism, too thoroughly evokes the British imperial self-importance the series commissioners seem to have had in mind. The livelier study shown on this book's cover, however,

may convey something of what Rothenstein himself perceived in the
Ajanta frescoes, "a great joy in the surpassing radiance of the face of the
world," as well as a sense of incompletion, of the possibility that the relationship between Britain and India might yet unfold on the footing of respect and mutuality that this depiction of the diplomatic encounter
implies.[9]

For C. H. Alexandrowicz, writing in Madras after India's independence,
the Roe embassy was emblematic of precisely such a legal disposition of
equality and mutual recognition and respect:

> Sir Thomas Roe on arriving in India found himself in a part of the world
> in which the exchange of ambassadors between rulers was based on a
> tradition as old as that in Europe. In spite of the difference between Eu-
> ropean and Asian habits and usages, the English ambassador had no dif-
> ficulty in speaking a common language of diplomatic custom with the
> Emperor and the authorities of the Empire. He emphasized in the ac-
> count of his embassy that he asserted his right to diplomatic privileges
> not on the basis of the custom of England, but of "the consent of the
> whole world." Neither had he any difficulty in securing for himself and
> his retinue treatment [in] accordance with the law of nations which the
> authorities of the receiving Empire accorded to him with all customary
> courtesy . . . it was obvious that mutual dealings took place on a basis of
> reciprocal acknowledgement of sovereignty and of the principles of the
> law of nations. The position remained the same up to the beginning of
> the nineteenth century.[10]

The encounter was more double-edged than Alexandrowicz would have
liked to admit. Indeed, observed one reviewer of the 1926 republication of
Roe's memoirs, which both Rothenstein and Alexandrowicz drew upon,
the English ambassador "judged the emperor, his son, and his ministers by
his own English standard—an error to which so many of our mistakes in
India have been due. . . . We wonder whether Roe's unflagging anxiety to
assert his dignity and claim respect (of the record of which we get rather
tired) did not strike the observant Oriental as savouring of pride. This attitude is apt to antagonize."[11] For Alexandrowicz, however, as I noted in the
Introduction, it was important in the moment of decolonization to be able
to establish legal precedent for the equal participation of postcolonial states
in international law: to show that when "a restricted number of European
powers proclaimed themselves as the founder group of the modern inter-

national society and assumed authority to admit new member States," they were resting their case on a historical fallacy.[12] Over the next two decades until his death in 1975, against the view that "New States are faced with the *fait accompli* of the existing international legal order and must accept its principles as they find them," Alexandrowicz added further legal and eventually political arguments to his historical case. He observed, in a nod to the positivist deference to state practice, that the practice of the New States "does not supply sufficient evidence of such a *fait accompli*."[13]

Alexandrowicz had in mind, above all, the efforts of postcolonial states to revise "Eurocentric international law" through their "overwhelming majority" in the General Assembly in the name of a New International Economic Order (NIEO). These included resolutions on permanent sovereignty over natural resources that limited the prerogatives of foreign investors against postcolonial states, and the adoption in 1974 of the Charter of Economic Rights and Duties of States by the United Nations Conference on Trade and Development, an organ of the General Assembly.[14] Alexandrowicz further suggested that the principles of self-determination, the universality of the law of nations, and "its non-discriminatory application irrespective of civilisation, religion, race or colour" were *jus cogens* norms: "peremptory norm[s] of general international law . . . from which no derogation is permitted," as described in article 53 of the 1969 Vienna Convention on the Law of Treaties.[15] In turning to *jus cogens*, Alexandrowicz was building on his own long-standing regard for what he saw as the natural law universalism of the pre-nineteenth-century law of nations. At the same time, he was following the efforts of representatives and lawyers from a number of Third World states during and after the Vienna Convention negotiations to make *jus cogens* a means by which "the 'paganism' of classical international law might finally be replaced with a genuinely inclusive and participatory order," as Umut Özsu has summarized the efforts of those lawyers.[16]

The NIEO moment marked a shift in Alexandrowicz's understanding of how international law, and the narration of its history, should relate to politics. He had long maintained that international law and lawyers could and should remain outside politics, restraining "power politicians" by clarifying the rules of international law and making it harder for them to justify their conduct by appeal to principle.[17] He had turned to the history of international law in order to expose the "fallacy" of Eurocentric positivism. Rather than understanding his legal arguments as serving the political goal of a more egalitarian world, he believed historical argument could establish as a matter of "objective" legal principle ("in consonance with the reality of events") that postcolonial states were equal members of a universal legal order.[18] With the NIEO, however, he came to see the necessary "transformation" of international law as something that could occur only through concerted action by postcolonial states. A new state was "hardly in a position" to challenge customary principles of international law when seeking to have its sovereignty recognized by an international community still dominated in so many ways by the former colonial powers. But collectively, through their "overwhelming majority" in the United Nations, they could force "the industrial powers . . . to face the reality of legal change."[19]

Alexandrowicz shared with other proponents of the NIEO the belief that the emancipatory possibilities of a universalist international law could be pursued by postcolonial states working in solidarity, despite the long-standing "co-option" of such principles by Western states and their ideologues.[20] In his 1979 *Towards a New International Economic Order,* arguably the most significant work written in defense of the NIEO, the Algerian jurist and diplomat Mohammed Bedjaoui used "the common heritage of mankind" as an example of a universalistic legal principle that, although "suspect" in light of its long abuse by imperial powers, might still be mobilized to egalitarian ends. He certainly recognized its ongoing vulnerability to abuse. The idea that the basins of the Amazon and Congo, as the world's largest reserves of oxygen, were a common human resource is, he argued, "in itself in no way outrageous." Yet the principle could readily be used to "aggravate domination patterns" as long as "nothing is said" about common human resources held or squandered by rich states, such as intellectual property or the earth's atmosphere.

For all their recognition of what Bedjaoui called the "seeming paradox" that international law, "an instrument of conservation[,] is entrusted with a task of transformation"—its own transformation as well as that of the global economic system—the NIEO's proponents were ultimately unable to resist Western states' use of international law to structure and justify their ongoing domination.[21] The NIEO's project was, in Sundhya Pahuja's judgment, an "exemplary instance in which the Third World or its champions have made an attempt to capture the potential offered by the universal promise of international law and in which that attempt has been subsumed by a logic of rule operative in terms of a claim to universality."[22] As Antony

Anghie similarly concludes of the failure of the NIEO's legal campaign, despite the "resourcefulness and innovation" with which the Global South sought to work within existing international institutions, "imperialism was too deeply entrenched in international law to be reformed by that very same law."[23] As the moment of the NIEO passed, international law's identity as an emancipatory project with an essentially European genealogy continued to shape most conceptions of international law, which often still overlook or elide the substantive inequalities inscribed in formally equal legal principles as well as the profound legal asymmetries imposed on postcolonial states during decolonization that continue to structure the global legal order.

International law is the product of a history at once distinctively European and also, often devastatingly, global: its history is a history of aspirations to universal validity that itself cannot be told impartially. "There is no space in international law," as Koskenniemi writes, that would not "involve a 'choice'—that would not be, in this sense, a politics of international law."[24] The history of international law, a history of universalism and hierarchy intertwined, represents an important space for the work of conceptualizing, and gaining critical purchase on, hierarchy in the international sphere. This is perhaps primarily because of the long-standing and ongoing role that law has played in structuring and justifying hierarchy and domination, and, as this book has argued, in occluding them. As Pahuja trenchantly puts the point, "not everyone has the luxury of disengagement with international law. For some—possibly most—of the world, if they don't do international law, international law will 'do' them."[25] Yet it is also because international law contains resources for critique and frameworks for envisioning greater justice and equity, as we see in the work of thinkers from Anquetil-Duperron to Hamdan Khodja and Henry Stanley, to C. H. Alexandrowicz and Mohammed Bedjaoui. If international law is a moral and political language we can hardly avoid, we can also try to better deploy it, in part by understanding its fraught past.

Notes

ONE   Introduction

1. Jean-Pierre Abel-Rémusat, "Discours sur le génie et les moeurs des peuples orientaux," in *Mélanges posthumes d'histoire et de littérature orientales* (Paris: Imprimerie Royal, 1843), 247–248. Unless otherwise noted, all translations are mine.

2. On participation by legal actors from the "semi-periphery" in the later period, see Arnulf Becker Lorca, *Mestizo International Law: A Global Intellectual History 1842–1933* (Cambridge: Cambridge University Press, 2014); Liliana Obregón, "Completing Civilization: Creole Consciousness and International Law in Nineteenth-Century Latin America," in *International Law and Its Others,* ed. Anne Orford (Cambridge: Cambridge University Press, 2006), 247–264; Cemil Aydin, *The Politics of Anti-Westernism in Asia: Visions of World Order in Pan-Islamic and Pan-Asian Thought* (New York: Columbia University Press, 2007); Lauri Mälksoo, *Russian Approaches to International Law* (Oxford: Oxford University Press, 2015); Umut Özsu, "From the 'Semi-Civilized State' to the 'Emerging Market': Remarks on the International Legal History of the Semi-Periphery," in *Research Handbook on Political Economy and Law,* ed. Ugo Mattei and John D. Haskell (Cheltenham, UK: Edward Elgar, 2015), 246–259; and Özsu, "Ottoman International Law?," *Journal of Ottoman and Turkish Studies Association* 3 (2016): 369–376.

3. Christopher Warren, *Literature and the Law of Nations, 1580–1680* (Oxford: Oxford University Press, 2015), 19–22.

4. As Christopher Tomlins has written of the colonial encounter in early America, legalities are "social products" that "supply the conceptual frames that we use to interpret practices and invent legalities for, and of, others." Tomlins, "Introduction: The Many Legalities of Colonization: A Manifesto of Destiny

for Early American Legal History," in *The Many Legalities of Early America,* ed. Christopher Tomlins and Bruce Mann (Chapel Hill: University of North Carolina Press, 2001), 2–3.

5. Uday Mehta, *Liberalism and Empire* (Chicago: University of Chicago Press, 1999); Jennifer Pitts, *A Turn to Empire* (Princeton, NJ: Princeton University Press, 2005); Jeanne Morefield, *Covenants without Swords* (Princeton, NJ: Princeton University Press, 2005); Morefield, *Empires without Imperialism* (Oxford: Oxford University Press, 2014); Karuna Mantena, *Alibis of Empire* (Princeton, NJ: Princeton University Press, 2009); Anthony Pagden, *Burdens of Empire* (Cambridge: Cambridge University Press, 2015); Duncan Bell, *Reordering the World* (Princeton, NJ: Princeton University Press, 2016).

6. Arjun Appadurai, "Trajectorism and the Making of Europe" (talk given at the conference "After Europe: Postcolonial Knowledge in the Age of Globalization," University of Chicago, 12 March 2010). See also Dipesh Chakrabarty, *Provincializing Europe: Postcolonial Thought and Historical Difference* (Princeton, NJ: Princeton University Press, 2000).

7. Martti Koskenniemi, *From Apology to Utopia: The Structure of International Legal Argument* (Cambridge: Cambridge University Press, 2005), 122–154; Koskenniemi, *The Gentle Civilizer of Nations* (Cambridge: Cambridge University Press, 2001); Antony Anghie, *Imperialism, Sovereignty, and the Making of International Law* (Cambridge: Cambridge University Press, 2005); Casper Sylvest, *British Liberal Internationalism, 1880–1930: Making Progress?* (Manchester: Manchester University Press, 2010); Sylvest, "'Our Passion for Legality': International Law and Imperialism in Late Nineteenth-Century Britain," *Review of International Studies* 34 (2008): 403–423; Gustavo Gozzi, "The Particularistic Universalism of International Law in the Nineteenth Century," *Harvard International Law Journal* 52 (2010): 73–86.

8. Sundhya Pahuja, *Decolonizing International Law* (Cambridge: Cambridge University Press, 2011), 1. Emmanuelle Jouannet similarly describes international law as "intrinsically ambivalent," "simultaneously an instrument of domination and an instrument of emancipation." Jouannet, *A Short Introduction to International Law* (Cambridge: Cambridge University Press, 2013), 1.

9. Recent critiques within international relations include Tarak Barkawi, "Empire and Order in International Relations and Security Studies," in *The International Studies Encyclopedia,* ed. Robert Denemark, vol. 3 (Chichester: Wiley-Blackwell, 2010), 1360–1379; David Long and Brian Schmidt, eds., *Imperialism and Internationalism in the Discipline of International Relations* (Albany, NY: SUNY Press, 2005); Philip Darby, ed., *At the Edge of International Relations: Postcolonialism, Gender and Dependency* (London: Pinter, 1997); L. H. M. Ling, *Postcolonial International Relations: Conquest and Desire between Asia and the West* (Basingstoke, UK: Palgrave, 2002);

Branwen Gruffydd Jones, ed., *Decolonizing International Relations* (Lanham, MD: Rowman and Littlefield, 2006).

10. James Tully, "On Law, Democracy and Imperialism," in *Public Philosophy in a New Key,* vol. 2 (Cambridge: Cambridge University Press, 2008), 127–128.

11. Benjamin Straumann, *Roman Law in the State of Nature: The Classical Foundations of Hugo Grotius's Natural Law* (Cambridge: Cambridge University Press, 2015); Benedict Kingsbury and Benjamin Straumann, eds., *The Roman Foundations of the Law of Nations* (Oxford: Oxford University Press, 2010).

12. Paulina Starski and Jörn Axel Kämmerer write that "a still open question is how to conceptualize and categorize legal relations that . . . sometimes still existed between European and non-European entities." Starski and Kämmerer, "Imperial Colonialism in the Genesis of International Law—Anomaly or Time of Transition?," *Journal of the History of International Law* 19 (2017): 50–69. I am interested in the somewhat different question of how thinkers at the time conceptualized them.

13. Francisco de Vitoria, *Political Writings,* ed. Anthony Pagden and Jeremy Lawrance (Cambridge: Cambridge University Press, 1991), 238. On the "Janus-faced" quality of reciprocity, see Matthew Craven, "What Happened to Unequal Treaties? The Continuities of Informal Empire," *Nordic Journal of International Law* 74 (2005): 335–382, at 380.

14. Gentili, *De iure belli libri tres,* ed. J. B. Scott, trans. J. C. Rolfe, 2 vols. (Oxford: Clarendon Press, 1933), 1:10, referring to Cicero, *Tusculan Disputations,* 1.13.30.

15. Waldron associates this view with English positivists such as H. L. A. Hart and traces it to Bentham's analytical separation of "expository" from "censorial" jurisprudence. Jeremy Waldron, *"Ius gentium:* A Defense of Gentili's Equation of the Law of Nations and the Law of Nature," in Kingsbury and Straumann, *Roman Foundations,* 283–296, at 286.

16. Waldron, *"Ius gentium,"* 296.

17. Relatedly, Koskenniemi has argued that naturalism and positivism should be seen as complementary rather than as oppositional, and that eighteenth-century German lawyers all "oscillated uncertainly between the relative emphasis" they laid on each. Martti Koskenniemi, "Into Positivism: Georg Friedrich von Martens (1756–1832) and Modern International Law," *Constellations* 15, no. 2 (2008): 189–207, at 192.

18. Robert Phillimore wrote that although international law is binding among "heathen" states, "unquestionably, however, the obligations of International Law attach with greater precision, distinctness, and accuracy to Christian States in their commerce with each other." *Commentaries upon International Law,* 4 vols., 2nd ed. (London: Butterworth, 1871–1874), 1:24.

19. For a recent argument for the first feature, see Larry Siedentop, *Inventing the Individual: The Origins of Western Liberalism* (London: Allen Lane, 2014).

20. Jean-Jacques Rousseau, *The Plan for Perpetual Peace, On the Government of Poland, and Other Writings on History and Politics,* ed. Christopher Kelly (Hanover, NH: Dartmouth College Press, 2005), 30–33.

21. Voltaire, "Rescript of the Emperor of China on the Occasion of the Plan for Perpetual Peace," in Rousseau, *The Plan for Perpetual Peace,* 50–52.

22. Teemu Ruskola, *Legal Orientalism: China, the United States, and Modern Law* (Cambridge, MA: Harvard University Press, 2013), 108, 132 (quoting Cushing).

23. See, e.g., Hedley Bull and Adam Watson, *Expansion of International Society* (Oxford: Clarendon Press, 1984); Adam Watson, *The Evolution of International Society* (London: Routledge, 2002), 258. Danielle Allen makes a compelling case for the critical lens of domination rather than that of exclusion in her "Response" in "Forum: Ferguson Won't Change Anything. What Will?," *Boston Review* (January 5, 2015).

24. Richard Tuck, "Alliances with Infidels in the European Imperial Expansion," in *Empire and Modern Political Thought,* ed. Sankar Muthu (Cambridge: Cambridge University Press, 2012), 61–83. Peter Borschberg makes a similar suggestion by showing how the Dutch secured their monopoly over East Asian trade not on the basis of first occupation, as the Portuguese had done, but rather precisely on the basis of treaties with local powers, treaties that Grotius argued the Dutch had a right to compel the Asians to honor. Borschberg is perhaps too magnanimous when he writes that "as a result of his efforts to safeguard the independence of Asian rulers from encroachments by Spain and Portugal, Grotius (perhaps quite inadvertently) lent his support to preparing the legal and commercial ground for almost three and a half centuries of Dutch colonial rule in Southeast Asia." Borschberg, "Hugo Grotius, East India Trade and the King of Johor," *Journal of Southeast Asian Studies* 30 (1999): 225–248, at 248.

25. See Saliha Belmessous, ed., *Empire by Treaty: Negotiating European Expansion, 1600–1900* (Oxford: Oxford University Press, 2014); Jeffrey Glover, *Paper Sovereigns: Anglo-Native Treaties and the Law of Nations, 1604–1664* (Philadelphia: University of Pennsylvania Press, 2014).

26. C. H. Alexandrowicz, *The European-African Confrontation: A Study in Treaty-Making* (Leiden: Sijthoff, 1973); Anghie, *Imperialism, Sovereignty,* 93–107; Mamadou Hébié, *Souveraineté territorial par traité: Une étude des accords entre puissances colonials et entités politiques locales* (Paris: Presses Universitaires de France, 2015); Isabelle Surun, "Une souveraineté à l'encre sympathique? Souveraineté autochtone et appropriations territoriales dans les traités franco-africains au XIXe siècle," *Annales. Histoire, Sciences Sociales* 69 (2014): 313–348; Mieke van der Linden, *The Acquisition of Africa (1870–1914): The Nature of International Law* (Boston: Brill, 2016). Jo-Anne Claire Pem-

berton has argued for the "theoretical impossibility of ceding sovereignty by means of a treaty," citing Rousseau on the Roman law principle that a sovereign cannot destroy his own sovereignty. Pemberton, "The So-Called Right of Civilization in European Colonial Ideology, 16th to 20th Centuries," *Journal of the History of International Law* 15 (2013): 25–52.

27. *Somerset v. Stewart* (1772), *English Reports* 98, 499–510, at 505.

28. Odette Lienau, *Rethinking Sovereign Debt* (Cambridge, MA: Harvard University Press, 2014).

29. Pufendorf named the concept in a 1675 essay, "De systematibus civitatem." Samuel Pufendorf, *Dissertationes academicae selectiores* (Frankfurt: Weidmann, 1678), 226–283. See also Martin Wight, *Systems of States* (Leicester: Leicester University Press, 1977), 21–45; David Armitage, "Modern International Thought: Problems and Prospects," *History of European Ideas* 41 (2015): 116–130; Armitage, *Foundations of Modern International Thought* (Cambridge: Cambridge University Press, 2013), 13; Richard Devetak, "Historiographical Foundations of Modern International Thought: Histories of the European States-System from Florence to Göttingen," *History of European Ideas* 41 (2015): 69; Peter Schröder, *Trust in Early Modern International Political Thought, 1598–1713* (Cambridge: Cambridge University Press, 2017); Andrew Fitzmaurice, "Sovereign Trusteeship and Empire," *Theoretical Inquiries in Law* 16 (2015): 447–471, at 449.

30. C. H. Alexandrowicz called this a "*pars pro toto* fallacy." "G. F. de Martens on Asian Treaty Practice," *The Indian Year Book of International Affairs* 13, pt. 2 (1964): 59–77, at 75n27; reprinted in Alexandrowicz, *The Law of Nations in Global History,* ed. David Armitage and Jennifer Pitts (Oxford: Oxford University Press, 2017), 191n37. See also Miloš Vec, "Universalization, Particularization, Discrimination," *InterDisciplines* 2 (2012): 79–102.

31. Martti Koskenniemi, "International Law in Europe: Between Tradition and Renewal," *European Journal of International Law* 16 (2005): 113–124, on the "messianic teleology" of "much Western legal cosmopolitanism"; Koskenniemi, "Legal Cosmopolitanism: Tom Franck's Messianic World," *NYU Journal of International Law and Politics* 35 (2003): 471–486.

32. Charles-Irénée Castel de Saint-Pierre, *Projet pour rendre la paix perpetuelle en Europe* (Utrecht: A. Schouten, 1713), xix–xxi. Translation from *A Project for Settling an Everlasting Peace in Europe* (London: J. W. and Sold, 1714), viii–ix.

33. Immanuel Kant, "Toward Perpetual Peace," in *Practical Philosophy,* ed. Mary Gregor (Cambridge: Cambridge University Press, 1999), 319–351 (describing a "federalism that should gradually extended over all states," 327). See also James Tully, "The Kantian Idea of Europe: Critical and Cosmopolitan Perspectives," in *The Idea of Europe: From Antiquity to the European*

Union, ed. Anthony Pagden (Cambridge: Cambridge University Press, 2002), 331–358. Jürgen Habermas has described the European Union as an "exemplary case" of "democracy beyond the nation-state." Habermas, *The Post-National Constellation: Political Essays,* trans. and ed. Max Pensky (Cambridge, MA: Harvard University Press, 2001), 88. See also John McCormick, *Weber, Habermas, and Transformations of the European State* (Cambridge: Cambridge University Press, 2007), 204.

34. Devetak, "Historiographical Foundations," 65; Andrew Fitzmaurice, *Sovereignty, Property, and Empire 1500–2000* (Cambridge: Cambridge University Press, 2014), 10; Keene, *Beyond the Anarchical Society: Grotius, Colonialism and Order in World Politics* (Cambridge: Cambridge University Press, 2002).

35. E.g., John Westlake, *Chapters on the Principles of International Law* (Cambridge: Cambridge University Press, 1894): "The society of states, having European civilisation, or the international society, is the most comprehensive form of society among men. . . . States are its immediate, men its ultimate members" (78); Lassa Oppenheim, *International Law* (London: Longmans, 1912 [1905]), 3–11; Wilhelm Grewe, *The Epochs of International Law [Epochen der Völkerrechtsgeschichte],* trans. Michael Byers (New York: de Gruyter, 2000 [1984]).

36. For critiques of the narrative placing the Westphalia treaties at the origins of modern international law, see Andreas Osiander, "Sovereignty, International Relations, and the Westphalian Myth," *International Organization* 55 (2001): 251–287; Benno Teschke, *The Myth of 1648: Class, Geopolitics, and the Making of Modern International Relations* (London: Verso, 2003); Stéphane Beaulac, *The Power of Language in the Making of International Law: The Word Sovereignty in Bodin and Vattel and the Myth of Westphalia* (Leiden: Martinus Nijhoff, 2004).

37. J. H. W. Verzijl, "Western European Influence on the Foundation of International Law," *International Relations* 1 (1955): 137–146, at 137, 146. See also Verzijl, *International Law in Historical Perspective,* 10 vols. (Leiden: A. W. Sijthoff, 1968–1979).

38. See also Robert H. Jackson, *Quasi-states: Sovereignty, International Relations, and the Third World* (Cambridge: Cambridge University Press, 1990); Stephen Neff, *Justice among Nations* (Cambridge, MA: Harvard University Press, 2014).

39. Watson, *Evolution of International Society,* 258.

40. Adom Getachew, *Worldmaking after Empire: The Rise and Fall of Self-Determination* (Princeton, NJ: Princeton University Press, 2018); Jean Allain, "Orientalism and International Law: The Middle East as the Underclass of the International Legal Order," *Leiden Journal of International Law* 17 (2004): 391–404; Anghie, *Imperialism, Sovereignty,* 196–272.

41. Watson, *Evolution of International Society,* 262; cf. Immanuel Wallerstein, *The Modern World System* (Berkeley: University of California Press, 2011); Andre Gunder Frank, *Re-Orient* (Berkeley: University of California Press, 1998); Barry Buzan and George Lawson, *The Global Transformation: History, Modernity, and the Making of International Relations* (Cambridge: Cambridge University Press, 2015). For a powerful argument that international law, like liberalism more broadly, came to seem coherent, normatively compelling, and indeed natural because it presupposed and helped to constitute a society premised on commodity exchange among formally free and equal individuals, see Robert Stern, "The Liberal *Nomos* of Empire: Extraterritoriality, Legal Orientalism, and the Universalization of 'Civilized' International Law in China" (PhD diss., University of Chicago, 2016).

42. For Vitoria, see Anthony Pagden, "Dispossessing the Barbarian: The Language of Spanish Thomism and the Debate over the Property Rights of the American Indians," in *The Languages of Political Theory in Early-Modern Europe,* ed. Anthony Pagden (Cambridge: Cambridge University Press, 1993), 79–98; Anghie, *Imperialism, Sovereignty,* 13–31; Martti Koskenniemi, "Empire and International Law: The Real Spanish Contribution," *University of Toronto Law Journal* 61 (2011): 1–36. On Grotius's legal ideas about and involvement with Dutch imperial activities in Asia, see Keene, *Beyond the Anarchical Society;* Borschberg, "Hugo Grotius, East India Trade"; Martine van Ittersum, *Profit and Principle: Hugo Grotius, Natural Rights Theories and the Rise of Dutch Power in the East Indies, 1595–1615* (Leiden: Brill, 2006); Eric Michael Wilson, *The Savage Republic: De Indis of Hugo Grotius, Republicanism, and Dutch Hegemony within the Early Modern World-System (c. 1600–1619)* (Leiden: Martinus Nijhoff, 2008); H. W. Blom, ed., *Property, Piracy, and Punishment: Hugo Grotius on War and Booty in* De iure praedae— *Concepts and Contexts* (Leiden: Brill, 2009). For a discussion of the broader tradition, see Richard Tuck, *The Rights of War and Peace* (Cambridge: Cambridge University Press, 1999). See also C. H. Alexandrowicz, "Grotius and India," *Indian Year Book of International Affairs* 3 (1954): 357–367; Alexandrowicz, "Freitas *versus* Grotius," *British Year Book of International Law* 35 (1959): 162–182, reprinted in Alexandrowicz, *Law of Nations in Global History,* 113–139.

43. Jörg Fisch, "Power or Weakness? On the Causes of the Worldwide Expansion of European International Law," *Journal of the History of International Law* 6 (2004): 21–25; Fisch, *Die europäische Expansion und das Völkerrecht. die Auseinandersetzungen um den Status der überseeischen Gebiete vom 15. Jahrhundert bis zur Gegenwart* (Stuttgart: Steiner, 1984).

44. Anghie, *Imperialism, Sovereignty,* 193; Yasuaki Onuma, "When was the Law of International Society Born? An Inquiry of the History of International

Law from an Intercivilizational Perpective," *Journal of the History of International Law* 2 (2000): 1–66; Martti Koskenniemi, *The Gentle Civilizer of Nations: The Rise and Fall of International Law 1870–1960* (Cambridge: Cambridge University Press, 2001); Gerry Simpson, *Great Powers and Outlaw States: Unequal Sovereigns in the International Legal Order* (Cambridge: Cambridge University Press, 2004); Anne Orford, *Reading Humanitarian Intervention: Human Rights and the Use of Force in International Law* (Cambridge: Cambridge University Press, 2003); Orford, *International Authority and the Responsibility to Protect* (Cambridge: Cambridge University Press, 2011); Orford, ed., *International Law and Its Others* (Cambridge: Cambridge University Press, 2006); Ruskola, *Legal Orientalism*; Becker Lorca, *Mestizo International Law*.

45. E.g., Georges Abi-Saab, *The United Nations Conference on Trade and Development: The Issues and their Significance* (Uppsala: Dag Hammarskjöld Foundations, 1968); Abi-Saab, "The Third-World Intellectual in Praxis: Confrontation, Participation, or Operation behind Enemy Lines?," *Third World Quarterly* 37 (2016): 1957–1971 (special issue devoted to TWAIL); R. P. Anand, *New States and International Law* (Delhi: Vikas, 1972); Jorge Castañeda, *México y el orden internacional* (México: Colegio de México, 1956); Castañeda, *Mexico and the United Nations* (New York: Manhattan Publishing Company, 1958 [1956]).

46. Bardo Fassbender and Anne Peters, eds., *The Oxford Handbook of the History of International Law* (Oxford: Oxford University Press, 2012), 4. On the resilience of Eurocentrism in the history of international law, see the symposium on the *Oxford Handbook* in *European Journal of International Law* 25 (2014), especially the contributions by Stefan Kirmse and Anne-Charlotte Martineau.

47. On the broader renaissance in the history of international thought, see especially Armitage, *Foundations,* and the forum on the book in *History of European Ideas* 41 (2015); Duncan Bell, "International Relations: The Dawn of a Historiographical Turn?," *British Journal of Politics and International Relations* 3 (2001): 115–126.

48. Koskenniemi has made the provocative argument that the doctrinal international law that developed beginning with the "men of 1873" was in important ways quite disconnected from the law of nations theories of the previous century. Martti Koskenniemi, "International Law and *raison d'état*: Rethinking the Prehistory of International Law," in Kingsbury and Straumann, *Roman Foundations,* 297–339, at 297. But nineteenth-century writers consistently cited Grotius, Pufendorf, Wolff, Vattel, and the broader *ius gentium* tradition as their intellectual forebears.

49. C. H. Alexandrowicz, "Doctrinal Aspects of the Universality of the Law of Nations," *British Year Book of International Law* 37 (1961): 506–515; Alexandrowicz,

Law of Nations in Global History, 168–179; David Armitage and Jennifer Pitts, "This Modern Grotius: An Introduction to the Life and Thought of C. H. Alexandrowicz," in Alexandrowicz, *Law of Nations in Global History,* 1–31.

50. Koskenniemi has gone so far as to say that "almost every jurist writing in the last half of the 19th century, and certainly most members of the *Institut [de droit international],* were overt or covert natural lawyers." Martti Koskenniemi, "Race, Hierarchy and International Law: Lorimer's Legal Science," *European Journal of International Law* 27 (2016): 415–429, at 416.

51. Henry Maine, *Ancient Law* (London: John Murray, 1870), 53. On the "doubled" sources of the *ius gentium* in Roman legal texts—a more speculative and "hellenic" natural law, and Roman positive law—see Peter Haggenmacher, *Grotius et la doctrine de la guerre juste* (Paris: Presses universitaires de France, 1983), 311–314.

52. See Annabel Brett, *Changes of State: Nature and the Limits of the City in Early Modern Natural Law* (Princeton, NJ: Princeton University Press), 13, on the implications of Vitoria's misremembering *inter omnes homines* as *inter omnes gentes.* See also Grewe, *Epochs of International Law,* 25; Brian Tierney, "Vitoria and Suarez on *ius gentium,* Natural Law, and Custom," in *The Nature of Customary Law: Legal, Historical, and Philosophical Perspectives,* ed. Amanda Perreau-Saussine and James Murphy (Cambridge: Cambridge University Press, 2007), 101–124; Peter Stein, *Roman Law in European History* (Cambridge: Cambridge University Press, 1999), 94–95 *(ius gentium),* 12–13 *(ius civile);* Kingsbury and Straumann, *Roman Foundations;* David Lupher, *Romans in a New World: Classical Models in Sixteenth-Century Spanish America* (Ann Arbor: University of Michigan Press, 2003); Anthony Pagden, *Lords of All the World: Ideologies of Empire in Spain, Britain, and France c. 1500–c. 1800* (New Haven, CT: Yale University Press, 1995).

53. Jeremy Bentham, *Introduction to the Principles of Morals and Legislation,* ed. J. H. Burns and H. L. A. Hart (London: Athlone, 1970 [1789]), 296. Bentham's term gradually came to replace "law of nations" as the standard term in the first decades of the nineteenth century. See Hidemi Suganami, "A Note on the Origin of the Word 'International,'" *British Journal of International Studies* 4 (1978): 226–232; David Armitage, "Globalizing Jeremy Bentham," in *Foundations,* 172–187.

54. Vattel cited Roman law precedent for thinking of the law of nations as that "generally acknowledged and adopted by all civilized nations." Emer de Vattel, preface in *Droit des gens, ou principes de la loi naturelle* (London, 1758 [actually Neuchâtel, 1757]). He cites Cicero, *De Officiis,* bk. 3, ch. 5, though Cicero does not use the word "civilized" in the quoted passage. Unless otherwise noted, I quote from the 1797 English translation of *Droit des gens* (hereafter cited as *DG*) reproduced in Vattel, *The Law of Nations,* ed. Béla Kapossy

and Richard Whatmore (Indianapolis, IN: Liberty Fund, 2008), citing book, chapter, and section number.

55. Grotius, *The Rights of War and Peace*, ed. Richard Tuck (Indianapolis, IN: Liberty Fund, 2005), bk. 1, ch. 1, §12; Thomas Hobbes, *Elements of Law*, ed. Ferdinand Tönnies (London: Cass, 1969), 75. See also Benjamin Straumann, *Roman Law in the State of Nature: The Classical Foundations of Hugo Grotius's Natural Law* (Cambridge: Cambridge University Press, 2015), 1.

56. James Muldoon, *Popes, Lawyers, and Infidels: The Church and the Non-Christian World 1250–1550* (Philadelphia: University of Pennsylvania Press, 1979). The opposing view that infidel rule and property was invalid, associated with the canonist Hostiensis (Henry of Segusio, a student of Innocent IV), had waned by the end of the fourteenth century. On the idea of the "*ius commune*" as a system of norms linking all Christians (and the crisis of that idea in the fifteenth century), see Manlio Bellomo, *The Common Legal Past of Europe 1000–1800*, trans. Lydia G. Cochrane (Washington, DC: Catholic University of America Press, 1995). On Dominican understandings of *dominium*, see Annabel Brett, *Liberty, Right and Nature: Individual Rights in Later Scholastic Thought* (Cambridge: Cambridge University Press, 1997).

57. Tuck, *Rights of War and Peace*, 27–29; Giulio Vismara, *Impium foedus: Le origini della "respublica christiana"* (Milan: A. Giuffrè, 1974); Garrett Mattingly, *Renaissance Diplomacy* (Boston: Houghton Mifflin, 1955); Mark W. Janis and Carolyn Evans, eds., *Religion and International Law* (Leiden: Martinus Nijhoff, 1999). For debate about the usefulness of Tuck's organizing distinction between theological and humanist traditions in early modern legal thought, see the essays in Kingsbury and Straumann, *Roman Foundations*.

58. See Noel Malcolm's incisive discussion in "Alberico Gentili and the Ottomans," in Kingsbury and Straumann, *Roman Foundations*, 127–144, and Malcolm's colloquial translation of the Latin at 127. On Gentili's admiralty court advocacy and his arguments' role in "constructing a global legal regime inhabited by states with imprecisely defined and fragmented sovereignty," see Lauren Benton, "Legalities of the Sea in Gentili's Hispanica Advocatio," in Kingsbury and Straumann, *Roman Foundations*, 269–282. See also Benedict Kingsbury, ed., *Alberico Gentili e il mondo extraeuropeo: Atti del Convegno, Settima Giornata Gentiliana, 20 settembre 1997* (Milan: A. Giuffrè, 2001); Kaius Tuori, "Alberico Gentili and the Criticism of Expansion in the Roman Empire: The Invader's Remorse," *Journal of the History of International Law* 11 (2009): 205–219; Schröder, *Trust*, 42–44.

59. Contrast Neff, who attributes universalism to Christianity and the West and hostility to infidels to Islam, in *Justice among Nations*, 59–60.

60. See G. W. Leibniz, "Mars Christianissimus," and *Caesarinus Fürstenerius*, in *Political Writings*, ed. Patrick Riley (Cambridge: Cambridge University Press,

1988), 121–145, 111–120. The phrase *"peste de mahométanisme"* appears in "Réflexions sur la guerre" (1687); Ian Almond identifies a "general mellowing of Leibniz's attitude to Islam from the beginning of the 1690s" in "Leibniz, Historicism, and the 'Plague of Islam,'" *Eighteenth-Century Studies* 39 (2006): 463–483. Almond, *History of Islam in German Thought: From Leibniz to Nietzsche* (New York: Routledge, 2010).

61. Andreas Osiander, *The States System of Europe, 1640–1990* (Oxford: Clarendon Press, 1994), 110; Denys Hay, *Europe: The Emergence of an Idea* (Edinburgh: Edinburgh University Press, 1957). For an astute reading of more localist and fragmentary accounts of Christendom / Europe in the 1590s (and the present), see Jane Pettegree, "Writing Christendom in the English Renaissance: A Reappraisal of Denys Hay's View of the Emergence of 'Europe,'" in *Europe and Its Others: Essays on Interperception and Identity,* ed. Paul Gifford and Tessa Hauswedell (Oxford: Peter Lang, 2010), 39–56. On Western European ambivalence about Russia's membership in the European community, see Pärtel Piirimäe, "Russia, the Turks and Europe: Legitimations of War and the Formation of European Identity in the Early Modern Period," *Journal of Early Modern History* 11 (2007): 63–86.

62. *Cobbett's Complete Collection of State Trials and Proceedings for High Treason and Other Crimes,* vol. 10 (London: Hansard, 1811), 392. The lawyer appealed to the authority of Grotius and argued that "the Indians have a right to trade here, and we there, and this is a right natural and human, which the Christian faith does not alter."

63. *DG,* bk. 2, ch. 13, §161.

64. See, for instance, Charles François Lefèvre de La Maillardière, *Précis du droit des gens, de la guèrre, de la paix, et des ambassades* (Paris: Quillau, 1775), x (where the author calls himself the "bee gathering the purified sugar" from Grotius, Vattel, Barbeyrac, Pufendorf, Burlamaqui, and others); Pierre Joseph Neyron, *Principes du droit des gens européen conventionnel et coutumier* (Bronswic: Librairie des orphelins, 1783), which cites, as sources of the "droit des gens européens," treaties, treaty collections, memoirs and negotiations, systems of this law, and political journals. For treaty collections Neyron cites Dumont, as well as "les Capitulaires des Francs rassemblés par Balluze, Muratori, Du Chesne, Freher, Leibnitz pour les anciens Traités. Outre cela Rymer pour l'Angleterre, Leonard pour la France, Bertodano pour l'Espagne, Faber & Lungi pour L'Allemagne." Johannes van der Linden, "On the Formation of a Select Law Library," in *Institutes of the Laws of Holland,* ed. and trans. Jabez Henry (London, 1828).

65. Jean Dumont, *Corps universel diplomatique du droit des gens, contenant un recueil des traitez . . . qui ont été faits en Europe,* vol. 1 (Amsterdam: Brunel, 1726), xv.

66. G. F. de Martens, *Summary of the Law of Nations, Founded on the Treaties and Customs of the Modern Nations of Europe: With a List of the Principal Treaties*, trans. William Cobbett (Philadelphia: T. Bradford, 1795), 5 (*a potiori*: from the strongest or the most important part). See also Karl-Heinz Ziegler, "The Peace Treaties of the Ottoman Empire with European Christian Powers," in *Peace Treaties and International Law in European History: From the Late Middle Ages to World War One,* ed. Randall Lesaffer (Cambridge: Cambridge University Press, 2004), 338–364; Guido Komatsu, "Die Turkei und das europäische Staatensystem im 16. Jahrhundert: Untersuchungen zu Theorie und Praxis des frühneuzeitlichen Völkerrechts," in *Recht und Reich im Zeitalter der Reformation: Festschrift für Horst Rabe,* ed. Christine Roll (Frankfurt am Main: Peter Lang, 1996), 121–144.

67. See *A Complete Collection of All the Marine Treaties Subsisting between Great-Britain and France, Spain, Portugal, Austria, Russia, . . . &c.: Commencing in the Year 1546, and Including the Definitive Treaty of 1763* (London: J. Millan, 1779), lv.

68. Paul Rycaut, *The History of the Present State of the Ottoman Empire*, 6th ed. (London, 1686 [1666]), 160–161.

69. Sir James Porter, *Observations on the religion, law, government, and manners of the Turks,* 2nd ed. (London: J. Nourse, 1771), 151.

70. Christian Wolff, *Jus gentium methodo scientifica pertractatum,* trans. Joseph H. Drake, 2 vols. (Oxford: Clarendon Press, 1934 [1764]), vol. 2 (translation), §§157–158. Wolff also held the practices of civilized states to be authoritative for less cultured nations (even if they were not to be imposed by force): "it is plain . . . that what has been approved by the more civilized nations is the law of nations" (Prolegomena, §§20–22). Donald F. Lach, "The Sinophilism of Christian Wolff (1679–1754)," *Journal of the History of Ideas* 14 (1953): 561–574, at 564; Travers Twiss, *The Law of Nations Considered as Independent Political Communities* (Oxford: Clarendon Press, 1884), xxvi.

71. *DG,* bk. 2, ch. 1, §16. On the universality of natural law, see also Vattel's 1742 essay "Dissertation on This Question: Can Natural Law Bring Society to Perfection without the Assistance of Political Laws?," trans. T. J. Hochstrasser, in Vattel, *The Law of Nations,* 773–781.

72. In addition to Wolff and Vattel, see, e.g., Richard Zouch[e], *Iuris et judicii fecialis, sive, juris inter gentes* [An exposition of fecial law and procedure, or of law between nations, and questions concerning the same], trans. J. L. Brierly, vol. 2 (Washington, DC: Carnegie Institution, 1911), pt. 1, §1.1: "That which natural reason has established among all men is respected by all alike, and is called the Law of Nations, as being a law which all nations recognize"; it includes both "the common element in the law which the peoples of single nations use among themselves" and the law observed between nations, or

"jus inter gentes." See also J. G. Heineccius, *A Methodical System of Universal Law; or, The Laws of Nature and Nations*, trans. George Turnbull, ed. Thomas Ahnert and Peter Schröder (Indianapolis, IN: Liberty Fund, 2008 [1741]), which asserts a universal law of nations based on the law of nature but says almost nothing about contemporary non-European nations, aside from a brief mention of systems of barter among "barbarous countries" in "Asia, Africa, and America" (bk. 1, ch. 13, §337).

73. Lauren Benton and Lisa Ford, *Rage for Order: The British Empire and the Origins of International Law, 1800–1850* (Cambridge, MA: Harvard University Press, 2016).

74. *Annuaire de l'Institut de droit international* (1877): 141. And see, e.g., Hans-Ulrich Scupin, "History of the Law of Nations: 1815 to World War I," in *Encyclopedia of Public International Law*, ed. Rudolph Bernhardt, vol. 2 (Amsterdam: North-Holland, 1992), 767–793. For skepticism about this narrative, see Koskenniemi, *Gentle Civilizer;* Casper Sylvest, "International Law in Nineteenth-Century Britain," *British Yearbook of International Law* 75 (2004): 9–70.

75. Twiss, *Law of Nations Considered as Independent Political Communities*, v.

T W O   Oriental Despotism and the Ottoman Empire

1. J. C. Hurewitz, "The Europeanization of Ottoman Diplomacy," *Belleten* 25 (1961): 455–466; Umut Özsu, "Ottoman Empire," in *The Oxford Handbook of the History of International Law*, ed. Bardo Fassbender and Anne Peters (Oxford: Oxford University Press, 2012), 429–448. Daniel Goffman proposes that "the Ottomans became part—perhaps even the core—of the diplomatic system that had arisen out of Italy in the fifteenth and sixteenth centuries." Goffman, *The Ottoman Empire and Early Modern Europe* (Cambridge: Cambridge University Press, 2002), 19–20; Goffman, "Negotiating with the Renaissance State: The Ottoman Empire and the New Diplomacy," in *The Early Modern Ottomans: Remapping the Empire*, ed. Virginia Aksan and Daniel Goffman (Cambridge: Cambridge University Press, 2007), 61–74.

2. Christian Windler has stressed the "analogous contradictions" on the part of both Europeans and the Ottoman dependency of Tunis: with "hostility in principle and the multiple forms of a pragmatic search for legal security" with regard to the other side. "Diplomatic History as a Field for Cultural Analysis: Muslim-Christian Relations in Tunis, 1700–1840," *The Historical Journal* 44 (2001): 79–106. See also Windler, "Towards the Empire of a 'Civilizing Nation': The French Revolution and the Ottoman Regencies in the Maghreb," in *International Law and Empire: Historical Explorations*, ed. Martti Koskenniemi, Walter Rech, and Manuel Jiménez Fonseca (Oxford: Oxford University Press, 2016), 201–223.

3. Ottomans used the term *"ahdname"* (derived, in a characteristically Ottoman mixture, from the Arabic *ahd,* oath or promise, and the Persian *name,* or letter; so, a "letter of promise," or a pledge) to refer to both commercial capitulations and peace treaties. See A. H. de Groot, *The Netherlands and Turkey* (Istanbul: Isis Press, 2009), 108; Hans Theunissen, "Ottoman-Venetian Diplomatics: The *Ahd-names," Electronic Journal of Oriental Studies* 1 (1998): 1–698; Feroz Ahmad, "Ottoman Perceptions of the Capitulations, 1800–1914," *Journal of Islamic Studies* 11 (2000): 1–20; Maurits H. van den Boogert, *The Capitulations and the Ottoman Legal System: Qadis, Consuls, and Beraths in the 18th Century* (Leiden: Brill, 2005); Turan Kayaoğlu, *Legal Imperialism: Sovereignty and Extraterritoriality in Japan, the Ottoman Empire, and China* (Cambridge: Cambridge University Press, 2010), 104–148; Halil Inalcik, "İmtiyazat," in *Encyclopedia of Islam,* 2nd ed. (Leiden: E. J. Brill, 1971), 1179.

4. Stanley, *The East and the West: Our Dealings with Our Neighbours* (London: Hatchard, 1865), 2. The original and now archaic meaning of the verb "capitulate" was likewise to "draw up articles of agreement; to propose terms; to treaty, parley, negotiate"; that meaning appears from the passages quoted in the *Oxford English Dictionary* to have been superseded in the eighteenth century by the now dominant meaning, "to surrender or yield."

5. Edhem Eldem, "Capitulations and Western Trade," in *The Cambridge History of Turkey,* ed. Suraiya N. Faroqhi, vol. 3 (Cambridge: Cambridge University Press, 2006), 297.

6. Alexander H. de Groot, "The Historical Development of the Capitulatory Regime in the Ottoman Middle East from the Fifteenth to the Nineteenth Centuries," in *The Ottoman Capitulations: Text and Context* (Naples: Oriente Moderno, 2004), 575–604, at 579.

7. See Philip Stern, *The Company-State: Corporate Sovereignty and the Early Modern Foundation of the British Empire in India* (Oxford: Oxford University Press, 2011); Siraj Ahmed, *Stillbirth of Capital: Enlightenment Writing and Colonial India* (Stanford, CA: Stanford University Press, 2012).

8. Ignace de Testa, *Recueil des traités de la Porte ottomane avec les puissances étrangères, depuis le premier traité conclu, en 1536, entre Suléyman I et François I jusqu'à nos jours* (Paris: Amyot, 1864); see also Karl-Heinz Ziegler, "The Peace Treaties of the Ottoman Empire with European Christian Powers," in *Peace Treaties and International Law in European History,* ed. Randall Lesaffer (Cambridge: Cambridge University Press, 2004), 338–364.

9. Travers Twiss held that the term "capitulations" was first used with respect to the 1535 agreement. Twiss, *The Law of Nations Considered as Independent Political Communities,* vol. 1 (Oxford: Clarendon Press, 1884), 463.

10. Pierre Bourdeille, seigneur de Brantôme, *Les vies des grands capitaines françois, Oeuvres complètes,* vol. 5, ed. Ludovic Lalanne (Paris: Renouard, 1869),

55, quoted by the nineteenth-century editor Charles Schefer, of Saint-Priest's *Mémoires sur l'ambassade de France en Turquie* (Paris: Leroux, 1877), iii. On Brantôme and more generally on early modern French-Ottoman relations, see Christine Isom-Verhaaren, *Allies with the Infidel: The Ottoman and French Alliance in the Sixteenth Century* (London: I. B. Tauris, 2011).

11. Krishan Kumar, *Visions of Empire* (Princeton, NJ: Princeton University Press, 2017), 93–97.

12. De Groot, "Historical Development of the Capitulatory Regime," 599.

13. Nabil Matar, *Turks, Moors and Englishmen in the Age of Discovery* (New York: Columbia University Press, 1999), 33–37; Jerry Brotton, *The Sultan and the Queen* (New York: Viking, 2016); Susan A. Skilliter, *William Harborne and the Trade with Turkey, 1578–1582: A Documentary Study of the First Anglo-Ottoman Relations* (Oxford: Oxford University Press, 1977); Ziegler, "Peace Treaties of the Ottoman Empire," 344–345.

14. Fatma Müge Göçek, *East Encounters West: France and the Ottoman Empire in the Eighteenth Century* (Oxford: Oxford University Press, 1987), 101.

15. Kumar, *Visions of Empire*, 74–144, esp. 119.

16. Mustafa Serdar Palabiyik, "The Emergence of the Idea of 'International Law' in the Ottoman Empire before the Treaty of Paris (1856)," *Middle Eastern Studies* 50 (2014): 233–251, at 236.

17. Rifa'at A. Abou-El-Haj, "Ottoman Diplomacy at Karlowitz," *Journal of the American Oriental Society* 87 (1967): 498–512, at 499.

18. Virginia Aksan, *An Ottoman Statesman in War and Peace: Ahmed Resmi Efendi, 1700–1783* (Leiden: E. J. Brill, 1995), 43.

19. Ziegler, "Peace Treaties of the Ottoman Empire," 355; Palabiyik, "Idea of 'International Law,'" 237–238. One grand vizier wrote to Mahmud I that despite the violation of religious law, alliances could be justified as for the "order of the state" (*nizam-ı mülk*). On the combination of Islamic legal sources and customary law as the basis for Ottoman conceptions of interpolity law, see Viorel Panaite, "Islamic Tradition and Ottoman Law of Nations," in *The Turks*, vol. 3: *The Ottomans*, ed. Hasan Celâl Güzel, C. Cem Oğuz, and Osman Karatay (Ankara: Yeni Türkiye Publications, 2002), 597–604.

20. Virginia H. Aksan, *Ottoman Wars 1700–1870: An Empire Besieged* (Harlow, UK: Pearson, 2007). On the contested Russian right of protection, see Roderic H. Davison, "'Russian Skill and Turkish Imbecility': The Treaty of Kuchuk Kainardji Reconsidered," in *Essays in Ottoman and Turkish History, 1774–1923: The Impact of the West* (Austin: University of Texas Press, 1990), 29–50.

21. Suraiya Faroqhi, *The Ottoman Empire and the World Around It* (London: I. B. Tauris, 2004), 182; Virginia Aksan, "Ottoman Political Writing, 1768–1808," *International Journal of Middle East Studies* 25 (1993): 53–69.

22. Mehmed Raşid, *Tarih-i Raşid*, vol. 5 (1660–1721), 213–214; quoted by Göçek, *East Encounters West*, 7. The report was translated into French and published in 1721 as *Nouvelle description de la ville de Constantinople avec la relation du voyage de l'ambassadeur de la Porte Ottomane et de son séjour à la cour de France* (Paris: Nicolas Simart, 1721), and again in 1757 as *Relation de l'ambassade de Mehemet Effendi à la cour de France en 1721, écrite par lui-même et trad. du turc*, Julien Galland (Constantinople and Paris: Ganeau, 1757).

23. Aksan, *Ottoman Statesman in War and Peace*, 46–99.

24. Şerif Mardin, "Some Notes on an Early Phase in the Modernization of Communications in Turkey," *Comparative Studies in Society and History* 3 (1961): 250–271, at 265.

25. *Account of the Mission of Yusuf Agha, Ambassador from Turkey to the British Court, Written by Himself*, trans. Joseph von Hammer (London: Royal Asiatic Society, 1833); Aksan, *Ottoman Wars*, 226–228; David Worrall, *Celebrity, Performance, Reception: British Georgian Theatre as Social Assemblage* (Cambridge: Cambridge University Press, 2013), 157–182; Mehmet Aladdin Yalçinkaya, "Mahmud Raif Efendi as the Chief Secretary of Yusug [*sic*] Agah Efendi, the First Permanent Ottoman-Turkish Ambassador to London (1793–1797)," *Ankara Üniversitesi Osmanli tarih Arastirma ve Uygulama Merkezi Dergisi (OTAM)* 5 (1994): 385–434.

26. Thomas Naff, "Reform and the Conduct of Ottoman Diplomacy in the Reign of Selim III, 1789–1807," *Journal of the American Oriental Society* 83 (1963): 295–315. For a more skeptical reading of Selim III's permanent missions as ill-coordinated "half measures," with continuous diplomacy more firmly instituted under Mahmud II in the 1830s, see Hurewitz, "Europeanization of Ottoman Diplomacy," 461–463.

27. James Gillray, "Presentation of the Mahometan Credentials—or—The Final Resource of French Atheists" (London: H. Humphrey, 26 December 1793), British Museum. Crouching around him, in Jacobin garb, are Charles James Fox, Richard Sheridan, and Joseph Priestly. Harriet Guest notes the "exaggerated manliness" of the emissary's "unmistakably phallic" credentials. Guest, *Empire, Barbarism, and Civilisation* (Cambridge: Cambridge University Press, 2007), 182–183.

28. "Manifesto of the Ottoman Sublime Porte relating to war against the French Republic," 9 September 1798, in Maurice Herbette, *Une ambassade turque sous le Directoire* (Paris: Perrin, 1902), 313–324, from the official French translation; a slightly different translation appears in Testa, *Receuil des traités*, 1:548; Pascal Firges, *French Revolutionaries in the Ottoman Empire* (Oxford: Oxford University Press, 2017), 37–58.

29. For a discussion of further documents and the relevant Ottoman terms—*hukuk-u-nas* (law of mankind), *hukuk-u ümem* (law of nations or communi-

ties), and *hukuk-u milel* (also translatable as law of nations)—see Palabiyik, "Idea of 'International Law,'" 239–241.

30. "Manifesto," in Herbette, *Une ambassade turque,* 318. See also Caroline Finkel, *Osman's Dream: The Story of the Ottoman Empire, 1300–1923* (London: John Murray, 2005), 396; Yasemin Saner Gönen, "The Integration of the Ottoman Empire into the European State System during the Reign of Selim III" (master's thesis, Boğaziçi University, 1991), 79.

31. Imperial firman of late August 1798, in Joseph Kabrda, *Quelques firmans concernant les relations Franco-Turques lors de l'expédition de Bonaparte en Égypte (1798–1799)* (Paris: Imprimerie Nationale, 1947), 71. Juan Cole, in *Napoleon's Egypt: Invading the Middle East* (New York: Palgrave Macmillan, 2007), 156–157, calls the document "remarkable in showing the reformist, civil mind-set of Selim III," in its appeal equally to the international criminality of the French invasion and to its assault on Islam.

32. Thomas Naff, "Ottoman Diplomatic Relations with Europe in the Eighteenth Century: Patterns and Trends," in *Studies in Eighteenth Century Islamic History,* ed. Thomas Naff and Roger Owen (Carbondale: Southern Illinois University Press, 1977), 88–107, at 106–107. See also Kahraman Şakul, "An Ottoman Global Moment: War of Second Coalition in the Levant" (PhD diss., Georgetown University, 2009).

33. De Groot, "Historical Development of the Capitulatory Regime," 600; Armand Goşu, *La troisième coalition antinapolienne et la Sublime Porte 1805* (Istanbul: Isis Press, 2003).

34. Kahraman Şakul, "What Happened to Pouqueville's Frenchmen? Ottoman Treatment of the French Prisoners during the War of the Second Coalition (1798–1802)," *Turkish Historical Review* 3 (2012): 168–195.

35. On the related question of the legal standing of the North African regencies of the Ottoman Empire, excluded by some authors under the description of *hostes humani generis,* and included within the scope of the law of nations by others, notably the Dutch jurist Cornelius van Bynkershoek (1673–1743), see Guillaume Calafat, "Ottoman North Africa and *ius publicum europaeum:* The Case of the Treaties of Peace and Trade (1600–1750)," in *War, Trade and Neutrality: Europe and the Mediterranean in the Seventeenth and Eighteenth Centuries,* ed. Antonella Alimento (Milan: FrancoAngeli, 2011), 171–187; Walter Rech, *Enemies of Mankind: Vattel's Theory of Collective Security* (Leiden: Martinus Nijhoff, 2013), 49–104.

36. Gabriel Effendi Noradounghian, *Recueil d'actes internationaux de l'Empire ottoman,* vol. 1: *1300–1789* (Paris: F. Pichon, 1897), 30. The first French commercial capitulation was issued in 1535; for the text of that agreement, see Noradounghian, *Recueil,* 83–87.

37. See James Porter, *Observations on the religion, law, government, and manners of the Turks,* 2nd ed. (London: J. Nourse, 1771), 362.

38. De Groot argues that some of the forms and language of reciprocal agreement observed by pre-Ottoman regimes in the Levant were adopted by the Ottomans despite their official policy of making unilateral grants. De Groot, "Historical Development of the Capitulatory Regime," 592, 595. See also Naff, "Ottoman Diplomatic Relations," 98.

39. Paul Rycaut, *The Capitulations and Articles of Peace between the Majestie of the King of England, . . . And the Sultan of the Ottoman Empire, as they have beene augmented, and altered in the times of every Embassadour: And as now lately in the city of Adrianople in the month of January 1661* (Constantinople: Abraham Gabai, 1663), 6 (emphasis added). The capitulations were renewed in January 1661 Old Style (O.S.), 1662 New Style (N.S.). See Sonia P. Anderson, *The English Consul in Turkey: Paul Rycaut at Smyrna 1667–1678* (Oxford: Clarendon Press, 1989), 30.

40. Noradounghian, *Recueil,* 277–306, at 285. As Halil Inalcik writes in his authoritative article on the capitulations, "It was tacitly understood that reciprocal advantages were expected in return for the privileges conceded, and that if these advantages failed to materialize, the Muslim ruler could claim that the preconditions of 'friendship and sincerity' had been broken"; reciprocity was, he writes, "a reality, from which the whole Empire benefited." Inalcik, "İmtiyazat."

41. Rycaut's text of the 1661 English capitulations indicates the many privileges added to the original 1580 agreement, from further protections for consuls serving under the ambassador (e.g., protection from being examined or placed under house arrest) to the privilege of moving goods within the empire without being taxed with further duties, to the privilege of making wine for private use. The 1740 French renewal likewise extended French privileges, for instance, granting to the French everything that had been accorded the Venetians. See Noradounghian, *Recueil,* 277–306, especially art. 28 at 285; van den Boogert, *Capitulations,* 9.

42. Joan-Pau Rubiés has argued that European treatments of oriental despotism were more responsive to realities about Asian societies than has often been assumed. Rubiés, "Oriental Despotism and European Orientalism: Botero to Montesquieu," *Journal of Early Modern History* 9 (2005): 109–180. See also Lucette Valensi, *The Birth of the Despot: Venice and the Sublime Porte* (Ithaca, NY: Cornell University Press, 1993); Gerald M. MacLean, *Looking East: English Writing and the Ottoman Empire before 1800* (Basingstoke, UK: Palgrave Macmillan, 2007), 61, 175.

43. Beginning with the third edition of 1670, the work was retitled *The History of the Present State of the Ottoman Empire,* and so it is easy to confuse it with his later *History.* Between 1670 and 1741 editions appeared in French, Italian, German, Dutch, Polish, and Russian. See Anderson, *English Consul in Turkey,*

24, 40–48, and Appendix 1. On Rycaut as a source for Montesquieu, see Ann Thomson, "L'Empire ottoman, symbole du despotisme oriental?," in *Rêver d'Orient, connaître l'Orient,* ed. Isabelle Gadoin and Marie-Elise Palmier-Chatelain (Paris: ENS Éditions, 2008), 177–196; Aslı Çirakman, *From the Terror of the World to the Sick Man of Europe: European Images of Ottoman Empire and Society from the Sixteenth Century to the Nineteenth* (Oxford: Oxford University Press, 2002).

44. See, e.g., Paul Rycaut, *The History of the Present State of the Ottoman Empire,* 6th ed. (London: R. Clavell, 1686), 406. All subsequent references are to this 1686 edition.

45. Rycaut, "Epistle to the Reader," in *Present State.*

46. In her *Turkish Embassy Letters,* which date from 1717–1718 but were first published after her death in 1762, Lady Mary Wortley Montagu would attest to her own eyewitness authority by questioning Rycaut's accuracy, as in: "Sir Paul Rycaut is mistaken (as he commonly is) in calling the sect *Muterin* (i.e. *the secret with us*) Atheists, they being Deists." *Letters of the Right Honourable Lady M—y W—y M—e: Written, during her travels in Europe, Asia and Africa, to persons of distinction,* vol. 2 (London: Becket and De Hondt, 1763), 7.

47. Linda T. Darling, "Ottoman Politics through British Eyes: Paul Rycaut's *The Present State of the Ottoman Empire,*" *Journal of World History* 5 (1994): 71–97.

48. Pierre Bayle, "Du Despotisme," in *Réponse aux questions d'un provincial* (Rotterdam: Reinier Leers, 1704), 263–296. See Richard Koebner, "Despot and Despotism," *Journal of the Warburg and Courtauld Institutes* 14 (1951): 275–302, at 300, stressing the significance of this novel *-ism,* noting that this was the first such term designating a political system, though it followed such terms as "Machiavellism," "atheism," and "nepotism."

49. Rycaut, "Epistle Dedicatory," in *Capitulations.*

50. Rycaut, *Capitulations,* 6–7.

51. Rycaut, *Present State,* 7–9. He noted that the "Grand Signior" assiduously respected religious property as distinct, "to the shame of our Sectaries in England, who violate the penetralia of the Sanctuary."

52. Rycaut, *Present State,* 3, 16.

53. Rycaut, "Epistle Dedicatory," and *Present State,* 3–5, 317.

54. "It is an ordinary saying among the *Turkish Cadees* and Lawyers, That *the Grand Signior is above the Law;* that is, whatsoever law is written, is controllable, and may be contradicted by him: his mouth is the Law it self, and the power of an infallible interpretation is in him." Rycaut, *Present State,* 9, 11 (emphasis in original).

55. Rycaut, *Present State,* 10–11. He quotes the rule, from Justinian's *Institutes* (2.17.8), "Et si legibus soluti sumus, tamen legibus vivimus" (although freed from the laws, yet kings live by the laws).

56. Rycaut cited chapter 19 of Machiavelli's *Prince,* contrasting the dependence of local powers on the Ottoman Empire's absolute ruler with the independent barons of feudal France (the latter was easier to conquer, but harder to keep once conquered), as well as the opening lines of Francis Bacon's essay "Nobility" for the somewhat more judgmental claim that "A Monarchy where there is no Nobility at all, is ever pure and absolute Tyranny, as that of the Turks." Rycaut, *Present State,* 128.

57. "And that such perfidiousness as this might not be Chronicled in future Ages, in disparagement of his Sanctity; he made it lawful for his Believers, in cases of like nature, when the matter concerned those who were Infidels, and of a different perswasion, neither to regard Promises, Leagues, or other Engagements." Rycaut, *Present State,* 182.

58. Rycaut, *Present State,* 179, 141–142 (emphasis in original). Here, as in the case of a number of his more derogatory claims about the legal system, Rycaut cites the sixteenth-century Dutch writer and imperial ambassador to Constantinople, Ogier Ghiselin de Busbecq.

59. Rycaut saw the elaborate ceremonies by which the sultan received ambassadors as designed to impress them into awed descriptions to their sovereigns of his wealth and power. Rycaut, *Present State,* 156.

60. "The Alcoran it self calls this Office inviolable; and it is a Turkish Canon, Elchi zaval yoketer, Do not hurt an Ambassadour, so that the Turks do confess themselves obliged by their own Law to Rules of Civilities, Courteous treatment and Protection of Ambassadours." Rycaut, *Present State,* 155.

61. Rycaut, *Present State,* 160–162.

62. Rycaut, *Present State,* 167–168, citing Busbecq (emphasis in original).

63. See Céline Spector, "Montesquieu, l'Europe et les nouvelles figures de l'Empire," *Revue Montesquieu* 8 (2006): 17–42. On the ideology of the British Empire as "commercial" and "free," see David Armitage, *The Ideological Origins of the British Empire* (Cambridge: Cambridge University Press, 2000).

64. Rycaut, *Present State,* 12.

65. Garcilaso de la Vega, *The Royal Commentaries of Peru in Two Parts* (London: M. Flesher, 1688). The book was said to have influenced Defoe's portrait of Robinson Crusoe; see Anderson, *English Consul in Turkey,* 267.

66. Though he cited Rycaut anonymously in the first edition of 1746, in a much expanded discussion in the 1776 edition, where the Ottoman chapter dwarfs the others, he extensively quoted Rycaut by name.

67. Gabriel Bonnot de Mably, *Le droit public de l'Europe, fondé sur les traitez conclus jusqu'en l'année 1740,* vol. 1 (The Hague: J. Van Duren, 1746), 284–285.

68. Mably, *Le droit public de l'Europe* (1746), 283, 269.

69. Gabriel Bonnot de Mably, *Le droit public de l'Europe fondé sur les traités* (Paris: Bailly, 1776), 347, 375.

70. Mably, *Le droit public de l'Europe* (1776), 353.

71. Nicolas-Antoine Boulanger's *Recherches sur l'origine du despotisme oriental,* published posthumously in 1761, is an influential and early use of the phrase; Boulanger criticized Montesquieu's reliance on climate and argued that instead history and human choices are the cause of differences among regimes, and that while monarchy is the only appropriate form of government for the human race, it was only to be found in Europe. The earliest uses I have found in French and English databases date from the 1750s; see, e.g., Gabriel François, abbé Coyer, *Dissertations pour être lues* (The Hague: Pierre Gosse, 1755), 21: "Si nous vivions sous le despotisme oriental, où l'on ne connoît d'autres loix que la volonté du souverain, d'autres maximes que l'adoration de ses caprices, d'autres principes du gouvernement que la terreur, où aucune fortune, aucune tête n'est en sûreté."

72. Voltaire, *L'A, B, C, ou dialogue entre A, B, C,* in *Political Writings* (Cambridge: Cambridge University Press, 1994), 97. The specialized use of the term "despot" to refer to European principalities dependent on the Ottomans, such as Wallachia, served as a kind of bridge between the more abstract ancient referents coming out of Aristotle and the application of the term to the Ottoman, Persian, and Mughal regimes.

73. François Fénélon, *Directions pour la conscience d'un roi* (The Hague: Neaulme, 1747), 88.

74. [Le Mercier de la Rivière], *L'Ordre naturel et essentiel des sociétés politiques* (Paris: J. Nourse, 1767), 166, 67. See also Robert Shackleton, "Les mots 'despote' et 'despotisme,'" in *Essays on Montesquieu and the Enlightenment,* ed. Robert Shackleton, David Gilson, and Martin Smith (Oxford: Voltaire Foundation, 1988), 482–485.

75. Voltaire, *Commentaire sur l'Esprit des loix de Montesquieu* (1777–1778), in *Les oeuvres complètes de Voltaire,* ed. Sheila Mason, vol. 80B (Oxford: Voltaire Foundation, 2009); see, e.g., 339–341 (on Rycaut and on the sultan's subjection to law and obligation to observe treaties), 356 (on several "just, generous, clement, liberal warriors" among Ottoman viziers), and 369 (on the "common sense, equity, and promptitude" of Turkish legal procedures).

76. Republics and despotisms were subject to their own instabilities, however: successful republics were vulnerable to either territorial overreach or corrupting luxury, and despotism, "corrupt by its nature," provokes rebellion. Charles-Louis de Secondat Montesquieu, *De l'esprit des lois,* in *Oeuvres complètes,* ed. Roger Caillois, vol. 2 (Paris: Gallimard, 1951), bk. 21, ch. 6; bk. 9, ch. 1. I use the (sometimes modified) translation from *The Spirit of the Laws,* ed. Anne Cohler, Basia Miller, and Harold Stone (Cambridge: Cambridge University Press, 1989). See also Michael Mosher, "Montesquieu on Empire and Enlightenment," in *Empire and Modern Political Thought,* ed. Sankar

Muthu (Cambridge: Cambridge University Press, 2012), 112–154, at 114, 148–149.

77. Montesquieu, letters 131 and 102 in *Lettres persanes*, in *Oeuvres complètes*, ed. Roger Caillois, vol. 1 (Paris: Gallimard, 1949), 129–373.

78. Montesquieu, *De l'esprit des lois*, bk. 8, ch. 8.

79. Rubiés, "Oriental Despotism"; Sharon Krause, "Despotism in *The Spirit of Laws*," in *Montesquieu's Science of Politics*, ed. David Carrithers, Michael Mosher, and Paule Rahe (Lanham, MD: Rowman and Littlefield, 2001), 231–272, at 251.

80. Denis de Casabianca, "Comment les régimes peuvent-ils être despotiques? Montesquieu et Boulanger," *Revue française d'histoire des idées politiques* 35 (2012): 37–50.

81. Montesquieu, *De l'esprit des lois*, bk. 2, ch. 1.

82. As Shackleton shows, early readers disagreed radically about whether the text was a defense or critique of monarchy. While most contemporary scholars read the work as a qualified critique that indicated the dangerous proximity of monarchy to despotism, Annelien de Dijn has argued that Montesquieu meant to defend the French monarchy as categorically different from despotism. De Dijn, "Montesquieu's Controversial Context: *The Spirit of the Laws* as a Monarchist Tract," *History of Political Thought* 34 (2013): 66–88.

83. J. De la Porte, *Observations sur L'Esprit des loix, ou l'art de lire ce livre, de l'entendre et d'en juger* (Amsterdam: Mortier, 1751); Claude Dupin, *Observations sur un livre intitulé: De l'Esprit des loix* (Paris: Guérin et Delatour, 1757–1758); François Risteau, *Réponse aux observations sur l'Esprit des loix*, reprinted in Montesquieu and Octavien de Guasco, *Lettres familières du président de Montesquieu, baron de la Brède, à divers amis d'Italie* (Florence, 1767). Montesquieu wrote to Risteau, "Un gouvernement qui est tout à la fois l'État et le prince vous paroît chimérique; je pense, au contraire, qu'il est très-réel & je crois l'avoir peint d'après la vérité." Montesquieu, *Oeuvres complètes*, 3 vols. (Paris: Nagel, 1950–1955), 3:1382. For discussion of the work's reception, see Casabianca, "Comment les régimes peuvent-ils être despotiques?"

84. Rycaut, *Present State*, 5.

85. "Some maintain that the very Oaths and Promises of the Grand Signior are always revocable, when the performance of his Vow is a restriction to the absolute power of the Empire." Rycaut, *Present State*, 9–11. Bayle, *Réponse aux questions*, 276; Montesquieu, *De l'esprit des lois*, bk. 3, ch. 9.

86. This was one of Anquetil's opening charges in *Législation orientale*. Abraham Hyacinthe Anquetil-Duperron, *Législation orientale* (Amsterdam: Marc-Michel Rey, 1778), 1. Krause perhaps more subtly argues that Montesquieu's argument assimilates subjects of despotism to brute nature by suggesting that

the fundamental laws of despotism are like laws of nature in the sense of necessary forces rather than of art and intelligence. See Montesquieu, *De l'esprit des lois*, bk. 1, ch. 1 on the difference between laws of nature and human laws; Krause, "Despotism," 237.

87. Montesquieu, *De l'esprit des lois*, bk. 2, ch. 5.

88. Montesquieu, *De l'esprit des lois*, bk. 2, ch. 4; bk. 3, ch. 10; bk. 5, ch. 16.

89. Montesquieu, *De l'esprit des lois*, bk. 5, ch. 14; bk. 4, ch. 2. Likewise, in monarchies, judges deliberate together, come to agreement, and modify their opinions to make them like the others'. This is not in the nature of republics (bk. 6, ch. 4); this is one respect in which republics bear some structural similarity to despotisms.

90. Montesquieu, *De l'esprit des lois*, bk. 9, ch. 4; bk. 5, ch. 14. Montesquieu also speculates that Asia's distinctive climatic profile drives interstate relations into a dynamic of conquest: "In Asia, the strong and the weak nations face each other . . . therefore, one must be the conquered and the other the conqueror. . . . This is the major reason for the weakness of Asia and the strength of Europe, for the liberty of Europe and the servitude of Asia" (bk. 17, ch. 3).

91. "If the prince is taken prisoner, he is supposed dead, and another ascends the throne. The treaties made by the prisoner are null; his successor would not ratify them" (Montesquieu, *De l'esprit des lois*, bk. 5, ch. 14).

92. As Mosher has noted, although Montesquieu recognized the imperial ambitions of European monarchies and was a sharp critic of Spanish depredations in the Americas, he argued that imperial aggrandizement (at least within Europe) was self-defeating for modern European states. Mosher presents Montesquieu as a "great anti-imperial thinker," but he also conveys the degree to which Montesquieu anticipated nineteenth-century imperial liberals in his apparent acceptance of "colonization that spreads enlightenment" as well as his approval of modern commercial colonization. Mosher, "Montesquieu on Empire and Enlightenment," at 134, 139.

93. Montesquieu, *De l'esprit des lois*, bk. 8, ch. 8.

94. Spector, "Montesquieu, l'Europe"; Mosher, "Montesquieu on Empire and Enlightenment," 145–154.

95. Porter, *Observations*. Another early critic was the political economist Johann Heinrich Gottlob von Justi, in his treatise *Vergleichungen der europäischen mit den asiatischen und andern vermeintlich barbarischen Regierungen* [Comparison of European with Asian and other supposedly barbarian regimes] (Berlin: Johann Heinrich Rüdiger, 1762), 51–52. See C. H. Alexandrowicz, "A Treatise by J. H. G. Justi on Asian Government," *The Indian Year Book of International Affairs* 9–10 (1960): 136–142, reprinted in Alexandrowicz, *Law of Nations in Global History*, 163–167.

96. Porter had a commercial background and had served on both commercial and diplomatic missions on the continent before his Constantinople post, where his appointment may have been due to his brother's connection by marriage to one of the leading "Turkey merchants"; he later became minister-plenipotentiary at Brussels. Alfred Wood, *A History of the Levant Company* (London: Oxford University Press, 1935).

97. Porter, *Observations*, xiv, 8–9.

98. William Robertson, *The history of the reign of the Emperor Charles V,* vol. 1 (London: A. Strahan, 1787), 224. "A state in which the sovereign possesses the absolute command of a vast military force, as also an extensive revenue at his disposal, in which the people have no privileges, and no share, either immediate or remote, in legislation, in which there is no body of hereditary nobility jealous of their rights and distinctions, to stand as an intermediate order between the prince and the people, cannot be distinguished by any name but that of despotism" (470 n43, §3 [note UU]).

99. Porter, *Observations*, xiv, 76–79 (on Ottoman laws to secure property and limit monarchic power).

100. "In despotic states, where there are no fundamental laws, neither is there a depository of laws. This is why religion has so much force in these countries; it forms a kind of permanent depository, and if it is not religion, it is customs that are venerated in the place of laws." Montesquieu, *De l'esprit des lois,* bk. 2, ch. 4.

101. The sultan must appeal to the ulema "for a sanction in every important act of state, whether relative to peace or war" and "cannot take the life of a single subject, without the Mufti's decree" (the Mufti being chosen "out of this hereditary order"). Porter, *Observations*, xxxii.

102. Porter, *Observations*, xix–xx.

103. Porter, *Observations*, xxxi, 76. He likewise disputed Montesquieu's denial of all rights of private property in the Ottoman Empire (49–53).

104. *Observations*, xxxiii–xxxiv (emphasis in original). His source is Marc-Antoine Laugier, *Histoire des négociations pour la Paix concluë à Belgrade,* vol. 1 (Paris: Duchesne, 1768), 157.

105. Porter, *Observations*, 152, 231–232.

106. Porter, *Observations*, 151.

107. Porter, *Observations*, 249, 245–246.

108. The only full-length biography is Raymond Schwab's *Vie d'Anquetil-Duperron* (Paris: Ernest Leroux, 1934). See also the engaging narrative in Anthony Pagden, *Worlds at War* (New York: Random House, 2008), 335–351.

109. For a brief biography and sources on Anquetil de Briancourt, see Anne Mézin, *Les consuls de France au siècle des lumières (1715–1792)* (Paris: Ministère des affaires étrangères, 1997), 98–100. For the broader context of the Com-

pagnie des Indes, see Kate Marsh, *India in the French Imagination* (London: Pickering and Chatto, 2009).

110. Lucette Valensi, "Éloge de l'Orient, éloge de l'orientalisme. Le jeu d'échecs d'Anquetil-Duperron," *Revue de l'histoire des religions* 212 (1995): 419–452.

111. William Jones's intemperate assault on the work, *Lettre à Monsieur A*** du P**** (London, 1771), is described by a recent biographer as having "blotted Jones's scholarly integrity as surely as it blighted the academic career of its addressee." Michael J. Franklin, *Orientalist Jones* (Oxford: Oxford University Press, 2011), 74.

112. Anquetil-Duperron, *Législation orientale,* v–vi. See also Siep Stuurman, "Cosmopolitan Egalitarianism in the Enlightenment: Anquetil-Duperron on India and America," *Journal of the History of Ideas* 68 (2007): 255–278; Frederick Whelan, "Oriental Despotism: Anquetil-Duperron's Response to Montesquieu," *History of Political Thought* 22 (2001): 619–647; Whelan, *Sultans and Savages: Enlightenment Political Thought and Non-Western Societies* (New York: Routledge, 2009), 78–102.

113. The title changed in the course of publication; see the "Avis du libraire" after the title page, *Législation orientale.* The complete manuscript title was *Le despotisme consideré dans les trois états ou il passe pour être le plus absolu, la Turquie, la Perse et l'Indoustan. Ouvrage dans lequel on prouve: 1) Que la manière dont jusqu'ici on a représenté le gouvernement despotique ne peut qu'en donner une idée absolument fausse, 2) Que dans les trois états qui viennent d'être nommés il y a un code de loix écrites qui obligent le prince aussi que les sujets, 3) Que dans ces trois états les particuliers one des propriétés, ou biens meubles et immeubles dont ils jouissent librement.* Bibliothèque nationale de France, Nouvelles acquisitions françaises 453. See the discussion in Franco Venturi, "Oriental Despotism," *Journal of the History of Ideas* 24 (1963): 133–142.

114. Anquetil-Duperron, *Législation orientale,* 34: "It is difficult to abase [*rabaisser*] the human species any further; there is nothing more than to reduce it to the condition of brutes; and this is what M. de M* does."

115. Anquetil-Duperron, *Législation orientale,* 66: "But is it fair [*de l'équité*] to attribute these evils to the constitution of the state?"

116. Anquetil-Duperron, *Législation orientale,* 29 (emphasis in original).

117. "Until now the Princes of the Orient have hardly ever been known but by qualities destructive to humanity. . . . it seems, based on the majority of the Writers of Europe, that the history of these vast countries is but that of a number of great brigands. . . . In numerous volumes, which present nothing but perfidies, usurpations, massacres, the reader is hard put to find a few pages on the laws of these peoples." Anquetil-Duperron, *Législation orientale,* 1.

118. Anquetil-Duperron, *Législation orientale,* 9.

119. Abraham Hyacinth Anquetil-Duperron, *Considérations philosophiques, historiques et géographiques sur les deux mondes,* ed. Guido Abbattista (Pisa:

Scuola Normale Superiore, 1993). This extensive ethnographic manuscript, presented over many sessions to the Académie des Inscription in 1780, remained unpublished in Anquetil's lifetime. Girolamo Imbruglia treats its themes in connection with *Législation orientale*, especially the claim that a society without law was an impossibility, in "Tra Anquetil-Duperron e *L'Histoire des Deux Indes:* Libertà, dispotismo e feudalismo," *Rivista storica italiana* 106 (1994): 140–193, at 142.

120. Whelan rightly and usefully calls Anquetil's critique of the theory of oriental despotism "ideology critique," in the sense that Anquetil "in effect accuses Montesquieu and his followers of presenting an ideology in the familiar sense of an ostensibly scientific doctrine whose covert purpose or effect is to promote a special interest or political programme." Whelan, "Oriental Despotism," 643. Teemu Ruskola analyzes such an ideology in the related context of U.S.–Chinese relations in *Legal Orientalism: China, the United States, and Modern Law* (Cambridge, MA: Harvard University Press, 2013).

121. Anquetil-Duperron, *Législation orientale*, 2: "The Publicists, drawing on travelers' reports, badly understood, form a system of Despotism that in reality exists nowhere"; thus Montesquieu's own sources often furnish counter-evidence to his theory.

122. Anquetil-Duperron, *Législation orientale*, vii.

123. Anquetil-Duperron, *Considérations philosophiques*, 15.

124. Behavior that Europeans call "deceit" [*fourberie*] when they see it in Persia becomes "skill, statecraft [*habilité, politique*]" when practiced by Europeans. Anquetil-Duperron, *Législation orientale*, 37.

125. Anquetil-Duperron, *Législation orientale*, 31–32 (emphasis in original).

126. Anquetil draws widely on sources that do not seem to share his project of rendering Muslim practices recognizable or sympathetic; he selects from travel works that have little to do with law, observations that support his argument, such as the remark that Ottoman legal officers are educated in seminaries where "the *Roman codes* and *pandects,* translated into the Arabic language, are taught and explained, as in the universities of Europe." Anquetil-Duperron, *Législation orientale*, 57, drawing on Thomas Shaw, *Travels, or, Observations relating to several parts of Barbary and the Levant* (London: A. Millar, 1757), 252.

127. Anquetil-Duperron, *Législation orientale*, 61. The question of the degree to which *kanun*, secular sultanic law, modified or overrode şeriat (Sharia) remains the subject of debate. See Kumar, *Visions of Empire*, 114–116.

128. Anquetil-Duperron, *Législation orientale*, 58. He quoted Porter's conclusion that many provisions of the Qur'an constitute a "strong barrier against despotism and corruption."

129. Anquetil-Duperron, *Législation orientale*, 55–56. He cites the treaty as printed in Paris in 1615 in French and Turkish. See *Articles du traicté faict en l'année*

mil six cens quatre, entre Henri le Grand roy de France, & de Navarre, et sultan Amat empereur des Turcs (Paris: l'imprimerie des langues orientales, 1615). Anquetil's reading is supported by recent scholarship.See Alexander H. de Groot, "Historical Development of the Capitulatory Regime," 576.

130. Anquetil-Duperron, *Législation orientale*, 55. For a contemporary English translation, see *The Koran*, trans. N. J. Dawood (New York: Penguin, 1993), 133.

131. Anquetil-Duperron, *Législation orientale*, 5–6. Less ironically he pointed to the Mughal reception of the embassy of Sir Thomas Roe as demonstrating, "by the respect that the Mughals have for foreigners, for Ambassadors, that they know the law of nations" (37).

132. Anquetil-Duperron, *Législation orientale*, 50–51. On La Croix, see John-Paul Ghobrial, *The Whispers of Cities: Information Flows in Istanbul, London and Paris in the Age of William Trumbull* (Oxford: Oxford University Press, 2013), 4.

133. Anquetil-Duperron, *Législation orientale*, vi.

134. Jacques-Benigne Bossuet, *Politique tirée des propres paroles de l'écriture sainte* (Paris: Pierre Cot, 1709), 395–397. Translation from Bossuet, *Politics Drawn from Holy Scripture*, ed. and trans. Patrick Riley (Cambridge: Cambridge University Press, 1990), 263–264. Richard Koebner notes that while Bossuet deliberately avoided the language of despotism in relation to Louis XIV, instead using *"arbitraire"* as the antithesis of legitimate absolutism, he clearly had Aristotle's account of despotic government in mind. Koebner, "Despot and Despotism," 295–296. Anquetil ignores Bossuet's attempted substitution of terms and recommends attention to the passage on "government despotism."

135. "Politique tirée de l'écriture sainte . . . Jugement porté sur cet ouvrage par Monsieur Anquetil Duperron" (1783, 1794); Bibliothèque Nationale de France, département des Manuscrits, cote Français 12838. I am grateful to Oliver Cussen for supplying me with images of the manuscript.

136. *L'Inde en rapport avec l'Europe*, vol. 1 (Paris: Lesguilliez frères, An VII de la République française [1798]), 85–89. Blake Smith, who discusses the radical shift in Anquetil's argument about Mughal legitimacy between *Législation orientale* and *L'Inde en rapport*, argues that in the first work Anquetil articulated for the public sphere a line of argument about the Mughal Empire that had been common among French agents in India—that the empire was legitimate, respectable, and nondespotic—just at the moment when those diplomats began to abandon such a view and seek allies among the Hindu states, especially the Marathas. Smith, "Diplomacy and Its Forms of Knowledge: Anquetil-Duperron, the Balance of Power, and India in the French Global Imaginary, 1778–1803," in *L'Inde des Lumières: discours, histoire, savoirs, XVIIe–XIXe siècle*, ed. Marie Fourcade and Ines Zupanov (Paris: Editions de l'École des hautes études en sciences sociales, 2013), 209–227.

137. Jules Michelet, *Bible de l'humanité* (Paris: F. Chamerot, 1864), 10–11; see also Valensi, "Éloge de l'Orient," 430.

138. Edward Said, "Raymond Schwab and the Romance of Ideas," *Daedalus* 105 (1976): 151–167, at 164. Said distinguished the "large vistas" opened by Anquetil from Jones's controlling efforts to "domesticate the Orient and thereby turn it into a province of European learning," but said nothing about Anquetil's own critique of Orientalist ideology. Said, *Orientalism* (New York: Vintage, 1979), 77–78.

139. Stuurman, "Cosmopolitan Egalitarianism," 278. See also his discussion of Anquetil in Stuurman, *The Invention of Humanity: Equality and Cultural Difference in World History* (Cambridge, MA: Harvard University Press, 2017), 319–322 and 339–341. Lucette Valensi, in contrast, in a rather hostile account that seems partly a reaction against what she sees as the hagiographic nature of earlier accounts, attributes Anquetil's failed reception to his grating narcissism and to what she considers the poor argumentation of *Législation orientale;* she does not credit the work's often acute irony. Valensi, "Éloge de l'Orient," 444.

140. August Wilhelm Heffter, *Le droit international de l'Europe* (Berlin: E. H. Schroeder, 1866), 35–36.

141. Turan Kayaoğlu, *Legal Imperialism: Sovereignty and Extraterritoriality in Japan, the Ottoman Empire, and China* (Cambridge: Cambridge University Press, 2010); Eliana Augusti, "From Capitulations to Unequal Treaties: The Matter of an Extraterritorial Jurisdiction in the Ottoman Empire," *Journal of Civil Law Studies* 4 (2011): 285–307; Richard Horowitz, "International Law and State: Transformation in China, Siam, and the Ottoman Empire during the Nineteenth Century," *Journal of World History* 15 (2004): 455–486.

THREE   Nations and Empires in Vattel's World

1. As David Armitage notes, "Franco Venturi had earlier pointed to the Seven Years' War—'a crisis of the whole of Europe'—as pivotal to the development of Enlightened cosmopolitanism." Armitage, *Foundations of Modern International Thought* (Cambridge: Cambridge University Press, 2013), 37, citing Franco Venturi, *Italy and the Enlightenment: Studies in a Cosmopolitan Century* (London: Longman, 1972), 18–20.

2. Jean-Jacques Rousseau, *Extrait du project de la paix perpetuelle de Monsieur l'abbé de Saint-Pierre* (n.p., 1761); Rousseau, *A Project for Perpetual Peace* (London: M. Cooper, 1761). It is difficult to ascertain the effects of the war on Rousseau himself, who was sheltered during the war in the territory of Neuchâtel by Frederick II.

3. Armitage, *Foundations,* 174–175.

4. Fred Anderson, *Crucible of War* (New York: Knopf, 2000), ch. 1; Franz A. J. Szabo, *The Seven Years' War in Europe, 1756–1763* (Edinburgh: Longman, 2008), ch. 1. As Richard Bourke has put it, "The war in Europe would be fought over the political economy of empire." Bourke, *Empire and Revolution: The Political Life of Edmund Burke* (Princeton, NJ: Princeton University Press, 2015), 165.

5. Emer de Vattel, *Droit des gens, ou principes de la loi naturelle* (London, 1758 [actually Neuchâtel, 1757]). Unless otherwise noted, I quote from the 1797 English translation of *Droit des gens* (hereafter cited as *DG*) reproduced in Vattel, *The Law of Nations,* ed. Béla Kapossy and Richard Whatmore (Indianapolis, IN: Liberty Fund, 2008), citing book, chapter, and section number.

6. See André Bandelier, "De Berlin à Neuchâtel: La Genèse du *Droit des gens* d'Emer de Vattel," in *Schweizer im Berlin des 18. Jahrhunderts,* ed. Martin Fontius and Helmut Holzhey (Berlin: Akademie Verlag, 1996), 45–56. Béla Kapossy likewise situates Vattel in the context of the Swiss Protestant republican tradition, arguing that he was as critical of "bankrupt Saxony" as of "militaristic Prussia." Kapossy, "Introduction: Rival Histories of Emer de Vattel's *Law of Nations,*" *Grotiana* 31 (2010): 5–21, at 8.

7. Adam Smith defended Prussia's move as an example of preemptive action justified "when one nation seems to be conspiring against another." Smith, *Lectures on Jurisprudence,* ed. R. L. Meek, D. D. Raphael, and P. G. Stein (Oxford: Oxford University Press, 1978), 546.

8. Note the inconclusive evidence of the series of volumes attributed to Vattel as a coeditor, called the *Mémoires pour servir à l'histoire de notre tems,* par l'Observateur hollandois, rédigez et augmentez part M.D.V. (Frankfurt and Leipzig: Aux dépens de la Compagnie, 1757–1758). These address both the American and the Asian theaters of the war in a way that may suggest greater attention to the war's extra-European facets than the *Droit des gens* implies.

9. He did observe, in arguing for the importance of precision and specificity in peace treaties, that if the negotiators of the Treaty of Utrecht had been more precise, "we should not see France and England in arms, in order to decide by a bloody war what are to be the boundaries of their possessions in America. But the makers of treaties often designedly leave them in some obscurity, some uncertainty, in order to reserve for their nation a pretext for a rupture:—an unworthy artifice in a transaction wherein good-faith alone ought to preside!" (*DG*, bk. 2, ch. 7, §92).

10 "C'est un traité systématique du Dr[oit] des gens, mais écrit dans un goût à le faire lire par des gens du monde," he wrote to his lifelong correspondent Samuel Formey, an author, journalist, and professor at the Collège français of Berlin, 17 February 1757. Emer de Vattel, *Emer de Vattel à Jean Henri Samuel Formey: Correspondances autour du* Droit des gens, ed. André Bandelier

(Paris: Honoré Champion, 2012), letter 65. In an earlier letter to Formey, Vattel had written of his aspiration to write a book "drawn from the works of Wolf [*sic*], but infinitely shorter, and stripped of that dryness which will eternally repel all the French." Letter 23, Dresden, 27 March 1747.

11. His more narrowly legal context has been called "l'École romande [i.e., francophone Swiss], protestante, du droit naturel," pioneered earlier in the century by Jean Barbeyrac, the translator and popularizer of Grotius and Pufendorf, and Jean Jacques Burlamaqui, professor of civil and natural law in Geneva. André Bandelier, introduction to Vattel, *Vattel à Formey*, vii.

12. Frank S. Ruddy, *International Law in the Enlightenment* (Dobbs Ferry, NY: Oceana, 1975), 283. See also Albert de la Pradelle, introduction to Vattel, *The Law of Nations* (Washington, DC: Carnegie Institution, 1916).

13. Vattel to Formey, Dresden, 21 September 1765, in Vattel, *Vattel à Formey*, letter 84. He also noted that, having been translated into German in 1760, the book was already being cited in Vienna as a "livre classique."

14. See C. G. Fenwick, "The Authority of Vattel," pt. 1, *American Political Science Review* 7 (1913): 395; Emmanuelle Jouannet, *Emer de Vattel et l'émergence doctrinale du droit international classique* (Paris: Pedone, 1998), 14–15; Frank S. Ruddy, "The Acceptance of Vattel," in *Grotian Society Papers 1972*, ed. C. H. Alexandrowicz (The Hague: Martinus Nijhoff, 1972), 177–196.

15. As Ruddy and others have noted, Vattel's was the text Jefferson chose for the education of students at the College of William and Mary in the Law of Nature and of Nations, and it remained so from 1779 to 1841, as it did at Dartmouth College from 1796 to 1828. Ruddy, *International Law in the Enlightenment*. See also Ian Hunter, "'A *Jus gentium* for America': The Rules of War and the Rule of Law in the Revolutionary United States," *Journal of the History of International Law* 14 (2012): 173–206.

16. Preliminaries in *DG*, §21. See also bk. 3, ch. 13, §195, and bk. 2, ch. 4, §54: "all [nations] have the right to be governed as they think proper, and . . . no state has the smallest right to interfere in the government of another."

17. *DG*, bk. 2, ch. 1, §7. He criticizes Grotius for licensing punishment of "transgressions of the law of nature" when these do not affect the rights or safety of the punisher.

18. *DG*, bk. 2, ch. 4, §§54–55. Vattel follows Montesquieu's account and language so closely here that although (like Montesquieu) he cites Garcilaso de la Vega, he may simply be drawing straight from Montesquieu; compare Montesquieu, *De l'esprit des lois*, in *Oeuvres complètes*, ed. Roger Caillois, vol. 2 (Paris: Gallimard, 1951), bk. 26, ch. 22. Garcilaso, though he portrays Atahualpa as a tyrant and usurper who had murdered his brother to illegitimately seize the throne, also describes the Spanish trial and execution of Atahualpa for murder as a travesty and records the protest of various Spanish

officials that "they had put a King to death, during the time that they had given their Parole to the contrary, and were under Obligations of Treaty, and Articles, for his Ransome." See Garcilaso de la Vega, *Royal Commentaries of Peru,* trans. Paul Rycaut (London: M. Flesher, 1688), 478 (bk. 1, ch. 37).

19. Preliminaries in *DG,* §§6, 27, 28 (emphasis in original).

20. For praise, see, e.g., Stephen Neff, *Justice among Nations* (Cambridge, MA: Harvard University Press, 2014), 194–198, and Jouannet, *Emer de Vattel.* Emmanuelle Jouannet reaffirms her views in "Les dualismes du *Droit des gens,"* in *Vattel's International Law in a XXIst Century Perspective,* ed. Peter Haggenmacher and Vincent Chetail (Boston: Martinus Nijhoff, 2011), 133–150.

21. T. J. Hochstrasser, for instance, argues that Vattel's "distinction between a necessary and voluntary law of nations is effectively an endorsement of current practice camouflaged by the supposedly self-enforcing sanction of conscience." Hochstrasser, *Natural Law Theories in the Early Enlightenment* (Cambridge: Cambridge University Press, 2001), 181. Contrast Peter Haggenmacher's contrary judgment that the "so-called voluntary law of nations" in Vattel does not proceed from the will of states but rather is rationally deduced from the "fundamental exigencies of their social relations" and so is really "pseudo-positive" law, "no less obligatory and necessary than the natural law of nations." Haggenmacher, "Le modèle de Vattel et la discipline du droit international," in Haggenmacher and Chetail, *Vattel's International Law,* 3–48, at 18–20.

22. Philip Allott, *Eunomia: A New Order for a New World* (Oxford: Oxford University Press, 2010 [1990]), 247–249. In such a vein, Cornelius van Vollenhoven argued that Vattel "gave a Judas-kiss to Grotius's system" and "enable[d] every state, affirming its sovereignty, to make war on every other state at all times, without being accountable to anyone." Vollenhoven, *The Three Stages of the Law of Nations* (The Hague: Nijhoff, 1912), 27–37.

23. Ian Hunter, "Vattel's *Law of Nations:* Diplomatic Casuistry for the Protestant Nation," *Grotiana* 31 (2010): 108–140, at 108. Hunter's own argument that Vattel strategically used the opposing principles of natural law and national sovereign as poles within which to create a space for "diplomatic casuistics" is discussed below.

24. C. H. Alexandrowicz, *Introduction to the History of the Law of Nations in the East Indies* (Oxford: Clarendon Press, 1967), 10. Ian Hunter and Tetsuya Toyoda have developed the latter interpretation, and other scholars assume it, as discussed below.

25. Preliminaries in *DG,* §28.

26. Preface in *DG.*

27. Sir William Scott in the *Maria,* in Christopher Robinson, *Reports of Cases Argued and Determined in the High Court of Admiralty,* vol. 1 (London,

1806), 340–378, at 363. He adds, "And to be sure the only marvel in the case is, that [Vattel] should mention it as a law merely modern, when it is remembered that it is a principle, not only of the civil law, (on which great part of the law of nations is founded,) but of the private jurisprudence of most countries in *Europe*."

28. On the centrality to Vattel's project of the conception of the state as moral person, see Ben Holland, "The Moral Person of the State: Emer de Vattel and the Foundations of International Legal Order," *History of European Ideas* 37 (2011): 438–445. Ian Hunter has argued that Vattel's apparently abstract state is implicitly more concretely a "Protestant territorial republic." Hunter, "Vattel's *Law of Nations*," 118–119.

29. For background, see E. Béguelin, "En souvenir de Vattel," in *Recueil de travaux* (Neuchâtel: Attinger, 1929); A. de Lapradelle, "Emer de Vattel," in *The Classics of International Law—Vattel,* ed. J. B. Scott, vol. 1 (Washington, DC: Carnegie Institution of Washington, 1916); Béla Kapossy and Richard Whatmore, introduction to Vattel, *Law of Nations,* ix–xx.

30. In Vattel's French, "un pays, dont la liberté est l'ame, le trésor & la loi fondamentale." *DG*, Preface. As Koskenniemi writes, "Grotius did not intend to write a textbook on 'the law of nations.' Instead, he was concerned to say a number of things about the legitimacy of war, in particular war waged by the United Provinces for access to the colonies." Martti Koskenniemi, "The Advantage of Treaties: International Law in the Enlightenment," *Edinburgh Law Review* 13 (2009): 27–67, at 51.

31. See Antony Anghie, "Vattel and Colonialism," in Haggenmacher and Chetail, *Vattel's International Law,* 237–253; Mark Hickford, "'Decidedly the Most Interesting Savages on the Globe': An Approach to the Intellectual History of Maori Property Rights, 1837–53," *History of Political Thought* 27 (2006): 122–167, at 132; Andrew Fitzmaurice, *Sovereignty, Property, and Empire 1500–2000* (Cambridge: Cambridge University Press, 2014).

32. Alexandrowicz, *Introduction to the History of the Law of Nations,* 9, quotes Vattel's precept that "all sovereign and independent states governing themselves 'by their own authority and laws' are ipso facto members of the natural Society of Nations" (*DG*, bk. 1, ch. 1, §4).

33. "The classic law had been definitely an obstacle to the policy of those European agencies in the East Indies which aimed at the elimination of subordinate Rulers from the family of nations. Vattel considered them part and parcel of the natural Society of Nations in which *de facto* sovereignty meant *de jure* sovereignty (*Droit des Gens,* Vol I, ch I)." Alexandrowicz, *Introduction to the History of the Law of Nations,* 153. Note that Vattel does not specifically refer to East Indian powers in the section Alexandrowicz cites.

34. Hunter, "A *Jus gentium* for America," 181; Kapossy, in "Rival Histories," offers a less polemical version of the argument that the Swiss Protestant republican tradition is a key context for Vattel's account of the state.

35. Tetsuya Toyoda, *Theory and Politics of the Law of Nations: Political Bias in International Law Discourse of Seven German Court Councilors in the Seventeenth and Eighteenth Centuries* (Leiden: Martinus Nijhoff, 2011), 177–179.

36. Kapossy, for instance, assumes that Vattel's account of interstate relations refers to a "European order," though he notes that recent scholarship has read thinkers from the Spanish scholastics to Pufendorf as "theorizing the emerging modern sovereign states against the backcloth of European imperialism." Kapossy, "Rival Histories," 12. Isaac Nakhimovsky describes the text as "an attempt to reconcile the workings of the European state system with the idea of international society embedded in the natural law tradition." Nakhimovsky, "Vattel's Theory of the International Order: Commerce and the Balance of Power in the *Law of Nations*," *History of European Ideas* 33 (2007): 157–173, at 158. Nakhimovsky uses the terms "global republic" and "European republic" interchangeably.

37. Ian Hunter, "The Figure of Man and the Territorialisation of Justice in 'Enlightenment' Natural Law: Pufendorf and Vattel," *Intellectual History Review* 23 (2013): 289–307, at 291.

38. See, e.g., Randall Lesaffer, "A Schoolmaster Abolishing Homework? Vattel on Peacemaking and Peace Treaties," in Haggenmacher and Chetail, *Vattel's International Law,* 354–384, at 354.

39. Martti Koskenniemi, "The Advantage of Treaties: International Law in the Enlightenment," *Edinburgh Law Review* 13 (2009): 27–67, at 38–40. See also Koskenniemi, "International Law and *raison d'état*: Rethinking the Prehistory of International Law," in *The Roman Foundations of the Law of Nations,* ed. Benedict Kingsbury and Benjamin Straumann (Oxford: Oxford University Press, 2010), 297–339, at 298.

40. In this less doctrinally precise usage, questions of the grounds, or legal nature, of the law of nations tend not to be addressed.

41. Michel de Montaigne, "Of Coaches" ("Des coches"), in *Essays,* trans. Donald M. Frame (Stanford, CA: Stanford University Press, 1958), 696.

42. Jean Bodin, *Les six livres de la république* (Paris: Jacques Du Puys, 1576), 255 (bk. 2, ch. 5).

43. "The character of ambassador was not a sufficiently august title to cover their rusticity. Wicquefort, in his treatise on the ambassador and his functions, speaks of them in such terms." Marquis d'Argens, *Lettres juives,* vol. 4 (Amsterdam: Paul Gautier, 1736), 325.

44. Gabriel Bonnot de Mably, *Des principes des négociations, pour server d'introduction au "Droit public de l'Europe"* (The Hague, 1757). Translation

from Mably, *The Principles of Negotiations: or, an Introduction to the Public Law of Europe Founded on Treaties, etc.* (London: James Rivington and James Fletcher, 1758), 37–38, 11, 26; *DG*, bk. 3, ch. 3, §47. Mably dated the origins of the system to the treaties of Westphalia: "The Treaties that preceded those of Munster and Osnabruck are monuments that a historian may consult but are largely useless for a *publiciste*"; that is, for the study of public law. Mably, *Le droit public de l'Europe fondé sur les traites* (Paris: Bailly, 1776 [1746]), v–vi. Peter Haggenmacher has noted, however, that Mably's idea of a public law of Europe initiated by those treaties is "entirely different from the supposed 'Westphalian Order'" commonly invoked as a backdrop to twentieth-century international law. Haggenmacher, "Le modèle de Vattel," *Vattel's International Law*, 3–48, at 48.

45. In a note added to the 1773 edition (Preliminaries in *DG*, §6n).
46. For influential strands of Roman thought, the Roman Empire was "not merely a political authority; it became the embodiment of the Stoic notion of the *koinos nomous*, the universal law for all mankind." Anthony Pagden, *Burdens of Empire* (Cambridge: Cambridge University Press, 2015), 9.
47. Fitzmaurice, *Sovereignty, Property, and Empire*, 10.
48. Preliminaries in *DG*, §§12, 26.
49. Hunter, "Vattel's *Law of Nations*," 129.
50. Hunter, "Vattel's *Law of Nations*," 114. See also Hunter's claim that Vattel's defense of this conception, "as in all such cases, amounts only to the declaration of his preference for a particular moral anthropology over rival ones" (113n17).
51. Richard Rorty argued similarly in that ultimately we can give no good reasons for our moral beliefs but can only assert that they are meaningful to us. Rorty, *Achieving Our Country: Leftist Thought in Twentieth-Century America* (Cambridge, MA: Harvard University Press, 1998).
52. Ian Hunter, "Kant and Vattel in Context: Cosmopolitan Philosophy and Diplomatic Casuistry," *History of European Ideas* 4 (2013): 477–502, at 499.
53. Preliminaries in *DG*, §§3, 18.
54. See Vattel's claim that the interpretation of treaties always requires inferences about the "just application" of general principles to particular cases, as well as about when to suspend the principle altogether: "If a case occurs, to which the well-known reason of a law or promise is utterly inapplicable, that case ought to be excepted, although, if we were barely to consider the meaning of the terms, it should seem to fall within the purview of the law or promise." *DG*, bk. 2, ch. 17, §292. Vattel was described in an English review of his *Questions de Droit Naturel* as "this ingenious and entertaining Casuist." *The Monthly Review* 28 (1763): 509.
55. Adam Smith, *Theory of Moral Sentiments,* ed. D. D. Raphael and A. L. Macfie (Oxford: Oxford University Press, 1976), VII.iv.7–37. See James Chandler,

England in 1819: The Politics of Literary Culture and the Case of Romantic Historicism (Chicago: University of Chicago Press, 1998), 312; I am indebted to his discussions of casuistry there and in Chandler, "On the Face of the Case: Conrad, *Lord Jim*, and the Sentimental Novel," *Critical Inquiry* 33 (2007): 837–864, as well as to many illuminating conversations.

56. Smith, *Theory of Moral Sentiments*, VII.iv.33–34. While Richard Tuck places Vattel in a strand of thought that includes Grotius and Locke, largely on the grounds of his support for expropriating the lands of nomadic peoples, a key respect in which he departs from Grotius and Locke is in this restriction of the right to execute the law of nature. Tuck, *Rights of War and Peace* (Cambridge: Cambridge University Press, 1999), 193.

57. Edmund Leites has argued that while a tradition of Protestant casuistry existed in the sixteenth and seventeenth centuries, by the eighteenth it had come to be rejected in favor of the self-reliant conscience. Leites, "Conscience, Casuistry, and Moral Decision: Some Historical Perspectives," *Journal of Chinese Philosophy* 2 (1974): 41–58, at 55.

58. Chandler describes casuistry as "a two-way movement in which now the general normative scheme, now the particular event or situation, is being tested." Chandler, *England in 1819,* 209. For the parallel dynamic in the law of nations, see Jeremy Waldron, "*Ius gentium*: A Defence of Gentili's Equation of the Law of Nations and the Law of Nature," in Kingsbury and Straumann, *Roman Foundations,* 283–296. Margaret Sampson argues that the Grotian tradition of natural law should be seen as a Protestant adaptation of Counter-Reformation casuistry. Sampson, "Laxity and Liberty in Seventeenth-Century English Political Thought," in *Conscience and Casuistry in Early Modern Europe,* ed. Edmund Leites (Cambridge: Cambridge University Press, 1988), 72–118. She argues that it was to (over)accentuate differences between Grotian natural law and Catholic casuistry that Henry Maine insisted in *Ancient Law* on the influence of Roman law on Grotius.

59. Jouannet, "Les dualismes du *Droit des gens,*" 147. Casuistry understood in this way likewise accords with Nakhimovsky's description of the function of the law of nations in Vattel: "to guide states' judgments of their utility so that the limitations they imposed on mutual aid were no greater than they absolutely had to be in order to assure their own liberty." Nakhimovsky, "Vattel's Theory of the International Order," 162. Jouannet praises the "very great practical success" of Vattel's treatise, though it is worth asking to what extent the *Droit des gens* was used in the way Vattel intended, as a guide to conscientious states or leaders. That it simply gave legal cover to statesmen to continue their destructive practices was the force of Kant's criticism in *Toward Perpetual Peace* of Vattel, with Grotius and Pufendorf, as "sorry comforters."

60. *DG*, bk. 2, ch. 1, §§15–16. In discussing Vattel's use of the phrase "*l'ennemi du Genre-humain*" (*hostis humani generis*), Daniel Edelstein notes its more

general usage in eighteenth-century French thought, attributing its currency to the theological resonance of the phrase given its use in Roman Catholic liturgies as a term for the devil. Edelstein, "War and Terror: The Law of Nations from Grotius to the French Revolution," *French Historical Studies* 31 (2008): 229–262, at 243. See also Walter Rech, *Enemies of Mankind: Vattel's Theory of Collective Security* (Leiden: Martinus Nijhoff, 2013).

61. See also *DG*, bk. 2, ch. 7, §94 (on the justice of China's former prohibition to foreigners to enter the country) and bk. 1, ch. 12, §148 (on the prudence of China's expulsion of European missionaries).

62. *DG*, bk. 2, ch. 12, §§162–164; *DG*, bk. 4, ch. 7, §103.

63. In *DG*, bk. 2, ch. 1, §4, Vattel gives two European examples of prudent and just leagues against aggressors: the United Provinces against Louis XIV, and Poland's rescue of Austria from the Turkish siege of Vienna, which saved "possibly all Germany, and his own kingdom."

64. *DG*, bk. 2, ch. 1, §§7, 15, 16.

65. *DG*, bk. 2, ch. 17, §273. See, e.g., Vattel's account of the "enormous abuses which the popes formerly made of their authority" by licensing Christian kings to break treaties, including one between the Polish king Vladislaus III and the Turkish sultan Murad II; the Polish king, having been freed by the pope from his oath, illegitimately renewed hostilities with Turkey and "paid dearly for his perfidy, or rather his superstitious weakness" (*DG*, bk. 2, ch. 15, §223). See also his account of the "perfidious Christien II." of Denmark (r. 1513–1523), who accepted assistance from the Swedes and then absconded with some of their hostages in violation of the "sacred faith" with which the hostages were given (*DG*, bk. 2, ch. 16, §248).

66. *DG*, bk. 2, ch. 17, §282.

67. Vattel canvassed histories of various non-European peoples for information on how they understood the law of nations, including two further references to the operation of the law of nations regarding ambassadors in Asia in his notes incorporated in the posthumous 1773 edition. The texts on which he based these notes were Marigny's *Histoire des Arabes* and La Croix's *Histoire de Timur-Bec* (Paris: A. Deshayes, 1722). La Croix used the language of the law of nations to describe principles insisted upon by Timur; but his text flags this as "the law of nations observed by the Tartars," whereas Vattel includes no such qualifier but seems to treat it as an instance of the universal law of nations.

68. *DG*, bk. 4, ch. 7, §103. The earlier paragraph on the Mexicans that he cites here (§84) is not backhanded in the same way, though it does highlight the restricted nature of the protection, noting that ambassadors "could not deviate from the high road without forfeiting their rights:—a prudent and judicious reservation" intended to prevent the abuse of ambassadorial privilege for the purpose of spying.

69. He implies a narrative of progress when he writes, of the unjust punishment by the victors of a governor who had obstinately defended a town under siege, "In the last century this notion still prevailed; it was looked upon as one of the laws of war, and is not, even at present totally exploded"; but his explicit point is that the ancients had superior principles on this question: "What an idea! to punish a brave man for having performed his duty! Very different were the principles of Alexander the Great, who spared some Milesians for their courage and fidelity." *DG*, bk. 3, ch. 8, §143. See also bk. 2, ch. 8, §112, on the survival of the "barbarous practice" of escheatage in a contemporary Europe "so enlightened and so full of humanity."

70. *DG*, bk. 2, ch. 1, §20.

71. *DG*, bk. 3, ch. 8, §148. John Millar's 1771 *Origin of the distinction of ranks* would famously place the rising "condition of women" at the heart of his account of societal development.

72. *DG*, bk. 1, ch. 8, §§97, 85. Britain's pamphlet wars over the East India Company's trade monopoly were to erupt only in the 1760s.

73. *DG*, bk. 1, ch. 23, §§281–287. On *Mare liberum*, see David Armitage, introduction to Grotius, *The Free Sea*, ed. David Armitage (Indianapolis, IN: Liberty Fund, 2004).

74. *DG*, bk. 3, ch. 3, §34. Daniel Edelstein has argued that a "horror of wartime atrocities," which "entailed an inversely proportional damnation of those who disrespected the law of nations . . . reached its apex in Vattel's *Droit des gens*." Edelstein, "War and Terror," 238. See also Edelstein, *The Terror of Natural Right: Republicanism, the Cult of Nature, and the French Revolution* (Chicago: University of Chicago Press, 2009), 39. But if Europeans seeking to vilify revolutionary France and deny it the protections of sovereignty could draw on this passage, Vattel was as readily cited by others in favor of negotiating for peace with France; see, e.g., the Earl of Lauderdale's speech of 5 June 1795, relying on Vattel for the claims that every self-governing nation is a sovereign state protected from intervention and "that foreign nations may receive Ambassadors and other Ministers, even from an usurper, and send such ministers to them." *Parliamentary Register* 42 (1794–1795). Vattel also names the German barbarians who "destroyed the Roman empire: nor was it till long after their conversion to Christianity that this ferocity wore off"; any humanizing effects Christianity might have are, he suggests, weak; *DG*, bk. 3, ch. 3, §34.

75. *DG*, bk. 2, ch. 7, §78. In contrast, the Dutch jurist Cornelius van Bynkershoek specified that the Barbary States were "entitled to the rights of independent states," even if they sometimes violated treaties or acted "with less justice than others," because perfect respect for treaties could not be expected of any state. Bynkershoek, *Quaestionum Juris Publici Libri Duo*, trans. Tenney Frank,

vol. 2 (Oxford: Clarendon Press, 1930 [1737]), 99. Note that Vattel illustrates his milder formulation of the nation whose "restless and mischievous disposition, ever ready to injure others" gives others a right to form a coalition against it with the example of Philip II of Spain (*DG*, bk. 2, ch. 4, §53).

76. Walter Rech argues that Vattel's originality lay in his argument for the collective enforcement of international law not for either moral or "theoretical" purposes (as in Wolff's account of a world state), but rather for "straightforwardly pragmatic" and utilitarian reasons of basic security; but he holds further that Vattel exhibited a "bias" against the Barbary regencies that anticipated nineteenth-century defenses of a civilizing mission in North Africa. Rech, *Enemies of Mankind.*

77. Preface in *DG*, bk. 1, ch. 1, §9, asserting that Neuchâtel, despite sharing a king with Prussia, retained "all its rights as a free and sovereign state." Frederick Whelan calls Vattel's conception of a generic type of sovereign state, given the heterogeneity of states around him, "a rather daring act of the theoretical imagination." Whelan, "Vattel's Doctrine of the State," *History of Political Thought* 9 (1988): 76–77.

78. See Daragh Grant, "Law, Sovereignty, and Empire in the Atlantic World" (unpublished paper, 2015).

79. See, e.g., Nakhimovsky, "Vattel's Theory of the International Order," arguing that Vattel saw the balance of power as the key device by which "a system of independent states could be prevented from destroying the natural society that united them" (160).

80. *DG*, bk. 3, ch. 3, §47.

81. *DG*, bk. 4, ch. 4, §37. For Vattel's precept about war *en forme* (that both sides in a publicly declared war should be considered, by one another and by outsiders, as presumptively just) to hold, those declaring war must present at least a plausible pretext for their cause: this is the "homage which unjust men pay to justice" (*DG*, bk. 3, ch. 3, §32). Sometimes, as in the case of Cortes, even this seemingly low bar is not met. For discussion, see Gabriella Silvestrini, "Justice, War, and Inequality: The Unjust Aggressor and the Enemy of the Human Race in Vattel's Theory of the Law of Nations," *Grotiana* 31 (2010): 44–68.

FOUR   Critical Legal Universalism in the Eighteenth Century

1. C. H. Alexandrowicz, "G. F. de Martens on Asian Treaty Practice," *Indian Year Book of International Affairs* 13, pt. 1 (1964): 74, reprinted in Alexandrowicz, *The Law of Nations in Global History*, ed. David Armitage and Jennifer Pitts (Oxford: Oxford University Press, 2017), 191.

2. Jennifer Pitts, *A Turn to Empire* (Princeton, NJ: Princeton University Press, 2005), 63–85. I argue there that Burke's appeals to the law of nature

and nations served as much to mark the expansive geographic scope of states' duties as to provide substantive content.

3. On traditions of legal pluralism, see Paul S. Berman, "Global Legal Pluralism," *Southern California Law Review* 80 (2007): 1155–1237; Sally Engle Merry, "Legal Pluralism," *Law and Society Review* 22 (1988): 869–896; Merry, *Colonizing Hawai'i: The Cultural Power of Law* (Princeton, NJ: Princeton University Press, 1999); Lauren Benton, *Law and Colonial Cultures: Legal Regimes in World History, 1400–1900* (Cambridge: Cambridge University Press, 2002); Lauren Benton and Richard J. Ross, eds., *Legal Pluralism and Empires, 1500–1850* (New York: New York University Press, 2013).

4. Sankar Muthu, *Enlightenment against Empire* (Princeton, NJ: Princeton University Press, 2003); Clement Hawes, *The British Eighteenth Century and Global Critique* (New York: Palgrave Macmillan, 2005); Frederick Whelan, *Enlightenment Political Thought and Non-Western Societies: Sultans and Savages* (New York: Routledge, 2009).

5. A. H. Anquetil-Duperron, dedication in *Législation orientale* (Amsterdam: Marc-Michel Ray, 1778), iii–iv. He called for the study of Asian languages, "because it contributes to our knowledge of lands that are more considerable than Europe, and it presents us with a grand survey proper to perfect the knowledge of mankind, and above all to assure the inalienable rights of humanity" (181).

6. Daniel O'Neill, *Edmund Burke and the Conservative Logic of Empire* (Berkeley: University of California Press, 2016), 68–75; Margaret Kohn and Daniel I. O'Neill, "A Tale of Two Indias: Burke and Mill on Empire and Slavery in the West Indies and Americas," *Political Theory* 34 (2006): 192–228.

7. Edmund Burke, "Address to the Colonists" (January 1777), in *The Writings and Speeches of Edmund Burke,* ed. Paul Langford, 9 vols. (Oxford: Oxford University Press, 1981–2015) (hereafter cited as *WSEB*), 3:281. Burke discussed Native Americans in speeches of the 1770s primarily in relation to whether it was appropriate for the British to deploy them in battle against the rebelling American colonists. The other major source of his thought on Native Americans is the cowritten book *Account of the European Settlements,* which cannot definitively be attributed to Burke; see [Edmund Burke and William Burke], *An Account of the European Settlements in America* (London: R. and J. Dodsley, 1757). See also Richard Bourke, *Empire and Revolution* (Princeton, NJ: Princeton University Press, 2015), 162–176.

8. A. H. Anquetil-Duperron, *Considérations philosophiques, historiques et géographiques sur les deux mondes,* ed. Guido Abbattista (Pisa: Scuola Normale Superiore, 1993).

9. He could also praise Hastings for having "established the British throne with majesty on the ruins of Mogol power." A. H. Anquetil-Duperron, *L'Inde*

en rapport avec l'Europe: Ouvrage divisé en deux parties (Paris: Lesguilliez frères, An VII de la République française [1798]), xxiv.

10. Nicholas B. Dirks, *The Scandal of Empire: India and the Creation of Imperial Britain* (Cambridge, MA: Harvard University Press, 2006); Robert Travers, *Ideology and Empire in Eighteenth-Century India: The British in Bengal* (Cambridge: Cambridge University Press, 2007), 220.

11. In 1762, the *Annual Register* (then under Burke's editorship) devoted considerable space to translated excerpts of Anquetil-Duperron's account of his voyage to India, with an introduction that lavishly praised his erudition and character. *The Annual Register; or, A View of the History, Politicks, and Literature of the Year 1762* (London, 1762), 103–112 [introduction], 112–129 [translation].

12. Sanjay Subrahmanyam, *The Portuguese Empire in Asia, 1500–1700: A Political and Economic History* (London: Longman, 1993); Om Prakash, ed., *European Commercial Expansion in Early Modern Asia* (Aldershot, UK: Variorum, 1997).

13. Philip J. Stern, *The Company-State: Corporate Sovereignty and the Early Modern Foundations of the British Empire in India* (Oxford: Oxford University Press, 2011), 9–10; Stern, "History and Historiography of the English East India Company: Past, Present, and Future!," *History Compass* 7 (2009): 1146–1180.

14. The decisive defeat of the French and their local allies at the Battle of Plassey (1757) led to the Company's acquisition of the diwani of Bengal (1765), powers of revenue collection and administration of justice delegated by the declining Mughal Empire that were widely understood as Company "sovereignty" over the vast territory. See Huw V. Bowen, "A Question of Sovereignty? The Bengal Land Revenue Issue, 1765–67," *Journal of Imperial and Commonwealth History* 16 (1988): 155–176. On the incompatibility of the interests of merchant and sovereign, see Adam Smith, *An Inquiry into the Nature and Causes of the Wealth of Nations,* ed. R. H. Campbell, A. S. Skinner, and W. B. Todd (Oxford: Oxford University Press, 1976), 637–641; Thomas Pownall, *The Right, Interest, and Duty of the State, as Concerned in the Affairs of the East Indies* (London: S. Bladon, 1773), 3–4.

15. Bowen, "A Question of Sovereignty?," 155.

16. *Journals of the House of Commons,* 42:666, quoted by P. J. Marshall in *The Impeachment of Warren Hastings* (London: Oxford University Press, 1965), 1. The trial itself began in 1788. See also Marshall, "Burke and Empire," in *Hanoverian Britain and Empire: Essays in Memory of Philip Lawson,* ed. Stephen Taylor, Richard Connors, and Clyve Jones (Woodbridge, UK: Boydell Press, 1998), 288–298; Geoffrey Carnall and Colin Nicholson, eds., *The Impeachment of Warren Hastings: Papers from a Bicentenary Commemoration* (Edinburgh:

Edinburgh University Press, 1989); David Musselwhite, "The Trial of Warren Hastings," in *Literature, Politics, and Theory: Papers from the Essex Conference, 1976–84,* ed. Francis Baker, Peter Hulme, Margaret Iversen, and Diana Loxley (London: Methuen, 1986), 77–103; Dirks, *Scandal of Empire;* Mithi Mukherjee, "Justice, War, and the Imperium: India and Britain in Edmund Burke's Prosecutorial Speeches in the Impeachment Trial of Warren Hastings," *History Cooperative Journal* 23 (2005): 589–630; Mukherjee, *India in the Shadows of Empire: A Legal and Political History* (Oxford: Oxford University Press, 2010); and Bourke's unrivalled account combining compelling interpretation of Burke's arguments with a meticulous narrative of events in *Empire and Revolution,* 627–775, 820–850.

17. "Questions of effeminacy, the decline of landed families, and the figuration of despotism as errant masculinity suddenly emerge as the substance of the Whig case against East India Company's flirtations with disturbing modes of sovereignty." Daniel O'Quinn, *Staging Governance: Theatrical Imperialism in London, 1770–1800* (Baltimore, MD: Johns Hopkins University Press, 2005), 124. See also Isaac Kramnick, *The Rage of Edmund Burke: Portrait of an Ambivalent Conservative* (New York: Basic Books, 1977); Regina Janes, "At Home Abroad: Edmund Burke in India," *Bulletin of Research in the Humanities* 82 (1979): 160–174; Frans De Bruyn, "Edmund Burke's Gothic Romance: The Portrayal of Warren Hastings in Burke's Writings and Speeches on India," *Criticism* 29 (1987): 415–438; Sara Suleri, *The Rhetoric of English India* (Chicago: University of Chicago Press, 1992); Nicole Reynolds, "Phebe Gibbes, Edmund Burke, and the Trials of Empire," *Eighteenth-Century Fiction* 20 (2007–2008): 151–176.

18. See especially Conor Cruise O'Brien, *The Great Melody: A Thematic Biography and Commented Anthology of Edmund Burke* (Chicago: University of Chicago Press, 1992); Frederick G. Whelan, *Edmund Burke and India: Political Morality and Empire* (Pittsburgh, PA: University of Pittsburgh Press, 1996); Uday Singh Mehta, *Liberalism and Empire* (Chicago: University of Chicago Press, 1999); David Bromwich, introduction to Edmund Burke, *On Empire, Liberty, and Reform: Speeches and Letters,* ed. David Bromwich (New Haven, CT: Yale University Press, 2000); Lida Maxell, *Public Trials* (Oxford: Oxford University Press, 2014); Bourke, *Revolution and Empire.*

19. E.g., F. P. Lock, *Edmund Burke,* 2 vols. (Oxford: Oxford University Press, 1998–2006), 2:468. Marshall notes that whereas the articles of charge were more concerned with public opinion, the articles of impeachment sought to establish a legal case (*WSEB,* 6:126). By the closing speech, when it was clear the legal case had been lost, moral argument again became paramount.

20. Mithi Mukherjee has compellingly proposed that Burke's conception of empire was primarily juridical, that he used a "discourse of empire as a

deterritorialized discourse of justice" and saw a "homology between the categories of justice and empire," though arguably she exaggerates the continuity
Burke saw between empire and justice, given his profound doubts about
whether the British Empire could in practice govern India justly. Mukherjee,
India in the Shadows of Empire, 7.

21. *WSEB,* 7:256, where he notes that the relevant facts have been established
during the trial.

22. Dirks, *Scandal of Empire,* 314; Travers, *Ideology and Empire,* 220.

23. As Richard Bourke has noted, the variability of spellings of Vattel's name
that we find in the newspaper records of Burke's speech suggests his relative
unfamiliarity to a British audience (the *Morning Herald,* 15 May 1781, quoted
Burke as citing "Votelle, the last and best writer upon the subject"; the *London
Chronicle* of 15 May 1781 had, "Vallette, a Swiss, the last writer on the law of
nations, who was an author of acknowledged reputation, had availed himself
of every former authority, and from his country was likely to be impartial").
Bourke, *Empire and Revolution,* 436–439.

24. "Letter to the Sheriffs of Bristol," in *WSEB,* 3:295; "Inquiry into the Seizure of
Private Property in St. Eustatius" (14 May 1781), in *The Speeches of the Right
Honourable Edmund Burke, in the House of Commons, and in Westminster-
Hall,* 4 vols. (London, 1816), 2:248–263, and "Motion for an Inquiry into the
Confiscation of the Effects Taken on the Island of St. Eustatius" (4 De-
cember 1781), 2:313–325.

25. Edward Keene has argued that as early as Grotius, we can find a bifurcated
notion of law and sovereignty, so that while sovereignty in Europe was seen
as unitary and absolute, the prerogatives of sovereignty in Asia were seen by
European theorists as divided between semi-sovereign Asian rulers and
European states and their agents. Edward Keene, *Beyond the Anarchical
Society: Grotius, Colonialism and Order in World Politics* (Cambridge:
Cambridge University Press, 2002).

26. See Vattel, introduction to *Droit des gens, ou principes de la loi naturelle*
(London, 1758 [actually Neuchâtel, 1757]), §§14–21. The law of nations is the
"science of the rights which exist between Nations or States, and of the
obligations corresponding to these rights" (§3). Recent challenges to such a
"monist . . . statist . . . and positivist" conception of law include William
Twining, *Globalisation and Legal Theory* (London: Butterworths, 2000),
and Robert Cover, "Nomos and Narrative," in Cover, *Narrative, Violence,
and the Law: The Essays of Robert Cover,* ed. Martha Minow, Michael Ryan,
and Austin Sarat (Ann Arbor: University of Michigan Press, 1993), 95–172.

27. On Vattel's influence on Burke, and Burke's late departures from Vattel
during the war with revolutionary France, see David Armitage, "Edmund
Burke and Reason of State," *Journal of the History of Ideas* 61 (2000): 617–634;

Armitage, *Foundations of Modern International Thought* (Cambridge: Cambridge University Press, 2013), 154–171; Iain Hampsher-Monk, "Edmund Burke's Changing Justification for Intervention," *Historical Journal* 48 (2005): 65–100; Isaac Nakhimovsky, "Carl Schmitt's Vattel and the 'Law of Nations' between Enlightenment and Revolution," *Grotiana* 31 (2010): 141–161.

28. Lauren Benton and Adam Clulow, "Legal Encounters and the Origins of Global Law," in *The Cambridge World History,* vol. 6, pt. 2: *The Construction of a Global World, 1400–1800 CE: Patterns of Change,* ed. Jerry H. Bentley, Sanjay Subrahmanyam, and Merry Wiesner-Hanks (Cambridge: Cambridge University Press, 2015), 80–100.

29. See Edmund Burke, "First Letter on a Regicide Peace" (1796), in *WSEB,* 9:248–251.

30. *WSEB,* 6:367. This is echoed in the closing speech: "We do contend that the Law of Nations is the Law of India as well as Europe, because it is the Law of reason and the Law of nature" (*WSEB,* 7:291).

31. E. A. Bond, ed., *Speeches of the Managers and Counsel in the Trial of Warren Hastings,* 3 vols. (London: Longman, Green, 1860), 3:175, 226–227, 344, 372–373. Hastings's lawyers cite Vattel in several of these instances.

32. *The Minutes of what was offered by Warren Hastings, Esquire, Late Governor General of Bengal, at the Bar of the House of Commons, upon the Matter of the Several Charges of High Crimes and Misdemeanors, Presented Against him in the Year 1786,* 2nd ed., 2 vols. (London: J. Debrett, 1786), 1:87 (emphasis in original).

33. *WSEB,* 7:262. For his praise of Halhed's compilation, see *WSEB,* 7:265–267. Burke ridiculed Hastings for forswearing that defense, then "get[ting] his Counsel [Edward Law] to resort to it again and to shew that India had nothing but arbitrary power for its Government." See *WSEB,* 7:261–262. F. P. Lock notes that a witness, Major Scott, claimed that Hastings had not even seen parts of this testimony before reading them to the Commons. Lock, *Edmund Burke,* 2:182. P. J. Marshall goes so far as to say that in these passages Burke was "probably destroying a target of his own construction" (*WSEB,* 7:267); but Hastings's defense contributed to the construct.

34. *WSEB,* 7:264–265, 285. The Holy Roman Empire served as one model of a system of plural legal orders to which Burke implicitly gestured in inviting his audience to imagine India on the model of Germany (*WSEB,* 5:390).

35. See, e.g., his letter to Nathaniel Smith introducing a translation of the *Bhagavad Gita,* in *The British Discovery of Hinduism in the Eighteenth Century,* ed. P. J. Marshall (Cambridge: Cambridge University Press, 1970), 184–191. On Hastings's patronage of Orientalist research, see P. J. Marshall, "Warren Hastings as Scholar and Patron," in *Statesmen, Scholars, and Merchants,* ed. J. S. Bromley and P. G. M. Dickson (Oxford: Clarendon Press, 1973).

36. Hastings to Lord Mansfield, Ft William, 21 March 1774, in G. R. Gleig, *Memoirs of the Life of the Right Hon. Warren Hastings,* vol. 1 (London: Richard Bentley, 1841), 399–404. Hastings went on, "It would be a grievance to deprive the people of the protection of their own laws, but it would be a wanton tyranny to require their obedience to others of which they have no possible means of acquiring a knowledge."

37. Robert Travers has described the legal reforms that Warren Hastings proposed in 1772 as an "uneasy partnership of constitutional variation and natural law." Hastings declared that Company policy should be "to let their laws sit as light on them as possible, and to share with them the Privileges of our own Constitution, where they are capable of partaking of them consistently with their other rights and the Welfare of the State." Travers, *Ideology and Empire,* 105–106, quoting BL Add. MSS 29,303 fos. 10r–11v.

38. See Benton, *Law and Colonial Cultures,* 133–149, on the legal arrangements Hastings supervised; on Hastings and Jones, see Bernard Cohn, *Colonialism and Its Forms of Knowledge: The British in India* (Princeton, NJ: Princeton University Press, 1996), 60–72.

39. Hastings, 1785 Minute, published as Appendix C, in S. C. Sanial, "History of the Calcutta Madrassa," *Bengal Past and Present* 8 (1914): 109.

40. See *WSEB,* 7:455, in the course of a discussion of the begums of Oudh: Hastings "seizes the goods of these Ladies and at your Bar he justifies it upon Mahometan law"; the Lords "have nothing but a quotation cut out with scissors out of the Mahometan law book."

41. E.g., *WSEB,* 7:452, where he deplores the fact that the "express regulation made in Parliament for the redress of the Natives" was made "an instrument for destroying the property real and personal of the natives."

42. *WSEB,* 6:347.

43. Arguing that the question of the begums' entitlement to property could not possibly be judged by the Lords, Burke said: "The parties are at a distance from you. They are neither represented by themselves nor any Counsel, Advocate, or Attorney, and I hope no house of Lords will ever judge upon the title of any human being, much less upon the title of the first women in Asia, shut up from you at nine thousand miles distance" (*WSEB,* 7:458).

44. See Benton, *Law and Colonial Cultures,* 147.

45. For Hastings's 1772 "Plan for the Administration of Justice," see "Seventh Report from the Committee of Secrecy," in *Reports from Committees of the House of Commons,* vol. 4 (London, 1804), 348–351.

46. Gleig, *Memoirs of Warren Hastings,* 400.

47. As Bernard Cohn has put it, Hastings held that British law was "too technical, too complicated, and totally inappropriate for conditions in India." Cohn, *Colonialism and Its Forms of Knowledge,* 66–68. In a similar

vein, Jones wrote to Burke that British law must not be imposed on India, for "a system of *liberty*, forced upon a people invincibly attached to opposite *habits*, would in truth be a system of tyranny." Garland Cannon, ed., *Correspondence of Sir William Jones*, vol. 2 (Oxford: Clarendon Press, 1970), 643–644.

48. As Robert Travers has argued, "In Hastings' view, "Mughal legality . . . was provisional and subordinate to the reserved and absolute powers of sovereignty." Travers, *Ideology and Empire*, 139–140.

49. *Journals of the House of Commons*, 41:696. This is in the section of the speech apparently drafted by Halhed.

50. Hastings, as quoted by Burke, "Speech in Reply," in *WSEB*, 7:259, citing *Journals of the House of Commons*, 41:489.

51. Lauren Benton has criticized conceptualizations of "plural legal orders as comprising a set of 'stacked' legal systems or spheres," which she argues pervades contemporary analysis of legal processes. Lauren Benton, "Beyond Legal Pluralism: Towards a New Approach to Law in the Informal Sector," *Social and Legal Studies* 3 (1994): 223–242. Burke's version of legal pluralism, however, which presupposes and searches for commonalities among legal systems, may fall afoul of Benton's strictures in other ways (see 224).

52. As Mithi Mukherjee argues, Burke staged a "convergence . . . between two independent traditions of jurisprudence," the "exclusively national" tradition of common law and the "international discourse" of natural law. Mukherjee, *India in the Shadows of Empire*, 32.

53. *WSEB*, 7:264–265. See also 7:272–276 outlining the constraints on rulers under Muslim laws. Hastings's defense quoted Montesquieu "to establish, in point of historical truth, that the government of Asia, before it was supplanted by the free government of Britain, was a government of misrule, producing no one benefit to the governed, but every species of vexation, cruelty, and oppression." Bond, *Speeches of the Managers*, 2:540. Richard Bourke argues that Montesquieu is an indispensable foil for Burke's diverse intellectual responses to empire. Bourke, *Empire and Revolution*, 19–23.

54. *WSEB*, 7:256. "That it is a refined, enlightened, curious, elaborate, technical Jurisprudence under which they lived, and by which their property was secured and which yields neither to the Jurisprudence of the Roman Law nor to the Jurisprudence of this Kingdom, formed and allowed to be, as it is, a basis and substratum to the manners and customs and opinions of that people, which is different. And we contend that Ms. Hastings was bound to know and to act by these Laws. And I shall prove that the very condition upon which he received power in India was to protect these people in their Laws and known rights" (*WSEB*, 7:285).

55. *WSEB*, 6:308.

56. *WSEB*, 7:256.

57. "Your Lordships will find Mr. Hastings considers all Treaties as being weakened by a considerable degree of natural doubt and invalidity, concerning their binding and conclusive force in such a state of things as exists in India" (*WSEB*, 7:393).

58. [House of Lords], *Minutes of the evidence taken at the trial of Warren Hastings Esquire, late Governor General of Bengal, at the bar of the House of Lords*, vol. 1 ([London], 1788), 23 (25 February 1788).

59. *WSEB*, 7:282.

60. *WSEB*, 7:290.

61. *Journals of the House of Commons*, 41:694–696; *WSEB*, 7:291 (citing Vattel, *Law of Nations*, bk. 1, ch. 16).

62. In the course of denouncing the Jacobins for having "demolished" the jurisprudence that France shared with "other civilized countries," Burke wrote, "I have not heard of any country [except France], whether in Europe or Asia, or even in Africa on this side of Mount Atlas, which is wholly without" institutions dedicated to the conservation of that universal jurisprudence. "First Letter on a Regicide Peace," in *WSEB*, 9:240.

63. *WSEB*, 7:291.

64. *WSEB*, 7:168.

65. "Opening of Impeachment"; while it is conceiveable that Burke intended "rights" (see *WSEB* 6:227n3), "rites" is a more plausible reading given Burke's insistence on shared "rights of natural equity," cited above.

66. *WSEB*, 7:168. See the excellent discussion of the *Report*, "Burke's most sustained legal writing," in Lock, *Edmund Burke*, 2:470–474. The idea of law as a flexible instrument that evolved in response to the demands of society was one that Burke had first explored in his early *Abridgment of English History* (1757).

67. "As Commerce, with its Advantages and its Necessities, opened a Communication more largely with other Countries; as the Law of Nature and Nations (always a Part of the Law of *England*) came to be cultivated; as an increasing Empire; as new Views and new Combinations of Things were opened, this antique Rigour and over-done Severity gave Way to the Accommodation of Human Concerns, for which Rules were made, and not Human Concerns to bend to them" (*WSEB*, 7:163).

68. Scott was generally referred to by later jurists as Lord Stowell, but since his relevant opinions were delivered before his peerage, I refer to him, as the documents do, as Scott. Henry J. Bourguignon, *Sir William Scott, Lord Stowell, Judge of the High Court of Admiralty, 1798–1828* (Cambridge: Cambridge University Press, 1987); R. A. Melikan, "Scott, William, Baron Stowell (1745–1836)," in *Oxford Dictionary of National Biography* (Oxford: Oxford

University Press, 2004); E. S. Roscoe, *Lord Stowell: His Life and the Development of English Prize Law* (Boston: Houghton Mifflin, 1916); Benton, "Toward a New Legal History of Piracy: Maritime Legalities and the Myth of Universal Jurisdiction," *International Journal of Maritime History* 23 (2011): 225–240, at 234.

69. Bourguignon, *Sir William Scott,* 37–38. Scott took his doctorate in civil law and joined the Doctors' Commons in 1779; he also held a readership in ancient history at Oxford from 1774 through 1785. As a civil lawyer, he practiced ecclesiastical law in addition to maritime law.

70. On the English civil law tradition, see Bourguignon, *Sir William Scott,* 1–30; Peter Stein, *Roman Law in European History* (Cambridge: Cambridge University Press, 1999); Stein, "Continental Influences on English Legal Thought, 1600–1900," in *The Character and Influence of the Roman Civil Law: Historical Essays* (London: Hambledon, 1988), 209–229; Daniel R. Coquillette, *The Civilian Writers of Doctors' Commons, London: Three Centuries of Juristic Innovation in Comparative, Commercial and International Law* (Berlin: Duncker and Humblot, 1988); G. D. Squibb, *Doctors' Commons: A History of the College of Advocates and Doctors of Law* (Oxford: Clarendon Press, 1977). On the awkward place of natural law in common-law thought such as Blackstone's, see David Lieberman, *The Province of Legislation Determined: Legal Theory in Eighteenth-Century Britain* (Cambridge: Cambridge University Press, 1989), 37–42.

71. I am grateful to Martti Koskenniemi for pressing me on this point. Scott's Oxford training included lectures in civil law by Thomas Bever that presented the law of nations as regulated by natural law. See Bourguignon, *Sir William Scott,* 36; Coquillette, *Civilian Writers,* 16–23.

72. William Scott to Henry Dundas, 1 June 1794, BL, Add MS. 38353, f. 88; extract of a letter from Dundas to General Sir Charles Grey, BL, Add MSS 38353, f. 86.

73. Scott's legal decisions are cited as they appear in Christopher Robinson, *Reports of Cases Argued and Determined in the High Court of Admiralty; Commencing with the Judgments of the Right Hon. Sir William Scott, Michaelmas Term 1798,* 6 vols. (London, 1799–1808), 1:349–350. Subsequent references follow the standard citation format for these volumes, e.g., *Maria (Paulsen)* (1799), 1 Rob. 349–350.

74. This occurred with respect to British Orders in Council regarding blockades on the open ocean, which Scott defended in Parliament, and deferred to in a series of legal judgments from 1807 to 1811, favoring British interests as a belligerent over neutral merchant ships. Bourguignon, *Sir William Scott,* 218–222, 270.

75. William Scott, motion on the Prize Agency Bill, 20 March 1805; Commons Debate, *Hansard* 1st ser., vol. 4, col. 62. The advertisement to Robinson's first volume of Scott's judgments similarly ties Britain's national honor to its courts' impartial adjudication of the law of nations: "The honor and interest

of our own Country are too deeply and extensively involved in its administration of the Law of Nations, not to render it highly proper to be known here
at home, in what manner and upon what principles its Tribunals administer
that species of law to foreign states and their subjects, whose commercial concerns are every day discussed and decided in those Courts" (1 Rob. v). Such
expressions corroborate the idea that we should locate the origins of
nineteenth-century international law in the institutions and practices of
British imperial order, as Lauren Benton and Lisa Ford argue in *Rage for
Order: The British Empire and the Origins of International Law, 1800–1850*
(Cambridge, MA: Harvard University Press, 2016).

76. *Flad Oyen (Martenson)*, 1 Rob. 141, 139.

77. *Flad Oyen (Martenson)*, 1 Rob. 139–140.

78. Here Scott argued that contracts denying wages to sailors on long journeys if
the ship did not return safely to London were unjust, even if the sailors freely
signed them. *Juliana (Ogilvie)* (1822), J. Dodson, *Reports of Cases Argued and
Determined in the High Court of Admiralty*, 2 vols. (London, 1815–1828) [2
Dod.], 521. See also Bourguignon, *Sir William Scott*, 71.

79. On the broader maritime context, see Martin Robson, *Britain, Portugal and
South America in the Napoleonic Wars: Alliances and Diplomacy in Economic
Maritime Conflict* (London: I. B. Tauris, 2011).

80. *The Helena (Heslop)* (1801), 4 Rob. 5–6.

81. *Twee Juffrowen (Etjes)* (1802), 4 Rob. 244: "With respect to what has been said
of a different understanding [of the law of nations] prevailing in [Prussia], I am
afraid it is not the only instance in which our exposition of the law of nations
differs."

82. When the dey of Algiers spoke of the property in question "*as his own,* [he]
spoke as Sovereigns are apt to speak . . . and I understand him therefore as
interposing rather to protect the interest of *his subjects,* than to assert any
private interests of *his own,*" and when his subjects "applied to their own government in the first instance instead of applying" to the British admiralty
court, they did no more than others had done. *Kinders Kinder* (1799), 2 Rob.
90–91 (emphasis in original).

83. *Kinders Kinder*, 2 Rob. 88.

84. "Upon such considerations, the Court has, on some occasions, laid it down
that the European law of nations is not to be applied in its full rigor to the
transactions of persons of the description of the present claimants, and residing in that part of the world. . . . it would be extremely hard on persons
residing in the kingdom of Morocco, if they should be held bound by all the
rules of the law of nations, as it is practiced among European states . . . they
may on some points of the law of nations, be entitled to a very relaxed application of the principles, established, by long usage, between the states of

Europe, holding an intimate and constant intercourse with each other." *The Hurtige Hane* (1801), 3 Rob. 325–326.

85. *The Fortune (Smith)* (1800), 2 Rob. 99.

86. *The Recovery (Webb)* (1807), 6 Rob. 348–349.

87. *The Manilla (Barret)* (1808). In *Reports of Cases Argued and Determined in the High Court of Admiralty; Commencing with the Judgment of the Right Hon. Sir William Scott, Easter Term 1808* (London: A. Strahan, 1812), 1–6.

88. Scott, *Manilla,* citing the *Dart* (in which an American ship trading with Haiti was seized by a British privateer for trading contraband of war with an enemy of Great Britain) and the *Happy Couple* (in which the judge of the vice-admiralty court in Halifax, Nova Scotia, deemed the ship a good prize on the grounds that France had never abandoned its claim to the colony and Britain had not recognized Haitian independence).

89. Julia Gaffield, *Haitian Connections in the Atlantic World: Recognition after Revolution* (Chapel Hill: University of North Carolina Press, 2015), 112–123. An Order in Council of July 1806 permitted the granting of licenses to British ships to trade in independent Haitian ports (those not under the "immediate Dominion and in the actual Possession of France or Spain"); another of February 1807 modified the language to "under control."

90. That it was not "merely military" was shown "by the clearances and other documents which are regularly made out in the name of Christophe the chief of this anomalous black government." *Manilla,* 3.

91. Burke, "Opening of Impeachment," in *WSEB* 6:365–366. Also see *Institutes political and military, written originally in the Mogul language by the great Timour, improperly called Tamerlane,* ed. Joseph White, trans. Major William Davy (Oxford: Clarendon Press, 1783).

92. But cf. Burke's influence on nineteenth- and early twentieth-century Indian nationalists, in Ganesh Prashad, "Whiggism in India," *Political Science Quarterly* 81 (1966): 412–431, and Mukherjee, "Justice, War, and the Imperium," as well as the references to Burke in the thought of nineteenth-century imperial critics (particularly regarding his respect for Indian civilization) as noted by Gregory Claeys, *Imperial Sceptics: British Critics of Empire, 1850–1920* (Cambridge: Cambridge University Press, 2010), 33, 61.

93. The East India Company and the Holy Roman Empire, for instance, were both being assimilated into the modern state at the turn of the nineteenth century. On the "contagion of sovereignty" that spread the Vattelian model of the free and equal state in the wake of the American Revolution, see David Armitage, *The Declaration of Independence: A Global History* (Cambridge, MA: Harvard University Press, 2006), 103–112.

94. For the argument that the economic and technological divergence began at the end of the eighteenth century, much later than nineteenth-century

observers convinced of Europe's cultural superiority were inclined to believe, see Kenneth Pomeranz, *The Great Divergence: China, Europe, and the Making of the Modern World Economy* (Princeton, NJ: Princeton University Press, 2000).

95. Quoted in John Sankey, "Lord Stowell," *Law Quarterly Review* 52 (1936): 327–344, at 336.

96. Travers Twiss, *The Law of Nations Considered as Independent Political Communities* (Oxford: Clarendon Press, 1884), 161.

FIVE   The Rise of Positivism?

1. Neff sees the decisive novelty of the "positive century" (1815–1914) as the "denial of the very existence of natural law," though he notes that many positivists "stopped short" of that denial. Stephen Neff, *Justice among Nations* (Cambridge, MA: Harvard University Press, 2014), 227.

2. By 1823, Bentham could write, "As to the word *international*, from this work, or the first of the works edited in French by Mr. Dumont, it has taken root in the language. Witness Reviews and Newspapers." Jeremy Bentham, *Introduction to the Principles of Morals and Legislation*, ed. J. H. Burns and H. L. A. Hart (Oxford: Oxford University Press, 1970), 297n.

3. E.g., Martti Koskenniemi, "International Law and *raison d'état*: Rethinking the Prehistory of International Law," in *The Roman Foundations of the Law of Nations*, ed. Benedict Kingsbury and Benjamin Straumann (Oxford: Oxford University Press, 2010), 297–339, at 298.

4. Edward Keene uses quantitative data treaty making to suggest that the "crucial period during the first half of the nineteenth century" was as significant a moment of transformation in attitudes about interstate relations as the latter half of the nineteenth century. Edward Keene, "The Treaty-Making Revolution of the Nineteenth Century," *International History Review* 34 (2012): 496.

5. Alexandrowicz's interest in the shift from naturalism to positivism lay primarily in the shift from universalism to Eurocentrism, and this chapter follows his lead in this respect.

6. On changes from one edition to the next in response to increasing contact with non-European states, see Gerrit W. Gong, *The Standard of "Civilization" in International Society* (Oxford: Clarendon Press, 1984), 26–29.

7. Vattel's text was also translated into Turkish in 1837, two years before the *Tânzimat* reforms began: Hüsrev Mehmed Paşa, the official who ordered the manuscript translation of books 3 and 4, had fought against the French in Egypt and later served as governor there. A decade later, the first work of international law published in Turkish, by the Viennese official Baron Ottokar

Maria Schlechta von Wschehrd, noted the distinction between natural and positive law of nations. See Mustafa Serdar Palabiyik, "The Emergence of the Idea of 'International Law' in the Ottoman Empire before the Treaty of Paris (1856)," *Middle Eastern Studies* 50 (2014): 242–245.

8. Abraham Hyacinthe Anquetil-Duperron, *L'Inde en rapport avec l'Europe* (Paris: Lesguilliez frères, An VII de la République française [1798]), 248.

9. Immanuel Kant, *Practical Philosophy*, ed. Mary Gregor (Cambridge: Cambridge University Press, 1996), 326 (8:354). On Voltaire's verdict after the start of the Seven Years' War that the "law of nations has become chimerical," and for his disparagement of Vattel in a letter to La Chalotais of 28 February 1763, see Dan Edelstein, "Enlightenment Rights Talk," *Journal of Modern History* 86 (2014): 530–565, at 536.

10. Jeremy Bentham, *The Works of Jeremy Bentham*, ed. John Bowring, 11 vols. (Edinburgh: W. Tait, 1843) 10:584. On Bentham's critique of the natural law tradition for confusing "that which ought to be" and "that which is," see David Armitage, "Globalising Jeremy Bentham," in *Foundations of Modern International Thought* (Cambridge: Cambridge University Press, 2013), 180–185.

11. Palmerston quoted the passage in response to Gladstone during a heated debate leading up to the first Opium War (27 July 1840; *Hansard House of Commons Debates,* vol. 55, cols. 1029–1054); Thomas De Quincey, "Goethe (review of *Wilhelm Meister's Apprenticeship)*," *London Magazine,* September 1824, 292.

12. "Elegy on the Death of Jean Bon Saint André," *The Anti-Jacobin, or Weekly Examiner,* 2:314–317 (14 May 1798), reprinted in *Poetry of the Anti-Jacobin* (London, 1799), 144–149. See Edward Hawkins, "Authors of the Poetry of the Anti-Jacobins," *Notes and Queries,* 1st ser., vol. 3 (3 May 1851), 348–349; Emily Lorraine de Montluzin, *The Anti-Jacobins, 1798–1800: The Early Contributors to the* Anti-Jacobin Review (New York: St. Martin's Press, 1988); John Strachan, "Poetry of the Anti-Jacobin," in *A Companion to Romanticism,* ed. Duncan Wu (Oxford: Blackwell, 1999), 191–198.

13. The *Saturday Review*'s 1883 (4 August) review of John Hosack's *On the Rise and Growth of the Law of Nations as Established by General Usage and by Treaties* noted that that the author "warns us indeed in his preface that it is not his object to compete with those eminent writers who have sought 'to lay down certain rules for the guidance of independent States as well in peace as in war.' He does not, it would seem, aspire to be cited by future consuls on future historic occasions, as when 'The Consul quoted Wicquefort.' . . . His aim is simply to describe what have been the actual practice and usages of nations in their transactions with each other."

14. "Vattel," in *Chambers's Encyclopaedia: A Dictionary of Universal Knowledge for the People,* 10 vols. (Philadelphia: J. B. Lippincott, 1870), 9:720; James

Lorimer, *Institutes of the Law of Nations* (Edinburgh and London: William Blackwood, 1883), 80–83.

15. Martens's Latin text was published 1785 and the French in 1789, from which this English translation by Cobbett was published in 1795. G. F. von Martens, *A compendium of the law of nations, founded on the treaties and customs of the modern nations of Europe,* trans. William Cobbett (London: Cobbett and Morgan, 1802 [1788]); I quote this 1802 translation unless otherwise noted. Martens taught at the University of Göttingen beginning in 1783 and later held several posts in Hanover and briefly in Napoleon Bonaparte's Kingdom of Westphalia.

16. Neff sees Martens as working "strongly in the spirit of Vattel," though he characterizes him as holding that there "was not, and could not be, any such thing as a universal law of nations." Neff, *Justice among Nations,* 199. Béla Kapossy likewise sees Vattel and Martens as sharing "a strong common ground," along with earlier figures in the German academic tradition such as Gottfried Achenwall and Johann Stephan Pütter, because, it seems, he treats Vattel as discussing a European political system rather than a universal law. Béla Kapossy, "Introduction: Rival Histories of Emer de Vattel's *Law of Nations,*" *Grotiana* 31 (2010): 5–21, at 15.

17. Martti Koskenniemi, "Into Positivism: Georg Friedrich von Martens (1756–1821) and Modern International Law," *Constellations* 15 (2008): 189–207, at 190.

18. Martens, *Compendium,* 10–11.

19. Moser's first work, *Anfangsgründe der Wissenschaft von der heutigen Staatsverfassung von Europa* (1732), was followed by various works on "Europäischen Völkerrechts" published into the 1770s. Martens also cited Achenwall, *Juris gentium Europ. practici primae lineae;* P. J. Neyron, *Principes du droit des gens Européens, conventionnel et coutumier* (1783); C. G. Gunther, *Grundris eines Europ. Völkerrechts* (1777); and Gunther, *Europäisches Völkerrecht in Friedenszeiten* (1787).

20. Martens, *Compendium,* 5, 27. He lists Turkey among the European powers at 33, 38, 42; he notes its practice sometimes as reflective of (220), sometimes as a departure from (232, 349) standard European practice. Keene has noted that patterns of treaty making between the Ottoman Empire and European states seem to have been unaffected by the 1856 Treaty of Paris that was often described by nineteenth-century observers as marking Turkey's entrance into the family of nations. Keene, "Treaty-Making Revolution," 475–500.

21. The English *Compendium* in a sense brought this tension between Martens's theory and his treaty collections into a single volume, by appending a list of "the principal treaties" from 1731 to 1802 that, like Martens's *Recueil des traités,* included many treaties with extra-European powers—a 1731 treaty between the States-General of Holland and the Kingdom of Algiers; a 1732 treaty be-

tween the Russian and Persian Empires; a 1737 treaty of commerce, and a 1739 defensive alliance, between the Swedish Crown and the Ottoman Porte.

22. He wrote of "the resemblance in manners and religion, the intercourse of commerce, the frequency of treaties of all sorts, and the ties of blood between sovereigns," though as we have seen, he recognized the regularity of treaties with states outside Europe. Martens, *Compendium*, 3, 27.

23. On Ompteda as an important German predecessor, see Alexandrowicz, "Doctrinal Aspects of the Universality of the Law of Nations," *British Year Book of International Law* 37 (1961): 506–515, reprinted in Alexandrowicz, *The Law of Nations in Global History*, ed. David Armitage and Jennifer Pitts (Oxford: Oxford University Press, 2017), 168–179. Alexandrowicz notes that the key late eighteenth-century German authors who addressed questions of the scope of the law of nations, Ompteda, Justi, and Martens, had connections to the British sovereign by way of Hanover, which may account for their greater attention to the kinds of extra-European interactions that British and French authors addressed more often than their continental counterparts.

24. Robert Ward, *An enquiry into the foundation and history of the law of nations in Europe: from the time of the Greeks and Romans, to the age of Grotius*, 2 vols. (Dublin, 1795), 1:xix. Ward's book earned "immediate notice and approval from the critics." *Annual Register* (1795), 174.

25. Edmund Phipps, *Memoirs of the Political and Literary Life of Robert Plumer Ward, Esq.*, vol. 1 (London, 1850), 1, 8–16.

26. Diego Panizza, *Genesi di una ideologia. Il conservatorismo moderno in Robert Ward* (Padua: CEDAM, 1997), 2, 57.

27. Phipps, *Memoirs*, 13–17.

28. E.g., Ward, *Enquiry*, 1:78. One of Ward's most emphatic criticisms reads, "The miserable departure of the French from that humanity which has constituted the distinguishing honour of modern warfare, however execrated by all good men, is considered by themselves an elevation of their character" (1:153); in the preface written just before publication, he adds, "The conduct of this nation is now *somewhat* mended, and . . . the points most complained of were the effects of the influence of a merciless tyrant, or of dark minded ruffians who have already, most of them, met their reward" (1:lvii–lviii) (emphasis in original).

29. Ward, *Enquiry*, 1:60.

30. "Burlamaqui contends, that variations, when they are cruel, are mere barbarous customs, from which all just and well-regulated Nations ought to abstain. But surely, when the very question is concerning the *universality* of a custom, and other customs are proved to exist; to get rid of them in this way, is a mere petitio principii; not to mention that the Nations thus adopting other Laws, have an equal right with any other, to call themselves (according

to their own ideas at least,) just and well-regulated" (Ward, *Enquiry*, 1:153) (emphasis in original).

31. See, e.g., Ward, *Enquiry*, 1:145–146 (here Ward is remarkably uncritical of his European sources).

32. Ward, *Enquiry*, 1:158, x–xi.

33. Ward, *Enquiry*, 1:35. Ward generally praised Vattel, though he questioned some of his judgments and noted that "if we differ [from Vattel] at all, it will only be in endeavouring to give something more definite and binding even than this assemblage of the laws of Nature and the laws of Man, as the *real* foundation of the Law of Nations." Ward, *Enquiry*, 1:27 (emphasis in original).

34. Ward, *Enquiry*, 1:36 (emphasis in original), 1:102 (emphasis in original), 1:144.

35. Ward, *Enquiry*, 2:322; 1:141.

36. For instance, Edward Coke's version of the prohibition, he argued, was based on biblical passages that should have been irrelevant to the modern European law of nations. Ward, *Enquiry*, 1:326.

37. Ward, *Enquiry*, 1:331–332, 162–163.

38. Ward, *Enquiry*, 1:36. Note George Canning's quip that Ward's "law books were as interesting as novels and his novels as dull as law books." Quoted by Clive Towse, "Ward, Robert Plumer (1765–1846)," in *Oxford Dictionary of National Biography* (Oxford: Oxford University Press, 2004). Joseph Chitty, in his list of works of jurisprudence that should be counted (alongside state practice) among the sources of "the positive Law of Nations generally and permanently binding upon all independent states," cites Ward's book a few times, calling it a work "of great ability, but not yet acknowledged to be such high general authority" as the earlier classics including Vattel. Emer de Vattel, *The Law of Nations; or, Principles of the Law of Nature, Applied to the Conduct and Affairs of Nations and Sovereigns,* ed. Joseph Chitty (London: S. Sweet, 1834), lv (note).

39. James Mackintosh, *A Discourse on the Study of the Law of Nature and Nations* (London, n.d. [1799]), 5. See Christopher J. Finlay, "James Macalister Mackintosh of Kyllachy (1765–1832)," in *Oxford Dictionary of National Biography* (Oxford: Oxford University Press, 2004); *Memoirs of the Life of the Right Honourable Sir James Mackintosh,* ed. Robert James Mackintosh (London: E. Moxon, 1835).

40. David R. Fisher, "Sir James Mackintosh," in *The History of Parliament: the House of Commons, 1820–1832,* ed. D. R. Fisher (Cambridge: Cambridge University Press, 2009); see http://www.historyofparliamentonline.org/volume/1820-1832/member/mackintosh-sir-james-1765-1832.

41. James Mackintosh, "Speech on Presenting a Petition from the Merchants of London for the Recognition of the Spanish-American States" (15 June 1824),

in *The Miscellaneous Works of the Right Honourable Sir James Mackintosh,* vol. 3 (London: Longman, 1846), 437–482, calling for recognition of independent Latin American states for the sake of British commerce. Mackintosh further argued that formal recognition of a former colony as an independent state can be granted only by the imperial power renouncing its authority; in relation to Spanish America, Great Britain could only grant "virtual" recognition, acknowledging the fact of their independence by sending and receiving diplomatic agents. But he proposed that to impose a demand on the new states that they earn recognition by demonstrating good government was to unfairly impose a condition that was never required among European states (441, 466).

42. Mackintosh, *Discourse* (1799), 5, 60–61. Editions of Vattel that began with Mackintosh's *Discourse* as a preface include French editions of 1830 and 1863, a Belgian edition of 1839, and a Spanish edition of 1836.

43. James Mackintosh, *A Discourse on the Study of the Law of Nature and Nations,* 3rd ed. (London: T. Cadell, 1800), 32n.

44. Henry Wheaton, *An Anniversary Discourse: Delivered before the New-York Historical Society, on Thursday, December 28, 1820* (New York: E. Bliss, 1821), quoting Mackintosh on Vattel at 42.

45. Henry Wheaton, *Histoire des progrès du droit des gens en Europe* (Leipzig: F. A. Brockhaus, 1841), 127.

46. Wheaton, *Anniversary Discourse,* 17–18. He added, manifestly falsely, given the extensive classical scholarship in the medieval Islamic world, that the Muslim world "caught no inspiration from the finished productions of classical genius."

47. "The European law of nations is mainly founded upon that community of origin, manners, institutions, and religion which distinguished the Christian nations from those of the Mahommedan world." Henry Wheaton, *History of the Law of Nations in Europe and America; From the Earliest Times to the Treaty of Washington, 1842* (New York: Gould, Banks and Co., 1845), 555.

48. Wheaton, *History,* 556. For the full passage, see Burke, "Speech on Conciliation with America," in *The Writings and Speeches of Edmund Burke,* ed. Paul Langford, 9 vols. (Oxford: Oxford University Press, 1981–2015), 3:125.

49. Wheaton, *Anniversary Discourse,* 22, 19 (emphasis in original).

50. Vattel, *The Law of Nations,* ed. Chitty. In a significant departure from Vattel, Chitty, citing Ward's *Enquiry,* asserted that when there was doubt about a legal principle, "Christianity . . . should be equally appealed to and observed by all as an unfailing rule of construction" (liv–lv).

51. In the last of three House of Commons debates of 17 June, 7 July, and 23 July 1845. Hansard, 3rd ser., vol. 82, cols. 970–1025. See also Mark Hickford, " 'Decidedly the Most Interesting Savages on the Globe': An Approach to the

Intellectual History of Maori Property Rights, 1837–53," *History of Political Thought* 27 (2006): 122–167.

52. See Elisabetta Fiocchi Malaspina, "La ricezione e la circolazione di 'Le Droit des Gens' di Emer de Vattel nel XIX siecolo," *Materiali per una storia della cultura giuridica* 43 (2013): 303–319; Malaspina and Nina Keller-Kemmerer, "International Law and Translation in the 19th Century," *Rechtsgeschichte. Zeitschrift des Max-Planck-Instituts für europäische Rechtsgeschichte* 22 (2014): 214–227.

53. Paul Pradier-Fodéré, ed., *Le droit des gens . . . par Vattel,* vol. 1 (Paris: Gillaumin, 1863), 498. Referring to the Treaty of Tianjin, he wrote, "The conquest by modern civilization of these two countries, so full of mystery, is one of the titles to glory of the year 1858 . . . in establishing new commercial relations everywhere, in bringing European mores to every shore, the European powers are propagating civilization in the most remote countries" (275–276).

54. See Emer de Vattel, *Droit des gens, ou principes de la loi naturelle* (London, 1758 [actually Neuchâtel, 1757]), bk. 1, ch. 8, §§92–95 and bk. 2, ch. 2, §25. Unless otherwise noted I quote from the 1797 English translation reproduced in Vattel, *The Law of Nations,* ed. Béla Kapossy and Richard Whatmore (Indianapolis, IN: Liberty Fund, 2008) (hereafter cited as *DG*), citing book, chapter, and section number. See also Li Chen, *Chinese Law in Imperial Eyes* (New York: Columbia University Press, 2016), 201–242.

55. E.g., James Matheson, *The Present Position and Prospects of the British Trade with China: Together with an Outline of Some Leading Occurrences in Its Past History* (London: Smith, Elder, 1836), 33–35. See also Lydia Liu, "Legislating the Universal," in *Tokens of Exchange: The Problem of Translation in Global Circulation* (Durham, NC: Duke University Press, 1999), 127–164. See also Samuel Warren, *The Opium Question* (London: James Ridgway, 1840), citing Vattel on the duty of nations to fulfill their engagements and arguing, notwithstanding Vattel's explicit principle that nations may choose not to participate in commerce and may change their commercial policy at any time without injuring their trading partners, that "the Chinese may possibly have been entitled originally to refuse any intercourse with us, either social or commercial; but they have long resigned such rights. They have invited our commercial intercourse. . . . They have led us to invest in it our capital to an enormous extent, and to erect a machinery for carrying on such commerce, which they cannot now shatter to pieces at their will" (101–103).

56. "Opium," in *Supplement to Mr. McCulloch's Commercial Dictionary* (London: Longman, Brown, Green, and Longmans, 1842), 72.

57. Teemu Ruskola discusses American public opinion in favor of the Chinese position and identifies the Treaty of Wanghia of 1844 as a turning point in American conceptions of Chinese legal standing. Teemu Ruskola, *Legal*

Orientalism: China, the United States, and Modern Law (Cambridge, MA: Harvard University Press, 2013), 123–130.

58. Adams's speech, delivered before the Massachusetts Historical Society in December 1841, was reprinted in part in *Chinese Repository* 11 (May 1842): 274–289, and then in full in "J. Q. Adams on the Opium War," *Proceedings of the Massachusetts Historical Society* 3rd ser., 43 (February 1910): 295–325. I quote from the 1910 version (307).

59. "J. Q. Adams on the Opium War," 311 (emphasis in original).

60. *Chinese Repository* 11 (May 1842), 289. On the distinctive role of missionaries in "producing the depravity of Chinese law" in order to demonstrate the urgency of conversion, see Jedediah Kronke, *The Futility of Law and Development: China and the Dangers of Exporting American Law* (Oxford: Oxford University Press, 2016), 29–70.

61. Citing Vattel on the "necessary" law of nations as the law of nature applied to inter-state relations, Adams made a distinctly unVattelian move with the qualification that the necessary law "can be enforced only between Nations who recognize that the State of Nature is a State of Peace" and that "Mahometan Nations" rejected that claim in principle. "J. Q. Adams on the Opium War," 306.

62. Captain T. H. Bullock, *The Chinese Vindicated, or Another View of the Opium Question, Being in Reply to a Pamphlet by Samuel Warren, Esq. Barrister at Law in the Middle Temple* (London: Allen and Co., 1840), 64–65; quoting *DG*, bk. 2, ch. 8, §101.

63. Chang Hsi-T'ung describes Parker's translation of Vattel as "very likely the earliest piece of literature on Western political science ever written in the Chinese language." Chang Hsi-T'ung, "The Earliest Phase of the Introduction of Western Political Science into China," *Yenching Journal of Social Studies* 5 (1950): 1–30, at 13. See also Immanuel C. Y. Hsü, *China's Entrance into the Family of Nations* (Cambridge, MA: Harvard University Press, 1960), 123–125; Lydia Liu, *The Clash of Empires: The Invention of China in Modern World Making* (Cambridge, MA: Harvard University Press, 2004), 118.

64. Peter Parker, "Tenth Report of the Ophthalmic Hospital, Canton, Being for the Year 1839," *Chinese Repository* 8 (1839–1840): 634–635.

65. Lydia Liu, "Legislating the Universal: The Circulation of International Law in the Nineteenth Century," in *Tokens of Exchange: The Problem of Translation in Global Circulations,* ed. Lydia Liu (Durham, NC: Duke University Press, 1999), 127–164, at 141.

66. Chang, "Earliest Phase," 14, 17; Jane Kate Leonard, *Wei Yuan and China's Rediscovery of the Maritime World* (Cambridge, MA: Harvard University Press, 1984), 93–120.

67. Martin explained in the book's English preface, "My mind at first inclined to Vattel; but on reflection, it appeared to me, that the work of that excellent and

lucid writer might as a practical guide be somewhat out of date." Quoted by Hsü, *China's Entrance*, 127.

68. Hamdan Khodja, *Aperçu historique et statistique sur la Régence d'Alger, entitulé en arabe Le Miroir* (Paris: Goetschy fils, 1833) (hereafter *Miroir*); *Le Miroir*, ed. Abdelkader Djeghloul (Paris: Sindbad, 1985), 194. Unless otherwise noted, I cite the modern (1985) edition. While many of his French contemporaries refer to him as Hamdan (or Si Hamdan), I follow Djeghloul in referring to him as Hamdan Khodja. Bentham wrote that Hamdan Khodja's "only son" studied for three years at a boarding school near London and was apparently able to pass in speech and writing for an Englishman. Jeremy Bentham, *Securities against Misrule*, ed. Philip Schofield (Oxford: Oxford University Press, 1990), 150.

69. See Abdeljelil Temimi, *Recherches et documents d'histoire Maghrébine: La Tunisie, l'Algérie et la Triploitane de 1816 à 1871* (Tunis: Université de Tunis, 1971), 166–171; Temimi, "À propos du *Miroir*," in *Recherches*, 109–171 at 112–113. For an account of Hamdan Khodja's two journeys to Constantine on behalf of the French, and the relevant documents, see Temimi, *Le beylik de Constantine et Hadj Ahmed Bey (1830–1837)* (Tunis: Revue d'histoire maghrébine, 1978), 101–126, and on Hadj Hassan, 159.

70. Although the title page of the work notes that it was "translated from the Arabic by H. D., Oriental," no original Arabic text of *Miroir* has been found. Abdeljelil Temimi surmises that others, whether Ottoman dragomans (translators) in Paris or Frenchmen, may have assisted Hassuna D'Ghies with the translation, but he has not recovered the identities of any other collaborators. See Temimi, "À propos du *Miroir*," 109–171 (and on possible collaborators, 116–119); Temimi, *Le beylik*, 101–126.

71. Hamdan Khodja, *Miroir*, 37–38. He charged that the French had supported the Greeks and Poles with funds seized from his "miserable country, although Algerians are also men" (236). Letter quoted in Georges Yver, "Si Hamdan ben Othman Khodja," *Revue Africaine* 57 (Algiers, 1913): 112.

72. Hamdan Khodja, *Miroir*, 32; Hamdan Khodja, "Réclamations," pièce 10, *Miroir* (1833), 426. *Miroir*'s call for Algerian national independence would not have sat well with the Ottoman authorities, and in his appeals to Ottoman correspondents, Hamdan Khodja emphasized the importance of saving Algeria from the rule of nonbelievers rather than its national independence. See, e.g., his August 1833 letter to the Sultan translated in Temimi, *Recherches*, 144–149.

73. On the meaning of the term "nation" in French discourse, see Hagen Schulze, *States, Nations and Nationalism* (Oxford: Blackwell, 1996); William F. Sewell, "The French Revolution and the Emergence of the Nation Form," in *Revolutionary Currents: Nation Building in the Transatlantic*

World, ed. Michael Morrison and Melinda Zook (Lanham, MD: Rowman and Littlefield, 2004), 91–125.

74. "Mémoire de Si Hamdan," Archives Nationales, F. 80 9, reprinted by Georges Yver, Revue Africaine 57 (Algiers, 1913): 122–138 (passage cited at 137).

75. Hamdan Khodja, Miroir (1833), 324.

76. "Mémoire," 36; Hamdan Khodja, Miroir (1833), 322; "Réfutation de l'ouvrage," in Hamdan Khodja, Miroir, 266. Le Miroir "always collectively represents the interests of the Moors and those of the Arabs; in thus employing the general denomination of Algerians, Hamdan purports to express the wishes and grievances of the whole population, whereas in reality nineteen-twentieths of the population have nothing in common with the Moors, not even religion, and their interests are entirely distinct"; "Réfutation," 294.

77. He argued that Islamic jurisprudence recognizes that laws cannot determine their own application in particular circumstances, and that this inevitable indeterminacy had been abused by particular sovereigns. Hamdan Khodja, Miroir, 112–113.

78. In a gesture of identification with his audience, Hamdan Khodja noted that when Algiers conquered Tunis in 1754, the Tunisians resented the Algerians just as the latter now did the French; the majority of honorable Algerians, he argued, disapproved of what had been done but felt powerless to stop it, and he imagined the same was now true of many of his French readers. Hamdan Khodja, Miroir, 142.

79. Bentham Papers, University College London, box 24, f. 529. The report was apparently drafted in January 1823 by D'Ghies, based on a letter from Hamdan Khodja. See Philip Schofield, "Editorial Introduction," in Bentham, Securities, xxxiii, and "D'Ghies to John Quincy Adams," in Bentham, Securities, 159–160.

80. Hamdan Khodja, Miroir, 262.

81. On Bentham's relationship with D'Ghies, see Schofield, "Editorial Introduction," xv–xxxvi, and Bentham's correspondence with and about D'Ghies, in Correspondence of Jeremy Bentham, vol. 11: January 1822 to June 1824, ed. Catherine Fuller, and vol. 12: July 1824 to June 1828, ed. Luke O'Sullivan and Catherine Fuller (Oxford: Oxford University Press, 2000, 2006). See also L. J. Hume, "Preparations for Civil War in Tripoli in the 1820s: Ali Karamanli, Hassuna D'Ghies and Jeremy Bentham," Journal of African History 21 (1980): 311–322.

82. Correspondence of Jeremy Bentham, 12:471 472 (emphasis in original).

83. Bentham's sense of the possibilities for innovation generated outside Europe stands in contrast to the more common European use of colonies as laboratories for governing and disciplinary techniques that were then imported back into the metropole. See, e.g., Timothy Mitchell, Rule of Experts:

Egypt, Techno-Politics, Modernity (Berkeley: University of California Press, 2002).

84. Jeremy Bentham, *Anarchical Fallacies,* in *Works of Jeremy Bentham,* 2:501, 494. Bentham similarly criticized the language of natural rights in the American Declaration of Independence in [Bentham,] "Short Review of the Declaration," in [John Lind and Jeremy Bentham,] *Answer to the Declaration of the American Congress* (London, 1776); for discussion, see David Armitage, *The Declaration of Independence: A Global History* (Cambridge, MA: Harvard University Press, 2007), 74–80.

85. Jeremy Bentham, "Emancipate your colonies!" (1793), in *Works of Jeremy Bentham,* 4:408, 416.

86. He described inhabitants of colonies such as Guernsey, Jamaica, Canada, and Bengal as "deprived of liberty in an international sense" because "the native . . . is subject to the controuling agency of such distant government." Bentham Papers, UCL, box 100, f. 168.

87. Jeremy Bentham, "International Law," 11 June 1827, British Library, Add MSS 30151, ff. 13, 15b.

88. Bentham, "International Law," f. 15b, 17.

89. Wheaton, *Elements of International Law,* 6th ed. (Boston: Little Brown, 1855), cxci.

90. Wheaton, *Elements,* 21.

91. Travers Twiss, "Preface to the Second Edition," in *The Law of Nations Considered as Independent Political Communities* (Oxford: Clarendon Press, 1884), v. This group, plus the Oxford professor Mountague Bernard, were the British members and associates of the Institute of International Law in its early years. See *Annuaire de l'Institut de droit international* 1 (Ghent: Bureau de la Revue de droit international, 1877), xiii–xv.

92. See, e.g., T. E. Holland's claim that jurisprudence is "not a science of legal relations *à priori,* as they might have been, or should have been, but is abstracted *à posteriori* from such relations as have been clothed with a legal character in actual systems, that is to say from law which has actually been imposed, or positive law. It follows that Jurisprudence is a progressive science." T. E. Holland, *The Elements of Jurisprudence* (Oxford: Clarendon Press, 1880), 8. John Burrow attributed the influence of evolutionary social theory in Victorian Britain precisely to the "tension between English positivistic attitudes to science on the one hand and, on the other, a more profound reading of history, coming to a large extent from German romanticism, which made the older form of positivist social theory, philosophic radicalism, seem inadequate." John Burrow, *Evolution and Society: A Study in Victorian Social Theory* (Cambridge: Cambridge University Press, 1966), xv.

SIX   Historicism in Victorian International Law

1. Travers Twiss, "Introduction to the Second Edition," in *The Law of Nations Considered as Independent Political Communities* (Oxford: Clarendon Press, 1884 [first published 1861–1863]), xvii. A "revised second edition" was published in 1875 with a different "second edition" preface and introduction; the historical narrative discussed here, in what Twiss calls the "introduction to the second edition," is in fact new to the 1884 edition, as is its preface. Twiss, who in 1849 had been appointed to the new chair in international law at King's College, London, and later held the Regius Professorship of Civil Law at Oxford, had in 1872 resigned all his offices in the wake of a scandal involving his wife. For discussion of the possible implications of his personal life for his career, particularly his willingness to serve the deeply problematic cause of the Belgian king Leopold's conquests in the Lower Congo valley, see Andrew Fitzmaurice, "The Resilience of Natural Law in the Writings of Sir Travers Twiss," in *British International Thought from Hobbes to Namier,* ed. Ian Hall and Lisa Hill (New York: Palgrave Macmillan, 2009), 137–160.

2. Twiss, *Law of Nations* (1884), xxviii. Twiss's reading of Wolff is novel; note, for instance, Wheaton's criticism, which takes for granted the universality of the *civitas maxima,* that Wolff "takes no pains to prove the existence of any such social union or universal republic of nations, or to show when and how all the human race became members of this union or citizens of this republic." Henry Wheaton, *Elements of International Law,* 6th ed. (Boston: Little Brown, 1855), 11. See the introduction in Wolff, *Jus gentium methodo scientifica pertractatum,* ed. Joseph Drake (Oxford: Clarendon Press, 1934), xlv. Wolff does distinguish between "civilized" and "barbarous" nations and argues that all nations ought to be cultured and civilized (*Jus gentium,* §§52–57). But his *civitas maxima* is explicitly a society "among all nations," without which "the universal obligation of all toward all would be terminated; which assuredly is absurd" (§7).

3. "The term 'Christian States' has been used here for the sake of convenience, as distinguishing the States of Europe which took part in or acceded to the Principal Act of the Congress of Vienna, from the Ottoman Porte, which was not a party to that Act." Twiss, *Law of Nations* (1884), xxxi. I discuss his anxieties further below, when addressing Twiss's report for the Institut de droit international's commission on the applicability of the law of nations to "Oriental" nations.

4. Twiss, *Law of Nations* (1884), xxxvii. Twiss refers here to his contemporary, the Russian legal theorist Frederic de Martens (not the G. F. von Martens discussed in Chapter 5). On Bluntschli's emphatically hierarchical conception

of the community of nations, see Georg Cavallar, *Imperfect Cosmopolis: Studies in the History of International Legal Theory and Cosmopolitan Ideas* (Cardiff: University of Wales Press, 2011), 117–121; Betsy Baker, "The 'Civilized Nation' in the World of Johann Caspar Bluntschli," in *Macht und Moral—Politisches Denken im 17. und 18. Jahrhundert*, ed. Markus Kremer and Hans-Richard Reuter (Stuttgart: Kohlhammer, 2007), 342–358.

5. Note the ambiguous scope of "mankind" in Twiss's claim that "The history of modern civilisation demonstrates [the Law of Nations'] existence, and the public opinion of mankind affirms its obligation." Twiss, *Law of Nations* (1884), xlii.

6. Twiss, *Law of Nations* (1884), xxxix.

7. The restricted view of the law of nations as solely European "leaves untouched the maxim of Natural Law, that plighted faith is to be maintained even towards semi-civilised peoples, who are outside the pale of contemporary international law." Twiss, *Law of Nations* (1884), xxxviii.

8. Twiss, *Law of Nations* (1884), xiii–xvi. See also Adam Hochschild, *King Leopold's Ghost* (Boston: Houghton Mifflin, 1999), documenting both the philanthropic language that Leopold and his agents used to justify their project and the extent of the Congo Free State's abuses.

9. Twiss, *Law of Nations* (1884), v; Casper Sylvest, "Foundations of Victorian International Law," in *Victorian Visions of Global Order,* ed. Duncan Bell (Cambridge: Cambridge University Press, 2007), 47–66.

10. He is listed as an honorary vice president of the association, along with a fellow diplomat from China, the "Marquis Tsêng," and representatives from Japan ("Jushie Woogeno Kagnori" [Kagenori Ueno]) and the Ottoman Empire / Egypt ("Nubar Pasha, Risa Pasha, Riaz Pasha"). See the association's *Report of the Sixth Annual Conference* (London, 1879).

11. Arnulf Becker Lorca, *Mestizo International Law* (Cambridge: Cambridge University Press, 2014), 3; David Dudley Field, in *Report of the Sixth Annual Conference,* 41.

12. Andrew Fitzmaurice argues that historians have understated the commitment to natural law among many nineteenth-century international lawyers. Fitzmaurice, "Resilience of Natural Law."

13. Twiss was professor of civil law at Oxford (1855–1870) and a celebrated practitioner in the civilian admiralty and ecclesiastical courts. Lorimer was Regius Professor of Public Law and the Law of Nature and Nations at the University of Edinburgh, where, given the role of civil law in Scots law, standard legal training included civil law.

14. The Chichele Professorship of International Law and Diplomacy was established at Oxford in 1859; the Whewell Professorship of International Law at Cambridge was founded in 1869. See Casper Sylvest, "International Law in

Nineteenth-Century Britain," in *British Yearbook of International Law 2004* (Oxford: Oxford University Press, 2005), 9–70.

15. His own successor, Lassa Oppenheim, wrote of him that "in a sense it may even be said that every living jurist is his pupil." Reprinted in John Westlake, *The Collected Papers of John Westlake on Public International Law,* ed. Lassa Oppenheim (Cambridge: Cambridge University Press, 1914), ix–x.

16. John Westlake, *Chapters on the Principles of International Law* (Cambridge: Cambridge University Press, 1894), v.

17. "To these studies I would add International Law; which I decidedly think should be taught in all universities, and should form part of all liberal education. The need of it is far from being limited to diplomatists and lawyers; it extends to every citizen." J. S. Mill, "Inaugural Address Delivered to the University of St. Andrews," in *Collected Works of John Stuart Mill,* 33 vols., ed. J. M. Robson and R. F. McRae (Toronto: University of Toronto Press, 1963–) (hereafter cited as *CW*), 21:246.

18. See, e.g., Maine's account of this history in Henry Maine, *International Law* (London: John Murray, 1888), 3–6.

19. Davide Rodogno, *Against Massacre: Humanitarian Interventions in the Ottoman Empire 1815–1914* (Princeton, NJ: Princeton University Press, 2012); Rodogno, "European Legal Doctrines on Intervention and the Status of the Ottoman Empire within the Family of Nations throughout the Nineteenth Century," *Journal of the History of International Law* 18 (2016): 5–41.

20. See Georgios Varouxakis, *Liberty Abroad: John Stuart Mill on International Relations* (Cambridge: Cambridge University Press, 2013), 26–40; David Armitage, *Civil Wars: A History in Ideas* (New York: Knopf, 2017), 172–174.

21. Martti Koskenniemi offers the authoritative account of the self-understanding of the international lawyers he calls the "men of 1873," the founders of the Institut, who saw the legal profession as the "conscience juridique du monde civilisé," as Article 1 of its founding statute put it. Koskenniemi, *The Gentle Civilizer of Nations: The Rise and Fall of International Law 1870–1960* (Cambridge: Cambridge University Press, 2001), 47. See also Miloš Vec and Luigi Nuzzo, eds., *Constructing International Law: The Birth of a Discipline* (Frankfurt am Main: Vittorio Klostermann, 2012).

22. On the role of the lawyers at the Berlin Conference, see Matthew Craven, "Invention of a Tradition," in Vec and Nuzzo, *Constructing International Law,* 363–403. On Sir Travers Twiss's assiduous work on behalf of the claims over the Congo made by the Belgian king Leopold II and his private association, the International African Association, see Andrew Fitzmaurice, *Sovereignty, Property and Empire, 1500–2000* (Cambridge: Cambridge University Press, 2014), 277–284.

23. Sir Richard Bethell, "Inaugural Address," in *Papers Read before the Juridical Society*, vol. 1 (1855–1858) (London: Stevens and Norton, 1858), 1–2.

24. Henry Maine, "The Conception of Sovereignty, and Its Importance in International Law," 16 April 1855, in *Papers Read before the Juridical Society*, 26–45, at 40.

25. Maine, *International Law*, 4.

26. His early biographer wrote that "before he went to Calcutta [in 1862] he had written a book on International law, the manuscript of which disappeared in his absence." Sir M. E. Grant Duff, *Sir Henry Maine: A Brief Memoir of His Life* (New York: Harper and Row, 1969), 69–73, quoted by Carl Landauer, "From Status to Treaty: Henry Sumner Maine's *International Law*," *Canadian Journal of Law and Jurisprudence* 15 (2002): 219–254, at 221.

27. See "Place and Time," the new critical edition of the essay, in Jeremy Bentham, *Selected Writings*, ed. Stephen Engelmann (New Haven, CT: Yale University Press, 2011), 152–219.

28. Wilfrid E. Rumble, *Doing Austin Justice* (London: Bloomsbury, 2005); Rumble, "Nineteenth-Century Perceptions of John Austin: Utilitarianism and the Reviews of *The Province of Jurisprudence Determined*," *Utilitas* 3 (1991): 199–216. Westlake began his 1894 *Chapters on the Principles of International Law* with an attempt to tread a path between the historical and analytical schools.

29. John Austin, *The Province of Jurisprudence Determined*, ed. Wilfrid E. Rumble (Cambridge: Cambridge University Press, 1995), 112. As Michael Lobban has noted, it was not so much Austin himself that the international jurists had to combat as it was "the spectre of the 'vulgar' Austin who seemed to many to dismiss international law as so much private opinion." Lobban, "English Approaches to International Law in the Nineteenth Century," in *Time, History and International Law*, ed. Matthew Craven, Malgosia Fitzmaurice, and Maria Vogiatzi (Leiden: Martinus Nijhoff, 2007), 65–90, at 80–84.

30. T. E. Holland, *Elements of Jurisprudence* (Oxford: Clarendon Press, 1880), 263. Casper Sylvest has described Holland as "more Austinian than Austin." Sylvest, "Foundations of Victorian International Law," 56.

31. Westlake, *Chapters on the Principles of International Law*, viii.

32. On historicism in this broader sense, Friedrich Meinecke's *Historism: The Rise of a New Historical Outlook* (London: Routledge, 1972 [first published in German, 1936]) is the classic account. James Chandler, *England in 1819* (Chicago: University of Chicago Press, 1998) deftly charts scholarly disagreements around Romantic historicism.

33. On Savigny (1779–1861), see Koskenniemi, *Gentle Civilizer*, 43–46 (which notes that Westlake's 1858 treatise on private international law "had been

systematically written to familiarize English jurists with continental scholarship, and Savigny in particular"); Luigi Nuzzo, "History, Science and Christianity: International Law and Savigny's Paradigm," in Vec and Nuzzo, *Constructing International Law,* 25–50; Fitzmaurice, *Sovereignty, Property and Empire,* 239–241.

34. Henry Maine, *Ancient Law: Its Connection with the Early History of Society, and Its Relation to Modern Ideas* (London: John Murray, 1861), 7. On Maine's critique of Austin, see Rumble, *Doing Austin Justice,* ch. 7, and Collini, Winch, and Burrow, who write that Maine "made of historical jurisprudence the perfect stick with which to beat the Utilitarians for the widely sensed failure of their 'abstract' method." Stefan Collini, Donald Winch, and John Burrow, *That Noble Science of Politics: A Study in Nineteenth-Century Intellectual History* (Cambridge: Cambridge University Press, 1983), 211.

35. See Maine, *Ancient Law,* 3. In *Ancient Law* Maine set out to deflate the universalist pretentions of the natural law tradition by identifying the historical origins of the modern law of nature in Roman law. He traced the transformation of the *ius gentium,* the rules that Romans applied to Italian tribes not subject to Roman civil law, into the broader *ius naturale,* which then acquired philosophical abstraction through the adoption of Stoic ideas of nature. See Karuna Mantena, *Alibis of Empire: Henry Maine and the Ends of Liberal Imperialism* (Princeton, NJ: Princeton University Press, 2010), 122–124.

36. Henry Maine, "Roman Law and Legal Education" (1856), in *Village-Communities in the East and West: Six Lectures Delivered at Oxford, to Which Are Added Other Lectures, Addresses, and Essays* (London: John Murray, 1881), 330–386, at 352.

37. Maine, *International Law,* 21. Identifying the law of nations with the law of nature was merely an old "habit" of European lawyers "for the purpose of giving it dignity."

38. Maine, *International Law,* 22–23, 51.

39. T. J. Lawrence, *Essays on Some Disputed Questions in International Law* (Cambridge: Deighton, Bell, 1885), 5.

40. Lawrence, *Disputed Questions,* 31–32.

41. Lawrence, *Disputed Questions,* 25.

42. Austin, *Province of Jurisprudence Determined,* 171–172 (emphasis in original). See also 177, comparing contemporary savage societies to "the German nations whose manners are described by Tacitus."

43. Henry Maine, "The Effects of Observation of India on Modern European Thought (Rede Lecture for 1875)," in *Village-Communities,* 203–239, at 238; J. S. Mill, "Review of Grote's *History of Greece*," in *CW,* 11:313.

44. James Lorimer, *The Institutes of the Law of Nations,* 2 vols. (London: Blackwood, 1883–1884), 1:102, 98.

45. Maine, "Effects of Observation of India," 238–239.

46. Maine, *Ancient Law*, 170 (emphasis in original).

47. Maine, *Ancient Law*, 22. As Maine later wrote, "the natural condition of mankind (if that word 'natural' is used) is not the progressive condition." Henry Maine, *Popular Government: Four Essays* (London: John Murray, 1886), 170. On the complexities of Maine's view of progress, see John W. Burrow, "Henry Maine and Mid-Victorian Ideas of Progress," and Krishan Kumar, "Maine and the Theory of Progress," both in *The Victorian Achievement of Sir Henry Maine: A Centennial Reappraisal*, ed. A. Diamond (Cambridge: Cambridge University Press, 1991), 55–69 and 76–87.

48. Maine, *Ancient Law*, 19–20.

49. Maine, *Ancient Law*, 23–24.

50. Mantena, *Alibis of Empire*, 83, 149, 187.

51. John Westlake, "Introductory Lecture on International Law, 17 October 1888," in *Collected Papers*, 393. The relevant "part of the world" was Europe, colonies of "European blood," and more recently, Japan.

52. William Edward Hall, *A Treatise on International Law*, 2nd ed. (Oxford: Clarendon Press, 1884), 40.

53. On the last, see Gerrit Gong's classic study, *The Standard of "Civilization" in International Society* (Oxford: Clarendon Press, 1984); Brett Bowden, *The Empire of Civilization: The Evolution of an Imperial Idea* (Chicago: University of Chicago Press, 2009).

54. J. S. Mill, "Civilization" (1836), in *CW*, 18:117.

55. Twiss, "Introduction to the Second [1875] Edition," in *Law of Nations* (1875), xli–xlii.

56. Twiss, "Introduction to the Second [1884] Edition," in *Law of Nations* (1884), xxxviii–xxxix.

57. John Westlake, "The Equality of States in Civilisation," in *Collected Papers*, 101.

58. Westlake, *Collected Papers*, 103–104.

59. J. S. Mill, "A Few Words on Non-Intervention," in *CW*, 21:119 (emphasis in original).

60. J. S. Mill, "Treaty Obligations" (1870), in *CW* 21:343–348, at 346; "Austin on Jurisprudence" (1863), in *CW*, 21:167–205, at 183. For an excellent discussion of Mill's acceptance of Austin's view of international law, see Varouxakis, *Liberty Abroad*, 19–25.

61. J. S. Mill, "Vindication of the French Revolution of 1848," in *CW*, 21:345.

62. Gong's *Standard of "Civilization"* too readily takes the lawyers' language of a standard at face value (see at 25). Koskenniemi has rightly noted the fluidity of the civilization "standard" and the mythical nature of the suggestion that non-Europeans had merely to meet some well-established set of criteria in order to gain all the rights of international legal personhood. Koskenniemi,

Gentle Civilizer, 103. Robert Phillimore, more explicitly than most, adhered to the idea that the European-international system of public law was fundamentally a Christian system. He oddly described the Treaty of Paris as "recognis[ing] the quasi-Christian *status* of the Turkish Empire." Phillimore, *Commentaries upon International Law,* 4 vols. (London: W. Benning, 1854–1861), 3:iv. Others tended to emphasize the ethical community that stemmed from religious agreement but did not logically require it.

63. See David Dudley Field, "Applicability of International Law to Oriental Nations" (presented to the IDI at The Hague, August 1875), in Field, *Speeches, Arguments, and Miscellaneous Papers,* vol. 1 (New York: D. Appleton, 1884), 447–456, at 447. Sir Travers Twiss served as commission president and rapporteur. *Annuaire de l'Institut de droit international* 1 (1877): 51. See also Koskenniemi, *Gentle Civilizer,* 31.

64. Field, "Applicability of International Law," 452–453. See also Luigi Nuzzo, *Origini di una scienza: diritto internazionale e colonialismo nel XIX siecolo* (Frankfurt am Main: Vittorio Klostermann, 2012).

65. *Annuaire de l'Institut de droit international* 6 (Turin session of 1882): 263.

66. *Annuaire* 3/4 (1880): vol. 1, 304.

67. *Annuaire* 1 (1877): 141–142. The questionnaire also posed what became the commission's primary question: whether special consular tribunals for Europeans living in Turkey, China, and Japan were justified, and if so, how they should be organized. See also Koskenniemi, *Gentle Civilizer,* 132–136.

68. Twiss wrote, "I am assured: First, that the difference between the ideas and beliefs of these nationals and ours are not such that it would be impossible to imagine admitting them into the general community of the law of nations"; and second, that China and Japan in particular "have the same ideas touching their obligations vis-à-vis foreign peoples and individuals, and these ideas are no different at base than the ideas of the European nations, regarding the essential principle of the European law of nations, that no power can relieve itself of treaty obligations without the agreement of the contracting parties." *Annuaire* 3/4 (1880): vol. 1, 302.

69. *Annuaire* 3/4 (1880): vol. 1, 305.

70. As Koskenniemi has put it, Hornung "lived securely in a prison-house of paternalism." Koskenniemi, *Gentle Civilizer,* 129. This paternalism is abundantly demonstrated in Hornung's multipart article "Civilisés et barbares," *Revue de droit international et de legislation comparée* 17 (1885): 5–18, 447–470, 539–560; 18 (1886): 188–206, 281–298.

71. Sir Travers Twiss was another of several figures with membership in both groups.

72. "Principles of International Law to Govern the Intercourse between Christian and Non-Christian Peoples" (summary of committee report presented

to the Association for the Reform and Codification of the Law of Nations, Antwerp, 30 August–3 September 1876), *Report of the Fifth Annual Conference* (London: W. Clowes, 1880), 57–58.

73. Joseph Parrish Thompson, "The Intercourse of Christian with Non-Christian Peoples (Presented at the Conference of the 'Association for the Reform and Codification of the Law of Nations,' at Bremen, September, 1876)," in *American Comments on European Questions, International and Religious* (Boston: Houghton, Mifflin and Company, 1884), 104–131, at 105–107. Compare Lorimer's account of Ashanti as archetypal savages who "proclaim themselves *hostes humani generis.*" James Lorimer, "Does the Corân Supply an Ethical Basis on Which a Political Superstructure Can Be Raised?," in *Studies National and International* (Edinburgh: W. Green, 1890), 133.

74. Sheikh Husein at Akaba reportedly refused to supply Thompson with a guide to Petra, outside his own territory, on the grounds that if Thompson were robbed or killed, word would reach England and the sheikh would pay with his life. Thompson observed: "Never was I so impressed with the omnipresence and majesty of that Public Law that holds even the Bedouins under its sway, and makes its presence felt even in the silence of the desert." Thompson, *American Comments,* 114–115.

75. Mill, "Non-Intervention," 21:118.

76. Twiss, "Rapport," *Annuaire* 5 (1881): 133. He refers to the "Hatti Cheriff of Gulhani" (hatt-ı şerif of Gülhane), 3 November 1839, part of the Tanzimât state reforms. See Inalcik, *Application of the Tanzimat and Its Social Effects* (Lisse, Netherlands: Peter de Ridder, 1976).

77. Twiss, *Law of Nations* (1881), 464–467.

78. Travers Twiss, *On International Conventions for the Maintenance of Sea-Lights* (London: William Clowes, 1879), 13.

79. International law, Kasson argued, recognized "the right of native tribes to dispose freely of themselves and of their hereditary title." Cited in Westlake, *Chapters on the Principles of International Law,* 139, and in Antony Anghie, *Imperialism, Sovereignty, and the Making of International Law* (Cambridge: Cambridge University Press, 2005), 93. Anghie argues that although Kasson's argument was greeted with mistrust by other lawyers at the congress, to the "extent that *any* remotely legal explanation could be given to the partition of Africa, it was based on his proposal" (95).

80. Andrew Fitzmaurice, "Equality of Non-European States in International Law," in *International Law in the Long Nineteenth Century,* ed. Inge Van Hulle and Randall Lesaffer (Leiden: Brill, 2018).

81. Twiss, *Maintenance of Sea-Lights,* 14–15; Fitzmaurice, "Equality of Non-European States."

82. Twiss, "Applicability of the European Law of Nations to African Slave States," *The Law and Magazine Review* 220 (May 1876): 409–437, at 410–411.

83. Twiss, *Maintenance of Sea-Lights,* 19.

84. Edward Hertslet, *The Map of Europe by Treaty,* vol. 2 (London: Butterworth, 1875), 1254–1255. "The Plenipotentiaries, then, unanimously recognize the necessity of revising the Capitulations, and decide upon recording in the Protocol their wish that a deliberation should be opened at Constantinople." *Protocols of Conferences Held at Paris Relative to the General Treaty of Peace* (London: Foreign Office, 1856), 59. Turan Kayaoğlu, *Legal Imperialism: Sovereignty and Extraterritoriality in Japan, the Ottoman Empire, and China* (Cambridge: Cambridge University Press, 2010), 122.

85. Andrew Cobbing, "A Victorian Embarrassment: Consular Jurisdiction and the Evils of Extraterritoriality," *International History Review* (2017): 1–19; Eliana Augusti, "The Ottoman Empire at the Congress of Paris, between New Declensions and Old Prejudices," in *Crossing Legal Cultures,* ed. Laura Beck Varela, Pablo Gutiérrez Vega, and Alberto Spinosa (Munich: Meidenbaur, 2009), 503–517. Madeleine Elfenbein argues for seeing the nineteenth-century transformation of Ottoman sovereignty not as a hollowing out but "as a dispersal along new networks of legitimacy created by international institutions," with 1856 as the moment at which that dispersal becomes "most legible in the historical record"; "No Empire for Old Men: The Young Ottomans and the World, 1856–1878" (PhD diss., University of Chicago, 2017), 29.

86. Phillimore, *Commentaries upon International Law,* 4 vols., 2nd ed. (London: Butterworth, 1871–1874), 1:xiv; Twiss, "Applicability of the European Law of Nations," 410.

87. James Lorimer, "Denationalisation of Constantinople" (lecture, November 1876), in *Studies,* 129. See also Lorimer, "Does the Corân," in *Studies,* 136.

88. Lorimer, *Institutes,* 1:123–124.

89. "It is plain," he argued, "that such tribunals constitute an *imperium in imperio,* and their existence in Turkey is a complete *reductio ad absurdum* of the 'integrity and independence of the Ottoman Empire.'" Lorimer, "Does the Corân," 144.

90. E.g., Lorimer, *Institutes,* 1:120–121 (attributing Disraeli's "imperialistic foreign policy" to his "Semitic sympathies"), 1:123 (excluding Turkey on racial grounds from international recognition), 1:228 (on the limited obligations of "higher races" to "inferior" and "retrograde" races). See also Martti Koskenniemi, "Race, Hierarchy and International Law: Lorimer's Legal Science," *European Journal of International Law* 27 (2016): 415–429.

91. Lorimer, "Prolegomena to a Reasoned System of International Law," in *Studies,* 156.

92. Lorimer, *Institutes,* 1:3–4, 133–135.

93. See Lorimer, "Reasons for the Study of Jurisprudence as a Science," in *Studies,* 37–52. See also Lorimer, *Institutes,* 1:77. One of Lorimer's Edinburgh colleagues remarked in an obituary that Lorimer had taught his students to resist

"the Austinian superstition long so dominant to the south of the Tweed." Robert Flint, "Biographical Notice," reprinted in Lorimer, *Studies*, xiv.

94. Lorimer, *Institutes*, 1:109.

95. Lorimer maintained that states are no more equal to each other in the "absolute" sense than individuals are: "They differ in powers, and consequently in rights." Lorimer, *Institutes*, 1:103. For analogous reasons, Lorimer was an advocate of plural voting and other means of granting greater political influence to worthier citizens.

96. Lorimer, "Prolegomena," 155.

97. On the other hand, Lorimer suggested that the notion that all of mankind ought ultimately to be self-governing was a peculiarly British notion, a kind of cultural prejudice. Lorimer, *Institutes*, 1:124.

98. Lorimer, "Denationalisation," 122, 127. In one of the passages that steer the essay in the direction of farce, Lorimer argues that the "whole yachting world" would flock to the new international city and elevate property values; this, along with secure property, religious freedom, and lower taxes, would secure the happiness and loyalty of the native inhabitants.

99. Ambitious claims were made that the mixed tribunals developing in Egypt in the 1870s could serve as the foundation for an international court. F. W. Newman (discussed below) regarded his proposed court to adjudicate disputes between the British Crown and the Indian princes as the possible basis for an international court. Newman, "Our Relation to the Princes of India," *Westminster Review*, o.s., 69 and n.s., 13 (1858): 477.

100. Gerry Simpson, "James Lorimer and the Character of Sovereigns," *European Journal of International Law* 27 (2016): 431–446. On Twiss's own use of a "racialized perspective upon international relations," see Fitzmaurice, "Equality of Non-European States."

101. Lorimer, "On the Distinction between International Recognition and Inter-ethnical Recognition," in *Institutes*, 1:93.

102. Lorimer, "Denationalisation," 129.

103. "It is too true that colonisation often acts as an improving influence only by improving those subjected to it off the face of the earth." Lorimer, *Institutes*, 1:229.

104. On "racial speculation" in the thought of other jurists, see Koskenniemi, *Gentle Civilizer*, 102–104. On race in Victorian discourse more broadly, see Patrick Brantlinger, *Taming Cannibals: Race and the Victorians* (Ithaca, NY: Cornell University Press, 2011); Nancy Stepan's classic *The Idea of Race in Science: Great Britain, 1800–1960* (London: Macmillan, 1982); and Duncan Bell, *Reordering the World: Essays on Liberalism and Empire* (Princeton, NJ: Princeton University Press, 2016), 182–207. The equivocal nature of the term "race" in this period makes it difficult to determine whether given instances

are intended to indicate biological difference; Hornung, to give one example, spoke of the "very intelligent races [in the Orient], who judge and condemn" European aggression and hoped that if Europeans set a better moral example "they would follow us in the path of civilization." *Annuaire* 3 / 4 (1879–1880): vol. 1, 307.

105. Maine, *Ancient Law,* 22.

106. Because "discipline . . . is an attribute of civilization," "none but civilized states have ever been capable of forming an alliance. The native states of India have been conquered by the English one by one." Mill, "Civilization," 18:122–123.

107. J. S. Mill, *On Liberty,* in *CW* 18:224. See also *Considerations on Representative Government,* in *CW,* 19:567. Uday Mehta has argued that liberal universalism, notably in Locke and Mill, distinguishes "between anthropological capacities and the necessary conditions for their actualization": while the capacities are acknowledged to be universal, various peoples are politically disenfranchised as not being in a position to realize those capacities. Mehta, *Liberalism and Empire: A Study in Nineteenth-Century British Liberal Thought* (Chicago: University of Chicago Press, 1999), 47.

108. For J. S. Mill's ambiguities on the subject of race, see Georgios Varouxakis, "John Stuart Mill on Race," *Utilitas* 10 (1998): 17–32. See also Mill's letter to Gustave d'Eichthal encouraging further study of racial difference (25 December 1840), in *CW,* 13:456.

109. T. J. Lawrence, *Principles of International Law* (London: Macmillan, 1895), 58–59.

110. John Westlake, "Territorial Sovereignty, Especially with Relation to Uncivilised Regions," in *Collected Papers,* 144–146.

111. Westlake, *Collected Papers,* 7.

112. Becker Lorca, *Mestizo International Law: A Global Intellectual History 1842–1933* (Cambridge: Cambridge University Press, 2014).

113. Andrew Fitzmaurice identifies August Wilhelm Heffter, Edward Creasy, and Charles Salomon as rare international lawyers who criticized both the idea of a civilizing mission and European imperial expansion: Fitzmaurice, "Scepticism of the Civilizing Mission in International Law," in *International Law and Empire: Historical Explorations,* ed. Martti Koskenniemi, Walter Rech, and Manuel Jiménez Fonseca (Cambridge: Cambridge University Press, 2017), 359–384.

114. The clever and eccentric Stanley, who became the third baron Stanley of Alderley (and the uncle of Bertrand Russell), edited a number of early modern European travel accounts for the Hakluyt Society. See Muriel E. Chamberlain, "Stanley, Henry Edward John, third Baron Stanley of Alderley and second Baron Eddisbury (1827–1903)," in *Oxford Dictionary of National Biography*

(Oxford: Oxford University Press, 2004); *The Amberley Papers: The Letters and Diaries of Lord and Lady Amberley,* ed. Bertrand Russell and Patricia Russell (London: Hogarth Press, 1937); and Stanley's obituary in the *Times,* 11 December 1903. Stanley was buried according to Muslim rites, his funeral presided over by the imam of the Turkish embassy.

115. Henry E. J. Stanley, ed., *The East and West: Our Dealings with Our Neighbours* (London: Hatchard, 1865), 13. The essays argued that Europeans had abused the capitulation regime, which was supposed simply to transfer to their consuls jurisdiction over Europeans who broke local laws, in order to violate altogether whatever local laws they chose.

116. Stanley, *East and West,* v–vi.

117. "The *Civis Romanus,* whose memory has been invoked in support of the widest demands that could be made in behalf of British residents in foreign states, enjoyed no such privileges or immunities." Stanley, *East and West,* 2.

118. Stanley, *East and West,* 120. Stanley repeatedly quotes Vattel as a model of international legal thought, here citing the Vattelian remark that "a dwarf is as much a man as a giant"; he also celebrated Vattel's criticism of the Spanish for bringing the Inca Atahualpa to trial on the ground that his polygamy and other domestic practices had violated the law of nations. Stanley, *East and West,* 129.

119. Stanley, *East and West,* 113–117.

120. "Mr. Layard's Remarks in the House of Commons," *The Times,* 13 July 1868, 8; "The East and the West," *The Times,* 24 August 1868, 4. Gallenga's proposed remedy was mixed tribunals developed truly jointly by European and Ottoman governments. I am grateful to Nicholas Mays of the *Times* archive for identifying Gallenga as the articles' author. Antonio Carlo Napoleone Gallenga (1810–1895) was a war correspondent and leader writer for the *Times* from 1859 through 1884; he also served as a deputy in the Italian parliament, under Cavour's influence, from 1854 to 1864; see the *Times* obituary, 19 December 1895.

121. "Mr. Layard's Remarks."

122. Andrew Cobbing has noted that while this vein of criticism had little effect on an "engrained official culture" in Britain, it "informed the outlook of states affected by consular jurisdiction," particularly Japan, where one of the pieces that appeared in Stanley's volume, Lord Grey's resolutions for the reform of extraterritoriality, appeared in the *Yokohama Commercial News* and was translated into Japanese. Cobbing, "A Victorian Embarrassment," 8.

123. For studies of British relations with the Indian princes in the first half of the nineteenth century, see the contemporary account by a British military officer, Captain J. Sutherland, *Sketches of the Relations Subsisting between the British Government in India and Different Native States* (Calcutta: G. H. Hutt-

mann, 1837); William Lee-Warner, *Protected Princes of India* (London: Macmillan, 1894); Urmila Walia, *Changing British Attitudes towards the Indian States, 1823-35* (New Delhi: Capital, 1985).

124. Francis W. Newman, "Our Relation to the Princes of India," *Westminster Review,* n.s., 13 (1858): 453–477, at 462; Newman, "Duties of England to India," *Fraser's Magazine* (December 1861), 674–689; Newman, "Indian Annexations: British Treatment of Native Princes," *Westminster Review,* n.s., 23 (January and April 1863): 115–157.

125. Newman, "Princes of India," 463–464 (emphasis in original). In other articles Newman analyzed more minutely the racism implicit or explicit in much British discussion of India; see especially "Duties of England," 675.

126. Newman, "Duties of England," 678–679. He added that since the English "have been unable to restrain their own police from deeds the most atrocious, we have no right . . . to indulge any scrupulous fear that natives may be unsuccessful in high office."

127. He pointed to the example of Ceylon, where limited participation in juries was soon extended to the entire (male) population, with none of the dire consequences predicted by the "fanatics of race." Newman, "Duties of England," 681.

128. Newman, "Princes of India," 454.

129. Twiss considered them "protected dependent states" with no international status; see Twiss, *Law of Nations* (1884), 27. Westlake denied that the language of international law when used vis-à-vis Indian states had any meaning, calling it simply empty rhetoric held over from an earlier era. See Westlake, "The Native States of India," in *Collected Papers,* 620–632. See also Westlake, *Chapters on the Principles of International Law,* 203–204.

130. T. J. Lawrence, "The Evolution of Peace," in *Disputed Questions,* 273, 276, 234.

131. As Westlake put it, "in the gradual improvement of international relations the precision and observance of rules is constantly on the increase, and that therefore those international rules which may already be ranked as law are typical of the subject, in that they are the completest outcome of a tendency which pervades the whole." Westlake, "Introductory Lecture on International Law," 402.

132. As Maine, Robert Phillimore, and Mountague Bernard wrote, as members of the 1876 Royal Commission on Fugitive Slaves, "International law . . . is not stationary; it admits of progressive improvement, though the improvement is more difficult and slower than that of municipal law, and though the agencies by which change is effected are different. It varies with the progress of opinion and the growth of usage." "Statement of Opinion on the Question of International Obligations, by Sir R. Phillimore, Mr. M. Bernard, and Sir H. S. Maine," *Report of the Commissioners, Minutes of the Evidence, and Appendix . . . Presented to Both Houses of Parliament by Command of*

Her Majesty (London: G. E. Eyre and W. Spottiswoode, for H. M. Stationery Office, 1876), xxv.

133. Koskenniemi, *Gentle Civilizer,* 47.

134. See Lawrence, "Evolution of Peace," 234–277.

135. Maine, *International Law,* 3.

136. Maine, *International Law,* 147–148.

137. W. E. B. Du Bois, "Of the Culture of White Folk," *Journal of Race Development* 7, no. 4 (April 1917): 434–447, at 437 (emphasis in original).

Epilogue

1. Roe's mission began in 1614 O.S. (hence the painting's title), or 1615 N.S., and lasted until 1619 N.S.; the durbar depicted took place in January 1616 N.S. The final work remains in St. Stephen's Hall; the study is held by Cartwright Hall Art Gallery in Bradford, England.

2. Michael Strachan, *Sir Thomas Roe, 1581–1644: A Life* (Salisbury, UK: M. Russell, 1989), 117, 291. Britain's character as an empire shaped by law is prominent in the series of eight works, which also include scenes of Queen Elizabeth commissioning Walter Raleigh to sail for America and the Parliamentary Union of England and Scotland in 1707—both, like Rothenstein's, centered on the handover of a formal document. Thanks to Emma Mackinnon for this observation.

3. W. G. Archer, "Sir William Rothenstein and Indian Art," *Art and Letters: The Journal of the Royal India, Pakistan, & Ceylon Society* 25 (1951): 1–7.

4. Rupert Richard Arrowsmith, "An Indian Renascence and the Rise of Global Modernism: William Rothenstein in India, 1910–11," *Burlington Magazine* 152, no. 1285 (April 2010): 228–235. See also Partha Mitter, *Art and Nationalism in Colonial India, 1850–1922* (Cambridge: Cambridge University Press, 1994), 309–314. Resisting earlier dismissals of Abanindranath's work as "kitsch," Ananya Vajpeyi reads his career as "a public argument about the reality of precolonial India and the necessity for a new, postcolonial India." Vajpeyi, *Righteous Republic: The Political Foundations of Modern India* (Cambridge, MA: Harvard University Press, 2012), 158.

5. William Rothenstein, *Men and Memories: Recollections of William Rothenstein* (New York: Coward-McCann, 1932), 232, 254.

6. Brajendranath Seal to Rothenstein, 14 September 1911, British Library, India Office Records and Private Papers, Mss Eur B213 / 1 / 8; I have transcribed as "phases" a word that is somewhat illegible. On the Universal Races Congress, see Gustav Spiller, ed., *Papers on Inter-Racial Problems Communicated to the First Universal Races Congress, Held at the University of London, July 26–29*

(London: P. S. King, 1911); Marilyn Lake and Henry Reynolds, *Drawing the Global Colour Line: White Men's Countries and the International Challenge of Racial Equality* (Cambridge: Cambridge University Press, 2008), 251–261.

7. Rothenstein to Dinesh Chandra Sen, 7 September 1914, British Library, India Office Records and Private Papers, Mss. Eur Photo Eur 478.

8. Tagore to Lord Chelmsford, Viceroy of India, 31 May 1919, in *Selected Letters of Rabindranath Tagore,* ed. Krishna Dutta and Andrew Robinson (Cambridge: Cambridge University Press, 1997), 223; Rothenstein to Tagore, 11 July 1919, in Mary Lago, *Imperfect Encounter: Letters of William Rothenstein and Rabindranath Tagore* (Cambridge, MA: Harvard University Press, 1972), 256 (ellipses in original).

9. William Rothenstein, "The Import of the Ajanta Paintings in the History of Art," in *Ajanta Frescoes,* ed. Christiana J. Herringham (London: H. Milford, 1915), 23. The final mural was constrained by "many rules regarding the size of figures and colour scheme"; personal communication, Jill Iredale, Curator of Fine Art, Cartwright Hall Art Gallery.

10. Alexandrowicz, "Mogul Sovereignty and the Law of Nations," *Indian Year Book of International Affairs* 4 (1955): 316–324, in Alexandrowicz, *The Law of Nations in Global History,* ed. David Armitage and Jennifer Pitts (Oxford: Oxford University Press, 2017), 64.

11. Charles Oldham ["C.E.A.W.O."] in *Journal of the Royal Asiatic Society of Great Britain and Ireland* 3 (July 1927): 618–621, reviewing William Foster, ed., *The Embassy of Sir Thomas Roe to India, 1615–1619* (Oxford: Oxford University Press, 1926).

12. Alexandrowicz, "Mogul Sovereignty," 63.

13. Alexandrowicz, "The New States and International Law" (1974), in Alexandrowicz, *Law of Nations in Global History,* 404.

14. Alexandrowicz, "Charter of Economic Rights of States" (1975), in Alexandrowicz, *Law of Nations in Global History,* 413.

15. Alexandrowicz, "New States and International Law," 409; Vienna Convention on the Law of Treaties, 1155 *United Nations Treaty Series* 344.

16. Umut Özsu, "*Jus Cogens* and the Politics of International Law," in *International Law and Empire: Historical Explorations,* ed. Martti Koskenniemi, Walter Rech, and Manuel Jiménez Fonseca (Oxford: Oxford University Press, 2017), 295–313, quoting "paganism" from Mohammed Bedjaoui, *Towards a New International Economic Order* (New York: Holmes & Meier, 1979), 98–101. Özsu himself observes that "*jus cogens,* and the kind of abstract universalism it exemplifies, has done precious little to reassure critics of its capacity to effect lasting and concrete change," 309.

17. "International Law: Need for Clarifying Rules Stressed," *The Hindu*, 13 February 1952, 7. See discussion in Armitage and Pitts, "This Modern Grotius: The Life and Thought of C.H. Alexandrowicz," in Alexandrowicz, *Law of Nations in Global History*, 21–23 and 30–31.

18. Alexandrowicz, "Doctrinal Aspects of the Universality of the Law of Nations" (1961), in Alexandrowicz, *Law of Nations in Global History*, 178.

19. Alexandrowicz, "New States and International Law," 409; Alexandrowicz, "Charter of Economic Rights of States," 413.

20. Bedjaoui, *Towards a New International Economic Order*, 224–236; Nils Gilman, "The New International Economic Order: A Reintroduction," *Humanity* 6 (2015): 1–16; Umut Özsu, " 'In the Interests of Mankind as a Whole': Mohammed Bedjaoui's New International Economic Order," *Humanity* 6 (2015): 129–143; Sundhya Pahuja, *Decolonizing International Law: Development, Economic Growth and the Politics of Universality* (Cambridge: Cambridge University Press, 2011), 95–171.

21. Bedjaoui, *Towards a New International Economic Order*, 235, 110.

22. Pahuja, *Decolonizing International Law*, 96.

23. Antony Anghie, "Legal Aspects of the New International Economic Order," *Humanity* 6 (2015): 145–158, at 146 and 147.

24. Koskenniemi, *From Apology to Utopia: The Structure of International Legal Argument; Reissue with New Epilogue* (Cambridge: Cambridge University Press, 2005), 596.

25. Sundhya Pahuja, "Changing the World: The Ethical Impulse and International Law," in *Who's Afraid of International Law?*, ed. Gerry Simpson (Clayton, Australia: Monash University Publishing, 2017), 21–42, at 35.

Acknowledgments

I thank the following journals and presses for permission to reprint material that first appeared in these articles and chapters: "Boundaries of Victorian International Law," in *Victorian Visions of Global Order: Empire and International Relations in Nineteenth-Century Political Thought*, ed. Duncan Bell (Cambridge: Cambridge University Press, 2007), 67–88, © Cambridge University Press 2007 (in Chapter 6); "Empire and Legal Universalisms in the Eighteenth Century," *American Historical Review* 117, no. 1 (February 2012): 92–121, © 2012 Oxford University Press (in Chapter 4); "The Critical History of International Law" (Review Essay), *Political Theory* 43, no. 4 (June 2015): 541–552, © 2015 SAGE Publications (in Chapter 1); "International Law," in *Historicism and the Human Sciences in Victorian Britain*, ed. Mark Bevir (Cambridge: Cambridge University Press, 2017), 237–261, © Cambridge University Press 2017 (in Chapter 6); and "International Relations and the Critical History of International Law," *International Relations* 31, no. 3 (September 2017): 282–298 (in Chapter 5).

This book is the culmination of over a decade's work, and I am thankful for the support of three institutions I have inhabited during that time and the animated intellectual environments all of them provided: the University of Chicago, Princeton University, and the Institute for Advanced Study in Princeton, where a fellowship year was indispensable to the project's development at its earliest stage. I am also grateful to audiences at many institutions for their warm welcomes, searching questions, and productive conversations as I developed the ideas in the book, including the Australian Association of European Historians, Brown University, Columbia University, Duke University, École des hautes études en sciences sociales, Harvard University, Indiana University at Bloomington, Loyola University School of Law, McGill University, Northwestern University, Oxford University, Princeton University, Queen Mary University of London, SciencesPo, Texas A&M University, the University of Amsterdam, the University of California–Berkeley, the University of Cambridge, the University of Helsinki, the University of London, the University of Toronto, the University of Virginia, the University of Wisconsin, Vanderbilt University, and of course the University of Chicago.

Andrew Fitzmaurice and Martti Koskenniemi read the entire manuscript and provided the most welcome possible feedback: searching, detailed, and constructive. I owe particular thanks to two groups whose ideas were indispensable at very different stages of the project. The lively and hospitable reading group on international law at New York University, convened by Benedict Kingsbury and Martti Koskenniemi, helped me find my way into the field from very much outside it. And, at a crucial moment in the book's composition, colleagues at Chicago— Daragh Grant, Patchen Markell, John McCormick, Sankar Muthu, Nathan Tarcov, Jim Wilson, and Linda Zerilli, along with David Armitage (for whose presence in Chicago for a quarter I am grateful to the Neubauer Collegium)—convened for a manuscript workshop, generously reading all of a very rough draft.

I am tremendously fortunate to have so many wise and generous friends and colleagues near and far, who have read parts of the project over the years and shared their critical insights, knowledge, and ideas, including Arash Abizadeh, Cliff Ando, Antony Anghie, William Bain, Gary Bass, Arnulf Becker Lorca, Nicole Beckman, Chuck Beitz, Duncan Bell, Lauren Benton, Richard Bourke, Annabel Brett, David Bromwich, Chris Brooke, Austin Carson, Dipesh Chakrabarty, Jim Chandler, Chiara Cordelli, Aurelian Craiutu, Maksymillian Del Mar, Madeleine Elfenbein, Stephen Engelmann, Matthew Fitzpatrick, Jill Frank, James Gathii, Adom Getachew, Stella Ghervas, Bob Gooding-Williams, Bernard Harcourt, Alex Haskins, Jared Holley, Douglas Howland, Iza Hussin, Duncan Ivison, Deme Kasimis, George Kateb, Edward Keene, Duncan Kelly, Benedict Kingsbury, Jed Kroncke, Matt Landauer, Randall Lesaffer, Jacob Levy, Catherine Lu, Steve Macedo, Emma Mackinnon, Karuna Mantena, Inder Marwah, Pratap Mehta, Charles Mills, Jeanne Morefield, Rosalind Morris, Sam Moyn, Jan-Werner Mueller, Isaac Nakhimovsky, Anthony Pagden, David Palfrey, Tejas Parasher, Philip Pettit, Stefano Recchia, Melvin Richter, Teemu Ruskola, David Scott, Tamsin Shaw, Mira Siegelberg, Céline Spector, Philip Stern, Benjamin Straumann, Casper Sylvest, Robert Travers, Richard Tuck, Jim Tully, Georgios Varouxakis, Michael Walzer, and Fred Whelan. I am grateful to Andrew Fitzmaurice, Katrina Forrester, Robin Law, Blake Smith, and Hans Theunissen for sharing their work prior to publication, and to Oliver Cussen for assistance with documents at the Bibliothèque Nationale. Chris Bayly, Istvan Hont, Tony Judt, and Robert Wokler were all wonderfully supportive at various stages of the book's evolution, and I regret that I was not able to complete it in time for them to see it.

My greatest debts in relation to this book are to David Armitage and Lisa Wedeen. David, with his gift for formulating questions and his tenacity in answering them, his deep and wide historical knowledge, and his intellectual generosity, has been a constant source of inspiration and guidance; the experience of working together on our volume of essays by C. H. Alexandrowicz was enlightening and invigorating at just the right moment. Lisa, my cherished and heroic writing partner for most of the decade I have been in Chicago, was indescribably generous with her time and (seemingly boundless) energy as she read innumerable drafts at every stage of draftiness and brought her theoretical acumen, political wisdom, and gift of expression to bear on every page I gave her.

Ian Malcolm has once again proven a superlative editor, whose knowledge, judiciousness, and interest in the book's argument improved it materially. I am grateful to John Donohue and Anne Davidson for their thoughtful and meticulous editing of the text, and to Thomas Broughton-Willett for the index.

Sankar Muthu has sustained me through another project with love, humor, marvelous meals, and a willingness to read chapters he's read in countless previous iterations with fresh eyes and spirited challenges. My parents-in-law, Muthu, who passed away as this book was going to press, and Jeya, have supported me and my work with great warmth and enthusiasm. To their abundant love, moral support, and thoughtful questions, my parents have added the gift of caring for my own children for long stretches and at conferences around the world, making it possible for me to think and write. This book is for Lucia and Nicholas, who have grown up with it and whose love and exuberance keeps me going.

Index

Abdülmecid I (Abdul Mejid), 169
Abel-Rémusat, Jean-Pierre, ix, 1
Abi-Saab, Georges, 16
Achenwall, Gottfried, 244n16
Adams, John Quincy, 135–136, 249n58, 249n61
African states and societies, 133, 176; and Berlin Conference (1884–1885), 16, 170; and Christian nations, 146; dispossession and subjugation of, 9; and Montesquieu, 49; and Rousseau, 7; and Saint-Pierre, 10–11; and slavery, 9; sovereignty of, 9; treaties with, 9; and Twiss, 169–170; and Westlake, 176–177
Ahmed Bey, 138
Ahmed I, 62
Ahmed Resmi, 34
Ajanta frescoes, 186, 188
Alabama, 155
Alexander the Great, 76
Alexandrowicz, Charles Henry, 16–17, 21, 71, 72, 73, 74, 92, 118, 178, 188–190, 191, 242n5, 245n23
Algeria, 112–113, 138, 142, 250n72, 251n76, 251n78
Algiers, 120, 138, 139, 140, 142, 240n82, 244n21, 251n78
Allen, Danielle, 196n23
Allott, Philip, 71
Amazon basin, 190
ambassadors, 210n41; inviolability of, 22, 85–86; and Muslim states, 83; and

Ottomans, 22, 39, 43–44, 56, 57, 85, 86; reports of, 33–34, 45; and Roe, 188; and Roman law, 18; in Vattel, 83, 85–86. *See also* consular jurisdiction; diplomacy
American Civil War, 155, 156
American Revolution, 69, 143; and Burke, 98
Americas: native peoples in, 5, 73, 176; and Vattel, 23, 70, 83. *See also* Native Americans
Amritsar massacre, 187
Anand, R. P., 16
Anghie, Antony, 190–191; *Imperialism, Sovereignty, and the Making of International Law*, 16
Anquetil-Duperron, Abraham Hyacinthe, 20, 24, 30, 38, 66–67, 93, 191, 214n86, 218n120, 218n126, 219n134, 219n136, 220n139; and Asia, 57; and Asian languages, 231n5; and Asian states, 63–64; and Bossuet, 64; and Boulanger, 59; and Burke, 67, 95, 99, 104, 115, 232n11; *Considérations philosophiques*, 59, 60; and Hastings, 231n9; and imperialism, 38, 94, 95; influence of, 115–116; *Législation orientale*, 29, 57–64; *L'Inde en rapport avec l'Europe*, 64; on Native Americans, 95; and Porter, 57, 61, 62; and Scott, 116; translation of *Zend-Avesta*, 57; on treaties and Ottoman Empire, 106; and universal sympathy, 63–64; and Vattel, 120
anthropology, 16, 65, 77, 153, 162, 175, 263n107